W9-CAZ-223

Praise for

# ALL THE
# SINGLE LADIES

---

"A monumental study of the political, economic, social, and sexual consequences of the rise of unmarried women."

—*New Republic*

"Personal and relatable. . . . [Traister's] assessment of single women's sex lives is so balanced and ordinary-sounding that it becomes extraordinary in a world where Tinder is supposedly bringing a dating apocalypse. . . . I'll swipe right on that message any day."

—*Washington Post*

"Though Traister is no longer one of us, she retains her memories and her empathy, as well as her feminist commitments. . . . Drawing on historical and contemporary sources, as well as her own reporting, she has produced a wide-ranging, insistently optimistic analysis of the role of single women in American society."

—*Chicago Tribune*

"I can't begin to count the number of conversations I've had in my adult life about my lack of enthusiasm to marry. . . . Thankfully, with the publication of Rebecca Traister's *All the Single Ladies: Unmarried Women and the Rise of an Independent Nation*, I can stop explaining and buy her book for all the busybodies in my happily unmarried life. Traister blends history, reportage and personal memoir to propose that the notion of marriage in American life has been and will be written by unmarried women."

—*Guardian* (U.S.)

"Traister is one of the sharpest journalists writing about feminism today, and her look into the link between eras with large numbers of unmarried women and periods of drastic social change is absolutely riveting. . . . It turns out the history of unmarried women in this country is a fascinating one, which Traister recounts in compulsively readable detail, combining facts with personal stories from single ladies across racial and financial spectrums. What's left after she joyfully dismantles conservative arguments about the death of wifely servitude is hope: 'Ring on it' or not, the paths open to women today are varied and bright."

—*Entertainment Weekly*

"The enormous accomplishment of Traister's book is to show that the ranks of women electing for nontraditional lives . . . have also improved the lots of women who make traditional choices, blowing open the institutions of marriage and parenthood. . . . This rich portrait of our most quietly explosive social force makes it clear that the ladies still have plenty of work to do."

—*Slate*

"In this intelligent book, Traister looks at the many reasons for choosing a path that would have been cultural and economic suicide 50 years ago. She wants single women to recognize themselves as a political force and to celebrate unmarried life for what it can be: an excellent option."

—*People*

"Wonderfully inclusive, examining single women from all walks of life—working-, middle-, and upper-class women; women of color and white women; queer and straight ones. . . . With *All the Single Ladies*, [Traister] brings her trademark intelligence and wit to bear, interspersing her own experiences and observations with dozens of interviews with women all over the country, plus historical context, from so-called Boston marriages (the nineteenth-century name for women who lived together) and the Brontë sisters to Murphy Brown and *Sex and the City*."

—*Elle*

"No husband, NP. . . . In *All The Single Ladies*, an exhaustive examination of independent women and how they shaped the world we live (and date) in today, Rebecca Traister explodes the centuries-old notion that marriage is compulsory to living a happy, fulfilled life and reveals the inestimable power of being blissfully unattached."

—*Cosmopolitan*

"*All The Single Ladies* is essential, careful, bold, and rigorous; it's a warning and a celebration, and I loved it."

—*Jezebel*

"[*All The Single Ladies*] has the potential to become a seminal text on female identity in the West. . . . Traister expertly paints a modern portrait of American life and how we got here, with an intersectional approach that accounts for class, race, and sexual orientation. Even more impressive is how Traister pushes a feminist agenda without the book ever feeling like it has an agenda, or that it's pointing the finger at the reader to make him or her feel guilty."

—*VICE*

"A well-written and unabashedly feminist analysis of the history and current situation of single women in America."

—*Newsday*

"Exploring all aspects of single life—social, economic, racial, and sexual—Traister's comprehensive volume, sure to be vigorously discussed, is truly impressive in scope and depth while always managing to be eminently readable and thoughtful."

—*Booklist* (starred review)

"[Traister is] a thoughtful journalist. . . . This fast-paced, fascinating book will draw in fans of feminism, social sciences, and U.S. history, similar to Gail Collins's *When Everything Changed*."

—*Library Journal*

"Incorporating a lively slew of perspectives of single ladies past and present, Traister conducts a nuanced investigation into the sexual, economic, and emotional lives of women in America and the opportunities available when marriage is no longer 'the measure of female existence.' . . . Traister is funny and fair in how she deals with the prevalent stereotypes and remaining stigmas attached to being an unmarried woman in society. . . . An invigorating study of single women in America with refreshing insight into the real life of the so-called spinster."

—*Publishers Weekly*

"Cogent and provocative. . . . A persuasive case for why unmarried women have grown into a potent political and social force. . . . Readers will also appreciate Traister's willingness to recount, with candor and humor, experiences in her own life that fit into the larger national story. This is a fascinating book—and an important one."

—*Bookmark/Politics & Prose Blog*

"Part social and cultural history, part anthropological and journalistic investigation, part memoir, and total investigation into the phenomenon and political power of single womanhood."

—*Flavorwire*

"Timely and important. . . . A significant addition to the literature of sociology and women's studies. . . . Clearly this book belongs right up there with those by Gloria Steinem, Gail Collins, and other feminist writers who shine a light on contemporary life as few others can."

—*New York Journal of Books*

ALSO BY REBECCA TRAISTER

*Big Girls Don't Cry:*
*The Election That Changed Everything for American Women*

# ALL THE
# SINGLE LADIES

Unmarried Women

and the

Rise of an Independent Nation

# REBECCA TRAISTER

SIMON & SCHUSTER PAPERBACKS

*New York   London   Toronto   Sydney   New Delhi*

Simon & Schuster Paperbacks
An Imprint of Simon & Schuster, Inc.
1230 Avenue of the Americas
New York, NY 10020

Copyright © 2016 by Rebecca Traister

All rights reserved, including the right to reproduce this book
or portions thereof in any form whatsoever. For information,
address Simon & Schuster Subsidiary Rights Department,
1230 Avenue of the Americas, New York, NY 10020.

First Simon & Schuster trade paperback edition October 2016

SIMON & SCHUSTER PAPERBACKS and colophon are
registered trademarks of Simon & Schuster, Inc.

For information about special discounts for bulk purchases,
please contact Simon & Schuster Special Sales at
1-866-506-1949 or business@simonandschuster.com.

The Simon & Schuster Speakers Bureau can bring authors to
your live event. For more information or to book an event, contact
the Simon & Schuster Speakers Bureau at 1-866-248-3049 or
visit our website at www.simonspeakers.com.

*Interior design by Joy O'Meara*

Manufactured in the United States of America

10 9 8 7 6 5 4 3 2 1

The Library of Congress has cataloged the hardcover edition as follows:

Names: Traister, Rebecca, author.
Title: All the single ladies : unmarried women and the rise of an
independent nation / Rebecca Traister.
Description: New York : Simon & Schuster, 2016.
Identifiers: LCCN 2015045131 | ISBN 9781476716565 (hardback) |
ISBN 9781476716572 (trade paperback)
Subjects: LCSH: Single women—United States—History. | Women—
United States—Social conditions. | Feminism—United States—
History. | United States—Civilization. | United States—History. |
United States—Social conditions. | BISAC: HISTORY / United States
/ 21st Century. | HISTORY / Social History. | SOCIAL SCIENCE /
Women's Studies.
Classification: LCC HQ880.4.U6 T73 2016 | DDC 306.81/530973—dc23
LC record available at http://lccn.loc.gov/2015045131

ISBN 978-1-4767-1656-5
ISBN 978-1-4767-1657-2 (pbk)
ISBN 978-1-4767-1658-9 (ebook)

*For my parents, who never
gave me a hard time about it*

# Contents

*Nellie Bly: "What do you think the new woman will be?"*
*Susan B. Anthony: "She'll be free."*

—1896

# A Note on Interviews and Attribution

While researching this book, I conducted interviews with close to one hundred women around the country. Some I sought out because their work corresponded to the issues I wanted to address; some had written affectingly on the topics of singlehood or marriage; some were friends or friends of friends; some were women I bumped into in airports; some were strangers I befriended because I wanted to include as broad a range of geographic, religious, economic, and racial experience as possible; some were women tracked down by my nimble research assistant, Rhaina Cohen. A few women got in touch with me after hearing through their own social or professional circles that I was writing about single women.

From those original hundred interviews, I wound up quoting the tales of about thirty women at length in these pages. Surely those thirty stories include an overrepresentation of people like me: It is fair to say that there are likely more college-educated feminists, writers, and New Yorkers here than most readers know in their real lives. But I have worked to ensure that these are not the only stories.

Nearly all of the interviewees agreed to be identified by their full names. Those who did not are referred to by their first or middle names only. Likewise, I deferred to individual preferences when it came to later references: Some women are called by their first names as their tales progress, reflecting the intimate nature of the stories they offer, some preferred to be called by their last.

The interviews took place between 2010 and 2015 and reflect the experiences and realities of the women at the time they were interviewed. During the fact-checking process, some of the interviewees who felt that their circumstances, perspectives, or thoughts on singlehood had changed significantly since the time of their interviews asked to update their status. I have included a "Where Are they Now?" section to account for their lives up through publication.

Finally, I did not set out to write a book that relies almost entirely on the words, scholarship, stories, and insight of women. In fact, when I realized, late in the process, that I had written more than three hundred pages of a book in which only a handful of men were cited, I felt bad. After all, men are socially, economically, and emotionally crucial to women and to the story of female independence, and they comprise half of the world that is being remade around us. But though they have been at the center of many female lives for many generations, men are not, as it turns out, at the center of the story I have laid out here.

# ALL THE
# SINGLE LADIES

# Introduction

I always hated it when my heroines got married. As a child, I remember staring at the cover of *The First Four Years*, willing myself to feel pleased—as I knew I was meant to—that Laura Ingalls had wed Almanzo "Manly" Wilder and given birth to baby Rose. I understood that despite the hail storms, diphtheria outbreaks, and other agrarian misery that Wilder chronicled in the last of her *Little House* books, Laura's marriage and motherhood were supposed to be read as a happy ending. Yet, to me, it felt unhappy, as if Laura were over. And, in many ways, she was.

The images on the covers of previous *Little House* books, drawn by Garth Williams in the editions I owned, had been of Laura in motion, front and center: gamboling down a hillside, riding a horse barefoot, having a snowball fight. Here she was, stationary and solidly shod, beside her husband; the baby she held in her arms was the most lively figure in the scene. Laura's story was coming to a close. The tale that was worth telling about her was finished once she married.

It was the same with *Anne of Green Gables'* Anne Shirley, whose days of getting her best friend Diana Barry drunk and competing at school with rival Gilbert Blythe were over when, at last, after three volumes of resistance and rejected proposals, she gave in and married Gilbert. Beloved Jo March, who, in *Little Women*, subverted the marriage plot by *not* marrying her best friend and neighbor Laurie, came to her clunky, connubial end by getting hitched to avuncular Professor Bhaer. And Jane

Eyre: Oh, smart, resourceful, sad Jane. Her prize, readers, after a youth of fighting for some smidgen of autonomy? Marrying *him*: the bad-tempered guy who kept his first wife in the attic, wooed Jane through a series of elaborate head games, and was, by the time she landed him, blind and missing a hand.

It was supposed to be romantic, but it felt bleak. Paths that were once wide and dotted with naughty friends and conspiratorial sisters and malevolent cousins, with scrapes and adventures and hopes and passions, had narrowed and now seemed to lead only to the tending of dull husbands and the rearing of insipid children to whom the stories soon would be turned over, in pallid follow-ups like *Jo's Boys* and *Anne of Ingleside*.

My dismay, of course, was partially symptomatic of the form. Coming-of-age-tales, *bildungsroman*, come to their tautological ends when their subjects reach adulthood. But embedded in the structure of both literature and life was the reality that for women, adulthood—and with it, the end of the story—*was* marriage.

Marriage, it seemed to me, walled my favorite fictional women off from the worlds in which they had once run free, or, if not free, then at least forward, with currents of narrative possibility at their backs. It was often at just the moment that their educations were complete and their childhood ambitions coming into focus that these troublesome, funny girls were suddenly contained, subsumed, and reduced by domesticity.

Later, I would learn that Shakespeare's comedies ended with wedlock and his tragedies with death, making marriage death's narrative equivalent and supporting my childhood hunch about its ability to shut down a story. My mother, a Shakespeare professor, would note wistfully to me that some of the Bard's feistiest and most loquacious heroines, including Beatrice in *Much Ado about Nothing*, ceased to have any lines after their dramatically conclusive marriage alliances.

Weren't there any interesting fictional women out there who *didn't* get married as soon as they became grown-ups, I wondered, even as a kid.

As I got older, I would discover that yes, there were plenty of stories about women who didn't get married. I would read about *Tar Baby*'s Jadine Childs, whose determination to flout gendered and racial expectations gets her cast out from her world, and about Theodore Dreiser's

Sister Carrie, who barters sex for capital gain and ends up empty. I'd read *Persuasion*, about Anne Elliot, who, unmarried at twenty-seven, veers perilously close to an economically and socially unmoored fate before being saved from the indignity of spinsterhood by Captain Wentworth. I'd read about Hester Prynne and Miss Havisham and Edith Wharton's maddening, doomed Lily Bart.

These were not inspiring portraits. Collectively, they suggested that women who remained unmarried, whether by choice or by accident, were destined to wear red letters or spend their lives dancing in unused wedding dresses or overdose on chloral hydrate. These characters might not have wed, but their *lack* of husbands constrained and defined them, just as surely as marriage would have.

They seemed to confirm Simone de Beauvoir's observation about real life women, which I would also, eventually, uncover: that, by definition, we "are married, or have been, or plan to be, or suffer from not being."

By the time I was on the verge of becoming a woman, ready to leave home for college, nothing could have been more implausible to me than the notion of becoming a wife to anyone anytime soon. By most accounts, marriage was coming to swallow me up in just a few short years. However, with my mind firmly absorbed by picking classes, worrying about roommates and keg parties and finding a job near campus, nothing could have seemed less likely.

At eighteen, I had never even had a serious boyfriend, and neither had any of my closest girlfriends. The people I knew who were my age in the early 1990s didn't really "date." We hung out, hooked up, drank beer, smoked cigarettes and pot and some of us, but by no means all of us, had sex. Very few got into heavy romantic relationships. Sure, perhaps I was just a misfit girl destined never to fall in love (a suspicion I logged many hours cultivating), let alone marry. But actually, I couldn't envision any of my girlfriends married anytime soon either.

I was on the verge of tasting meaningful independence, of becoming myself. The notion that in a handful of years, I might be ready, even eager, to enter a committed, legal, purportedly permanent relationship with a new family and a new home was patently absurd.

Yet this was what had happened to practically every adult I knew in the generation before mine. Growing up in rural Maine, my mother had already had one serious boyfriend by the time that she turned eighteen. Many of the women with whom she'd gone to high school were married—or pregnant and on their way to getting married—by the time she'd left for college. As an undergraduate in the early 1960s, my mother would serve as a student guide to Betty Friedan when she visited campus to discuss *The Feminine Mystique*; she would also go on to marry my father at twenty-one, days after her graduation, before getting her Masters and her PhD. My aunt, five years my mother's junior, had had a series of high-school swains before meeting my uncle in college and marrying him at twenty-three, also before getting her PhD. In this, my mother and aunt were not unusual. My friends' mothers, my mother's friends, my teachers: Most of them had met their spouses when in their early twenties.

Throughout America's history, the start of adult life for women—whatever else it might have been destined to include—had been typically marked by marriage. As long as there had been such records kept in the United States, since the late nineteenth century, the median age of first marriage for women had fluctuated between twenty and twenty-two. This had been the shape, pattern, and definition of female life.

History suggested that beyond the kegs and term papers in my immediate future, perhaps even tied up with them, the weird possibility of marriage loomed. It loomed, in part, because there weren't very many appealing models of what other kinds of female life might take its place.

## A Dramatic Reversal

I began work on this book seventeen years after I went to college, in the weeks before getting married at the age of thirty-five. Impending marriage did not, happily, feel like any sort of ending for me, but neither did it feel like a beginning.

By the time I walked down the aisle—or rather, into a judge's chambers—I had lived fourteen independent years, early adult years that my mother had spent married. I had made friends and fallen out with friends, had moved in and out of apartments, had been hired, fired, promoted, and quit. I had had roommates I liked and roommates I didn't like and I had lived on my own; I'd been on several forms of birth control and navigated a few serious medical questions; I'd paid my own bills and failed to pay my own bills; I'd fallen in love and fallen out of love and spent five consecutive years with nary a fling. I'd learned my way around new neighborhoods, felt scared and felt completely at home; I'd been heartbroken, afraid, jubilant, and bored. I was a grown-up: a reasonably complicated person. I'd become that person not in the company of any one man, but alongside my friends, my family, my city, my work, and, simply, by myself.

I was not alone.

In fact, in 2009, the proportion of American women who were married dropped below 50 percent.[1] And that median age of first marriage that had remained between twenty and twenty-two from 1890 to 1980?[2] Today, the median age of first marriage for women is around twenty-seven, and much higher than that in many cities. By our mid-thirties, half of my closest girlfriends remained unmarried.

During the years in which I had come of age, American women had pioneered an entirely new kind of adulthood, one that was *not* kicked off by marriage, but by years and, in many cases, whole lives, lived on their own, outside matrimony. Those independent women were no longer aberrations, less stigmatized than ever before. Society had changed, permitting this revolution, but the revolution's beneficiaries were about to change the nation further: remapping the lifespan of women, redefining marriage and family, reimagining what wifeliness and motherhood entail, and, in short, altering the scope of possibility for over half the country's population.

For the first time in American history, single women (including those who were never married, widowed, divorced, or separated) outnumbered married women. Perhaps even more strikingly, the number of adults younger than thirty-four who had *never* married was up to 46 percent,[3] rising twelve percentage points in less than a decade. For women under thirty, the likelihood of being married had become astonishingly small: Today, only around 20 percent of Americans between the ages of eighteen and twenty-nine are wed,[4] compared to the nearly 60 percent in 1960. In a statement from the

Population Reference Bureau, the fact that the proportion of young adults in the United States that has never been married is now bigger than the percentage that has married was called "a dramatic reversal."[5]

For young women, for the first time, it is as normal to be unmarried as it is to be married, even if it doesn't always feel that way.

British journalist Hannah Betts wrote in 2013, "Ask what has changed most about society during my lifetime and I would answer: the evolution from the stigmatised 'spinsters' of my childhood . . . to the notion of the 'singularist,' which is how I would currently define myself at 41."[6]

Young women today no longer have to wonder, as I did, what unmarried adult life for women might look like, surrounded as we are by examples of exactly this kind of existence. Today, the failure to comply with the marriage plot, while a source of frustration and economic hardship for many, does not lead directly to life as a social outcast or to a chloral hydrate prescription.

It is an invitation to wrestle with a whole new set of expectations about what female maturity entails, now that it is not shaped and defined by early marriage.

In 1997, the year that I graduated college, journalist Katie Roiphe wrote about the befuddlement felt by her generation of unmarried women. Four years earlier, Roiphe had published *The Morning After*, a screed against campus date-rape activism rooted firmly in her belief in the sexual agency and independence of college-aged women. However, as Roiphe and her compatriots closed in on thirty, many living unmarried into their second decade of adulthood, she argued that they were feeling the long-term effects of that independence and longing instead for the "felicitous simplicities of the nineteenth-century marriage plot."[7]

> *People live together and move out. They sleep together for indefinite periods. They marry later. They travel light. I recently overheard a pretty woman at a party say, not without regret, 'When our mothers were our age, they had husbands instead of cats." She is one of the many normal, pulled-together people I know inhabiting the prolonged, perplexing strip of adolescence currently provided by this country to its twenty- to thirty-year olds. The romantic sensibility—*

*cats or husbands?—is fragile and confused. We go to parties and occasionally fall into bed with people we don't know well, but we also have well-read paperbacks of Austen's* Mansfield Park *or* Emma *lying open on our night tables: the dream of a more orderly world.*

The unmarried state that Roiphe viewed as a kind of disorder was in fact a *new* order, or at least a new normal, in which women's lots in life were not cast based on a single binary (husbands *versus* cats). Instead, women's paths were increasingly marked with options, off-ramps, variations on what had historically been a very constrained theme.

While Roiphe may have felt herself in a prolonged period of adolescence because marriage had not yet come along to mark its end, she was in fact leading a very adult life, with a romantic history, an undergraduate education at Harvard, and a thriving career. The liberating point was that Roiphe's status and that of her cohort didn't hinge on the question of whether they had husbands or cats. It didn't have to, because they had jobs. They had sex lives. They had each other. They inhabited a universe that Jane Austen, for whose "orderly world" Roiphe claimed to pine, could never have imagined: Austen's novels had been as much ambivalent cries *against* the economic and moral strictures of enforced marital identity for women than they were any kind of reassuring blueprint for it.

Contemporary, unmarried life may have felt—to Roiphe and to many single women who continue to come after her—a lot more complicated, confusing and scary than the simpler single option on offer to women of previous generations. But the wholesale revision of what female life might entail is also, by many measures, the invention of independent female adulthood.

### The Single Ladies

This independence can be punishing. Many single women are poor or struggling. Almost 50 percent of the 3.3 million Americans now earning minimum wage or below are unmarried women.[8] Many of them live, often with children, in communities where unemployment, racial and class discrimination, and a drug war that puts many young men in prison combine to make the possibilities of stable marriages scarce, making singlehood less of a freeing choice than a socially conscripted necessity. More than half of unmarried young mothers with children under the age of six are likely to live below the poverty line, a rate that is five times the rate of the corresponding population of married women.[9]

Yes, many single women, across classes and races, would *like* to marry, or at least form loving, reciprocal, long-term partnerships, but have not found mates who want the same thing, or who can sustain it. Some are lonely.

Many women, unmarried into their thirties, living in geographic, religious, and socio-economic corners of the country where early marriage remains a norm, as well as many women who remain single less by choice than by circumstance, into their forties, fifties, and sixties, do not feel as though they are living in a new, singles-dominated world. They feel ostracized, pressured; they are challenged by family and peers.

However, statistically, across the country, these women are not alone. Their numbers are growing by the year. There were 3.9 million more single adult women in 2014 than there were in 2010.[10] Between 2008 and 2011, the rate of new marriage fell by 14 percent for those who had not completed high school and by 10 percent for those with at least a bachelor's degree.[11]

In the course of researching this book, I spoke to scores of American women from different backgrounds and classes and faiths and races about their experiences of living singly.

"We all expected to be married at twenty-six," said Kitty Curtis, a New Jersey hairstylist who is, at twenty-six, not married. "I don't really know anyone who is married," she said. "And the ones I do know, there's a sense that it's weird, strange. It's a foreign idea to be married before thirty." Meaghan Ritchie, a fundamentalist Christian college student from Kentucky, told me that she will not marry before she's at least twenty-two, because she believes that dropping out of college—as her mother did to marry her father—would not be an economically sound idea. Amanda Neville, a thirty-five-year-old New Yorker, flew to Russia to adopt a daughter, who is deaf, within a year of opening a wine store and beginning a new relationship with a boyfriend. Ada Li, a manicurist from China living in Brooklyn, told me that her decision to wait until her late thirties to marry and have a child was what made her life in the United States happy and free.

Some women actively decided against early marriage, in part out of fear that matrimony would put a stop to their ambitions. "The moment I saw that ring," wrote Jessica Bennett, a journalist who turned down a proposal at twenty-four, "I saw dirty dishes and suburbia . . . I saw the career I had hardly started as suddenly out of reach . . . the independence I had barely gained felt stifled. I couldn't breathe." Some are sad to not yet have found mates, like Elliott Holt, a forty-year-old novelist who told me, "I guess I just had no idea, could never have predicted, how intense the loneliness would be at this juncture of my life." And others, including Susana Morris, a thirty-two-year-old English professor in Alabama, are less worried about themselves than they are about how concerned everyone *else* is about them. "What's anxiety provoking is that every time you open a magazine or a book or turn on the television, there's someone telling you there's something wrong with you as a black woman—you're too fat, too loud, don't nobody want to marry you. *That* is anxiety producing!"

These women are not waiting for their real lives to start; they are living their lives, and those lives include as many variations as there are women.

To be clear, the vast increase in the number of single women is to be celebrated not because singleness is in and of itself a better or more desirable state than coupledom. The revolution is in the expansion of options, the lifting of the imperative that for centuries hustled nearly all (non-enslaved) women, regardless of their individual desires, ambitions, circumstances, or the quality of available matches, down a single highway toward early heterosexual marriage and motherhood. There are now an infinite number of alternate routes open; they wind around combinations of love, sex, partnership, parenthood, work, and friendship, at different speeds.

Single female life is not prescription, but its opposite: liberation.

This liberation is at the heart of our national promise, but that promise of freedom has often been elusive for many of this country's residents. This makes it all the more important to acknowledge that while the victories of independent life are often emblematized by the country's most privileged women, the war was fought by many Americans who have always had far fewer options to live free: women of color, poor, and working-class women.

## The Epoch of Single Women

When I began writing, I intended this to be a book of mostly contemporary journalism, an account of how generations of single women living at the turn of the twenty-first century were, by delaying or abstaining from marriage, reshaping the nation's politics and families. In short, while I understood it to be built on political gains made in previous eras, I believed that I was chronicling a mass behavioral revolution staged by women of my era.

What I learned, as I began my research, is that while this moment *is* unprecedented in terms of its size, thanks to women's contemporary ability to live more economically and sexually autonomous lives than ever before, it is certainly not without historical precedent. Today's unmarried and late married women are walking a road toward independence that was paved by generations of American women who lived singly when it was far harder to do so than it is today. Crucially, many of those radically single and late-married women were the ones who were able to devote their unmarried, nonmaternal lives to changing the nation's power structures in ways that might better support today's army of free women.

In 1877, the never-married suffragist, abolitionist, and labor activist Susan B. Anthony gave a speech called "The Homes of Single Women." In it, she prophesied that the journey toward gender equality would necessarily include a period in which women stopped marrying. "In woman's transition from the position of subject to sovereign, there must needs be an era of self-sustained, self-supported, homes," said Anthony.[12]

She continued, clairvoyantly:

*As young women become educated in the industries of the world, thereby learning the sweetness of independent bread, it will be more and more impossible for them to accept the . . . marriage limitation that "husband and wife are one, and that one the husband. . . ." Even when man's intellectual convictions shall be sincerely and fully on the side of Freedom and equality to woman, the force of long existing customs and laws will impel him to exert authority over her, which will be distasteful to the self-sustained, self-respectful woman. . . . Not even amended constitutions and laws can revolutionize the practical relations of men and women, immediately, any more than did the Constitutional freedom and franchise of Black men transform white men into practical recognition of the civil and political rights of those who were but yesterday their legal slaves.*

And so, Anthony predicted, logic would lead us, "inevitably, to an *epoch of single women.*"

Here we are.

Smack in the middle of Anthony's imagined epoch, an era in which—like the one in which Anthony herself lived—the independence of women is a crucial tool in their long struggle toward a more just and equitable position in the world.

# CHAPTER ONE

# Watch Out for That Woman: The Political and Social Power of an Unmarried Nation

The contemporary wave of single women was building in the very same years that I was heading off to college, though I hadn't realized it. The early 1990s was the period in which reverberations of the social and political revolutions of my mother's generation were manifesting as swiftly changing marriage and reproductive patterns, which, in turn, would create a current of political possibility for independent women in America.

On October 11, 1991, a thirty-five-year-old law professor, Anita Faye Hill, appeared before the Senate Judiciary Committee to testify about the sexual harassment she'd experienced while working for Clarence Thomas, a D.C. Circuit Judge nominated by President George H. W. Bush to fill the Supreme Court seat of the retiring civil rights hero, Thurgood Marshall. A native of rural Lone Tree, Oklahoma, Hill was the youngest of thirteen children raised by Baptist farmers; her grandfather and great-grandparents had been slaves in Arkansas. She was valedictorian of her high-school class and attended Yale Law School, worked for Thomas at both the Department of Education and the Equal Employment Opportunity Commission, and taught contract law at the University of Oklahoma. She was not married.

As cameras recorded every second, broadcasting to a rapt and tense nation, Hill sat before the all-white, all-male Senate Judiciary Panel and told them in a careful, clear voice of the sexually crude ways in which Thomas had spoken to her during the years she worked for him; she detailed her former boss's references to pornographic movie stars, penis size, and pubic hair in professional contexts. In turn, she was pilloried by the conservative press, spoken to with skepticism and insult by many on the committee, and portrayed by other witnesses as irrational, sexually loose, and perhaps a sufferer of *erotomania*,[1] a rare psychological disorder that causes women to fantasize sexual relationships with powerful men.

Wyoming Senator Alan Simpson questioned Hill's "proclivities" (a term that the conservative columnist William Safire suggested was "a code word for homosexuality"[2]). One pundit, David Brock, called Hill "a little bit nutty and a little bit slutty." Called in front of the committee after her testimony, John Doggett, a former classmate of Thomas's and an acquaintance of Hill's, described Hill as "somewhat unstable" and surmised that she had "fantasized about my being interested in her romantically." He guessed, based on their brief social interactions, "that she was having a problem with being rejected by men she was attracted to;" at another point, Doggett noted that Hill "seemed to be lonely in this town."

As Hill would later write of her experience, "Much was made in the press of the fact that I was single, though the relevance of my marital status to the question of sexual harassment was never articulated."[3]

The relevance of her single status was how it distinguished her from established expectations of femininity. Hill had no husband to vouch for her virtue, no children to affirm her worth, as women's worth had been historically understood. Her singleness, Hill felt at the time, allowed her detractors to place her "as far outside the norms of proper behavior as they could." Members of the Judiciary, she wrote, "could not understand why I was not attached to certain institutions, notably marriage," and were thus left to surmise that she was single "because I was unmarriageable or opposed to marriage, the fantasizing spinster or the man-hater."

The lingering assumption—born of the same expectations that I had chafed at as a kid, reading novels—was that the natural state of adult womanhood involved being legally bound to a man. Perhaps especially in the comparatively new world of female professional achievement, in which a woman might be in a position, as an equivalently educated professional peer of a judicial nominee to the Supreme Court, to offer testimony that could imperil his career, marriage remained the familiar institution that might comfortably balance out this new kind of parity, and would offer the official male validation and abrogate her questioners' ability to depict her as a spinster fantasist.

In raising questions about her marital status and her mental stability, Hill wrote, senators were "attempting to establish a relationship between marriage, values, and credibility" and prompt people to wonder "why I, a thirty-five-year-old Black woman, had chosen to pursue a career and to remain single—an irrelevant shift of focus that contributed to the conclusion that I was not to be believed."

Indeed, Hill's testimony was *not* believed by the members of the committee, at least not enough to make an impact on their decision. Clarence Thomas was confirmed to the Supreme Court days after her appearance before the Judiciary.

But Hill was not some contemporary Hester Prynne, doomed to a life in exile. Instead, her appearance had a lasting impact on the country and its power structures. The term *sexual harassment* entered the lexicon and the American consciousness, allowing women, married and single, to make sense of and lodge objections to workplace harassment; it offered us a view of how behavior long viewed as harmless was actually a form of discrimination and subjugation that hurt women as a class.

Just as long-lasting was the impact that the vision of Hill's being grilled by a panel of white men had on America's representative politics. In 1991, there had been only two women serving in the United States Senate, an embarrassing circumstance that the hearings put in stark national relief. A photograph published by the *New York Times* showed a group of Congress's few female representatives, including Patricia Schroeder and Eleanor Holmes Norton, running up the Capitol steps to stop the proceedings to demand that Hill be allowed to testify.

The spectacle of Hill's treatment by the committee spurred a reckoning with the nation's monochromatic and male representative body. The year after her testimony, an unprecedented number of women ran for the Senate. Four of them won. One, Washington's Patty Murray, has repeatedly explained that the Thomas hearings had helped spur her to political action; "I just kept looking at this committee, going 'God, who's saying what I would say if I was there,'" she's said. "I mean, all men, not saying what I would say. I just felt so disoriented."[4] Another, Carole Moseley Braun of Illinois, became the first (and, so far, only) African-American woman elected to the Senate. They called 1992 "The Year of the Woman."

Though Hill's life and career were certainly upended by the attention (as well as by the death and rape threats) that came in the wake of her testimony, they were not cut short or ended. She was not permanently ostracized, professionally or personally. Today, she teaches law at Brandeis and lives in Boston with her partner of more than a decade.

Part of the reason that Hill was not wholly written off as a social aberration was because by the early 1990s, she wasn't. A generation of women was, like Hill, living, working, and occupying public space on its own. The percentage of women between the ages of thirty-five and forty-four who were married had fallen from about 87 percent in 1960 and 1970 to 73 percent in 1990.[5]

"Women began, in the nineties, to embrace their own sexuality and sexual expression in a different way," Hill told me in 2013. Hill may have looked little like the recent past, but she was very much the face of the future, surely part of what made her discomfiting enough to send senators into paroxysms. As Alan Simpson urged the committee, citing the many warnings he claimed to have received about Hill, "Watch out for this woman!"[6]

In the early 1990s, there were so many women to watch out for.

## The Great Crossover

Less than a year after the Thomas hearings, Vice President Dan Quayle gave a campaign trail speech at the Commonwealth Club in San Francisco, during which he offered his theory on what was behind the Los Angeles race riots that had followed the verdict in the Rodney King trial. The "lawless social anarchy that we saw," Quayle argued, "is directly related to the breakdown of the family structure." To illustrate this point, Quayle took an unexpected turn, laying into a television character.

The eponymous heroine of CBS's *Murphy Brown*, played by Candice

Bergen, was about to give birth to a baby without being married—or romantically attached—to the child's father. Quayle was concerned that in doing so, Murphy, who he noted "supposedly epitomizes today's intelligent, highly paid professional woman," was "mocking the importance of fathers by bearing a child alone and calling it just another lifestyle choice."[7] Quayle's comments would land him, fictional Murphy Brown, and her fictional baby, Avery, on the front of the *New York Times*, making the character's unmarried status far more emblematic than it would have been otherwise.

Of course, Quayle's concern hadn't really been about Murphy; he had been unspooling some classic conservative rhetoric about how welfare programs discourage marriage when he'd thrown his pop-culture curveball. Quayle's anxiety over the possibility that new models of motherhood and womanhood, unhooked from marriage, might be taking hold across income brackets was palpable. A new reality was setting in: If women *could* live independently, many would do so, and as they did, men would become less central to economic security, social standing, sexual life, and, as it turned out, to parenthood.

Though Quayle surely didn't realize it at the time, 1992 was at the heart of what researchers would later dub "the great crossover."[8] Not only were the early nineties the years during which the marriage age was rising; they were the point at which the marriage age was rising *above* the age of first birth.

It was the reversal of a very old cultural and religious norm, purportedly a bedrock of female identity and familial formation, though not always a reflection of real life, in which premarital sex and pregnant brides had always existed. However, officially, public codes of respectability had held that marriage was to precede childbearing. Now, that sequence was being scrambled, and amongst the many Americans panicking about it were the men who had long enjoyed relatively unchallenged control of politics.

Two years after Quayle's speech, Pennsylvania senate candidate Rick Santorum gave a speech again emphasizing the link between unmarried motherhood and social chaos, claiming that "We are seeing the fabric of this country fall apart, and it's falling apart because of single moms." In

1994, Jeb Bush, son of former president George H. W. Bush, then running for governor in Florida, said that women on welfare "should be able to get their life together and find a husband" and, soon after, published a book in which he argued that the reason young women have babies outside of wedlock is because "there is no longer a stigma attached to this behavior," suggesting that maybe the stigma should return.

In 1993, Bill Clinton appointed Joycelyn Elders, an outspoken advocate of humane drug laws and abortion rights, as Surgeon General of the United States. The following year, at a United Nations conference on AIDS, Elders caused a scandal by voicing her support of teaching masturbation as part of sex education. It was a perfectly sane message, especially in the context of the AIDS epidemic. But so freighted was Elders's simple advocacy of independent sexual pleasure, achievable without a partner and with no chance of procreation, that the president who had appointed her asked her to resign.

It was a fraught period, Anita Hill told me in 2013, in which some Americans were "still trying to hold on to the idea that we lived in the 1950s, this *Leave It to Beaver* world." This imagined white universe, in which sex was hetero and always procreative and women were wives and mothers who lived in middle-class comfort and embraced designated gender roles, had "never actually existed for most women," Hill said, but was held up as an American ideal.

Now, even in pop culture, *Leave It to Beaver* had given way to the irreverent *Roseanne*, the sitcom about a working-class nuclear family in which the eponymous heroine joked of her (loving) marriage as "like a life sentence with no hope for parole." More broadly, nuclear families were being joined on television by a flood of images of women unbound from marriages and families altogether. Beginning in 1993, Queen Latifah anchored a group of Brooklyn roommates on FOX's *Living Single*; the next year, NBC answered with the white, Manhattan version: *Friends*. From 1994 to 1996, journalist Candace Bushnell penned a weekly newspaper column called "Sex and the City;" it would go on to become a book and a smash HBO series.

Terri McMillan's *Waiting to Exhale*, a 1992 novel about four female friends, some recently jilted, juggling the personal and the professional, remained on the bestseller list for months, and would be made into a movie. Four years later, British writer Helen Fielding published *Bridget Jones's Diary*, and was credited with kicking off a new publishing genre, "chick lit," devoted to the stories of women, whom Bridget's best friend would, in self-parody, describe as "a pioneer generation daring to refuse to compromise in love and relying on our own economic power."

As the millennium dawned, it was impossible to watch out for all the women who were coming to change America.

## Strange Stirrings

If women slowed their rush to the altar in huge numbers starting in the 1990s, their *ability* to do so was built directly on political, economic, social, and sexual victories won by the previous generation, during what is commonly known as the Second Wave of the women's movement. Several Second Wave feminists would remind me pointedly during my research for this book that my generation had far from invented contemporary habits of marital abstinence or delay; by many measures, theirs had.

And, to some degree, they're right: Many women whose consciousness had been raised and opportunities expanded by feminism actively decided, for political and personal reasons, to postpone or forego marriage.

They didn't do so in numbers large enough to create a demographic earthquake, to change the marrying behaviors of the masses, at least not right away. Because while its victories would transform the landscape in ways that would make it far more possible for my generation to delay marriage, the Second Wave was not built on opposition to marriage, but rather a desire to address its suffocating circumstances.

*The problem lay buried, unspoken, for many years in the minds of American women. It was a strange stirring, a sense of dissatisfaction, a yearning that women suffered in the middle of the twentieth century in the Unites States. Each suburban wife struggled with it alone. As she made the beds, shopped for groceries, matched slipcover*

*material, ate peanut-butter sandwiches with her children, chauf-*
*feured Cub Scouts and Brownies, lay beside her husband at night,*
*she was afraid to ask even of herself the silent question "Is this all?"*[9]

Is this all? Betty Friedan's first paragraph sliced the mid-century American situation for middle-class white women to its quick: assert- ing that the ennui, anger, and unhappiness experienced by millions of American women was the product of the "millions of words" spilled by ex- perts assuring women that "their role was to seek fulfillment as wives and mothers." These sages had spent a decade and a half, Friedan reported, telling women "how to catch a man and keep him . . . that truly feminine women do not want careers, higher education, political rights—the inde- pendence and the opportunities that the old-fashioned feminists fought for." Those women who'd been raised with the limited scope of female possibility offered by mid-twentieth century America, Friedan argued, believed that "All they had to do was devote their lives from earliest girl- hood to finding a husband and bearing children."

*The Feminine Mystique* would sell 1.4 million copies of its first pa- perback printing and, though its popularity was likely a symptom of the fact that Friedan's ideas were already in circulation and gaining steam in other quarters, it would be widely credited as having kicked off the Sec- ond Wave.[10] Early marriage and domestic confinement were so pervasive for middle-class white women in the middle of the twentieth century that the nation's most mass, conscious move to emancipate women erupted directly in response to it.

Yet, funnily enough, as the legal scholar Rachel Moran argues, while the feminist movement of the 1970s was in part a "direct response to these conditions of early and pervasive marriage," the ironic side effect was that *single* women had almost no place in the underpinnings of the movement.

As much as *The Feminine Mystique* was a cry against the limitations that early marriage and motherhood imposed on women, it did not as- sume (or even consider) that marriage itself was the problematic element, or that it might ever be optional for women. Friedan's vision of female empowerment entailed the expansion of activity *outside* the domestic sphere, but it did not question the primacy of that sphere itself.

Friedan's reflexive connections between male attention and female fulfillment—as well as the rather dim regard in which she held most single women—are evident throughout her book.[11] "Strangely, a number of psychiatrists state that, in their experience, unmarried women patients were happier than married ones," writes Friedan with obvious perplexity. Elsewhere, she cites Susan B. Anthony as the early feminist who most closely resembled the myth of the "embittered shrew," conceding (generously, she must have thought) that while Anthony "felt betrayed when the other [suffragists] started to marry and have babies," she did not end up some "bitter spinster with a cat."

When Friedan, who would co-found and become the first president of the National Organization for Women in 1966, was asked about NOW's mission in a television interview, she replied that the group's message was about revising the "conditions that prevent women from easily combining marriage and motherhood and work."[12] The group's mission statement amplified this intention, noting that NOW did "not accept the traditional assumption that a woman has to choose between marriage and motherhood, on the one hand, and a serious participation in industry or the professions on the other . . . We believe that a true partnership between the sexes demands a different concept of marriage, an equitable sharing of the responsibilities[13] . . ." It was (and remains!) a revolutionary vision, but the organization was not the National Organization of *Married* Women, and yet there was no hint of recognition that not every woman's life would (or should) include marriage and children, in that order.

This was only one way in which Friedan's vision was blinkered.

In addition to her inability to conceive of middle-class white women who might not *want* the youthful unions into which they were being nudged, Friedan also didn't consider the population of American women who were already altering marriage patterns, who had in recent years been marrying at declining rates and at later ages, who had been working outside the home for longer than that, supporting themselves and sometimes their children, both alongside, and independent of, husbands. Friedan did not include black women in her vision.

Black women, who experienced both gender and racial wage discrimination, who were less likely than their white peers to have college educations or economic power, and whose families and potential husbands were also less likely to have college educations or economic power, were also far less likely than white women to have the *choice* of not working outside their homes. They were therefore far less likely to experience the kind of domestic disenchantments from which Friedan's readers suffered.

Black women had in fact already made some of the very points for which Friedan was being hailed. Philadelphia lawyer Sadie Alexander had argued in the 1930s that women yearned to "place themselves again among the producers of the world" by involving themselves in work "that resulted in the production of goods that have a price value."[14] Not only would this increase women's status and security in the world, Alexander argued, in advance of Friedan, but "the satisfaction which comes to the woman in realizing that she is a producer makes for peace and happiness, the chief requisites in any home."

Even worse was that at practically the same moment that Friedan was being credited with jump starting the women's movement by advocating extramarital wage-earning that black women had been doing for generations, black women were being blamed for a different sort of social disruption. Two years after the publication of *The Feminine Mystique*, women whose experiences had foregrounded its philosophies were at the center of a national conversation about the devolution of the black family unit and the social and economic blight it was presumed to have precipitated.

In 1965, Assistant Secretary of Labor and future New York Senator Daniel Patrick Moynihan released a report called "The Negro Family: The Case for National Action." It was, in some ways, a thoughtful account of the systemic racial inequality that had plagued the nation since its founding, with Moynihan arguing that "the American Republic, which at birth was flawed by the institution of Negro slavery, and which throughout its history has been marred by the unequal treatment of Negro citizens" long had fallen short of "the full promise of the Declaration of Independence." Moynihan rightly acknowledged the development of middle-class white suburbs and abandonment of poor cities to African-Americans as having created a class chasm between the races, noting that "because of this new housing pattern—most of which has been financially assisted by the Federal government—it is probable that the American school system has become *more*, rather than less segregated in the past two decades."

Yet, despite these insights into the unequal histories and prospects of

America's black and white populations, Moynihan boiled his argument down to one, punishing point: that the root of black poverty lay with the breakdown of marital norms for which nonconforming women were responsible. The "deterioration of the Negro family," Moynihan argued, was tied to the high number of dissolved marriages, illegitimate births and the fact that "almost one-fourth of Negro families are headed by women."

There was some logic here: In economically unstable communities, raising children on single, low incomes is an inherently unstable proposition. But there was no consideration that those single incomes were a result as much as a cause, that reduced economic opportunity made marriage a less beneficial option for women, that women's work outside the home was, rather than a detriment, key to keeping disadvantaged black communities and families afloat. Instead, Moynihan positioned female independence from men and dominance within the family at the center of a "tangle of pathology" that created "a matriarchal structure which, because it is out of line with the rest of American society," and its *patriarchal* structure, "seriously retards the progress of the group as a whole."

## Comfort to the Singles

In the burgeoning feminist movement, the voices of figures more radical than Friedan began to get more notice for their arguments that women should not simply move toward the workforce, but away from marriage as the ratifying stamp of female worth.

In 1969, University of Chicago sociology professor Marlene Dixon wrote that "the institution of marriage is the chief vehicle for the perpetuation of the oppression of women . . . In a very real way the role of wife has been the genesis of women's rebellion throughout history." The next year, feminist Sheila Cronan wrote, "Since marriage constitutes slavery for women . . . Freedom for women cannot be won without the abolition of marriage." Radical feminist writer Andrea Dworkin famously commented that "Marriage as an institution developed from rape as a practice."

In 1970, the median age of first marriage for women remained under twenty-one, and 69.4 percent of Americans over the age of eighteen were married.[15] This is remarkable, in part, because of other social and political upheavals already well underway: In 1960, the FDA had approved the birth control pill for contraceptive use, an early step toward (or symptom of) what would become the sexual revolution. And, in 1969, the Stonewall riots had kicked off a gay rights movement that would be driven explicitly by the fight for acceptance by women and men who had no desire to partner with members of the opposite sex.

The emergence of gay women as a political faction was not an altogether welcome development within the Second Wave. Friedan herself would famously refer to lesbians as a "lavender menace" and, in later years, would voice her loathing[16] of women she called "man-hating" feminists, whose "down-with-men, down-with-marriage, down-with-childbearing rhetoric and actions" threatened to wrest control of feminism from "women who wanted equality but who also wanted to keep on loving their husbands and children."[17]

In fact, for some time, the intersections of the gay rights and women's rights movements seemed mostly to provide evidence both of the strength of homophobia amongst social progressives and gender iconoclasts, and of how inconceivable it remained even to many 1970s feminists that heterosexual women might live willingly single: The only way some feminists were able to absorb the notion of a woman who didn't necessarily want to marry a man was to understand her as homosexual.

At least until Gloria came along.

In the early 70s, feminism got a new and powerful popularizer, a woman who would come to stand (insufficiently and often to her own dismay) for the diverse, cacophonous, flawed, and multifaceted movement whose sometimes spiky messages she was so capable of transmitting smoothly to the broader public.

Gloria Steinem had come to New York from her native Toledo, and began a successful career as a writer for print and television; she was mentioned alongside other "new journalism" stars like Tom Wolfe, and was a stylish darling of New York's 1960s media scene, often photographed in the company of well-known men, many of whom she was dating.

Steinem was late to feminism. In 1962, she'd written a story about contraception that laid out the ways in which women were asked to choose between career and marriage; the next year she did an undercover exposé of Hugh Hefner's sex-themed *Playboy* clubs. However, her political engagements were with the Democratic Party, the civil rights, and antiwar movements; they didn't yet extend to the burgeoning women's movement. In 1963, the year that the *Feminine Mystique* was published, Steinem had written *The Beach Book*, a guide to travel and tanning that featured a foil cover flap that readers might use to catch rays.

Even without a raised consciousness, Steinem's life, by the late 1960s, served as a striking emblem of the era's new possibilities for women: She was unmarried, widely traveled, professionally successful, and open about her sexual appetites. In a 1968 television interview, Canadian broadcaster Moses Znaimer asked thirty-four-year-old Steinem about her reputation as a "chick with a good sense of the vibrations;" he questioned how she'd gone undercover at *Playboy,* since he "thought you had to be stacked to be a bunny girl;" he asked if she cooked (she was ironing in the interview). He asked her if she ever wanted to marry.

"Eventually," Steinem replied, "but it keeps receding two years into the comfortable distance." Did she think about it a lot? Yes, she said. "You imagine what it would be like to be married to people you're going out with . . . maybe it's a lady's thing . . . You think, 'Let's see, my name would be Gloria Burgermeister. . . . nah.'" In the interview's final question, Znaimer asks Steinem what she wants to be "when you grow up."

"Free," Steinem replies, "and old . . . and a little mean."[18]

A year later, Steinem wrote a piece called "After Black Power, Women's Liberation," in which she reported on the growing feminist movement. That same year, while covering an abortion speak-out in Greenwich Village, Steinem, who had had an abortion in Europe in her early twenties, experienced a conversion.

Within months, she was testifying in front of the Senate Judiciary on behalf of the Equal Rights Amendment; she co-founded, along with Shirley Chisholm, Bella Abzug, Myrlie Evers, Fanny Lou Hamer, and Friedan, the National Women's Political Caucus. In 1971, she and Letty Cottin Pogrebin launched *Ms.* magazine, the title of which rejected the notion that marital status should be the identifying feature of a woman.

Steinem's most powerful gift was her ability to synthesize radical sentiments into appealingly pithy, era-defining sound bites.

"We are becoming the men we wanted to marry," she said, clarifying that an opposition to marriage need not be about the rejection of men or love, but rather about the filling out and equaling up of female life. "A woman needs a man like a fish needs a bicycle," she was often credited with coining (actually, the phrase came from Australian educator Irina Dunn[19]). More sharply, Steinem argued that marriage rendered women "half people," and once explained that she had not married, and would not marry, because, "I can't mate in captivity." It was a funny line, borne of deep dissatisfactions and anger over the way life had been until now.

Not everyone was charmed.

"I guess [she] gave some comfort to the singles," Betty Friedan would later say of Steinem. "But really, Gloria was a phony. She always had a man. And I used to catch her hiding behind a *Vogue* magazine at Kenneth's having her hair streaked."[20]

Steinem herself made the same point to me in 2012, noting that she had been "somewhat protected" from certain kinds of man-hating caricature and denigration because "I always had a man in my life." However, that was part of what made her so useful when it came to offering a more fetching vision of unmarried life than had previously been available. Steinem's beauty, her independence, her unapologetic heterosexual appetites, and her steady stream of suitors could not easily be written off as *froideur*, as man-hating, as homosexuality. What was so disruptive about Steinem, and other women who were living like her, whether or not they had men on their arms, was that it seemed she just really enjoyed being free.

More young unmarried women were about to join her, thanks to two landmark cases decided in the early seventies.

The Supreme Court had made birth control legal for married couples in the 1965 case, *Griswold v. Connecticut*, basing its decision on the opinion that a ban violated the privacy of the marital bedroom's "innermost sanctum." But, for single women, the relevant decision came seven years later. In 1972's *Eisenstadt v. Baird*, the Court struck down a law that prohibited the sale of contraception to unmarried persons, thus affirming "the right of the *individual*, married or single, to be free from unwarranted governmental intrusion into matters so fundamentally affecting a person as the decision whether to bear or beget a child."

The decision affirmed both parties within a heterosexual union as individual entities with rights, a break from some long-standing principles of marital law, which had, in various forms over two centuries, meant that women forfeited many elements of their identities and their liberties upon marrying. "The marital couple is not an independent entity with a mind and heart of its own," wrote Justice William Brennan in his decision, "but an association of two individuals each with a separate intellectual and emotional make-up." It was like a legal equivalent of *Ms. Magazine*: the recognition that Americans' rights should neither be circumscribed nor made more expansive based simply on whether they were wed. As the historian Nancy Cott writes, by "refusing to deny single persons the privacy that married couples were granted, [*Eisenstadt*] moved toward displacing marriage from the seat of official morality."[21]

One year later, the court ruled in *Roe v. Wade* that abortion was legal. The decision affected married and single women equally. But, for the unmarried, legal abortion provided yet another tool to protect their ability to live outside of marriage.

By 1973, the *idea* of independent womanhood was worming its way into the national imagination persistently enough that *Newsweek* published a cover story that fulsomely asserted that "singlehood has emerged as an intensely ritualized—and newly respectable—style of American life. . . . It is finally becoming possible to be both single and whole."[22] And, in 1974, Congress passed the Equal Credit Opportunity Act, making it easier for women to secure credit cards, bank loans, and mortgages, and to buy their own homes.

While the women's movement had not been explicitly driven by efforts to advocate for single women, what it had succeeded at doing, via its impact on politics, economics, and the law, was to create options besides or in advance of marriage. With every passing year in the 1970s, there were simply more ways to valorize female existence: more jobs to apply for, flings to have, money to earn.

As these new temptations clashed with the retro realities of marriages begun in a pre-feminist era, the divorce rate skyrocketed, hitting close to

50 percent through the late 1970s and 1980s. The divorce boom had a huge impact on never or not-yet married women. First, it created more single people, helping to slowly destigmatize the figure of the woman without a ring on her finger. It also forced a very public reckoning with marriage as an institution of variable quality. The realization that a bad marriage might be bad enough to cause a painful split provided ammunition to those women who preferred to abstain from marriage than to enter a flawed one.

What the women's movement of the 1970s did, ultimately, was not to shrink marriage, or the desire for male companionship, as a reality for many women, but rather to enlarge the *rest* of the world to such an extent that marriage's shadow became far less likely to blot out the sun of other possibilities. As legal scholar Rachel Moran writes, "One of the great ironies of second-wave feminism is that it ignored single women as a distinct constituency while creating the conditions that increasingly enabled women to forego marriage."[23]

At the conclusion of the 1970s, the number of never-married persons was at its lowest[24] ever (mostly because the calculation included the enormous swell of married, now divorcing, Baby Boomers), but the rate of women who were getting married was beginning to slow noticeably, and the median age of first marriage had inched up to twenty-two.

In 1981, Ronald Reagan cruised into the Oval Office on a wave of aspersions cast on women he depicted as relying on government assistance in place of husbands, or in his parlance, "welfare queens." His ascension had come on the back of, and in tandem with, the rise of the New Right, an alliance of fiscal and social conservatives aligned around a commitment to religious righteousness and reversing the victories of twentieth-century social progressives. He struck the Equal Rights Amendment from the Republican Party's platform, where it had remained since 1940; he supported the so-called Human Life Amendment, which would have banned almost all abortions, and defined life as beginning at fertilization.

It was morning in post-feminist America, and the backlash, against the women's movement and the single women whose swelling numbers seemed to emblematize its success most uncomfortably, was in full force. In 1985, a study conducted by male researchers from Harvard and

Yale concluded that a never-married, university-educated forty-year-old woman had only a 2.6 percent chance of ever marrying. It spurred *Newsweek* to publish its infamous cover story "The Marriage Crunch," in which it made the famously inaccurate claim that single women at age forty were more likely to be killed by terrorists than to marry. *People* published photos of unmarried celebrities under the headline "Are These Old Maids?"[25] and warned that "most single women over thirty-five can forget about marriage." The social and cultural resistance to the spurning of marriage was evident.

And yet, women kept right on *not* marrying. In 1990, the median age for first marriage for women jumped to nearly twenty-four, the highest it had been in the century in which it had been recorded.

The future had arrived. With it had come echoes of the past advances of unmarried women, this time threatening the status quo with the sexual and economic power won for them by previous generations. Rising to meet them would be new iterations of old political and cultural opposition, figures anxious to corral these Amazons back into the marital fold.

## Now

Abstention from or delay of marriage may have been a conscious choice for some women in the 1970s and 1980s, but it has now simply become a mass behavior. The most radical of feminist ideas—the disestablishment of marriage—has, terrifyingly for many conservatives, been so widely embraced as to have become habit, drained of its political intent, but ever more potent insofar as it has refashioned the course of average female life. The independence of women from marriage decried by Moynihan as a pathology at odds with the nation's patriarchal order is now a norm.

By 2013, about half of first-time births were to unmarried women; for women under thirty, it was almost 60 percent.[26] The same year, the National Center for Family and Marriage Research released a study that revealed the marriage rate to be the lowest it had been in over a century.[27] "Marriage is no longer compulsory," the co-director of the NCFMR said in a statement about the study. "It's just one of an array of options."

That array of options is pretty stunning compared to the narrow chute of hetero marriage and maternity into which most women were herded just a few decades ago. Millions of women now live with, but do not marry, long-term partners; others move in and out of sequential monogamous relationships; live sexually diverse lives; live outside of romantic or sexual relationships altogether, both with and without children; marry or enter civil unions with members of the same sex or combine some of these options.

The journey toward legal marriage for gays and lesbians may seem at odds with what looks like a flight *from* marriage by heterosexuals. But in fact, they are part of the same project: a dismantling of the institution as it once existed—as a rigidly patrolled means by which one sex could exert legal, economic, and sexual power over another—and a reimagining of it as a flexible union to be entered, ideally, on equal terms.

Taken together, these shifts, by many measures, embody the worst nightmare of social conservatives: a complete rethinking of who women are and who men are and, therefore, also of what family is and who holds dominion within it . . . and outside it. The expanded presence of women as independent entities means a redistribution of all kinds of power, including electoral power, that has, until recently, been wielded mostly by men.

### Single Women Voters

In 2012, unmarried women made up a remarkable 23 percent of the electorate. Almost *a quarter* of votes were cast by women without husbands, up three points from just four years earlier. According to Page Gardner, founder of the Voter Participation Center, in the 2012 presidential election, unmarried women, who have a vested stake in their own economic and reproductive rights, drove turnout in practically every demographic, making up "almost 40 percent of the African-American population, close to 30 percent of the Latino population, and about a third of all young voters."

Single women helped put Barack Obama back in the White House;

they voted for him by 67 to 31 percent, while married women voted for Romney. In the 2013 Virginia race for governor, the Democratic candidate beat his Republican rival, carrying women by nine points, but single women by what the *New York Times* called[28] "a staggering 42 percentage points." Unmarried women's political leanings are not, as has been surmised in some quarters, attributable solely to their racial diversity. According to polling firm Lake Research Partners, while white women as a whole voted for Romney over Obama, *unmarried* white women chose Obama over Romney by a margin of 49.4 percent to 38.9 percent.[29] In 2013, columnist Jonathan Last wrote about a study of how women aged twenty-five to thirty voted in the 2000 election. "It turned out," Last wrote in the *Weekly Standard*, "that the marriage rate for these women was a greater influence on vote choice than any other variable" measured.[30]

The connection between single female life and electoral engagement is no wonky secret. As one 2014 *New York Times* story began, "The decline of marriage over the last generation has helped create an emerging voting bloc of unmarried women that is profoundly reshaping the American electorate."

Conservatives are so aware of this that antifeminist pundit Phyllis Schlafly claimed in 2012 that President Obama was working to keep women unmarried by giving away so many social services to them. "President Obama is simply trying to promote more dependency on government hand-outs because he knows that is his constituency,"[31] Schlafly said. This is how scary single women are today, and how badly Republican politicians want to lash out at them: During the October 2012 presidential debate between Mitt Romney and Barack Obama, when the candidates were asked about how they might stem the tide of gun violence, Romney replied that a major step in curbing "the culture of violence" in the United States was to "tell our kids that before they have babies, they ought to think about getting married to someone." Apparently, anyone (of the opposite sex) will do.

As the second decade of the twenty-first century has worn on, politicians of all stripes, aware of the political power of the unmarried woman yet seemingly incapable of understanding female life outside of a marital context, have come to rely on a metaphor in which American women, no longer bound to men, are binding themselves to government. During the lead-up to the 2014 midterms, Fox News pundit Jesse Watters, referring to unmarried women as "Beyoncé Voters," alleged that "they depend on government because they're not depending on their husbands. They need things like contraception, health care, and they love to talk about equal pay." Meanwhile, some young conservatives at the College Republican National Committee took a less scolding approach, cutting a series of television ads that imagined a single female voter trying on wedding dresses in the spirit of TLC's reality show "Say Yes to the Dress," except in the ads, the dress was actually a Republican gubernatorial candidate to whom this would-be-bride was pledging herself. Meanwhile, the liberal leaning *Cosmopolitan Magazine* launched a Get Out the Vote initiative that included a social-media–spread "Save the Date" notice for November 4, Election Day. It came with the unsubtle message, "You and the polls are getting hitched."

Joel Kotkin, a professor of urban development, argued in *The Daily Beast* that the power of the single voter is destined to fade, since single people "by definition . . . have no heirs,"[32] while their religious, conservative, counterparts will repopulate the nation with children who will replicate their parents' politics, ensuring that "conservative, more familial-oriented values inevitably prevail." Kotkin's error, of course, is both in assuming that unmarried people do not reproduce—in fact, they are doing so in ever greater numbers—but also in failing to consider whence the gravitation away from married norms derived. A move toward independent life did not simply emerge from a clamshell: It was born of generations of dissatisfaction with the inequities of religious, conservative, social practice. Why should we believe that children born to social conservatives will not tread a similar path, away from conservative values, as the one walked by generations of traditionally raised citizens before them? The impulse toward liberation isn't inoculated against by strict conservative backgrounds; it's often inculcated by them.

What all the electoral hand-wringing reveals is the seriousness of anxieties about how, exactly, independent women might wield their unprecedented influence, if only they came out to vote in full numbers, which they too often fail to do.

Unmarried women are among the voters who are hardest to pull to the polls. In part because they are often poor, many of them overworked single mothers with multiple commitments, low-paying jobs that don't permit them time to stand in line at the voting booth, or women for whom social policy has already failed so badly that they might not even see the point of voting. According to Page Gardner, in 2016, "For the first time in history, a majority of women voters are projected to be unmarried." Yet going into the last presidential election season, nearly 40 percent of them had not registered to vote.[33]

And yet, even with only a relatively small percentage of them voting, these single American women have already shown that they have the power to change America, in ways that make many people extremely uncomfortable.

## Co-eds, Sluts, and Marriage Cures

In 2012, a then-unmarried Georgetown law student, Sandra Fluke, testified about the insurance regulations being proposed for women buying birth control. Fluke's argument barely touched on issues of sexual freedom; it was instead about money, wages, education, about the rights that women have to live multi-faceted lives—the kinds that are now more possible, since marriage has become decentralized as the defining experience of female adulthood—without being taxed extra to control their reproduction.

When he tore into Fluke's testimony in a lengthy on-air rant, conservative radio host Rush Limbaugh couldn't seem to get past his spluttering fury at the fact that she was arguing for her rights to a product that would enable her to have unmonitored amounts of sex. Limbaugh turned promptly to eroticized denigration of the independent woman in a way that recalled the treatment of Anita Hill twenty years earlier. On his syndicated radio show, Limbaugh called Fluke a "slut" and a "prostitute;" "so much sex," "so much sex," "so much sex," he repeated, extending his condemnation to envelop Fluke's generational cohort, the "co-eds" who hook up "with as many partners as they want . . . Whatever, no limits on this." Limbaugh said "unlimited" repeatedly, conveying his unmistakable fury that women had successfully conspired to evade the restraints that marriage and custom used to provide.

Fluke, and the growing power of other independent women she seemed to represent, was an irritant to these conservatives. More than that, they feared, she might be contagious . . . positively pestilential.

A writer at *The American Spectator* called Fluke, whom he took care to refer to as *Mizz*, "the model Welfare Queen for the 21st Century;" and warned of "how many thousands of" her ilk "are graduating this year to enter government jobs or political campaigns. They will be spreading their ideas to all within hearing."[34]

Less than a week after his Fluke attack, Limbaugh was tearing into a book on food politics written by another young woman when he paused to ask on air: "What is it with all these young, single, white women?"

Watch out for these women, these men were saying. They are everywhere.

And for those unmarried women who are not privileged white law students like Fluke, the ones over whom lawmakers can more easily exert punishing power, there is no end to the rhetorical and policy attempts to stuff them back inside a marital box and lock them there.

The idea that the decline in marriage—as opposed to broken social safety networks and economic policies that benefit the wealthy, the white, and the educated over the poor—is the source of inequality in our still fundamentally unequal world has lit a fire under Republicans in the early decades of the twenty-first century. As Florida Republican Marco Rubio has opined, "the greatest tool to lift children and families from poverty . . . isn't a government spending program. It's called marriage."[35] Rubio's early competitors for the 2016 Republican nomination included Rick Santorum and Jeb Bush, politicians who have been campaigning on the denigration of single women since the Great Crossover of the mid-1990s.

In 2013, Mitt Romney's tone on the subject of early marriage became almost mournful, as he reported to graduates of Southern Virginia University during a commencement address there that "[S]ome people could marry, but choose to take more time, they say, for themselves. Others plan to wait until they're well into their thirties or forties before they think about getting married. They're going to miss so much of living, I'm afraid." [36]

This edged toward another arm of sociopolitical and economic anxiety about the growth in population of single women: the failure of these women to have enough babies.

"The root cause of most of our problems is our declining fertility rate," wrote columnist Jonathan Last, perhaps not coincidentally the same man who has studied marital status as the biggest determining factor in partisan affiliation, in a *Wall Street Journal* column pegged to his 2012 book, *What to Expect When No One's Expecting*.

The warning reverberated in many venues, and critics fretted that women's increasing ability to devote portions of their adulthood to things other than marriage and motherhood is diminishing our national prospects. The *New York Times* conservative columnist Ross Douthat wrote a piece entitled, "More Babies, Please" in which he called "the retreat from child rearing" a "decadence" and "a spirit that privileges the present over the future" and "embraces the comforts and pleasures of modernity, while shrugging off the basic sacrifices that built our civilization in the first place." Douthat was not specific about *whose* sacrifices had been so central to the steady repopulation of the nation, but Last himself was much more direct. Detailing the reasons for the falling number of babies, some of which he took care to call "clearly positive," Last wrote of how "Women began attending college in equal (and then greater) numbers than men" and how "more important, women began branching out into careers beyond teaching and nursing." Finally, he wrote, "the combination of the birth-control pill and the rise of cohabitation broke the iron triangle linking sex, marriage and childbearing." [37]

Economist Nancy Folbre, responding to demographic Chicken Littles in the *New York Times*, wrote that she knew "of no historical evidence that either the productivity or the creativity of a society is determined by the age structure of its population." [38] But the anxiety may not have stemmed from historical evidence as much as it did from historical yearning: for a time before what Last described as "the iron triangle" linking women, marriage, and reproduction had been dismantled.

Whether those who worried were concerned about too many babies or too few babies, women living in poverty or women enjoying power, they all seemed to return to the same conclusion: Marriage must be reestablished as the norm, the marker and measure of female existence, against which all other categories of success are weighed.

## The Story of Single Women Is the Story of the Country

The funny thing is that all these warnings, diagnoses, and panics—even the most fevered of them—aren't wholly unwarranted. Single women *are* upending everything; their growing presence has an impact on how economic, political, and sexual power is distributed between the genders. The ability for women to live unmarried is having an impact on our electoral politics. The vast numbers of single women living in the United States are changing our definitions of family, and, in turn, will have an impact on our social policies.

The intensity of the resistance to these women is rooted in the (perhaps unconscious) comprehension that their expanded power signals a social and political rupture as profound as the invention of birth control, as the sexual revolution, as the abolition of slavery, as women's suffrage and the feminist, civil rights, gay rights, and labor movements.

Crucially, single women played a huge part in all of those earlier ruptures. Though it may feel as though the growing numbers of unmarried women and the influence they wield have shaken the nation only in the past five decades, in fact, the story of single women's nation-shaping power is threaded into the story of the nation itself.

Women, perhaps especially those who have lived untethered from the energy-sucking and identity-sapping institution of marriage in its older forms, have helped to drive social progress of this country since its founding.

# CHAPTER TWO

# Single Women Have Often Made History: Unmarried in America

In 1563, England's House of Lords petitioned its Queen: "That it please your Majesty to dispose yourself to marry, where you will, with whom you will, and as shortly as you will." The monarch was Elizabeth Tudor, England's "Virgin Queen," who ruled from 1558 to 1603 and refused, to her death, to marry. Elizabeth considered several marriage proposals, some of which would have forged valuable international alliances, but remained independent, proclaiming after Parliament's first entreaty to her in 1558 "I have long since made choice of a husband, the kingdom of England," explaining in another instance her desire to remain unencumbered: "I will have here but one mistress and no master." She is reported to have said to a foreign emissary, "If I am to disclose to you what I should prefer if I follow the inclination of my nature, it is this: beggar-woman and single, rather than queen and married."[1]

The truth was that it would have been much harder for a beggar woman to have remained single than it was for Elizabeth. As historians Judith Bennett and Amy Froide observed in their study of single women in early Europe, "Women almost never found occupations that paid as well as the work of men," making life outside of marriage almost impossible, but, among elites, "wealthy heiresses who controlled their own destinies were better able than other women to forego marriage." They cite Elizabeth as "an obvious example of the link between female control of property and singleness."[2]

If Elizabeth is an example of how rare it was for centuries of women to flourish outside of marriage, she's also an example of the degree to which those women who contrived to remain single often found themselves better able than their married counterparts to exercise some control over their own fates, and, in extraordinary cases, to leave their marks on the world.

For most women, there were simply not other routes, besides marriage, to economic stability, to a socially sanctioned sexual and reproductive life, to standing within communities. But it was simultaneously true that to have a husband (and, in turn, children, sometimes scads of them) was to be subsumed by wifeliness and maternity. More than that, it was a way to lose autonomy, legal rights, and the capacity for public achievement. Of the few women who managed to leave a historical trace, usually from wealthier castes, a great number turn out to have been single, or, at the very least, single for the period during which they carved out space for themselves in the remembered world.

Writers and artists, including painter Mary Cassatt, poets Emily Dickinson and Christina Rossetti, novelists Anne and Emily Brontë, Willa Cather, Catharine Maria Sedgwick, and prolific African-American writer Pauline Hopkins, never married. Many of the women who broke barriers in medicine, including doctors Elizabeth and Emily Blackwell and nurses Florence Nightingale, Clara Barton, and Dorothea Dix, remained single. Social reformers including Jane Addams, Susan B. Anthony, Frances Willard, Alice Paul, Mary Grew, and Dorothy Height, and educators like Catharine Beecher and Mary Lyon—none had husbands.

That doesn't mean that many of these women didn't have sexual or domestic entanglements, or long-term, loving commitments to men or to other women, though some of them did not. It's that they did not match society's expectations by entering an institution built around male authority and female obeisance.

As Anthony would tell the journalist Nellie Bly, "I've been in love a thousand times! . . . But I never loved any one so much that I thought it would last. . . . I never felt I could give up my life of freedom to become a man's housekeeper. When I was young, if a girl married poor, she became a housekeeper and a drudge. If she married wealth, she became a pet and a doll. Just think, had I married at twenty, I would have been a drudge or a doll for fifty-five years."[3]

Of course, some married women also enjoyed successes unusual for their gender and their time: writers Elizabeth Gaskell and Harriett Beecher Stowe were not only married; they were great proselytizers of the institution's benefits for women. But many married women could, and did, acknowledge that wedlock, in its traditional form, took women out of the public world. Elizabeth Cady Stanton, nineteenth-century women's rights reformer and married mother of seven, was wry about the tolls of home life; she joked in a letter after not having heard from Anthony for a while: "Where are you, Susan, and what are you doing? Your silence is truly appalling. Are you dead or married?"[4]

Common amongst prominent women who did wed, including activists such as Ida B. Wells, Angelina Grimké and Pauli Murray; writers including George Elliot, Margaret Fuller, and Zora Neale Hurston; artists Frida Kahlo and Georgia O'Keefe; actress Sarah Bernhard; and aviator Brave Bessie Coleman were alliances that were unconventional for their times: open, childless, brief, or entered into late, after the women had established themselves economically or professionally, and thus could find partners more willing to accept them as peers, not appendages.

However, creative paths to evading the onerous limitations of traditional wifedom were not plentiful. Marriage, in the varied ways in which it has been legally constructed over centuries, has been extremely useful in containing women and limiting their power. That usefulness has meant that social, political, medical, and cultural forces have often worked to make life *outside* marriage difficult. So, while women who have remained single, on purpose or by accident, may have retained some power and self-determination, they rarely, in the past, escaped social censure or enjoyed economic independence.

To trace their difficult paths through the history of the United States is to recognize challenges and resistance to single female life that will be uncannily familiar to today's single women: Women, it turns out, have been fighting their own battle for independence, against politicians, preachers, and the popular press, since our founding. Not only that: Women living singly in America over the past two centuries have been partly responsible for the social and economic upheavals that have made the possibility of independent life for *today's* single women so much more plausible.

## (Marital) Independence and the New World

In the early colonial United States, an absence of established European government led to a preoccupation with the family as the locus of social control. In Plymouth, in the Massachusetts Bay Colony, Connecticut, and New Haven during the seventeenth century, unmarried people were required to live with families that were "well governed" by a church-going, land-owning man. New Haven decreed in the 1650s that persons "who live not in service, nor in any Family Relation" could become a source of "inconvenience, and disorder" and that each family's "Governor" would be licensed to "duly observe the course, carriage, and behaviour, of every such single person." Unmarried women were expected to maintain a servile domestic identity and never enter the world in a way that might convey independence.[5]

In Salem, town fathers very briefly allowed unmarried women their own property until the governor amended the oversight by noting that in the future, it would be best to avoid "all presedents & evil events of graunting lotts unto single maidens not disposed of."[6] Because, as historian Alice Kessler-Harris has observed, the possibility of land ownership created a path to existence outside of marriage, other colonies "began to recognize that giving land to women undermined their dependent role" and thus took measures to curtail the option. In 1634, a bill was introduced to the House of Delegates in Maryland proposing that land owned by a spinster must be forfeited, should she fail to marry within seven years.[7]

Almost the only kind of woman who might assert individual power was the wealthy widow, afforded social standing since she'd *been* married and was a legal inheritor of money or property, but left without master. This was rare. Most widows were poor, with no means to support themselves or their dependents, and lived at the mercy of their communities for help in feeding and housing themselves and their families.

Mostly, unmarried women were considered a drain on society and on the families with whom they were forced to find refuge.

The term *spinster* was derived from the word *spinner*, which, since the thirteenth century in Europe, had been used to refer to women, often the widows and orphans of the Crusades, who spun cotton, wool, and silk. By the sixteenth century, spinster referred to unmarried women, many of whom made themselves valuable in households by taking on the ceaseless, thankless work of textile manufacture into old age.[8]

In the New World, "spinster" gained a more precise meaning: in colonial parlance, it indicated an unmarried woman over the age of twenty-three and under the age of twenty-six. At twenty-six, women without spouses became *thornbacks*, a reference to a sea-skate with sharp spines covering its back and tail. It was not a compliment.

Boston bookseller John Dunton wrote in 1686 that "an old (or Super-annuated) Maid, in Boston, is thought such a curse as nothing can exceed it, and look'd on as a dismal spectacle."[9] But in fact, the "dismal spectacle" of unmarried womanhood was quite rare in the colonies. Many more men than women were settlers, creating a high sex ratio, in which men outnumber women, a dynamic that usually results in high marriage rates and low marriage ages. As Benjamin Franklin noted in 1755, "Hence, marriages in America are more general, and more generally early, than in Europe."

The early American attitude toward marriage, and men's and women's roles within it, corresponded to a doctrine of English common law known as *coverture*. Coverture meant that a woman's legal, economic, and social identity was "covered" by the legal, economic, and social identity of the man she married. A married woman was a *feme covert* and a single woman was a *feme sole*. William Blackstone's *Commentaries on the Laws of England* interpreted coverture as meaning that "the very being or legal existence of the woman is suspended during the marriage, or at least is incorporated and consolidated into that of the husband: under whose wing, protection, and cover, she performs every thing. . . . A man cannot grant any thing to his wife, or enter into covenant with her: for the grant would suppose her separate existence; and to covenant with her, would be only to covenant with himself."

Coverture encompassed what legal historian Ariela Dubler has called "a stunning array of status-defining legal restrictions" that prevented wives from keeping their own wages, entering contracts or bringing legal action.[10] "In its strictly economic aspect the traditional marriage contract resembled an indenture between master and servant," writes historian Nancy Cott.[11] And while scholars have shown that many women in Europe and the New World found ways to exert agency, both within their homes and in the outside world, the foundational inequities of marital law made it a battle.

For those *feme soles* who escaped coverture, there were other impediments to thriving. Puritan women enjoyed no sexual liberty; the legendary preacher Cotton Mather railed against those who displayed "sensual lusts, wantonness and impurity, boldness and rudeness, in Look, Word or Gesture."[12] There were a few poorly paid professions at which they could earn a subsistence; they might be midwives, seamstresses, caretakers, governesses, or tutors, all jobs that mirrored broader ideas about women's nature.

The colonies' violent break from England, the American Revolution, on which the nation was officially founded and its rules encoded, complicated gender relations. For one thing, it drained households of their able-bodied men, who fought the British in the 1770s, the 1780s, and in the War of 1812. These conflicts, followed by an era defined by the idea of Manifest Destiny, which would draw men west and leave tens of thousands of women back east, upended sex ratios across the country.

But the rethinking of women's relationship to marriage wasn't just about numbers. The end of the eighteenth century was a time of political instability; the War of American Independence was followed by the French Revolution, which helped spawn the Saint Domingue revolution that freed slaves and established the Republic of Haiti in 1804. Power structures were crumbling under the weight of Enlightenment-era notions about liberty, personal freedom, and representation. In England, author Mary Wollstonecraft (who would herself marry late and have one child out of wedlock) challenged the French philosopher Jean-Jacques Rousseau's vision of women as submissive to their husbands, declaring war in 1792's *A Vindication of the Rights of Woman* on "the sensibility that led [Rousseau] to degrade woman by making her the slave of love" and instead pushing for female education and independence.

"The egalitarian rhetoric of the Revolution provided the women's rights movement with its earliest vocabulary," historian Mary Beth Norton argues,[13] while Lee Virginia Chambers-Schiller describes how, "beginning in about 1780 women in the middle and upper classes . . . manifested a dramatic new form of female independence. In increasing numbers, the daughters of northeastern manufacturers, merchants, farmers, and 'poor professionals' rejected the 'tie that binds.'"[14]

The language of individual liberty was sharply at odds with the limitations put on some of America's inhabitants not just by marriage, but by the other institution that ensured the new nation's economic stability and white men's power within it: slavery.

Marriage and slavery were not equivalent practices. Slaves were chattel, counted in the Constitution as three-fifths human; they could be purchased and sold and had no rights over their own bodies. Marriage, while a contract by which one party *lost* rights and identities, was one that free women, acknowledged as human beings, officially entered into of their own accord (though any number of economic, familial, or community pressures may have been brought to bear). Through marriage, wives gained economic advantage, the rights of inheritance; they also enjoyed social and religious ratification and an increase in status.

But the intersections of slave and marital law illustrate the ways in which political, social, and sexual power over a population can be enforced by both pressing marriage and by forbidding it, as well as how systems of racism and sexism doubly oppressed black women. In the antebellum United States, marriages between slaves were not legally sanctioned, which both prevented the formation of respectable unions and allowed owners to have sexual relations with slaves without violating a marital bond.[15] Conversely, some slave owners pushed slaves into unwanted marriages, perhaps to produce more enslaved children or to concretize family ties that might discourage escape. "[W]hen they could not marry whom they chose under circumstances of their own choosing, some enslaved people chose not to marry at all," historian Frances Smith-Foster writes, citing Harriet Jacobs, a slave who, prevented from marrying the free man she loved and told to choose a husband from among her owner's other slaves asked, "Don't you suppose, sir, that a slave can have some preference about marrying?"[16]

Of course, enslaved women and men fell in love, married on their own terms, and created loving families all the time. But those families were often separated by sale; women and children were raped and bore children by their owners and their owners' sons. Control over women's marital and reproductive lives was one of the surest ways to suppress their power.

There were pockets of the rapidly changing nation in which remaining single seemed to have been a plausible, if not easy or enjoyable, option for some women. At the turn of the nineteenth century, New Orleans saw an influx of refugees from Haiti, increasing the population of *gens de couleur libre*, or free blacks. Free women of color were permitted to inherit, own property, businesses, and slaves; it was not expected that they would marry. The comparative economic and sexual liberty experienced by these *libre* women provided them some incentive to steer clear of what free Maria Gentilly, who, after a husband squandered her estate, sued to recover it in the 1790s,[17] called "the yoke of matrimony."[18]

## Industry, Expansion, Exploration, and Agitation

The late eighteenth century transition from an agrarian to an industrial economy precipitated a practical rethinking of male and female roles, at least in middle class households. Women's lives, long given over to the reproduction of human beings and the in-home production of food, clothes, and linens, suddenly had more space in them, thanks to the availability of commercially produced food and textiles. Improved medicine, decreased child mortality rates, longer life spans, and less farmland to work meant a need for fewer children.

The re-jiggering of roles in a young nation required new thinking about how women might be valued. The first third of the nineteenth century, with its mass religious revivals and a burgeoning women's magazine business, had new tools with which to communicate revised ideas about womanly virtue and value. From the pages of *Godey's Lady's Book* blared a new model of aspirational upper-class femininity and attitude about female purpose that historians now refer to as the Cult of Domesticity. The wealthy, white American wife, relieved of her responsibilities for at-home production, became responsible for scrupulously maintaining a domicile that served as the feminized inverse of the newly bustling, masculine public space. The domestic sphere was re-imagined as a pious haven and moral refuge from the universe of business, industrial, and civic participation into which men were venturing.

Published in 1829, *The Young Lady's Book* asserted that "Whatever situation of life a woman is placed, from her cradle to her grave, a spirit of obedience and submission, pliability of temper, and humility of mind, are required from her."[19] Everyday tasks were made more time-consuming and taxing, so as to better fill the days of women who might otherwise grow restive and attempt to leave the house. As *Godey's Lady's Book* helpfully informed readers, "There is more to be learned about pouring out tea and coffee than most young ladies are willing to believe."[20] And Catherine Beecher, a pioneer in education and strong proponent of education in the domestic arts, wrote in her 1841 book, *A Treatise on Domestic Economy,* that when a girl learned to do the laundry, she was "initiated into the arts and mysteries of the wash tub."[21]

But as the eighteenth century wore on and the marriage rates began to drop for those women on the east coast left without the men who'd headed west, the increasing numbers of unmarried women had to be comfortably folded back into a social structure that relied on domesticity as its principle mode of female control; this need produced early nineteenth century rhetoric that historians now call the Cult of Single Blessedness. The ideas that undergirded Single Blessedness were that women unmarried by chance or by choice had their own acceptably submissive purpose. The "singly blessed" were presumed to be pious vessels whose commitment to service, undiluted by the needs of husbands or children, made them perfect servants of god, family, and community. Women without husbands were often expected to care for the sick and destitute within their communities, and were expected to care for aging parents as married siblings headed off to tend new families.

Calling single women a "corps de reserve," nineteenth-century preacher George Burnap conveyed the dismal logic of Single Blessedness in his *Lectures on the Sphere and Duties of Woman and Other Subjects.*[22]

Just "as no wise general brings all his forces into the field at once, but keeps back a part to supply deficiencies," Burnap wrote, "so are unmarried women stationed . . . to take the places of those who . . . refuse to do their duty." While couples were out enjoying life's pleasures, he noted, single ladies were "toiling over those household duties which the gay and thoughtless have forgotten, or are watching by the bed side of pain and death."[23] Wheee!

Even the most dastardly efforts to redirect nondomestic ambitions into service could not bottle up all of the energies of the nineteenth century's women, especially those who, absent husbands and children to tend to, were swiftly expanding the scope of their professional and intellectual ambitions. Maria Mitchell, a female astronomer from Massachusetts, predicted of woman: "once emancipate her from the 'stitch, stitch, stitch,' and she would have time for studies which would engross as the needle never can."[24]

Louisa May Alcott, perhaps the century's best known literary agitator against the confinements of matrimony and a strenuous proponent of independent life for women, agreed. The daughter of a transcendentalist reformer and a social worker, Alcott had decided as a child that she had no wish to marry, a conviction that remained firm throughout her adulthood. In 1868, Alcott described "all the busy, useful independent spinsters" she knew, and argued both that "liberty is a better husband than love to many of us" and that "the loss of liberty, happiness, and self-respect is poorly repaid by the barren honor of being called 'Mrs.' instead of 'Miss.'"[25]

Alcott's determination to make herself economically independent stemmed perhaps from her family's economic need. Alcott worked as a teacher, nurse, seamstress, governess, writer, maid, and magazine editor to help support her parents and siblings. Alcott's path was an exceptional one; she managed to help provide for her family, but then went further, establishing *herself* as economically autonomous and experiencing contemporary renown as the author of *Little Women*, *Little Men*, and dozens of other stories and books. Yet for for the vast majority of her contemporaries, creative vocations were barely remunerated hobbies, bearing little resemblance to what we think of today as "careers." Even for the most ambitious, talented, and successful women, there was scant chance of attaining anything comparable to the status accorded male peers, and little possibility of earning a stable living.

Teaching didn't offer much job security and was poorly paid, but it was a growing field. Industrialization had meant that many more children no longer needed to work fields and could thus attend school and stay longer. Literacy rates in the United States had increased dramatically between the late 1700s and mid-1800s and the expansion of primary and secondary schools created a need for educators. Women, already comfortably regarded as nurturers to children, could fill the void. Journalist Dana Goldstein writes that, in 1800, 90 percent of American school teachers were men. By 1900, three-quarters of them were women, more than half of them single, since a set of policies known as "marriage bars," which allowed school districts to fire married women or deny them tenure, made it largely impossible for women to continue teaching after they were married in many states.[26] As Goldstein points out, education pioneers including Horace Mann and the never-married Catharine Beecher "explicitly conceived of teaching as a job for spinsters," an occupation that could "ease the stigma of being unwed"[27] and permit unmarried women to nurture young children and thus fulfill their domestic calling, even without offspring of their own.

The outbreak of the Crimean War in 1853 soon drew women into another profession, nursing. The industrial revolution also meant the proliferation of mills, many of which—like the textile-producing town of Lowell, Massachusetts—were staffed almost exclusively by young, unmarried women. Domestic service was the last choice of many and, therefore, often the job left to the poorest, often women of color.

In these contexts, and in others, including the religious revivals of the mid-nineteenth century, which encouraged a moral conscientiousness and concern with the improvement and uplift of society, women were encountering each other outside of the domestic sphere.

As the nation grew, the question of whether new territories would be slave or free was forcing a crisis. Women, meeting each other in schools and factories, where many of them were likely to be young and single, were participating in that conversation and coalescing around a handful of social movements that would alter the future of the nation.

## Woman Will Occupy a Large Space

In a 1840 letter to the *The Lowell Offering*, the publication of the Massachusetts mill town that employed thousands of young, single women and would become one of the birth places of the later labor movement, a correspondent named Betsey claiming to be "one of that unlucky, derided, and almost despised set of females, called spinsters, single sisters, lay-nuns . . . but who are more usually known by the appellation of Old Maids" argued that it was "a part of [God's] wise design that there should be *Old Maids*," in part because "they are the founders and pillars of anti-slavery, moral reform, and all sorts of religious and charitable societies."[28]

Here was the idea of service and moral uplift brought into disruptive relief: What if women, in service to greater and moral good, did not submit themselves to a larger power structure, but instead organized to overturn it?

Frederick Douglass would write in 1881, "When the true history of the antislavery cause shall be written, woman will occupy a large space in its pages; for the cause of the slave has been peculiarly woman's cause."[29] And many of the women who had time and ability to devote themselves to the cause of emancipation were women without husbands or families, at least during the time of their activism. These women included abolitionists Susan. B. Anthony and Sarah Grimké, neither of whom would ever marry, but also Sarah's sister Angelina, who had already drawn public attention for fiery antislavery speeches before she married a fellow abolitionist at age thirty-three.

Abolitionist thinking naturally overlapped women's rights advocacy. Antislavery reformers including Anthony and the Grimkés, as well as Elizabeth Cady Stanton, Lucretia Mott, Sojourner Truth, Harriet Tubman, Maria Stewart, and Lydia Maria Child, fought first for abolition, but soon broadened their attentions to address the persistent legal, social, and civil subjugation of women. They worked alongside men, including William Lloyd Garrison, who spoke up in defense of female abolitionists not permitted to enter the World Anti-Slavery Convention in London in 1840, and Frederick Douglass, one of the thirty-two men to sign 1848's Declaration of Sentiments, the document drawn up in Seneca Falls, New

York, which laid out one of the early blueprints for the emancipation of women.

Not all the women in these movements were single. But the perceived overlap between singlehood and the antislavery movement was strong enough that some early abolitionist women were accused of wanting to free slaves so that they might marry black men.[30] And many reformers *were* single, or at least excruciatingly aware of the gender limitations of the marriage model. When abolitionist and suffragist Lucy Stone married Henry Blackwell in 1855, the couple asked their minister to distribute a statement protesting marriage's inequities. It read, in part: "While acknowledging our mutual affection by publicly assuming the relationship of husband and wife . . . this act on our part implies no sanction of, nor promise of voluntary obedience to such of the present laws of marriage, as refuse to recognize the wife as an independent, rational being, while they confer upon the husband an injurious and unnatural superiority." Stone kept her last name, and generations of women who have done the same have been referred to as "Lucy Stoners."

An awareness of potentially injurious dynamics of marriage also undergirded the burgeoning movement to make alcohol illegal. Led by both single activists, notably Frances Willard, and married women, the temperance movement aimed to cut down on the drunken indolence (at best) and violence (at worst) of husbands by prohibiting the sale and consumption of alcohol. There may be no greater testament to the suffocating power of marital expectation than the fact that, for a time, the *banning of booze* seemed a more practical recourse against spousal abuse than the reform of marriage law or redress of inequities within the home.

## Civil War

About three million men left home to fight in The Civil War; more than 600,000 of them died, on the battlefields and of disease, many tended to by women who joined the war effort on both sides by working as nurses. The experience of single life and widowhood became far more common for America's women, both during the war and in the years that followed.

In 1865, the governor of Massachusetts proposed the transport of some of the 38,000 "excess" women in his state to Oregon and California, where women were in short supply. The state legislature demurred, revealing how swiftly society had come to rely on the labors of unmarried women: Should all the damsels of New England be deported, the legislature argued, "the whirring music of millions of spindles would be silent as a sepulchre, while the mistresses of more than 100,000 dwellings would be in consternation from the catastrophe of such a withdrawal of one, two, or three or more domestics from their premises."[31]

For middle-class reformers in the years after the war, writes the historian Rachel Seidman, new ideas about how "women *should not* be dependent on men," began to take hold, while for working-class women, there was a new consciousness about how—with husbands, fathers and brothers at war or out west—they "*could not*" be dependent on men. These women went to work in ever greater numbers, and that wage-earning in turn awakened in them an awareness of gendered and class injustices.

A former teacher, Virginia Penny, wrote an 1869 book, *Think and Act*, about the challenges of income inequality facing working women who were increasingly living independent of men. She pushed for equal-pay protections from the government, and even suggested taxing better-compensated single men to help support unmarried women. Around the same time, Aurora Phelps of the Boston Working Women's League petitioned for "Garden Homesteads," government-subsidized tracts of land near Boston to be given to unmarried women willing to work them; an imagined East Coast equivalent to the land being given away in the west as part of the Homestead Act.[32] These proposals certainly weren't going anywhere. But single women were beginning to enter policy debates about how to make room for them in the world.

Some women went west themselves. Lee Virginia Chambers-Schiller reports that prior to 1900, around 10 percent of land claims in two Colorado counties were filed by unmarried women, some of whom—like South Dakota homesteader "Bachelor Bess" Corey—were more interested in the land-grab than the man-grab. When Oklahoma's Cherokee Strip was opened to homesteaders in 1893, Laura Crews raced her horse seventeen miles in under an hour to claim the piece of land that she would tend herself for years before oil was discovered on the property.[33]

Crews would be the last participant of the Cherokee land run to die, in 1976, at age 105, unmarried.[34]

This small but nearly unprecedented opportunity for independent women to buy property and keep it wasn't simply a real estate issue; land ownership had been long linked to political enfranchisement. America's first voters were not just white men, but white men who owned property; in England in 1869, unmarried women with property had been granted the right to vote in local elections. And the first women to petition for the franchise were women who had managed to acquire property: unmarried Margaret Brent was Maryland's first female landowner and, in the 1640s, requested two votes in local civil proceedings.

Perhaps not coincidentally, many of the Western territories in which women staked out land were places in which woman suffrage would precede passage of the nineteenth amendment. Women could vote in Wyoming, Utah, Washington, Montana, Colorado, Idaho, California, Arizona, Kansas, Oregon, Nevada, Oklahoma, South Dakota, Michigan, and Alaska before 1920, while women in the more urban, established Eastern states (save for New York) had to wait for the Constitution to change.

The social crusades of the nineteenth century were made possible by the changing nature of female engagement with the world and new ideas about identity and dependence. The rate of American spinsterhood hit its first peak at 11 percent for American women born between 1865 and 1875.[35]

## Mannish Maidens, Bread and Roses

By the end of the nineteenth century, the country was awash in fears of insurrection by increasingly independent populations of women and newly freed slaves.

In addition to participating in social movements, women had been pushing themselves further educationally than ever before. The demand for teachers meant that teaching academies, known as "normal schools," proliferated. Private colleges for wealthier women had begun to open, starting with Mt. Holyoke in 1837, Vassar in 1861, Wellesley in 1870, and Smith in 1871. Bryn Mawr was founded in 1885, and, in ten years, was under the stewardship of its second president, M. Carey Thomas, a suffragist who would explain to her mother in a letter that since "marriage means loss of freedom, poverty, and a personal subjection for which I see absolutely no compensation . . . Thee must make up thy mind, sweetest mother, to have one old maid daughter."

The Morrill Act, in 1862, had established land-grant colleges, including agricultural and mechanical schools in the West and Midwest, where curricular flexibility permitted more women to be admitted alongside men.[36] In 1884, the Industrial Institute and College in Mississippi (originally the Mississippi Industrial Institute and College for the Education of White Girls) became the first state-funded university for women's higher education.[37] Spelman, the historically black women's college founded by two unmarried women, opened its doors in 1881.

But the insurgent liberty of people whose enforced subservience had until recently undergirded the country's power structure provoked a new, more damning wave of anti-spinster argument that ever more directly linked social disruption to unmarried women. These "mannish maidens"[38] had not just missed out on, but were, in fact, *unfit* for, family life. Responding to Susan B. Anthony's temperance work in 1853, the *New York Sun* published a screed noting that, "The quiet duties of daughter, wife or mother are not congenial to those hermaphrodite spirits who thirst to win the title of champion of one sex and victor over the other."

The imagined connection between social agitation and an unmarried state was so firm that even married activists got tarred as single, frigid, or unmarriageable. An 1838 edition of the *Mother's Magazine* asserted of women like the Grimké sisters (one of whom, Angelina, wed that same year and would go on to have three children; the other, Sarah, had already turned down at least one marriage proposal), "These Amazonians are their own executioners. They have unsexed themselves in public estimation, and there is no fear that they will perpetuate their race."[39]

Perhaps in response to women's move away from marriage, law and custom began to make slightly more room for female independence within the institution, though it was a battle. Women had been petitioning for Married Women's Property Acts and privy examination acts, which allowed a judge to speak privately with a wife outside the presence of her husband, and by 1839, courts had begun to grant them, kicking off the gradual overturn of *coverture* that would take more than a century. In the late 1860s, Myra Bradwell petitioned for a law license and argued that the 14th Amendment protected her right to practice. The Illinois Supreme Court rejected her petition, ruling that because she was married she had no legal right to operate on her own. When she challenged the ruling, Justice Joseph Bradley wrote in his decision, "It certainly cannot be affirmed, as a historical fact, that [the right to choose one's profession] has ever been established as one of the fundamental privileges and immunities of the sex." Rather, Bradley argued, "The paramount destiny and mission of women are to fulfill the noble and benign offices of wife and mother."[40]

Meanwhile, the legal system was cracking down on anything that would help women evade or exert control over those "benign offices." The Comstock Act of 1873, along with a series of state laws implemented soon after, made it illegal to distribute any materials deemed "obscene," including birth control and educational material about contraception. States were outlawing abortion, which until then had been legal under some circumstances; by 1880, the procedure was mostly prohibited, except to save the life of the woman.

In the same period, scientists around the world were working to justify the continued subjugation of women and nonwhites by making medical claims as to their inferior capabilities.

German scientist Carl Vogt wrote, in 1864, "The grown-up Negro partakes, as regards his intellectual faculties, of the nature of the child, the female, and the senile white." Gustave Le Bon, a prominent social psychologist, wrote in 1879 that "In the most intelligent races . . . there are a large number of women whose brains are closer in size to those of gorillas than to the most developed male brains. This inferiority is so obvious that no one can contest it for a moment; only its degree is worth discussion." Le Bon conceded that "Without a doubt there exist some distinguished women, very superior to the average man, but they are as exceptional as the birth of any monstrosity, as, for example, of a gorilla with two heads; consequently, we may neglect them entirely."[41]

There was no doubt about a fear of rebellion that lay just beneath these diagnoses. As Le Bon wrote, "A desire to give [women] the same education . . . is a dangerous chimera . . . The day when, misunderstanding the inferior occupations which nature has given her, women leave the home and take part in our battles; on this day a social revolution will begin, and everything that maintains the sacred ties of the family will disappear."[42]

The American medical establishment built on European pronouncements to rationalize their recommendations to keep women's lives small, confined, and attached to men. In his 1873 *Sex in Education; or A Fair Chance for the Girls*, Harvard professor Edward Clarke argued that the female brain, if engaged in the same course of study as the male, would become overburdened and that wombs and ovaries would atrophy.[43] Chambers-Schiller reports that in the medical establishment, "a painful menopause was the presumed consequence of reproductive organs that were not regularly bathed in male semen."

Yet for all of this, women kept on not marrying and they kept on bucking for change.

### The Progressive Era

The Progressive Era, from about 1890 to 1920, which coincided with the years in which American women were less likely to marry than ever before, was a moment of enormous political and social foment. These decades included defining fights for fair labor practices and reform of the tax code and public education, and a campaign against lynching, which in the south had become a deadly method of addressing the growing power of African-Americans.[44]

Immigrants from Europe were flooding East Coast cities, some moving toward the Midwest, while the Japanese population was growing on the West Coast. Chinese immigration had been halted, but Chinese communities already in the country continued to expand. The American puzzle became more intricate; fights for unionization were linked to the suffrage campaign, which, in turn, influenced the push for prohibition and the struggle to implement new social welfare measures. All these battles were tied to a stream of technological innovations that made new professions possible, and employed new populations of Americans, in turn pulling them into the labor, suffrage, education, and civil rights struggles of the day.

Young women, many forced by financial crises in 1873 and 1893 to seek employment, arrived in cities looking for professional opportunities that were rapidly becoming more diverse. The retail market for factory-made goods, alongside inventions such as the typewriter and telephone, created jobs for women as shop girls, typists, telephone operators, and secretaries. In 1870, professional women accounted for less than seven percent of the nonagricultural female workforce; that percentage would more than double by 1920.[45]

Many women, especially poor immigrant women who labored in factories, worked long hours, seven days a week, in terrifying, unregulated firetraps. The deplorable conditions experienced by millions of female workers were at the roots of the labor struggle, which would be spurred forward in large part by unconventionally wed, or unwed, women.

"The first industrial strikes in the United States [were] led and peopled by women," writes historian Nancy Cott, reporting on the account from a Boston newspaper of one of the first "turn-out" strikes in Lowell, Massachusetts in the 1830s, in which, "One of the leaders mounted a pump and made a flaming Mary Woolstonecraft [sic] speech on the rights of women."[46]

Most of the women who were working in factories were young and unmarried. According to historian Kathy Peiss, four-fifths of the 343,000 women working for wages in New York City in 1900 were unmarried.[47] "The Uprising of 20,000" was a 1909 walkout of female factory workers who made blouses called "shirtwaists." The Uprising was organized by the International Ladies' Garment Workers' Union and kicked off by twenty-three-year-old Ukrainian immigrant Clara Lemlich, then unmarried, who told a crowd of shirtwaist workers: "I am a working girl, one of those striking against intolerable conditions." That campaign lasted twelve weeks and resulted in union agreements with nearly all shirtwaist manufacturers save a few, including the Triangle Shirtwaist Factory, where two years later, 146 workers, all but seventeen of them women, and most younger than thirty and unmarried, would perish in a fire, unable to escape the building, which was locked to keep workers inside and prevent them from stealing.

Another participant in the Uprising was Russian-Polish immigrant and labor organizer and suffragist Rose Schneiderman, who would never marry. Her 1911 speech, in which she implored, "The worker must have bread, but she must have roses, too" became the mantra of the 1912 Bread and Roses strike of female textile workers in Lawrence, Massachusetts, and an anthemic phrase in the labor and women's movements that were to come. Elizabeth Gurley Flynn, a radical socialist who married at seventeen, but separated from her husband two years later, organized mining and textile strikes around the country and was arrested multiple times. She was dubbed by the writer Theodore Dreiser "an East Side Joan of Arc," memorialized in a popular song called "The Rebel Girl;" she was a founding member of the ACLU.

While factory unionizers often focused on the physical dangers in workplaces, the labor movement in education concerned itself primarily with fair pay. The never-married Margaret Haley, known in the press as the "Lady Labor Slugger," led the Chicago Teachers' Federation, one of the more militant teaching unions in the nation. She contested assumptions that female teachers could be paid less after a 1910 National Education Association survey found that they were often primary earners, either as single women or the sole supports of parents and siblings. Haley understood that since women couldn't vote, teachers needed to align with the male labor movement, and decided to join her 97 percent female union to the blue-collar Chicago Federation of Labor, remaking teacher unionism as an urban political force and getting herself dubbed by a conservative, anti-labor businessman, a "nasty, unladylike woman."[48]

By 1920, nearly 40 percent of black women worked for wages, compared to about 18 percent of white women; a 1919 study showed that the typical black laborer in New York City was young, unmarried, and had at least a grammar school education. Historian Paula Giddings describes how, "For the first time [black women] were permitted to use machinery, and some even found jobs as clerks, stenographers, and bookkeepers. These new opportunities had a salutary effect which went beyond better wages." It remained true, however, that even as opportunities expanded, black women were following in the professional wake of their white sisters, taking jobs only as white women fought for and eventually won better opportunities. Black women got stuck with the hottest, dirtiest and most unsafe jobs in factories, and as Giddings writes, "they were paid from 10 to 60 percent less than ill-paid White women."[49]

During these same years, other reformers—many of them suffragists, socialists, and labor agitators—were building the Settlement House Movement, creating residential spaces where rich and poor might come together to better understand and address class and racial injustice and pacifism. Chicago's Hull House, founded by two never-wed activists, Jane Addams and Ellen Gates Starr, provided everything from childcare to continuing education.

Settlement Houses were, in many cases, designed as sustainable places where single and divorced women might find community and a respectable life structure outside marriage; they were also a breeding ground for progressive economic policy. Frances Perkins, who worked at Hull House, would marry at thirty-three (and fight in court to keep her name), and remain the sole breadwinner for her family. Perkins would go on to become Franklin Delano Roosevelt's secretary of labor and the creator of Social Security. Florence Kelley, a suffragist, socialist, civil rights leader, and labor organizer who opposed child labor and sweatshops, fought for minimum wage laws and petitioned the Illinois legislature for eight-hour workdays for women and children; after leaving her husband, she moved to Hull House and then to the Henry Street Settlement, founded by the never-married social activist Lillian Wald, in New York.

The labor and Settlement House movements merged with the ongoing suffrage fight in natural ways. As Clara Lemlich explained, "The manufacturer has a vote; the bosses have votes; the foremen have votes; the inspectors have votes. The working girl has no vote."

An older generation of activists, including Anthony and antilynching crusader Ida B. Wells, teamed with younger women who also picked up strategies from England's radical feminists. Alice Paul and Lucy Burns, both unmarried, were often described as being of "one mind and spirit;" they picketed the White House and staged hunger strikes in the name of voting rights. In later years, Paul would draft the Equal Rights Amendment, which read, simply, "Men and women shall have equal rights throughout the United States and every place subject to its jurisdiction;" it would be introduced to every Congressional session from 1923 until 1972, when it finally passed but was not ratified by the states. (It has been reintroduced, though never passed, in every session since 1982).

But the biggest victory would change the gender politics of the country forever. In 1919, Congress passed the 19th Amendment; it was ratified by the states in 1920. For the first time in America's history, its female citizens could legally (if not practically, in the Jim Crow South) vote.

Over a century in which women had exercised increasing independence, living more singly in the world than ever before, the movements that independent women had helped to power had resulted in the passage of the 14th, 15th, 18th and 19th Amendments to the Constitution.

They had reshaped the nation.

## The New Women: Backlash and Redirection

The twentieth century dawned on a cultural landscape that was as remade as the political one.

Electric street lamps had come to cities around the country, creating "white ways" that made it feel safer for women to be on the streets at night. This development changed the kinds of jobs women could work, as well as the ways in which they could spend money and leisure time. Working-class young women in cities may have struggled economically, but the lit streets, Nickelodeons, Vaudeville houses, bowling alleys, music and dance halls that began to proliferate meant that these women (and men), according to Kathy Peiss, "spent much of their leisure apart from their families and enjoyed greater social freedom than their parents or married siblings, especially married women." Young women "Putting on finery, promenading the streets, and staying late at amusement resorts became an important cultural style for many working women."[50]

Peiss writes of the drive of some working-class women toward increased social and sexual freedoms, noting that single working women "were among those who flocked to the streets in pursuit of pleasure and amusement, using public spaces for flamboyant assertion." Although these so-called "rowdy girls" were vulnerable to public censure for immorality, Peiss writes, "young women continued to seek the streets to search for men, have a good time, and display their clothes and style in a public arena."[51]

African-Americans continued the great migration from the south into northern cities, while new waves of immigrants from Eastern Europe poured into New York City. Blacks and immigrants began to mix in urban centers, not always peaceably. But the coming together of different kinds of people helped the sharp class and ethnic lines begin to blur, if only slightly, producing new, liberated fashions in dress and entertainments.

Syncopated rhythms, rooted in the black neighborhoods of New Orleans, led to ragtime-era dance crazes, which in turn gave way to sexually expressive fads like the Charleston and the Black Bottom that would take hold in the Jazz Age. Working women of New York's Bowery and West Village began to experiment with cropped hair and shorter hemlines that made it easier and safer for them to work in factories; as they became more visible on sidewalks and in public gathering places, middle- and upper-class women began to mimic their styles. Women were soon unburdening themselves of fashions that had, in the nineteenth century, weighed an estimated thirty pounds, turning to shorter skirts and looser fits.[52]

In 1914, as courtship rituals moved away from family homes or closely watched community dance halls, the *Ladies' Home Journal* used the term "dating" in its modern sense. Couples could engage more easily in sexual experimentation, and Stephanie Coontz reports that ninety-two percent of college girls surveyed in the 1920s said they had participated in sexual, below-the-neck fondling, and that, by this time, "young middle-class men were more likely to lose their virginity with women of their own class than with prostitutes."[53]

As centuries of repression began to give way, reformers took up the fight to make contraception more accessible. That sex might be a pleasurable option for women without the high risk of pregnancy created room for both married and extramarital sexual liberty, the possibility of trying out multiple partners, of blissfully inconsequential experimentation, or simply of bearing fewer children and enduring fewer dangerous pregnancies.

The fight to exert control over reproduction drew the attention of anarchist activists including the Russian-born Emma Goldman. Married twice herself, Goldman was a believer in free love and an early proponent of gay rights; she was also a vociferous critic of marriage, which she felt condemned women "to life-long dependency, to parasitism, to complete uselessness, individual as well as social." As a nurse and midwife on the Lower East Side in the 1890s, Goldman had waged war on the Comstock Laws that barred the distribution of information about contraception and abortion. By the early twentieth century, she was smuggling diaphragms and cervical caps into the United States from Europe. She was also mentoring a young nurse and bohemian, Margaret Sanger.

Sanger, a married mother whose own mother had been pregnant eighteen times in twenty-two years and had died early of cervical cancer and tuberculosis, began writing pieces about sexual education for the socialist magazine *New York Call* in 1912. The next year she began work at the Henry Street Settlement and soon separated from her husband. In 1914 she published a newsletter called *The Woman Rebel*, which proclaimed that every woman should be "absolute mistress of her own body" and as such, should avail herself of contraception, which Sanger referred to as "birth control."

In 1916, Sanger opened a family planning clinic in Brownsville, Brooklyn; it was raided by police after ten days and Sanger spent thirty days in prison. Five years later, the same year that Sanger and her husband finally divorced, she would found The American Birth Control League, which would later become the Birth Control Federation of America, and, in 1942, would be renamed the Planned Parenthood Federation of America.

The slow reveal of female flesh, the lightening of a limiting wardrobe, the early acknowledgements of female sexual drive, the push for more accessible means of preventing pregnancy . . . together they began to send a popular message: that abstinence from marriage no longer necessarily meant abstinence from sex, or from fun. The popular press in the early twentieth century called the educated, politicized, wage-earning, sexually liberated female "the new woman."

She wasn't popular with everyone.

"In our modern industrial civilization, there are many and grave dangers to counterbalance the splendors and the triumphs," President Theodore Roosevelt said at the beginning of a 1905 speech to the National Congress of Mothers.[54] One of these dangers was the existence of women "who deliberately forego . . . the supreme blessing of children."

Roosevelt had become fretful after the 1890 census showed a declining birthrate[55] and began to worry about "race suicide," the idea that a white Anglo-Saxon failure to reproduce would damage the nation. Roosevelt, who supported suffrage and women's involvement in labor, nonetheless blamed the declining fertility rate on those white women whose professional, political, and other nondomestic commitments were leading them to start families late and not at all. "A race is worthless," Roosevelt railed, "if women cease to breed freely."

After Roosevelt left office, he continued to express his anxiety, clarifying that it was not over "pauper families with excessive numbers of ill-nourished and badly brought up children" but rather with "voluntary sterility among married men and women of good life . . . If the best classes do not reproduce themselves the nation will of course go down." Roosevelt's distinctions were rooted in the readily expressed racism of his time and in animosity toward Japanese and Chinese immigrants on the West Coast, whose comparative fecundity seemed to threaten the whiteness of the nation. But they were also an expression of judgment against the women exercising new forms of public autonomy. "It is the bare truth," Roosevelt continued, "to say that no celibate life approaches such a life in point of usefulness, no matter what the motive for the celibacy—religious, philanthropic, political, or professional."

Roosevelt's concerns were an inversion of the racial politics that would be echoed fifty years later by Moynihan, and mirror the arguments made more recently by population *agonistes*, including Jonathan Last and Ross Douthat. Different iterations of these anxieties, shaped by era and prevalent racial attitudes, share close ties: They home in on a resistance by women to wifeliness and motherhood as not simply *a* problem, but *the* problem imperiling their nation or race.

"The race, the race! Shouts the king, the president, the capitalist, the priest," wrote Emma Goldman in 1911, "The race must be preserved, though woman be degraded to a mere machine . . . and the marriage institution is our only safety valve against the pernicious sex awakening of woman."

At the end of the nineteenth century, writes Chambers-Schiller, "the singlehood of women became a politically charged issue from which it was clearly understood that spinsterhood and independence were linked." This recognition, she continues, "inspired a political and cultural backlash which, in the 1920s, returned women to marriage and domesticity."

## Marriage Dislodged

In 1924, the *Yale Review* posthumously published a piece by the sociologist William Sumner, who argued that the industrial age's new opportunities for women had "dislodged marriage from its supreme place in their interest and life plan. This is the greatest revolution in the conditions of the marriage institution . . . in all history . . . the importance of the fact that for great numbers of [women] it is no longer the sum of life to find husbands can easily be appreciated."[56]

The dislocation of marriage as the single path for women—not to mention the impact that these unmarried women, independently and in concert with each other as colleagues and activists, were having on politics, professions, and populations—was a threat that drew further cultural blowback.

The reverberations were sometimes hilariously obvious: Suffragists had often staged political "pageants" in which they wore sashes emblazoned "Votes for Women." But 1921, the year following the ratification of the 19th Amendment, brought a perversion of this display: the debut of the Miss America pageant, in which unmarried women showed off their decidedly *apolitical* attributes in competition against, as opposed to collaboration with, each other.[57]

The growing field of psychology provided a new, credentialed venue for the pathologizing of unmarried women. One of Sigmund Freud's adherents, Austrian physician and psychologist Wilhelm Stekel, claimed in a 1926 book, *Frigidity in Woman in Relation to Her Love Life*, that "Marriage dread and aversion to childbearing afflict particularly our 'higher' social circles; increasing numbers of girls belonging to the 'upper strata' remain single. . . . They are 'emancipated;' they are growing self-reliant, self-sufficient and, economically, too, they are becoming more and more independent of the male."

Rates of singlehood were dropping from their turn-of-the-century highs and, with them, marriage ages. While the fertility rate would dip during the Depression, the 1930s would include a widespread backlash not just against the sexual liberties of the Jazz Age, but against the politics of independent female reformers of the progressive age.

These attacks were sometimes lodged, as they are today, by women who had managed to see the domestic light from their own professional, political perches. Rose Wilder Lane, the Libertarian journalist and daughter of Laura Ingalls Wilder (Baby Rose!), had worked outside the home throughout her adult life, but wrote a *Ladies Home Journal* article in 1936 called "Woman's Place Is In The Home." In it, she argued that feminist agitation had dangerously diminished the importance of the "deep-rooted, nourishing and fruitful man-and-woman relationship." A woman's real career, wrote Lane, the journalist, "is to make a good marriage."[58]

## Marry Early and Often

The back-to-back crises of the Depression and World War II drove many women, married and single, into the workforce. For some white middle-class women who had never before had to work for wages, this was new. For the many black women who had always worked, the opportunity for skilled jobs, albeit for less money than their white counterparts, expanded.

But the patriotic step back, as soon as the economy rebounded and soldiers returned, was harsh, and brought with it a whole new brand of enforced domesticity.

Thanks to the GI Bill, veterans (or at least white veterans, who were far more likely to be admitted to universities) were eligible for college educations that could propel them into the coalescing white middle class. Meanwhile, the federal government underwrote loans and built up a suburban infrastructure that would house the millions of children women were busy making, in what could become America's enormous baby boom. It was a neat, elliptical system. Advertisers sold women and men on an old, cult-of-domesticity-era ideal: that the highest female calling was the maintenance of a domestic sanctuary for men on whom they would depend economically. In order to care for the home, these women would rely on new products, like vacuum cleaners and washing machines, sales of which would in turn line the pockets of the husbands who ran the companies and worked in the factories that produced these goods.

The consumerist cycle both depended on and strengthened capitalism, and thus worked to allay other postwar anxieties about nuclear attack and Communism, both of which had become linked to fears about the power of women's sexuality run amok. Historian Elaine Tyler May reports that "non-marital sexual behavior in all its forms became a national obsession after the war," and marriage, in tandem with the repudiation of women's recent advances, was the cure.[59]

The mid-twentieth century push for white women was not simply to marry, but to marry *early*, before gaining a taste for independent life. A 1949 American Social Hygiene Association pamphlet advised, sixty years in advance of Mitt Romney's touting of youthful wedlock, that "Marriage is better late than never. But early marriage gives more opportunity for happy comradeship . . . for having and training children . . . promoting family life as a community asset, and observing one's grandchildren start their careers."[60]

By the end of the 1950s, around sixty percent of female students were dropping out of college, either to marry or because the media blitz and realignment of expectations led them to believe that further education would inhibit their chances of finding a husband. Secondary education, which had expedited women's autonomy in the previous century, now worked, in part, to abrogate it. In his 1957 *Harpers* piece, "American Youth Goes Monogamous," Dr. Charles Cole, president of Amherst College, wrote that "a girl who gets as far as her junior year in college without having acquired a man is thought to be in grave danger of becoming an old maid." Cole sadly compared his female students, now in search of fiancés, to the women he'd taught in the 1920s, who he recalled attended college in hopes of launching a career, not finding a mate.[61]

In Barnard's graduating class of 1960, two-thirds of seniors were engaged before graduation and, as Gail Collins reports, at pregraduation parties, betrothed students were given corsages while singles were offered lemons.[62]

In these years, around half of those brides were younger than twenty[63] and 14 million women were engaged by the time they were seventeen.[64] Gloria Steinem, born in 1934, recalled to me that, in her heavily Polish neighborhood in Toledo, Ohio, most women got married in high school. "I just didn't know that you could live without getting married, unless you were crazy," Steinem said of her youth, recalling a cousin who had never married, worked with the Red Cross in Europe, and had been regarded as mentally unstable. "That was my image of the alternative," Steinem said.

She remembered going to a Polish wedding reception at a bar where, "even though I was a very young teenager, I noticed that the bride was very depressed." Steinem finally approached and asked what was wrong, to which the sad bride replied, "You don't understand. I'm twenty." The expectation, Steinem explained, was that "you were supposed to get married at sixteen or seventeen and she'd been unable to find a proper husband. Now she was twenty, and they had married her off to some guy who was younger, which was terrible."

Women who were educated, thanks to the propulsive victories of a previous generation, were sometimes left confounded by the regressive pressures of the society in which they lived. Author Judy Blume has described how, as a college student with literary ambitions, she gave in to the expectation to marry young. Pregnant by the time she earned her degree, Blume recalled the dismay with which she "hung [her] diploma over the washing machine."[65] And as writer Nora Ephron explained in a 1996 commencement address at her *alma mater,* Wellesley College, about her own graduating class of 1962: "We weren't meant to have futures, we were meant to marry them. We weren't meant to have politics, or careers that mattered, or opinions or lives; we were meant to marry them. If you wanted to be an architect, you married an architect."

Both Ephron and Steinem wound up engaged before graduation. Ephron would write of her betrothal as "an episode that still embarrasses me" and describe her once-affianced as "a total fool. . . . who ran the hero-sandwich concession at Harvard Business School and whom for one moment one December in New Hampshire I said—as much out of politeness as anything else—that I wanted to marry." She did not marry him.

Steinem explained that she, in fact, loved her college fiancé, with whom she would remain friends and enjoy a decades-long on-and-off affair. But she found the idea of marriage "profoundly depressing," and realized that "as wonderful as he was, it was a really bad idea. He hunted, he skied. All these things that I never wanted." She accepted his proposal, she said, because she simply "didn't know what else to do." Finally, as graduation and marriage loomed, Steinem escaped to another continent. "Part of the reason I went to India," she said, "was because I was trying not to get married to this extremely tempting man and I knew I had to go very very far away. So I left my engagement ring under his pillow and left. Not very wonderful."

## Recontainment

The domesticity of the 1950s has long been understood both as a reaction to the Depression and the World Wars, especially World War II, and the flooding into the working world of women in wartime. But it wasn't just about nudging women off factory floors and selling them blenders; it was also about forcing marriage back down the throats of women who had spent a century purging it as the central element of their identity.

Or, rather, it was about forcing marriage back down the throats of *some* women.

While marriage rates for middle-class white women soared through the 1940s and 1950s, for black women, mid-twentieth century conditions were very different. Since emancipation, black women had married earlier and more often than their white counterparts. In the years directly after World War II, thanks to the return of soldiers, black marriage rates briefly increased further.[66]

However, as white women kept marrying in bigger numbers and at younger ages throughout the 1950s, black marriage rates began to decrease, and the age of first marriage to climb.[67] By 1970, there had been a sharp reversal: Black women were not marrying nearly as often or as early as their white counterparts.

It was nothing as benign as coincidence. While one of the bedrocks of the expansion of the middle class was the aggressive reassignment of white women to domestic roles within the idealized nuclear family, another was the exclusion of African-Americans from the opportunities and communities that permitted those nuclear families to flourish.

Put more plainly, the economic benefits extended to the white middle class, both during the New Deal and in the post-World War II years, did not extend to African-Americans. Social Security, created in 1935, did not apply to either domestic laborers or agricultural workers, who tended to be African-Americans, or Asian or Mexican immigrants. Discriminatory hiring practices, the low percentages of black workers in the country's newly strengthened labor unions, and the persistent (if slightly narrowed[68]) racial wage gap, along with questionable practices by the Veterans Administration, and the reality that many colleges barred the admission of black students, also meant that returning black servicemen had a far harder time taking advantage of the GI Bill's promise of college education.[69]

Then there was housing. The suburbs that bloomed around American cities after the war, images of which are still summoned as symbols of midcentury familial prosperity, were built for white families. In William Levitt's four enormous "Levittowns," suburban developments which, thanks to government guarantees from the VA and the Federal Housing Association, provided low-cost housing to qualified veterans, there was not one black resident.[70] Between 1934 and 1962, the government subsidized $120 billion in new housing; 98 percent of it for white families. Urban historian Thomas Sugrue reports that, in Philadelphia, between the end of the war and 1953, "only 347 of 120,000 new homes built were open to blacks." As Sugrue writes, this disparity created a demand for housing that exceeded the supply, prices shot up for black buyers, and African-American residents were forced to live "crammed into old and run-down housing, mainly in dense central neighborhoods" that had been abandoned by white residents moving out to the suburbs. Banks routinely refused mortgages to residents of minority neighborhoods, or offered loans at prohibitively usurious rates meant to reflect the imagined risk of lending to African-Americans.[71]

The new freeways that threaded the suburbs to the urban centers where residents made their livings were often built by razing black neighborhoods; those roads regularly cut off black residents from business districts and the public transportation that might connect them to jobs and public services. Postwar "urban renewal" projects purportedly intended to create public housing for poor Americans often involved the dismantling of nonwhite communities and the relocation of minorities to poorly served areas.

When blacks *were* able to compete with whites by gaining employment that might otherwise have gone to whites, buying houses near white enclaves, attempting to vote or enroll in white schools or interact with white women, the response, especially in the postwar Jim Crow South, was often violent. It was an era of voter intimidation, lynching, cross burning, and property destruction by the Klan.

These maneuvers cemented a cycle of economic disadvantage that made marriage—especially the kinds of traditionally patriarchal marriages that white women were being shooed into—less practical. If black women were working all day (often scrubbing the homes of white women), it was impossible for them also to fulfill the at-home maternal ideal for which white women were being celebrated. If black men had a harder time getting educations and jobs, earning competitive wages or securing loans, it was harder for them to play the role of provider. If there were no government-subsidized split-levels to fill with publicly educated children, then the nuclear family chute into which white women were being funneled was not open to most black women. There simply weren't the same incentives to marrying early or at all; there were fewer places to safely put down roots and fewer resources with which to nourish them.

It's not that black women simply *happened* not to experience mid-1950s domesticity; they were actively barred from it, trapped in another way: walled off in underserved neighborhoods by highways that shuttled fairly remunerated white husbands back to wives who themselves had been walled off in well-manicured, stultifying suburbs.

As progress and regress tend to work, these double-edged recontainment efforts quelled the emerging power of women and African-Americans, two historically marginalized populations who had seen enormous gains at the end of the nineteenth and beginning of the twentieth centuries. As the country stitched itself back together after Depression and war, threatening upstarts were being cleared from the field so that America's white men might reclaim their grip on power.

But the funny thing about backlash is that, sometimes, it backfires.

The stuffing of middle-class American women back into the box of early marital expectation and domestic confinement—a box that chafed all the more thanks to the revolutionary opportunities that had so recently been made available to their mothers and grandmothers—by the 1960s had created a world so airless that it was nearly destined to combust, more forcefully than ever before.

"The problem lay buried, unspoken, for many years in the minds of American women . . . 'Is this all?'" began *The Feminine Mystique*, two years before Senator Daniel Patrick Moynihan bemoaned the fact that "almost one-fourth of Negro families are headed by females."

The winding road that America's women had taken around and outside marriage had led them to emancipation, to suffrage, to fairer labor practices, and higher education. The stifling resistance that they met in the midst of the twentieth century in fact set the stage for the social movements that eventually landed us here, edging toward the middle of the twenty-first century, with more than fifty percent of women unmarried.

Today's *free women*, as Gloria Steinem might say, are reshaping the world once again, creating space for themselves and, in turn, for the independent women who will come after them.

This is the epoch of the single women, made possible by the single women who preceded it.

# CHAPTER THREE

# The Sex of the Cities:
# Urban Life and Female Independence

Susana Morris is an English professor at Auburn University in Alabama. Born in 1980, and raised in Connecticut and Ft. Lauderdale, she attended college at Mt. Holyoke, in Massachusetts. Afterward, she considered getting her PhD in Boston, Chicago, and at Notre Dame, before finally settling on Emory University in Atlanta. The reasons were partly practical—Emory had offered her a good deal—but they were also geographic. Morris had loved her time as an undergraduate in rural New England, where she'd discovered Emily Dickinson and enjoyed the crisp autumns. But, in her twenties, she said, heading into the next phase of her adulthood, she craved something else. "I consciously moved to Atlanta to move to a chocolate city," she told me.

Atlanta was by no means a perfect place when she arrived there in 2002, she said, recalling its class contrasts, how mansions sometimes sat next door to crack houses. But it was also going through what Morris called its "Renaissance as black Hollywood." The city, with a high concentration of historically black colleges and big universities, drew young, ambitious students and was cementing itself as a center for African-American entrepreneurs, artists, activists, and educators. "There were black people everywhere," said Morris, "and they were doing big things, and no one was surprised." Morris's life soon filled with friends, museums, theater, clubs where women got in free before eleven. Very few of her fellow graduate students were married, she recalled. "We were young, single, having a good time," she continued. "There was just something about being in a city of fierce, single black women."

That something reminded her of *Sex and the City*, a show she had watched in syndication with her Dominican, lesbian Mt. Holyoke room-mate, both of them understanding that the women on screen did not represent them at all, yet enjoying it nonetheless. The vivid energy of *Sex and the City*, for all its broad, white strokes, was what Morris found in Atlanta. "There is this thing," Morris said of that energy. "It's having friends, going on the town, living it up, finding a network of women." She paused. "I just can't speak highly enough of my young independent life, my youth, in Atlanta."

I can name the moment that I first felt—or recognized—what Morris described: I was thirty, eating in a casual restaurant in Manhattan with one of my colleagues and closest friends. We were exchanging stories about work and men, about friends and our families. A male-female cou-ple nearby got into a nasty fight—someone overturned a plate of food onto someone else—and the hubbub prompted us to look around the restaurant. Aside from the tussling duo, the rest of the tables, probably twenty in all, were filled with women.

There were women in pairs, women in groups, women in their twen-ties, thirties, forties; there were white women, black women, Latina and Asian women. A few looked fancy, a few like they had stepped out of the L.L. Bean outlet; most were dressed as if they had simply come from an office, as we had. What struck me, as I scanned the tables, almost not believing that there could be so few men around me, was that until I'd looked up because of the romantic kerfuffle, the scene had struck me as so average, so unremarkable, that I hadn't even noticed that I was dining in an apparently Amazonian enclave.

It was the city in which I had lived for almost a decade, and the straight romantic couple was the aberration, not the norm. All around me were women drinking, laughing, telling each other stories. They were spending money, talking, maybe making decisions in consultation with each other: about jobs, family, life, sex and love, about where to eat, drink and dance, what movies to see, what books to read. They—*we*, actually—were sucking up every bit of energy from this city's sidewalks, populating its streets and its theaters and its office buildings and apartments, giving the city its character and its rhythm and its beauty and its speed.

Big cities, with their phallic, skyscraping tributes to man's triumphs over nature and free markets, are designed to make us think of masculinity. But the glinting glass pinnacles and flashing stock tickers obscure the fact that most cities gain their hard edges and steely characters from the women who have long inhabited them.

More than just any women: Cities have long provided safer harbor for, and have in turn been shaped by, single women.

Cities are chock-full of single people, male and female: never married, divorced, widowed, and separated. While more than 25 percent of people across the United States live alone, metropolises like Cincinnati, St. Louis, Pittsburgh, Seattle, and Denver boast single-dwelling households that comprise more than 40 percent of their total populations. According to Census data,[1] Susana's Atlanta has the highest share of residents living alone, at 44 percent; Washington D.C. and its surrounding suburbs clock in at about the same. According to sociologist Eric Klinenberg's book, *Going Solo*, in Manhattan, the percentage of solo-dwellers climbs to around 50 percent.[2]

Never-married women made up 41.7 percent of the New York City's female population in 2010, up from 38.7 percent in 2006.[3] Consider what that means: More than four in ten women living in the five boroughs have never married. In Boston, more than half of women (55 percent) have never been wed, a statistic that reflects the city's huge population of students, but is not wholly explained by it. The median age for first marriage for Boston's women is around thirty, among the highest in the country.[4]

The correlation between cities and comparatively high numbers of single female residents is long-standing and worldwide. As historians Judith Bennett and Amy Froide have written, approximately twenty percent of the women in Florence in the early fifteenth century were single women and, in Zurich by the end of the fifteenth century, "nearly half of all women had never taken a husband."[5]

Why are there, why have there always been, so many single people in cities? Mostly because, throughout history, cities have meant jobs.

In early modern Europe, as soon as any kind of nonagricultural opportunity materialized, women would decamp from the countryside to villages and towns where they could find jobs lace-making or spinning. In these more populated areas, there was the possibility of socializing with other women, earning wages, meeting a wider variety of potential mates, and living, even briefly, outside the power of a husband or a father.

In turn, these migrations of women would precipitate a rise in the marriage age, an increase in the percentage of women who never married at all, and a drop in reproduction. Higher concentrations of women skewed the gender ratio and made husbands harder to find. However, it was also true that by leaving the rural areas where they were more closely watched by fathers and local clergy, women gained a minuscule whiff of liberation: the chance to postpone, if often only for a short time, their inevitable futures as economically dependent wives and mothers. Historian Maryanne Kowaleski cites scholars who report that, in early modern Europe, even women working apparently thankless jobs as servants in cities including Rotterdam and London "may actually have preferred to remain single because of the security and independence a life in service offered them."[6]

These patterns of migration and behavior were repeated on larger scales as agrarian economies gave way to industrialized ones. In the nineteenth century United States, new mills and factories, especially in New England, actively recruited young women as cheap labor. Improvements in infrastructure—better roads, canals, and the railroad boom—made it easier for women to leave rural homes and head to growing cities to work as seamstresses and milliners, governesses and laundresses. Many of the poorest women, including free blacks in the north and south, worked in domestic service for the growing class of urban industrialists.

These female laborers were far from carefree. Poorly remunerated and overworked, their behaviors were monitored by bosses, neighbors, clergy, and boardinghouse mistresses. But the concentration of them within cities, where they could encounter a wider variety of potential partners and friends and earn even scant wages, meant that for the first time in the United States, single women were taking up space in economic, public spheres.

The work that drew women was often unrewarding and physically difficult. In *City of Women: Sex and Class in New York 1789–1860*, historian Christine Stansell looks at the 1805 New York census and finds a few women working as grocers, fruit sellers, tavern and shopkeepers; many more held jobs as seamstresses. Laundering, Stansell writes, was always needed in a filthy city, but was work often left to black women, since it involved physically demanding, scalding, freezing labor.[7]

Still, hundreds of unmarried women and girls arrived[8] in New York every week in the mid-nineteenth century, as immigrants from the countryside and from across oceans. Both white and black women experienced the professional shifts into urban spaces, but their circumstances differed. In her 1925 essay "The Double Task: The Struggle of Negro Women for Sex and Race Emancipation," writer Elise McDougald focused on women in Harlem because, she felt that, in the predominantly black northern Manhattan neighborhood, "more than anywhere else, the Negro woman is free from the cruder handicaps of primitive household hardships and the grosser forms of sex and race subjugation. Here, she has considerable opportunity to measure her powers in the intellectual and industrial fields of the great city." McDougald describes Harlem women working in previously impenetrably white, male fields: as probation and corrections officers, in libraries and bacteriology labs, in the garment industries and branches of the public health system. But McDougald notes, ". . . even in New York, the general attitude of mind causes the Negro woman serious difficulty. She is conscious that what is left of chivalry is not directed toward her. She realizes that the ideals of beauty, built up in the fine arts, have excluded her almost entirely."[9]

## Noisy and Bold

Letty Cottin Pogrebin graduated from Brandeis in 1959, and came to Manhattan in search of a bohemian life, settling into an apartment across the street from playwright Edward Albee. When her car was stolen, she bought a motor scooter. One of her boyfriends bought her a pet duck, whom she named "Moses," and then, because she took to it so quickly, a pet rabbit, Buckety. In her teens and early twenties, Pogrebin worked her way up in the publicity and subsidiary rights departments of the publishing industry, eventually earning a salary that was "unheard of" for a young woman, and in charge of promoting Helen Gurley Brown's *Sex and the Single Girl*, among other best sellers.

She was a Jewish girl from Queens whose mother had left an abusive first marriage, worked in the garment industry, and then had become a middle-class housewife before dying of cancer when Pogrebin was a teen. Yet in Manhattan, Pogrebin didn't have to be defined by her family or personal history. She could reinvent herself, tool around with ducks and rabbits and motor scooters, have lots of sex, and move ahead in a job that allowed her to tape pill capsules to press releases for *The Valley of the Dolls*. "I just had the most magical sixties," Pogrebin said of her days as a young single woman in the city. "Quite simply, I wanted to be Holly Golightly. And I felt I was doing really well at it."

Today, as always, women arrive in cities in search of work and money. But they also come, then stay, for the fun.

In metropolises, women are more likely to find a deep and diverse pool of romantic and sexual prospects, and to encounter a combination of community and anonymity that unburdens them of centuries of behavioral expectations. Cities have come to stand, in the cultural imagination, for sex and excitement and power. That they draw women toward these things makes them a catalyst for women's liberation, and for a reimagining of what it might mean for women to have full lives.

Urban landscapes often physically force people of different classes, genders, races, and religions to mix and to meet in the public spaces that they share with each other. At the end of the nineteenth and turn of the twentieth century, crammed tenements often became so fetid with disease that healthy residents exploded out of them by necessity, gathering on sidewalks, hanging out of windows and on stoops, socializing in public thoroughfares. Young people, often living with multiple generations in a single flat, sought relief from airless rooms by meeting up with each other in large groups on the Bowery.

Kathy Peiss writes of the working-class leisure activities and marketplaces of early twentieth century New York, noting that "Streets served as the center of social life in the working-class districts . . . Lower East

Side streets teemed with sights of interest and penny pleasures: organ grinders and buskers played favorite airs, itinerant acrobats performed tricks, and baked-potato vendors, hot-corn stands, and soda dispensers vied for customers."[10] Working women had to traverse streets to get to jobs, early morning and late-night shifts. As the sight of them became more common, less freighted with sexual hang-ups and musty expectations of propriety, the more acceptable the notion of women as part of the urban fabric became.

In an 1896 interview with Nellie Bly, Susan B. Anthony kvelled about the habit of women bicycling. "I think it has done more to emancipate women than anything else in the world," she said, "I stand and rejoice every time I see a woman ride by on a wheel. It gives woman a feeling of freedom and self-reliance. It makes her feel as if she were independent."[11]

Women began promenading without shame, publicly socializing and visiting the parks erected to be the lungs of industrialized cities. The outdoors offered opportunities to push social and sexual boundaries, and young people, writes Peiss, "used the streets as a place to meet the other sex, to explore nascent sexual feelings, and carry on flirtations, all outside the watchful eyes and admonitions of parents."[12] So liberating was a life lived in the urban wild that the YWCA worried, Peiss reports, about how "young girls . . . in this unconventional out-of-door life, are so apt to grow noisy and bold."

By the turn of the twentieth century, writes Betsy Israel in her book *Bachelor Girl*, "so many single girls were visibly out there—working, eating in restaurants, dancing—that it became harder to immediately categorize them."[13] This inability to immediately affix women with rigid class identity or expectation meant an increased potential for personal reinvention and flexibility amidst crowds of new people.

### Urban Drawbacks

Alison Turkos was born in 1988 in Underhill, Vermont, a town with fewer than 3,000 residents and zero traffic lights. In high school and college, she said, she didn't have much of a romantic life; she was working through questions about her identity and sexuality. When she moved to New York City to work in reproductive health activism, she said, "I discovered this incredible community of queer men and women and this whole gender-queer population." It was so freeing, she said, that it allowed her to feel more confident about who she was, and to come out as queer, first to her family, then to the people in her hometown.

Of course, the endless appeal of a city life has drawbacks, as Alison observed, noting that as much as she loves living independently in New York, there's an insatiability that she finds discomfiting. "Everyone always feels that they can do better appearance-wise, or find someone who makes more money or is more intellectually stimulating. There's always going to be someone or something who's more enticing, more interesting."

The madding crowds of people and of possible diversions can be overwhelming. From many urban interviewees, I heard repeated complaints of how hard it is to meet appealing mates, especially (for hetero women) as historic migration patterns hold and many cities remain home to more women than men.

Typically, single men outnumber single women where they always have: in many Western cities that once drew homesteaders and are now home to the tech industry. Eastern cities, including Boston and Atlanta, still have bigger populations of women. There are around 150,000 more single women living in New York City than there are single men,[14] while the dearth of women in Alaska has long been so pronounced that Oprah Winfrey did a handful of shows about Alaskan bachelors throughout the 1990s.

For those heterosexual women who hope to find partners, these numbers are often cited as the grim dead end of youthful urban jollity. As a twenty-two-year-old in my first steady job out of college, a divorced colleague in her forties regularly made me swear, as we chain-smoked in our office and gossiped about men, that if I hadn't married by the time I was twenty-eight, I would decamp for less urban climes. "You don't want to be one of those women," she'd say darkly. "The ones who stay after it stops being fun."

Ten years later, into my thirties and still having fun, I had dinner with a friend who'd lived in New York, but dispatched for New Orleans in her mid-thirties, where she'd promptly fallen in love. "As soon as you cross to the other side of the Hudson," she'd told me, "you'll meet a man." More recently, while chatting with a group of women about the difficulty, especially for successful black women, of meeting a man in New York, MSNBC host and political scientist Melissa Harris-Perry cracked: "Just go stand in a mall in North Carolina." Worried that that her remark had sounded glib, Harris-Perry later elaborated: "When I say if you stand in a mall you can get a husband, I'm not saying it's a *good* husband or one you'd want to marry." She added, even more seriously, that what she meant to convey was her sense that, "in my experience, marriage is an expectation and a desire of young adulthood for both men and women in the South. Men are actually wanting and expecting to marry and seeing marriage as a sign of full achieved adult manhood."

Precisely. And if the reluctance of most women to go stand in the mall but, instead, to tough it out (or live it up) in largely single cities tells us one thing, it's perhaps that these women are not really living their lives to find husbands who make such firm connections between marriage and adulthood.

Journalist Jen Doll wrote in *The Village Voice*, in a very fine piece about the varied pleasures of being single in New York City: "That, to a large extent, is why we live here. It's not because we wanted to settle down with the patient and reliable plod-along schmo, and have babies and live in a three-bedroom house with a two-car garage where we peaceably grill in the summer and make casseroles in winter until we die. It's not because we wanted our lives charted out before we lived them."

Doll's view was one that the journalist Juliet Wilbor Tompkins had scoffed off a century before, in an essay called, "Why Women Don't Marry," in which she wrote of young single women: "They are very happy. . . . with their battle cry of freedom! To their ignorance, life offers an enchanting array of possibilities. They see ahead of them a dozen paths and have but contemptuous pity for the woman of the past who knew but one dull highway."

Whether Tompkins was correct about the contemptuous pity, what's true today, especially in light of more contemporary possibilities, is that that one dull highway is simply not for everyone. To that end, cities permit a degree of self-selection; they siphon from the nonurban dating pool many of those who might rather be working or playing or sleeping with someone else. Perhaps the distractible and sexually voracious actually *shouldn't* be committing to the people they'd rather be doing something else than committing to, and cities offer a place for them to live and thrive.

When we cast, as we so often do, the choice not to permanently partner as a failure or as a tragedy, we assume partnership as a norm to which everyone should or must aspire. But cities allow those who might have made restless, dissatisfied, always hungry-for-something-else mates who caused their partners unhappiness to exit the marriage highway, veering instead onto paths that take them to places that they'd rather be.

It's not such a bad thing to always have something to do, someone to meet, work to complete, trains to catch, beers to drink, marathons to run, classes to attend. By the time some women find someone to whom they'd like to commit and who'd like to commit to them, perhaps it's not such a bad thing that they will have, if they were lucky, soaked in their cities and been wrung dry by them, that those who marry later, after a life lived single, may experience it as the relief of slipping between cool sheets after having been out all night. These same women might have greeted entry into the same institution, had they been pressured to enter it earlier, with the indignation of a child being made to go to bed early as the party raged on downstairs.

And, if marriage never happens, or before it happens, what's also true is that some women simply want to stay and keep playing. As Doll wrote, "We don't know what we want. And so we want a little bit of everything, over and over again." In Doll's formulation, "our status as single, independent, financially solvent New York women. . . . has us sitting on a mountain of unprecedented options. Options: Those are exciting. So we want all the options, bigger and better and faster and shinier, or taller or sexier or stronger or smarter, and yet somehow also different and completely our own. We want the tippy-top of what we can get—Why shouldn't we?"

## Infrastructure and Community

Letisha Marrero's parents had grown up in New York City. They were Puerto Ricans who were determined to give their children an American identity; they moved their family to a California suburb. Letisha came back to New York as soon as she could, working her way up at celebrity magazines, buying herself an apartment on the city's Upper West Side, dating but never finding anyone to whom she connected. When she was thirty-five, she became pregnant with a man she was about to break up with and decided to have the baby on her own.

Suddenly, the city to which she had been so driven became inhospitable. Seeking financial security, she sold her small Manhattan apartment, using the money to pay cheaper rent in a gentrifying neighborhood in Brooklyn. However, when she had her daughter, with no partner and a job that didn't allow her the flexibility she needed to raise her child, she found herself pushed into increasingly underdeveloped areas, trying to find the combination of community she loved and the safety she sought as a single mother. "I didn't want to be a pioneer," said Letisha. "Gunshots did not have any appeal to me whatsoever. I decided we had to get out somehow."

When Letisha was laid off from a job in 2009, she realized that she had to move. She and her daughter Lola went to Virginia, closer to family and to Lola's father. Some of the relief she's felt since leaving the city, she said, has felt like "leaving an abusive relationship. It's like 'Oh! Not everything has to be a struggle! I don't have to lug my groceries up five flights of stairs!'" Getting her daughter into good New York City schools, and into the gifted programs in the public system was, she said, "a fight every single term. I didn't have the money and wouldn't want to pay $25,000 for my kid to go to elementary school, and here I don't have to fight to get her a good education." She and Lola live in an apartment complex in Virginia, and Letisha now finds herself considering the appeals of yards and grills that prompted her parents to put down suburban roots.

Letisha also misses New York, and what it offered her as a single mother, even at the same time that it made it impossible for her to stay. "In New York, everybody on the corner knew who I was," she said. "Oh, that's the brown woman with the baby and the dog." This sense of community was comforting, and felt safe, even in the neighborhoods that she understood to be unsafe. One of her apartments, Letisha recalled, was "right next to a shady bodega," but she said, "Never once did I feel unsafe in there." She said she was never harassed on the street, often felt like the shop owners who sat outside on sidewalks served as an informal neighborhood watch, and felt comfortable enough with her neighbors, in each of her New York apartments, that she could ask for help getting groceries and a stroller up the stairs. She sometimes even left Lola in a store with neighbors while she ran across the street to pick up her laundry. "The attitude was: She's one of us and we take care of our own," she said. "I never felt like I was going to be in any danger. But you can't control the shootings, and I wouldn't go to block parties."

In her Virginia apartment complex, Letisha said, none of her neighbors acknowledge each other.

For single women, with or without children, cities offer domestic infrastructure. The city itself becomes a kind of partner, providing for single women the kind of services that women have, for generations, provided men. Male participation in the public sphere has long been enabled by wives who cooked, mended, did laundry and housekeeping. When men were single (and when they weren't) another low-paid female population worked as their maids, laundresses, seamstresses, secretaries, and prostitutes.

Until recently, there was not a reverse set of services available to most single women. For the well-off, at least, cities go some way toward rectifying that, starting perhaps with providing residents with smaller living spaces that require less cleaning and maintenance. In a city, you are more likely to have a super to perform maintenance and, if you are affluent, a doorman to collect packages, groceries, and greet your guests. There are shops and carts on every corner devoted to preparing morning coffee and hot breakfasts for people on the way to work. It's in cities that there is a stereotype about high-flying young women who use ovens to store sweaters: a testament both to the lack of closet space and the fact that reasonably priced take-out food of nearly every ethnicity is available around the clock; in cities, the work of food preparation that for generations fell to women becomes remarkably more negotiable. There are laundromats and tailors. There are neighbors to help with childcare; roommates with whom to split rents and electric bills. All these things make city living a partial answer to a question sociologist Arlie Hochschild has posed: "The homemaker of the 1950s is no longer at home, and so we must ask, 'Who is going to do her work?'"[15]

And that's to say nothing of the other structural components of a metropolis: the walkable access to multiple entertainments, to bars and clubs and movie theaters and gyms and basketball courts and parks. There is the public transport, the trains and subways and buses and trolleys that can get you to jobs and friends and family cheaply and (usually) swiftly.[16]

Even for those who can't easily avail themselves of the higher-end urban perks, the dense population allows for things like the "neighborhood watch" aspect that Letisha discussed: the streets lined with nosy neighbors, residents sitting on sidewalks in lawn chairs, paying attention to everyone who passes. In apartment complexes where residents know each other, there can be more off-the-cuff childcare options, more people from whom to borrow a cup of sugar.

The big populations of urban centers still create more jobs: often, yes, grossly underpaid jobs delivering take-out and washing gym towels for the more affluent, but still, more jobs than are available in rural communities, from which you might have to drive miles to get to the nearest mall or amusement park or hospital that might employ you.

In fact, one worry goes, cities might *promote* more prolonged independence by providing the kinds of amenities and support that one might otherwise require a mate to enjoy.

Speaking about her perceptions of different regional marriage patterns, Melissa Harris-Perry described to me how the girlfriends with whom she'd attended college in the south had mostly married early, while those she met later while working at Princeton remained single. It left her with the impression that "high-achieving black women marry in their twenties in the South" but far later in the North. Wondering why this was the case, Harris-Perry recalled a friend whom she described as "a classic fifty-year-old New York bachelor," who had once explained his persistent singlehood by noting "that on any day he could have his laundry done, he could get food in the middle of the night if he was hungry, he could go out and sit in the park, or he could go to a show; the proximity of all the services, arts, and cultural events, plus a wide variety of people to be dating made marriage not particularly interesting."

The notion that women too might get from urban homes what, in another era, they got—or what men got—from marriage is a radical, progressive revision of what marriage means. Cities allow us to extract some of the transactional services that were assumed to be an integral, gendered aspect of traditional marriage and enjoy them as *actual* transactional service, for which we pay. This dynamic also permits women to function in the world in a way that was once impossible, with the city serving as spouse, and, sometimes, true love.

Dodai Stewart grew up in New York. Her father, a doctor who was twenty years older than her mother, died when Dodai was a teenager, and her mother has never remarried. Dodai has been in and out of several relationships with men she had every intention of marrying, but, for a variety of reasons, it's never come to pass. Just after she turned forty, Dodai told me, "My long-term relationship is with New York. Definitely. I write about the city. I photograph the city. The city is Girlhattan."

Dodai remembered one of her exes, a San Franciscan who told her that he couldn't wait to get married and have a lawn. Dodai never wanted a lawn. He didn't know what the old punk nightclub CBGB was; he couldn't manage to distinguish, either culturally or geographically, between uptown and downtown. Dodai couldn't take it. "When you don't understand my city," she said, "you don't understand me." She chose New York over the man. She feels strongly that the city is a more rewarding mate. "The city talks to you all the time," she said. "It leaves you messages. You walk by graffiti, and everything changes suddenly because you read something that speaks to you. New York is a character in my life."

The fact that Dodai was raised in New York, by a mother who has lived independently here for more than twenty years, may make it easier for her family to understand her independent path. For those urban dwellers raised in earlier-marrying regions and amongst earlier-marrying friends, the dynamics can be trickier.

## Urban Myths

Nisha, from suburban Napierville, Illinois, described to me the disjuncture she feels between her life in her hometown and her life in Washington, D.C., as a twenty-four-year-old who works in social media and is in a relationship but remains unmarried. She's begun to note that some of her friends and high-school classmates are marrying, but her social circles in Washington and New York, where she also works, remain single. In the city, she said, her friends "are focusing on our careers and enjoying city life, but some of my friends from home are wondering when their boyfriends might propose."

Everyone she knows in D.C., Nisha told me, has both a day job and side projects and social calendars so packed that it's difficult for her to imagine meeting any old-fashioned marital milestones. She thinks that, in five years, her perspective will be different. "There is that invisible line of thirty," she said. "When women get close to thirty is when people start to wonder about you." Her parents, immigrants from India, have said to her that they hope she doesn't wait that long. But, she added, they also understand that in a new economy, it's "not smart for a woman to be financially dependent on a man."

Of course there are millions of single women who never leave, or indeed who move in a reverse migratory pattern, from cities to suburban and rural areas. And, while the age of marriage is rising everywhere, in the places where people tend to marry earlier, the stigma of remaining unmarried can be strong.

Kristina is a thirty-five-year-old archaeological lawyer who lives in Bismarck, North Dakota. She was born and raised in Philadelphia, and because of the ever-changing, regional nature of her work and studies, has lived as an adult in Massachusetts; Dallas, Texas; Carlsbad, New Mexico; Reno, Nevada; Rhode Island; Fairfield, Connecticut; Farmington, New Mexico; and Missoula, Montana.

With her vast geographical range, Kristina could say with confidence that, "being single is a handicap in the more rural places." When she told friends that she was moving from Missoula to Bismarck, many expressed concern that she'd be moving to a more urban area without a husband for protection. She told me that her response was often, "I moved from Connecticut to New Mexico by myself, and you're worried about the high crime rate in *Bismarck?*"

As Kristina began to make friends in North Dakota, she said, some people expressed shock that she wasn't married and had never been married. She also reported that, on several occasions, after being asked if she were hitched and replying no, people would respond by saying "Oh, I'm so sorry." But as an inhabitant of a place where early marriage is the norm, even she has internalized some of the prejudice and alarm about people she meets who remain unmarried. If she meets a man her age who has never wed, she said, "My red flags are all over the place. 'What's wrong with you? I know *I'm* single, but I'm feisty from the East Coast. Now you explain yourself to me.'" She thinks that if she lived in a city, she'd be more comfortable dating single men, because the swifter normalization of single adult life in cities makes the men who are single seem more . . . normal.

What's true is that women (and men) are marrying later all over the nation, not just in the cities, even though it can sometimes feel that way. The conscious embrace of unmarried life—or at least a gimlet-eyed critique of the early marriage model as opposed to a romanticizing of it—is far from exclusively urban. In 2013, twenty-four-year-old Kacey Musgraves from Golden, Texas, was nominated for an American Country Music Award for Best Female Vocalist. Her song, "Merry Go 'Round," begins: "If you ain't got two kids by twenty-one/You're probably gonna die alone/Least that's what tradition told you," and then continues to convey doubt about what that tradition gets you: "We get bored, so, we get married, Just like dust, we settle in this town . . . We think the first time's good enough/ So, we hold on to high school love."

## Rooms of Their Own

For poor women, communal living, no matter your marital status, has long been a necessity. In 1855, of four hundred single women on a New York City census sampled by historian Christine Stansell, only eleven lived alone.[17] Piled into tight rooms in narrow tenements with siblings, cousins, parents, and grandparents is how most working women lived in cities until relatively recently, and how many poor and immigrant families still live around the country.

Even those who were forced to, or longed to, break from the multigenerational living arrangement could not easily set up house on their own. Fears about controlling sexuality, enforcing moral codes, and keeping women safe meant that for generations, many wage-earning girls lived in boarding houses; activist Virginia Penny wrote in 1863, "Many of these shop girls sleep half a dozen to a garret."[18] That garret was usually closely monitored by older women who kept strict curfews and policed the virtue of their lessees with parental zeal.

Historian Joanne Meyerowitz writes of how, in 1891 Chicago, the matron of the Home for Self-Supporting Women contacted the Illinois Humane Society, who, in turn, contacted a young female resident's stepmother to get permission for the young woman to go out with a man from her South Dakota hometown. The stepmother thanked the organizations for protecting her stepdaughter from "the many traps and snares of the city."[19]

But the primal urge for women to carve out some space to call their own is familiar to anyone who has read Virginia Woolf.

Nineteenth century physician Harriot Hunt, who lived contentedly with her parents, and then a married sister, said, "It cripples one not to have a home of one's own."[20] And Louisa May Alcott wrote longingly, at age twelve, of a seemingly impossible fantasy: "I have been thinking about my little room, which I suppose I shall never have. I should want to be there about all the time, and I should go there and sing and think." Alcott was one of the few women eventually able to afford her own space, and would later describe herself, as a kind of spider, needing "to be alone to spin."[21]

While poor men, like their working-class sisters, also crowded into tenement spaces with families or coworkers, more affluent single gentlemen, whose rights to inherit property and earn rent money were less tenuous, had a wider array of options. They could live in apartment houses and in clubs, their domestic (and presumably sexual) needs attended to

by paid help. In Manhattan, by the end of the nineteenth century, between a third and a half of men over age fifteen were unmarried, and
many lived on their own. One bachelor wrote of his accommodations in a
gentlemen's club: "Each member is as much at home as if he were in his
own castle; the building . . . is kept with the same neatness, exactness,
and comfort as a private dwelling. Every member is a master, without any
of the cares or troubles of a master."[22]

It sounds nice! And, for a long time, there was simply no female equivalent. But as more women came to cities not simply to work as domestics,
but in the newly developing female professions, there had to be space for
them to live.

Built in 1903, the twelve-story Martha Washington Hotel was one of
the first complexes designed to individually house women who were arriving in New York to find work.[23] When the building was landmarked in
2012, the *New York Times* described the era as one in which "single professional women had a difficult time finding places to live in which they
were free from the suspicion of immoral behavior." Even in the Martha
Washington, which first admitted five hundred residents, and would go
on to house stenographers, editors, and a lawyer who would become the
first woman appointed a magistrate in New York, there were strict rules:
Men were not permitted beyond the first floor and, at first, male bellhops
were required to carry all heavy luggage; in 1904, fourteen women replaced those bellhops.

In 1906 the Trowmart Inn was built to house single women in Greenwich Village, and erected for "the class who labors for a small wage, and
whose parents have no home within the city." The Trowmart had no cur-
few, and was in fact expressly designed as a way station on the path to the
altar. Its founder told the *New York Times* that he intended to create a place
where men could court women, since an inability to live independently
also meant structural obstacles when it came to dating, romance, and sex.
As the *Times* described it, "Girls of gentleness and refinement do not care
to be courted upon the open highway, nor in public parks, and thus the
world is filling with spinsters who . . . had they a proper place in which to
entertain their admirers, would develop into happy, excellent wives and
still happier mothers." The Trowmart's founder said that he'd be pleased,

in the *Times*'s words, "if the girls have a happy home, and if a number of marriages accrue each year from the Trowmart Inn."

These establishments helped create a path for women who wanted to live on their own, giving way to slightly more glamorous options, like The Barbizon, a "Club Residence for Professional Woman" built in 1927, which, while featuring tiny, Spartan rooms, also began to provide some of the services of older gentlemen's quarters. The *Chicago Tribune* reported of the Barbizon as it was being built that it was "especially designed for business and professional women with such unique features as a gymnasium, swimming pool, studios and other conveniences usually found only in men's clubs." Two years later, the *Times* reported on the "modern Amazons" who were enjoying the Barbizon's athletic facilities, and noted that "it has been said that in their clubs women have more liberty than men."

By the middle of the twentieth century, it was far easier for women to find their own apartments, with roommates chosen through newspaper ads. But the possibility of living alone remained such a passionate fantasy that Betsy Israel described how to her, even in the 1980s, the phrase "rent-stabilized" was "a lot more exciting, filled with more possibility and the hint of adulthood, than 'marry me.'"[24]

Just before I graduated from college, a friend and I visited New York, where I was already planning to live, and met up with her sister, a successful woman several years older than we, who rented a studio on the city's Upper West Side. When I arrived to meet my friend and her sister, my friend explained apologetically that I could not come into her sister's apartment; she had a rule that no one but blood relations or lovers could enter the space. It was one room, it was all the privacy she had in the world, and she guarded it with what, to my young mind, was almost incomprehensible ferocity.

The growing number of women looking for a few square feet of their own has had an impact on urban planning. In 2013, the Museum of the City of New York presented an exhibition, in partnership with the Citizens Housing & Planning Council and the Architectural League of New York, called "Making Room," whose mission was to showcase design solutions "to better accommodate New York City's changing, and sometimes surprising, demographics, including a rising number of single people." The exhibit featured the designs of 325-square-foot apartments, roughly the size of the spaces that former New York City mayor Michael Bloomberg touted as part of his encouragement of new "micro-apartments" designed to house the city's growing number of single people.

In Washington, D.C., a DuPont Circle mansion is being converted into ninety-two apartments averaging about 350 square feet each;[25] a 2012 cluster of tiny 150 to 250 square-foot houses in an alleyway was designed to demonstrate how small living can provide a model for the future.[26] Meanwhile, the boom in micro-apartments in Seattle, where demand is so great that older, larger homes are being demolished to make room for 200 square-foot units with shared kitchens, has been dramatic enough to draw protest. One resident told *The Seattle Times*, "We're not concerned with who these people [renting micro-apartments] are, but with how many there are. This is a massive increase in density."[27]

In Dolores Hayden's classic book, *The Grand Domestic Revolution*, the urban historian looks at how the architecture of familial homes worked to separate women from each other and confine them to individual duties. Charlotte Perkins Gilman, author of the feminist utopian novel *Herland*, dreamt of kitchen-free homes for women who would be cooked for by paid staff, while the nineteenth century reformer and feminist Melusina Fay Peirce led a cooperative housing movement that argued that the segregation of women as cooks and mothers in separate houses was an impediment to equality.[28]

As increasing numbers of contemporary women enjoy lives untied from the kitchens and nurseries that once confined their forerunners, they are accidentally fulfilling these older activist fantasies, in which cooking and leisure spaces are shared, and independent adults are engaging in communal experiments in domestic life, no spouses required.

## Cautionary Tales

With liberty comes risk. Anonymity and freedom may be sweet relief, but they also create space for danger: sexual vulnerability, higher incidences of violent crimes, greater proximity to illegal activity.

In earlier eras, one of the greatest risks run by women who lived on their own in cities, or who roomed with other women, was the possibility of being taken for a prostitute. Or of being forced, by a combination of poverty and the urban market, to *become* a prostitute.

In 1832, New York's Magdalene Society issued the (possibly false) alarm that "We have satisfactorily ascertained the fact that the numbers of females in this city who abandon themselves to prostitution is not less than TEN THOUSAND!!!!"[29] In Chicago, women who lived in the cheapest and most transient parts of town, the "furnished room districts," were expected to augment their income through hooking. One observer of such a neighborhood in the early twentieth century, said, "an attractive woman who does not 'cash in' is likely to be considered a fool by her neighbors."[30]

But the varied mores of cities also provided women the shelter of forgiveness and redemption and reinvention, possibilities that were often lacking in smaller, rural environs. It was the city's permissiveness, the room it made for varied choices and self-correction, Christine Stansell argues, that made it such a crucial organ for the expansion of female potential. "Therein lies the importance of its tenements, sweatshops, promenades and streets for the history of American women."[31]

In discussions about femininity and urban life, there are entrenched arguments about whether it's cities that lead women astray, or the women themselves who bring temptation to metropolises. As cities teem with more single, increasingly powerful, women, the occasional tales of their sad ends get set up by the press as emblematic, and in them it is often easy to find the suggestion that in daring to live confidently and independently, women have overreached.

In the 1890s, the poster child for the phenomenon was a young Texan, Ada Baeker, who'd traveled to New York at the urging of a female relative, only to find herself so cut off from human connection in the cold metropolis that she tried twice to kill herself. Her story was covered breathlessly by tabloid newspapers of the time, trotted out as a cautionary tale of what happens to women who veer perilously into lonely and unmonitored urban waters.[32]

About a hundred years later, a female jogger in Central Park was raped and beaten nearly to death. The victim was later revealed to be Trisha

Meili, a white, unmarried twenty-eight-year-old investment banker who had graduated Phi Beta Kappa from Wellesley, and had graduate degrees in art and business from Yale. She was a near-perfect embodiment of the expensively educated, high-earning independent women beginning to populate New York at the tail end of the 1980s. She'd been using the park, part of the internal infrastructure that makes cities so livable, to exercise: She was fully engaged in the symbiosis between single women and their cities when she was assaulted. The crime (for which five young black men were wrongly imprisoned) was among the most widely covered stories of that year.

In 1999, Kendra Webdale, a thirty-two-year-old from upstate New York, who was reported to have thrived on New York City's "parks and museums, on its mix of people and possibilities," was killed in one of the places where people mix, pushed in front of a subway by a schizophrenic man with a history of attacking women.[33] In 2006 came the murder of a woman in the top 5 percent of her graduate school class in criminal justice, Imette St. Guillen; she'd been out drinking late with her best friend, insisted on staying out on her own late into the night, and was raped and killed by a bar bouncer.

The media messages about these crimes—always more breathless than coverage of tragedies that befall poor women or women of color, which is often nonexistent—have been clear. The women for whom cities increase economic and social empowerment are put at risk in these metropolises. The things these threatening women come to cities to enjoy on their own: the fun, the freedom, the sexuality, the trains that carry them to work, and the sidewalks on which they gather and the parks in which they run; the very places that support their independence and in which they are free also make them vulnerable. The power that women gain from their degrees or salaries will not protect them from the brutal attacks to which their gender—and their aloneness—makes them prey.

### One Great Love

I moved to New York in 1997, settling against my will in then-unfashionable Brooklyn, because I could not afford to live in Manhattan. Rudolph

Giuliani, who at that point had been mayor for three years, was fascistically scrubbing New York of its porn theaters, homeless people, and the men who washed car windows with squeegees. New York City's police force grew by 35 percent in the 1990s and, under Giuliani's tenure, cops developed a reputation for violent aggression, especially against black men. His policies, alongside a reduction of urban crime across the country, combined with the steady deregulation of Wall Street and a booming tech industry to bring a wealthier population to New York. Cheap, left-leaning gay enclaves became the gut-renovated playgrounds of investment bankers; former meat-packing districts that had once housed single women at the Trowmart and, within recent memory, been prostitution hubs, were now home to cavernous clubs that served stratospherically priced drinks. I could only afford Brooklyn.

When, in those early years, I read Joan Didion's postmarital Dear John letter to the city, "Goodbye to All That," I felt not an iota of recognition. Didion writes of the feeling that she "could stay up all night and make mistakes, and none of them would count," and of how her love for New York was not some colloquial affection, but rather that "I was in love with the city, the way you love the first person who ever touches you and you never love anyone quite that way again."

Far from confident that my mistakes would not count against me, when I arrived in New York City after college, I felt constantly on the verge of losing my place there, fearful that one wrong turn would get me kicked out. If I saw the city as a partner in those early days, it was as a chilly and slightly abusive one. Strapped and lonely, my roommate—a friend from Eastern Tennessee who had challenged her family's assumptions by coming to the big city—and I spent that first year eating two-dollar spicy dumplings and drinking beer on our couch, watching old episodes of *The X-Files,* and asking each other how we'd ever make friends.

In addition to my resentment at being forced to live in Brooklyn, I also, in my first years there, nursed a seething grudge against *Sex and the City,* which had just started its run on HBO. The network would regularly paper the entire metropolis with ads featuring its quirky heroine in her tutu, getting splashed by street water. I didn't hate the show because I thought it was bad; in fact, I had barely even seen it. And I didn't object to its message; I understood, from afar, that it stood, imperfectly, for a new era of female possibility.

What I didn't appreciate was that *Sex and the City* fast became the measure by which every urban-dwelling unmarried woman would be sized up and written off by friends and family. I stopped being able to count the number of people who confidently informed me that my life was "just like *Sex and the City*."

Never mind that, for large portions of my twenties, I was having exactly no sex. Never mind that while the show relied on expansive closets and sky-high heels as metaphors for the more meaningful spaces and heights now occupied by contemporary women, I spent the years that it aired broke (not poor . . . but broke); in fact, the reason I rarely watched *Sex and the City* was that I could not afford cable.

Even if I had been better-paid, better-shod and more frequently laid, I likely would have still resented the comparisons. In part, because I knew how limited this vision of modern femininity was—so many white women with so much money—but mostly because I suspected that when people told me that my life was like *Sex and the City*, it was likely that they didn't intend it as a kindness.

Television critic Emily Nussbaum, who was also a single woman in New York during *Sex and the City*'s run, told me that she was always "very excited by people saying 'your life is like *Sex and the City*.'" Before that, she remembered, they'd just say, "'Your life is like a 'Cathy' cartoon." Cathy was a newspaper comic strip, written by Cathy Guisewhite, that ran from 1976 to 2010, and chronicled its protagonist's diets, dull boyfriend, and unrewarding job. And, yes, it had for a long time provided one of the nation's only popular models of what unmarried life for women might entail. As Nussbaum would write in a *New Yorker* piece about *Sex in the City*, shortly after our conversation, "better that one's life should be viewed as glamorously threatening than as sad and lonely."[34]

Nussbaum also reveled in the fact that people were put off by *Sex and the City*. "I really loved how scary it was to people," she told me. Compared to earlier depictions of single women as determined and lovable, or sad and desperate, the sexually voracious Carrie and Samantha frightened men. Nussbaum continued, "The show knew Carrie was fucked-up and flawed, that she wasn't some sweet plucky avatar of 'Why can't she find love?' It was refreshing because it set the stage for women to be flawed, angry, strange, needy and otherwise nonadorable."

The complexities of the women in *Sex and the City* helped make them synonymous with the city, which is one of the reasons that in time, I grew to appreciate it more. Because I knew how flawed, angry, strange, and otherwise nonadorable a place New York City could be, even after its pleasures eventually began to reveal themselves to me.

Five years after I moved to New York, I was able to leave roommates behind and rent my own alcove studio, and my relationship with New York changed almost instantly. In my own apartment, I became happier than I had ever been. My flat was small and not fancy, but I loved every inch of it. I used to have nightmares about having accidentally given up that apartment; in the dreams, I'd be looking into it through its big windows, desperate to get back in.

Getting my own place coincided with an expansion of my social sphere, an increased ease in my professional life; I'd never felt more formed, more adult, and more at home than I did on the first morning I awoke in that apartment. If *Sex and the City* used shoes and closets and cocktails as material emblems of larger freedoms, I reveled in my own pricey symbolism; 450 square feet of unrenovated rental apartment.

However, while I was conducting interviews for this book, journalist Jessica Bennet described to me one of her lasting memories of single urban despair: After having broken up with her long-term boyfriend, she recalled the sense of exhaustion, defeat, and loneliness she felt while trying to lug an air conditioner up four flights of stairs to her apartment. As she spoke, she provoked in me a very vivid memory:

I'm standing outside a Lowe's Hardware store, just four blocks from the new apartment—my very own apartment—into which I have recently moved and which I adore. It's early summer, five-and-a-half years after my arrival in New York, and I have never felt so happy, so capable. But it's so hot, over 100 degrees. And the air conditioner is so heavy. I can't pick it up, let alone carry it home. I'm so happy, I tell myself. I'm so capable. But I'm so tired. And so lonely.

Who's going to help me? Not the city—this great city, with its independence and its friends and its spaces—the city is what got me into this mess. With its no cars and its sweltering pavement and its steep stoops and its array of similarly unmarried friends, who are wonderful but who also don't have cars, and are, also, in the midst of this unexpected heat wave, wrestling their own air conditioners into windows and weeping with the hot, sweaty solitude of it.

No, the only thing I want at that moment is a partner: not someone to do this for me, exactly, but to do it with me. I am twenty-seven years old and I want a goddamn husband.

And, at almost exactly the moment that I think this, perhaps even utter it under my breath, a taxi driven by a woman—still a rarity in New York—drops off another Lowe's customer. I look longingly at the car and the driver rolls down her window and asks if I want to get in. I don't have cash. Do I have cash at home? She asks. Yes. This woman gets out of the cab, helps me lift the air conditioner into the trunk. When she pulls up at my apartment, my new landlord is there, smoking a cigarette on the stoop. He helps me the rest of the way.

I scoot back out to pay the cabbie and thank her. "You looked stuck," she says in an Eastern European accent. "Sometimes, you just need a lift."

*Sex and the City* got unlocked from HBO and began airing in syndication at around the same time that I moved into my own apartment. I never did watch the series all the way through, but enjoyed the episodes I'd land on. For a while, it seemed that I always flipped to the same one, about Fleet Week. It was a half hour that ended with Carrie riffing on Didion, opining that if "You only get one great love, New York may just be mine."

I loved that line. By the time I carved out my own space in the metropolis, I had come to agree with it.

# CHAPTER FOUR

# Dangerous as Lucifer Matches: The Friendships of Women

In 2009, two women living in Washington, D.C., were invited to a *Gossip Girl* viewing party. Ann Friedman, then twenty-seven, arrived with a boyfriend; Aminatou Sow, then twenty-four, was wearing a homemade "Chuck + Blair" shirt, in reference to two of the show's nubile protagonists. They noticed each other right away.

Amina said she knew immediately that Ann—funny, tall, loquacious—was someone she wanted in her life. Even as they left the party that first night, she hoped that Ann and her then-beau would be walking in her direction; They weren't. "I remember being really heartbroken," Amina said. But when she got home, she discovered that Ann had already friended her on Facebook and knew then that they were "meant to be."

In a bit of social kismet, both women were invited to another event the very next day. They started hanging out all the time, discovered they shared pop culture and fashion interests. Ann was a journalist, Amina a digital strategist; as a way to get to know each other, they started a pop culture blog, called "Instaboner," that chronicled their literary, political, and stylistic obsessions. "We learned to speak the same language," said Amina.

"We were instantly close," agreed Ann, in a separate interview.

Though their connection wasn't sexual, the process of falling for each other was almost romantic. With Amina, Ann said, she found "the thing I always wanted but didn't get from relationships with men: pushing me to

be better without seeming like they were constantly disappointed in me."
She very quickly began to rely on Amina for emotional support, personal
advice, and professional counsel. "All these things people say they turn to
a partner for, I turn to Amina for," said Ann.

Among the largely unacknowledged truths of female life is that
women's primary, foundational, formative relationships are as likely to be
with each other as they are with the men we've been told since childhood
are supposed to be the people who complete us.

Female friendship has been the bedrock of women's lives for as long
as there have been women. In earlier eras, when there was less chance
that a marriage, entered early, often for practical economic and social
reasons, would provide emotional or intellectual succor, female friends
offered intimate ballast.

Now, when marriages may ideally offer far more in the way of soulful
satisfaction but increasingly tend to begin later in life, if at all, women
find themselves growing into themselves, shaping their identities, dreams
and goals not necessarily in tandem with a man or within a traditional
family structure, but instead alongside other women. Their friends.

Aminatou Sow was born in Guinea. The daughter of a Muslim dip-
lomat father, her mother one of the first women to get an engineering
degree in Guinea, Amina grew up in Nigeria, Belgium, and France, and
attended the University of Texas at Austin. She moved back to Belgium
briefly after college, to care for her father and siblings after the sudden
death of her mother, but soon returned to the United States for work,
and, within nine months, received female genital mutilation asylum that
enabled her to stay.

Ann Friedman was raised in Eastern Iowa. Her parents are Catholic,
and she went to the University of Missouri.

"I grew up in this very international world," said Amina. "Ann is a
Midwestern girl. In lots of ways we're so far apart. There are a lot of
things about us that complement each other and a lot of things we don't
see eye to eye on."

Among the things they had in common was their interest in and commitment to personal independence.

For Amina, whose parents were the first in their families to marry for love and not as part of an arranged union, and whose grandfather had three wives and twenty-one children, living alone, unmarried, into her late twenties is an almost political statement. Singlehood, she said, simply "isn't part of the world where I come. It is a thing that never, ever happens." She is the first woman in her family to live alone, the first to make as much money as she does.

Ann, who broke up with the boyfriend she'd brought to the *Gossip Girl* party several months after she and Amina became friends, has found enormous satisfaction in her adult singleness. In large part, she said, that's because in the years she's spent officially uncoupled, she's found that friendships have become paramount. "There is not a romantic relationship or a sexual relationship with a man that has even come close in two years," she said. Both women believe in what they call "chosen families."

"I don't mean just on a feminist or academic level," Ann clarified, "I mean that I believe if you choose to invest in people, the people you invest heavily in heavily invest in you, and that is emotionally sustaining." It's an idea that is gaining some ground in scientific circles. As Natalie Angier reports, after years of anthropologists dismissing nonblood familial ties as "fictive kin," researchers have "recently pushed back against that distinction, arguing that self-constructed families are no less real or meaningful than conventional ones," and are beginning to refer to them as "voluntary kin."[1] The distinction between voluntary kin and what we think of as regular friendship, Angier writes, is that the relationships "often become central to one's identity [and] may serve important life functions: They may provide a sense of belonging, as well as financial and emotional relief."

Ann described her friends, Amina chief among them, as "my emotional support, my everything." And Amina said, "I always tell Ann she's the single most important relationship in my life, not to put pressure on her, but because it's true. It feels like I've known her forever."

A couple of years after Ann and Amina began to twine their lives around each other, Ann decided to leave Washington to pursue a work opportunity. The separation was devastating.

Amina remembered, in detail, the things they did together to gear up for her best friend's departure: the packing and the deaccessioning of Ann's stuff and the good-bye partying. On the morning that Ann set off across the country—moving first to Austin, Texas, then on to Los Angeles—Amina recalled how hard she cried. "I went and got coffee at seven in the morning, and I was hysterical," she said. "It was one of the hardest things I've ever done."

I knew exactly how she felt.

## Sara

Sara and I met as office peons in 1999, but did not instantly hit it off. After several years of distant socializing through our shared network of friends, we found ourselves sitting together at a party after we'd both been through romantic breakups. Comparing notes on our recently smashed hearts, we began to build a relationship of our own.

We became friends in a period of our lives when the demands of our jobs were just heating up, when the roots we were putting down in the city were just getting deep. Sara and I each had lots of commitments, lots of ambitions; we were lucky enough to be engaged by our work. In each other, we found respite, recognition, a shared eagerness to relax, take stock, and talk about it all. We became each other's party dates, point people. My colleagues knew Sara, Sara's colleagues knew me; we each knew everything about the other's colleagues. We knew all of each other's family stories and, eventually, we knew each other's families.

My relationship with Sara had a low-slung thrum of beer, cigarettes, and the kind of quotidian familiarity we think of as being available mostly to long-term mates, or possibly siblings. Sure, we talked about crushes, unspooled tales of unrequited desires, described exciting or ill-advised hookups, and guided each other through the visceral mishaps, from missed periods to condoms lost within bodily recesses, to which the female body is regularly subjected. But the sheer volume of time we spent talking meant that those exchanges represented a tiny fraction of our interactions.

In truth, we were often more likely to compare weird rashes or spend hours sorting out our work drama than we were to talk about, say, our own orgasms or anyone else's penis. We helped each other find new apartments and get raises. We advised each other on budgeting, obsessed about presidential elections, shared books and went to the movies, dealt with exterminators, and watched awards shows together.

When it comes to friendships, even amongst the most tightly knit, exclusivity isn't required. As Ann would say to me, "The good thing about female friendships is that they're not exactly *Highlander*. It's not like 'there can only be one.'"

So, it's not even that we were "best friends." Or rather, we each had lots of "bests." Together, Sara and I shared a close network of four other friends with whom we vacationed, but we also maintained separate relationships with our own circles. I had my friends from home and college, the colleagues to whom I had become close, and one married friend with whose family I spent a lot of time. Sara had her Pittsburgh people, her own college crowd, and her own work friends. Even when we weren't close to each other's friends, we knew all about them; we were all kind of in it together.

Without realizing it, we were recreating contemporary versions of very old webs of support. Historian Carroll Smith-Rosenberg has written, in references to women's relationships of the nineteenth century, "Friends did not form isolated dyads but were normally part of highly integrated networks."[2]

Friendships provided the core of what I wanted from adulthood—connection, shared sensibilities, enjoyment—and, as Ann said about her friendship with Amina, a big part of what I'd wanted from romantic and sexual relationships with men, but had not yet experienced. Unlike my few romances, which had mostly depleted me, my female friendships were replenishing, and their salubrious effect expanded into other layers of my life: They made other things I yearned for, like better work, fairer remuneration, increased self-assurance, and even just *fun* seem more attainable.

Female friendship was not some consolation prize, some romance also-ran. Women who find affinity with each other are not settling. In fact, they may be doing the opposite, finding something vital that was lacking in their romantic entanglements, and thus setting their standards healthily higher.

"I'm just not sure there's somebody for everybody," says Amina, of her view of finding future partnership. "But also all of those things you're supposed to get out of a male partner I get out of my friendships, not just Ann. I had to build this family for myself. And I'm deeply invested in that for myself. It's where I bring my grievances; it's where I go to get healed. I just don't know if that's sustainable in a partnership with a man. And it's also just not a priority. My friends are my first priority. "

Four years after we first met, the man Sara had been seeing was offered a great job in Boston. They dated long distance for a year. But then they had to make a decision; he was intent on staying in Boston, despite the fact that it was not a city that offered her much professional opportunity.

Watching Sara wrestle with her choices was painful. She was thirty. She loved New York. She had a great, well-paying job. She was crazy about her apartment. She adored her friends. But she also cared for her boyfriend; she wanted to try to make a life with him, to see what happened.

It was the kind of upheaval, smack in the middle of adulthood, which was messy enough to make me consider, back then, the wisdom of early marriage. When we're young, after all, our lives are so much more pliant, can be joined without too much fuss. When we grow on our own, we take on responsibility, report to bosses, become bosses; we get our own bank accounts, acquire our own debts, sign our own leases. The infrastructure of our adulthood takes shape, connects to other lives; it firms up and gets less bendable. The prospect of breaking it all apart and rebuilding it elsewhere becomes a far more daunting project than it might have been had we just married someone at twenty-two, and done all that construction together.

The day Sara moved to Boston, after weeks of packing up and giving away her stuff, a bunch of friends closed up the U-Haul and gave long hugs and shouted our goodbyes as she drove off. When she was gone and I was alone, I cried.

Make no mistake: I believed that Sara should go. I wanted her to be happy and I understood that what we wanted for ourselves and for each other were not only strong friendships and rewarding work and good times, but also warm and functional relationships with romantic and sexual partners. Both of us were clear on our desires for love, commitment, family. The only way to build all those things, I thought at the time, was to leave independent life behind.

I didn't want to think of our friendship, our multi-textured life together, as some stand-in or placeholder for "realer" relationships with partners, but it was undeniable that part of what we did for each other was about practicing and preserving intimacy in our lives—remembering how to share and bicker and compromise and connect, how to work through jealousy and be bored together—even during years when we did not have traditionally romantic partners with whom to learn these human skills.

What's more, we pushed each other to become hardier versions of ourselves, more able (and, I suspected, more likely) to form healthy, happy alliances with partners. Friendship had helped make Sara's relationship possible; through one particularly self-pitying lens, I saw it as the rocket that propelled a shuttle into orbit . . . and then, inevitably, fell away. I was able to identify with Amina's story about Ann's move a decade later because, for me, Sara's departure was among the hardest losses of my adult life, far more destabilizing than my earlier breakup with a boyfriend.

Long before I ever considered that I'd one day be writing this book, I tried to make sense of my grief by writing a story called "Girlfriends Are the New Husbands." In it, I argued that while women no longer necessarily matured in the context of marriages, we did not spend our adult years alone, but instead became each other's de facto spouses.

When I sobbed to another, usually Eeyoreish, friend—a mentor about ten years my senior, who had herself been single deep into her thirties—she surprised me by assuring me: "Don't worry, she'll come back." Oh, I know, I said, she'll be back to visit, but it won't be the same. "No," my friend said more firmly. "She'll come back. Her life is here."

I was completely flummoxed by her confidence. Sara wasn't coming back. You don't come back. I knew this from way back, from Laura Ingalls and Anne Shirley and Jo March; I knew it in my bones. We might have postponed fate, but marriage remained women's ultimate destination, the tractor beam that would eventually pull us all in.

Sara and I were, to some degree, over.

## She Is My Person

The sadness Amina felt when Ann left didn't dissipate quickly. She started going to therapy again, since "the one person I would talk to wasn't there." Feeling that her social fabric in Washington D.C. had unraveled, Amina began to make plans to leave the city. "Ann was the center," she said. "And without her, there was not a lot there for me."

There was little chance that Ann, who had a big job in Los Angeles and was falling in love with her new city, was going to return east. Amina recalled a road trip they took together out west; Ann had gotten California plates and was glowing with affection for her new-found home. Amina remembered telling her, "It's stupid beautiful watching you fall in love with California; it's like watching the Grinch's heart grow."

When a member of a romantic couple gets a great job in another part of the world, there is usually at least discussion of whether the partner will accompany her or him; when a spouse has a yearning to live north and another spouse south, there is, typically, negotiation about where, or if, they will settle as a unit.

Given the way we're taught adulthood is supposed to unfold, the idea of figuring friends into life's trickiest logistical equations sounds silly. You can't—and aren't supposed to—build your lives around friendships, but rather around families, marriages, jobs, *maybe* aging parents . . .

But for Ann and Amina, the friendship does factor in their ideas about the future. Relocation has been discussed. "I'm getting really tired of this long-distance relationship and soon one of us is going to move for the other person," said Amina. Ann concurred, but it was hard for Amina to find a job that made the move a realistic option. Amina moved to New York, Ann's least favorite city, in 2013. They tried not to let six weeks go by without seeing each other. In 2014, Amina took a job in northern California.

"She's the person I text all day," said Ann. "If she didn't hear from me for a day, you could basically assume I was dead." When Ann spent a year as a boss, she was careful never to talk to her colleagues about her romantic or her sex life, but, she said, "They all knew Amina was my person."

"It's really important that my coworkers know Ann," said Amina. "You have to know the place that Ann occupies because people only talk about their significant others; I don't even think I say she's my best friend because it's so much more than that to me. She is the person I talk about every day. She is my person."

Though Amina said that there is no connection, this formulation—"She is my person"—echoes language used on the television drama *Grey's Anatomy*. The show's central relationship was the nonsexual but deeply loving friendship between two surgeons, Meredith and Cristina, tough women who argued and competed with each other, shared beds and booze, who disliked hugging and cheap sentiment, and were obsessive about their work and their love lives, and who referred to each other lovingly and possessively as "my person." It probably matters that *Grey's* was the creation of Shonda Rhimes, prolific writer and director of so many television shows about diverse and complicated women that her entertainment empire is often referred to as if it is some fantasized island of female power: Shondaland. Rhimes is the unmarried mother of three.

Intimacies between women who are each other's "person" have long played a crucial role in society, especially for women who have lived outside of traditionally married family units. The scholar Sharon Farmer has written that medieval Parisian "single women sometimes found practical, economic, and emotional support in their companionships with other unattached women,"[3] and notes that Parisian tax records offer evidence from the thirteenth and fourteenth centuries of women living, working, and being assessed together.

The closeness of unmarried women to each other was so recognizable that tight friendship (and often bedfellowship) between maidens was often used as a plot device by Shakespeare, whose heroine, Helena, of *A Midsummer Night's Dream*, describes herself and Hermia, with whom she shares an "ancient love" as being, "Two lovely berries moulded on one stem . . . with two seeming bodies, but one heart." In nineteenth century America, when westward expansion created a dearth of potential husbands on the East Coast, the social and adult domestic partnerships of women proliferated to the point that they became known colloquially as "Boston marriages."

As interactions between young women at boarding schools and

women's colleges became more frequent, the tightly cathected relationships they formed as teenagers became so accepted that there was a term for their connection: they were "smashed." As Betsy Israel writes, "smashed" pairs were thought of by their approving parents as something like "best friends going steady, and, once smashed, they'd learn trust, loyalty, tolerance, patience" from each other. The practicing of these behaviors on each other was all supposed to be in service of their later marital unions, Israel notes, "even if those who wed never felt quite the same about their husbands."

The scholar Carroll Smith-Rosenberg argues in her 1975 essay, "The Female World of Love and Ritual: Relations Between Women in 19th Century America," that the centrality of women's relationships with each other was determined in part by the rigidly patrolled divide between the male and female spheres in earlier centuries, creating what she called the "emotional segregation of men and women."[4]

Women often lived together, within multigenerational family housing, or in sex-segregated schools, boarding houses, or in factory dormitories like those in Lowell, Massachusetts. They guided each other through emotional and physical maturation, bonded over their experiences of courtship, marriage, and childbirth and, as Smith-Rosenberg writes, "lived in emotional proximity to one another." Marriage between these women and men who had been raised separately and educated and trained for public life, meant that "both women and men had to adjust to life with a person who was, in essence, a member of an alien group."[5] As Smith-Rosenberg writes, "While closeness, freedom of emotional expression, and uninhibited physical contact characterized women's relations with one another, the opposite was frequently true of male-female relationships."

Friendships often provided women with attention, affection, and an outlet for intellectual or political exchange in eras when marriage, still chiefly a fiscal and social necessity, wasn't an institution from which many might reasonably expect to glean sexual or companionate pleasure. Because these relationships played such a different role from marriage in a woman's life, it was quite realistic for commitments between women to persist as central after the marriages of one or both of them. Even the happiest of married women found something in their associations with other women that they did not have with husbands. As Elizabeth Cady Stanton, devotedly wed and mother of five, once said of her activist partner, Susan B. Anthony, "So closely interwoven have been our lives, our purposes, and experiences that [when] separated, we have a feeling of incompleteness."

It was not only women who turned often to their own sex for practical and tender fulfillments. In the early male-dominated Southern colonies, some men lived together on tobacco plantations and were referred to as "mates."[6] Abraham Lincoln shared a bed for several years with his friend Joshua Speed, to whom he wrote in 1842, "You know my desire to befriend you is everlasting."[7] And, according to *The Atlantic*, President James Garfield's attachment to his college buddy Harry Rhodes was so deeply felt that he once wrote, "I would that we might lie awake in each other's arms for one long wakeful night."[8]

The language of sentiment between same-sex friends—not to mention references to embracing, touching and snuggling in bed—suggests to many modern readers that the women (and men) in question were engaged in what we'd now understand as homosexual relationships. And some surely were. But the concept of homosexuality as a sexual identity really only emerged in the early twentieth century, making it largely impossible to retrospectively evaluate the nature of many close, even physically expressed, same-sex bonds.

Certainly, there were women who were both cognizant and vocal about their fealty to other women, in love and in life partnership. In her 1889 autobiography, reformer Frances Willard, who only had committed emotional and domestic relationships with other women, wrote that "The loves of women for each other grow more numerous each day . . . In these days when any capable and careful woman can honorably earn her own support, there is no village that has not its examples of 'two heads in counsel,' both of which are feminine."[9]

Others tried to clearly distinguish between carnal and romantic impulses. Margaret Fuller, Transcendentalist writer and literary critic, who had a lengthy epistolary friendship with Caroline Sturgis, and who at the end of her life entered a passionate affair with a man she may have married, wrote, in reference to another intense alliance with a woman, "I loved Anna for a time with as much passion as I was then strong enough to feel . . . This love was a key which unlocked for me many a treasure which I still possess, it was the carbuncle which cast light into many of the darkest caverns of human nature." But at the same time, Fuller argued that while it is "so true that a woman may be in love with a woman, and a man with a man," such relations are "purely intellectual and spiritual, unprofaned by any mixture of lower instincts."[10]

Smith-Rosenberg argues that a contemporary preoccupation with individual psycho-sexual dynamics was, for a long time, part of what obscured a larger social and political context in which to examine women's friendships. While the erotic dimensions of women's relationships to each other may well have mattered to the women themselves, the official distinction between gay or straight seems hardly crucial to those of us examining the place of women as supports in each other's lives.

And what we know today—when gay and lesbian identities are far more recognized than in earlier eras—is that women still form intensely emotional, often physical bonds that might easily be understood from a distance as homosexuality, but which aren't necessarily sexual.

When I was in junior high, I had Judy, with whom, a century before, I would have been said to have been "smashed." And while we never went in much for hugging, hair-braiding, or any of the other fleshy communions common to budding girlfriendships, we certainly experienced a chaste version of puppy love.

Neither of us had boyfriends (or girlfriends), and there's a compelling argument that we didn't precisely *because* we poured so much of ourselves into each other, but I think the reverse was true: We were adolescents, full of energy and self-interest and the incandescent urge for human connection. When no well-matched romantic interests came along to light us up, we focused our teenaged high beams on one another, composing volumes on our affections in birthday cards and yearbook messages and notebooks traded between classes. We shared inside jokes and argued about the war in the Persian Gulf and watched *When Harry Met Sally* and nursed jealousies, of interloping friends and even of changing tastes that might lead us to cease to perfectly mirror each other.

What criteria do we apply to properly designate the nature of "real" partnership? Do two people have to have regular sexual contact and be driven by physical desire in order to rate as a couple? Must they bring each other regular mutual sexual satisfaction? Are they faithful to each other? By those measures, many heterosexual marriages wouldn't qualify.

Marriage and its ancillary, committed dating, are simply not the only relationships that sustain and help to give shape, direction, and passion to female life, at least not for all women.

If there are broad distinctions to be made between the nature of same-sex female pairs versus heterosexual ones, it's that the same-sex unions have not entailed one of their members being automatically accorded more power, status, or economic worth based entirely on gender.

## Shrieking Sisterhoods

Bettina Chen and Alice Brooks met at Stanford, where they were both getting master's degrees in engineering after having been undergraduates at Caltech and at MIT, respectively. "There weren't many girls around," said Chen, of how they first came to notice each other. "We had a lot of things in common and we connected, being girls from tech schools. And we wanted to try to make more room for women around us."

The women became close and talked a lot about their experiences in male-dominated engineering circles, wondering what they might do about pulling more young women into their field. They began comparing notes about the factors that led them to engineering. Bettina had played with the hand-me-down Legos and Lincoln Logs of her older brothers, boys to whom those building and architectural toys were marketed. Alice, meanwhile, recalled having asked for a Barbie one Christmas, and having received instead, a saw, which she used to make her own toys, including a doll and a dinosaur.

As their friendship deepened, Brooks said, they vacationed together and realized that they spent time easily in each other's company; they figured that that meant they could work together. The two women have since created their own company, producing a set of engineering toys,

Roominate, marketed directly to young girls. It's a company born not only out of a collaboration between women, but intended to bring more women into the male-led world in which its founders encountered each other.

Historically, women have pushed each other into, and supported each other within, intellectual and public realms to which men rarely extended invitations, let alone any promise of equality. It was, after all, pairs of women who tended to found settlement houses and colleges together, who partnered around activism and academia. Female protesters, scholars, scientists, and artists found each other, compared notes, exchanged ideas, and collaborated to become the backbone of the suffrage and temperance movements, and key to abolition. The shared, as opposed to individual, experience of workplace danger and injustice led to women's collective labor actions and the formations of the earliest women's unions.

The power of collaboration and closeness between women has caused no end of anxiety. Nineteenth century antifeminist journalist Eliza Lynn Linton referred to groups of women, especially participants in the suffrage movement, as "shrieking sisterhoods."

Perhaps nervousness about the disruptive power of female association is partly why, a couple of decades into the twentieth century—after the massive political and sexual upheavals of the progressive era—the efforts to re-center women's lives around marriage included a new level of public suspicion and aspersion cast upon female friendships.

In the 1920s, perhaps not coincidentally, around the time of the passage of the 19th Amendment, the term "lesbian" began to be used popularly to indicate a class of single women with close bonds to each other. By the end of the 1920s, American psychoanalysts "were warning that one of the most common 'perversions of the libido' was the tendency of teenage girls to fix their 'affections on members of the same sex,'" writes Stephanie Coontz. "Such perversions, they claimed, were a serious threat to normal development and to marriage." The fix, Coontz writes, was to discourage social unions between women, and to encourage instead more free-wheeling experimentation between the sexes: Dating.[11]

Instead of pairing off with each other and causing trouble, women were prodded, from a young age, to pursue men. Men had their own responsibility in securing the exclusive attentions of young women: Beaus were increasingly supposed to provide not just money and status, but companionship and sociability that women had in previous decades found with female friends, friends with whom they were now in competition for the attentions of these men.

Caricatures of young women's relationships with each other began to change: No longer sentimental sweethearts who might collude and commiserate dangerously, they were portrayed in popular culture as being in perpetual Betty-and-Veronica hair-pulls with each other over coveted male attention. This view of women as competitors has extended beyond the prize of romantic affirmation. As new, but too few, public avenues for professional advancement began to open later in the twentieth century, the idea of factory workers laboring shoulder to shoulder gave way to popular visions of shoulder-padded professional dragon ladies eager to get in good with male bosses and dispatch with the female colleagues or underlings who might challenge them for the meager crumbs of power on offer. And backstabbing stereotypes weren't always so far removed from reality: Power structures have long been built, in part, on the energies of disempowered people vying with each other for the scant chance of advancement.

Finding a balance between camaraderie, support, and self-interest has remained challenging, especially when we find ourselves, today, working alongside, and becoming close to, women who are also competing with us for raises, for better shifts, for promotions. One woman told me, while I was writing this book, about a falling-out with a close friend in the same field in the wake of a professional triumph; her friend had difficulty containing her jealousy. As this woman observed, sadly, "We have years of practice with women competing over men, but now we find ourselves competing with our girlfriends over jobs."

It's not just jobs and men. As more things become available to more women, whether those things are luxuries like travel or nice homes, or too-scarce necessities like education or reliable childcare, the variety of things that women may find to resent about their lots, compared to the lots of their female peers, has only expanded.

Ann and Amina have developed what they call "Shine Theory," as an attempt to redress the now-entrenched model of women as meowing competitors. "When we meet other women who seem happier, more successful, and more confident than we are, it's all too easy to hate them for it," Ann has written, because we understand it to mean that "There's less for us." The solution, she advises, is, "when you meet a woman who is intimidatingly witty, stylish, beautiful, and professionally accomplished, befriend her. Surrounding yourself with the best people doesn't make you look worse by comparison. It makes you look better."

## Marital Rifts

Before the Skyping and texting and shared Tumblring that provide today's female friends their expressive channels, there were letters. In fact, epistolary communications provide the skeleton of much of what we know not only about specific friendships between women and also about the circumstances and perspectives of women whose lives might otherwise have slipped out of public view. They also offer us one of the best windows we have on how women have viewed their marriages and their friendships, and the struggle to make space for both.

A faithful and prolific correspondent, *Jane Eyre* novelist Charlotte Brontë accepted the proposal of her father's curate, Arthur Bell Nicholls, whom she did not love, when she was thirty-eight. She understood that marrying Bell would, as she wrote to a friend, secure her father "good aid in his old age." In this admission and others, Brontë was frank with her female confidantes.

"What I taste of happiness is of the soberest order," Brontë wrote to one friend in 1854, of her decision to marry. "My destiny will not be brilliant, certainly, but Mr. Nicholls is conscientious, affectionate, pure in heart and life . . . I am very grateful to him." She went on, in another missive, to explain that her betrothal had cemented many previous suspicions about marriage. "I know more of the realities of life than I once did," wrote Brontë. "I think many false ideas are propagated . . . those married women who indiscriminately urge their acquaintances to marry [are] much to blame. For my part I can only say with deeper sincerity and fuller significance—what I always said in theory—Wait."

It was clear that Brontë felt the loss of freedom palpably after her marriage. "[T]he fact is my time is not my own now;" she wrote. "Somebody else wants a good portion of it—and says we must do so and so. We do 'so and so' accordingly, and it generally seems the right thing—only I sometimes wish that I could have written the letter as well as taken the walk."

Several weeks later, Brontë wrote to her best friend, Ellen (Nell) Nussey, that her husband "has just been glancing over this note—He thinks I have written too freely . . . I'm sure I don't think I have said anything rash—however you must burn [triple underlined] it when read. Arthur says such letters as mine . . . are dangerous as Lucifer matches—so be sure to follow a recommendation he has just given [to] 'fire them'—or 'there will be no more.' . . . I can't help laughing—this seems to me so funny, Arthur however says he is quite serious and looks it, I assure you—he is bending over the desk with his eyes full of concern."

That concern only became fiercer as the weeks went on. "Dear Ellen," Brontë wrote a week later, "Arthur complains that you do not distinctly promise to burn my letters . . . He says you must give him a plain pledge to that effect—or he will read every line I write and elect himself censor of our correspondence. . . . You must give the promise—I believe—at least he says so, with his best regards—or else you will get such notes as he writes . . . plain, brief statements of facts without the adornment of a single flourish."

Nussey finally responded to Brontë's husband, "My dear Mr. Nicholls, As you seem to hold in great horror the *ardentia verba* [burning words] of feminine epistles, I pledge myself to the destruction of Charlotte's 'epistles' henceforth, if You pledge yourself to no censorship in the matter communicated."

Nicholls agreed. Nussey, much to her personal credit and to history's benefit, never burned the letters. Less than a year later, Brontë, who had written to Nussey that "it is a solemn and strange and perilous thing for a woman to become a wife," became an embodiment of one of the literal perils of wifeliness; she died, likely while pregnant, at thirty-eight.[12]

Marriage, in one manner or another, can have a deleterious impact on female friendship.

Sarah Steadman is a twenty-nine-year-old middle-school teacher in Vernal, Utah. She spoke of her mixed feelings at having seen so many of her friends, especially in early-marrying Utah, where those who share her Mormon faith wed early, driving the state's marriage age as low as anywhere in the nation. When Sarah's best friend from high school married in her early twenties, Sarah was happy for her. "I loved the guy," she said. "I had actually set them up." And yet, she said, "it was kind of devastating. I felt like I had lost her in my life, even though we're still good friends. It's never the same way that it was, completely, because they have their new life."

One of the most gutting moments of my thirty-third year came during the period in which two of my dearest, most beloved friends were getting married months apart. At one of the events to celebrate them, I was passed a message book in which I espied one of my best friends writing to the other about how grateful she was that they were "taking this step together." When I saw it, I felt as if I'd been punched in the stomach.

We were all friends together, a triad, equals. We had varied careers, ambitions, styles, impulses, sexual tastes. It was true that both of these women happened to be getting married and I happened to be single, but I hadn't, until that moment, conceived of their experiences as particularly parallel; their relationships were so different, their partners so different, even their weddings different. But this expression made me see the world in a new way. I may have still been their age, their confidant, their social peer, their neighbor, their friend, but here was an evocation of a shared step that perhaps they saw—and I suddenly felt—as a step away from me.

Elliott Holt is a novelist who lives in Washington, D.C.; she has two sisters, went to an all-girls school, and describes herself as one of those women whose most intimate relationships have been with other women. When she was in her twenties, she recalled to me, she and her friends often saw each other several times a week; they hung out and talked deep into the night. By the time they were in their thirties, some of her closest compatriots had begun to peel off into couples, saving to buy apartments and have children; they stopped going out as much. Now that she's forty, and nearly all of her closest girlfriends have partners and children, she said, she is lucky to catch up with them every three or four months. "I feel completely out of sync with my peers," Elliott said, "And I love them so much!"

As the only single woman in her social circle, Elliott said, "I always joke that I feel like a foreign exchange student: I do speak the language: I have nieces; I've been in people's weddings! But I'm kind of shut out." Her married friends used to invite her to social events but, eventually, she said, the invitations dwindled. She assumes that this is because her friends realized that all they talked about were kids and husbands and houses, and that they didn't want to subject her to it. But what they don't understand, she thinks, "is that I'm trying to figure out where the community is where I *do* belong. It's tricky to confess you're not sure where you fit without sounding like you're whining about not having a partner."

Elliott recently spoke to an ex-boyfriend who told her that she needed to make friends who were in their twenties or their seventies. And she's tried. On a work visit to New York she met a group of young women who invited her out with them. She had a nice time, until, she recalled, "at eleven-thirty, they said they were going to head somewhere else and I had the sense that the night was just starting, and was going to end at two in the morning." Elliott felt the decade and a half that separated them keenly. "I was born when Nixon was president," she said. "And they'd go out and take smoke breaks and I thought, 'Oh my god, you guys smoke! My friends all quit at twenty-nine!' I had a drink and a half, but I was tired and out of sorts." Elliott went home.

### Sara, Again

Six months after she moved to Boston, Sara came back.

She came back for many reasons and after an enormous amount of difficult decision making. She came back because the relationship she'd traveled to Boston for wasn't fulfilling. More importantly, she came back for the very reason my Eeyoreish friend had predicted: that the life she'd left in New York—her work, her city, her friends—*was* fulfilling. She came back for herself.

It was remarkable. I was sad that her relationship hadn't worked out, but happy that she had built a life on her own that was satisfying and welcoming enough to provide her with an appealing alternative to it. And I was thrilled to have her back.

But spaces can creep up between friends just as easily as they do in marriages; gaps yawn open just as they do with lovers. Sara and I were still close; we still talked and drank and watched awards shows and traveled together. But maybe because she was nursing painful wounds as she rebuilt her New York life, and was resistant to simply falling back into her old patterns; maybe because, after the pain of having to say good-bye, I was gun-shy about giving myself over so completely, our friendship was never again *quite* as easy, quite as effortless as it had once been.

Then, a couple of years after her return, it was I who fell in love. It was I who suddenly couldn't go out multiple nights a week with my girl-friends, because I had met a man with whom—for the first time in my life—I wanted to spend my nights.

We have no good blueprint for how to integrate the contemporary intimacies of female friendship and of marriage into one life. In this one small (but not insignificant) way, I think nineteenth-century women lucky, with their largely sucky marriages and segregation into a subjugated and repressed gender caste. They had it easier on this one front: They could maintain an allegiance to their female friends, because there was a much smaller chance that their husband was going to play a competitively absorbing role in their emotional and intellectual lives. (Though, admittedly, as Charlotte Brontë and Nell Nussey demonstrate, even a loveless marriage could put a crimp in communicative freedoms).

When I met Darius and fell in love with him, I was stunned by how much time I wanted to spend with him, and also by the impossibility of living my social life as I had before. I could not drink beer at the end of most workdays with Sara or eat dinner every other night with my friend Geraldine; I could not spend my weekends hashing over everything that had happened that week with my cousin Katie. I couldn't do those things because, if I had, I wouldn't have been spending most of my time with this wonderful guy who, in a remarkable turn of events, I also wanted to have sex with. And once I took out the constancy of communication with my friends, the dailyness and all-knowingness, the same-boatness, the primacy of our bonds began to dissipate.

The worrywarts of the early twentieth century may have been right about the competitive draw of female friendship, about the possibility it might inhibit or restrain a desire for marriage, especially bad marriages. But the real problem with having friendships that are so fulfilling that you prefer them to subpar sexual affiliations is that when you actually meet someone you like enough to clear the high bar your friendships have set, the chances are good that you're going to *really* like him or her. That's what happened to me.

It's not that I loved my friends any less. They are still my friends; I love them and I miss the everydayness of what we used to have. I feel guilty, but here was the truth, for me: I couldn't maintain the level of immersion in my friendships and immersion in what was to become my marriage, because I had been, in many senses, very happily married to my friends.

There has not yet been any satisfying way to recognize the role that we play for each other, especially now, as so many millions of us stay unmarried for more years. Because whether through our whole lives, or through decades at the beginning of them—and, often, at the end of them, after divorces or deaths—it's our friends who move us into new homes, friends with whom we buy and care for pets, friends with whom we mourn death and experience illness, friends alongside whom some of us may raise children and see them into adulthood. There aren't any ceremonies to make this official. There aren't weddings; there aren't health benefits or domestic partnerships or familial recognition.

And when those friendships change—when one friend moves or marries or dies—there aren't divorce settlements, there aren't specially trained therapists, there isn't alimony; there's not even a section in the greeting-card aisle to help us navigate it.

That's what makes the stories that women tell about their friendships—in letters to each other, in novels, and now on television shows and in movies—so powerful. It's part of what I loved about *Jane Eyre*, in which Jane's friendship with the consumptive and ill-fated Helen Burns saves her from boarding school solitude, about Anne Shirley, who finds her "bosom friend" and "kindred spirit" in schoolmate Diana Barry, and announces in her youth, "Diana and I are thinking seriously of promising each other that we will never marry but be nice old maids and live together forever."

Popular culture offers us visions of female friendship, and also, simply, of single women who can keep us company and perform a public, performed version of the thing that flesh-and-blood friends have done: reassure unmarried women that their lives are real and full and worth telling stories about.

## That Girl in Popular Culture

In 1962, Helen Gurley Brown, a forty-year-old Arkansas native who had worked her way up as an advertising copywriter and was certainly *not* a member of what would soon become the women's movement, published a blockbuster book. The slightly trashy paperback had none of the heft of *The Feminine Mystique*, which would be published the next year, but it addressed a constituency that Friedan would barely acknowledge. It was called *Sex and the Single Girl* and was a frank guide for unmarried, sexually adventurous women. It presumed that single women were motivated largely by their hunt for husbands, but, Gurley Brown believed, they should be having fun and feeling good about themselves along the way.

"If you can forget the stultifying concept that there are appropriate years for certain endeavors (like getting married) and appropriate days for being gay and merry (like Saturday nights) and use these times without embarrassment or self-pity to do something creative and constructive . . . I believe half your single girl battle is over," Brown wrote. She called the single years "very precious . . . because that's when you have the time and personal freedom for adventure" and took a rather pragmatic view of marriage, which she called "insurance for the worst years of your life."

The book caused a stir in the mainstream media. Letty Cottin Pogrebin, who would go on to co-found *Ms. Magazine* with Gloria Steinem, was, in the early sixties, a publishing publicity executive in charge of promoting *Sex and the Single Girl*. She told me of first reading the manuscript and thinking, "This is fantastic; this is my life."

Other books were beginning to present stories about what twentieth-century female life, unhooked from marriage, might look like. Rona Jaffe's *The Best of Everything* (1958) was a *sturm-und-drang* yarn about unmarried girls in clerical jobs, while Mary McCarthy's *The Group* (1963), was about more privileged young women, also grappling with sex, birth control, lesbianism, rape, work, and friendship. Norman Mailer would diss *The Group* by sneering at its author—in the style of men put out by powerful women of every era, apparently—that she was "a duncey broad . . . in danger of ending up absurd, an old-maid collector of Manx cats."[13] (McCarthy was, in fact, four times married.)

In 1966, a twenty-nine-year-old actress, Marlo Thomas, daughter of Hollywood comedian Danny Thomas, was trying to land a sitcom vehicle. Frustrated by anodyne scripts, Thomas would later recall, she asked a group of executives, "Have you ever thought about doing a show about a young woman who is the *focus* of the story? As opposed to being the daughter of somebody or the wife of somebody or the secretary of somebody? About *her* dreams, about something that *she* wants out of life?"[14] According to Thomas, the executive responded, "Do you think anybody would be *interested* in a show like that?" Thomas gave him a copy of *The Feminine Mystique* and soon after, ABC green-lighted a half-hour television program (produced by Thomas) about Ann Marie, an unmarried actress with an apartment of her own. Thomas originally wanted to title the series *Miss Independence*, but producers dubbed it *That Girl*.

Thomas, who would become active in the women's movement, was so driven to keep her peppy confection focused on a woman living on her own terms and *not* alongside a husband that, when ABC wanted to renew *That Girl*, Thomas declined. She felt that Ann, whose relationship with boyfriend Donald appeared unconsummated, was no longer a realistic representation of how American women were living. When executives wanted to end the series' five-year run with Ann and Donald's wedding, Thomas again balked: She did not want to send a message that women's stories always lead to marriage. Instead, *That Girl*'s 1971 finale was about the couple getting trapped in an elevator on the way to a women's liberation meeting.

The year before *That Girl* went off the air, its brawnier successor had kicked off. *The Mary Tyler Moore Show*, which would run from 1970 to

1977, was about a television journalist who breaks up at thirty with a boyfriend whom she put through medical school. Mary Richards moves to Minneapolis, finds work at a local station, and befriends her neighbor, Rhoda Morgenstern, to whom she opines in an early episode, "If there's one thing that's worse than being single, it's sitting around *talking* about being single."

Nancy Giles, a fifty-two-year-old unmarried comedian, actress, and television commentator told me that she loved *Mary Tyler Moore* because Mary "didn't end up married, and she was in the newsroom; she was a working person with bills and rent." More than that, her narrative let millions of women know that new opportunities for hat-tossing self-sufficiency were not only possible, but might be desirable. Television news anchor Katie Couric, for years television's highest paid journalist, told me in 2009 that Mary was one of her role models. "I know it sounds crazy," she said, "but I saw this woman out on her own, making a life for herself, and I always thought: I want into that."

Of course, popular culture has also been the most visible and widely absorbed vehicle for backlash—of both the gentle and punishing sort—*against* independent women. As women's liberation slid into Reagan-era, socially conservative, decline, movies reflected increasing anxiety about the growing population of unmarried women by again reflecting them as solitary, sad, and occasionally monstrous.

In 1988's *Crossing Delancey*, Izzy Grossman, a single bookstore employee whose old-world *bubbe* hires a professional *yenta* to set her up with a pickle salesman, is warned that "No matter how much money you got, if you're alone, you're sick!" (Izzy ends up with the pickle guy). At around the same time, Glenn Close warned ominously that she was "not going to be ignored," as the murderously single, lonely Alex in *Fatal Attraction*, who, after a one-night stand with a married man, covets his nuclear family so intensely that she—the unstable element of unmoored femininity—sets out to destroy it. When Alex meets her final judgment, it's the traditional wife who metes it out: shooting her until she bleeds out *and* drowns in a bathtub, in one of the most gruesome punishments of nonconforming femininity ever committed to celluloid. "The best single woman is a dead one," wrote feminist critic Susan Faludi of the movie.

Probably the most progressive film portrayal of a libidinously liberated single woman in the 1980s came from director Spike Lee, and his 1986 film, *She's Gotta Have It*. Lee's heroine, Nola Darling, a sex-loving woman whose reluctance to commit to one man leads her to take three lovers, embodies a bracingly nonjudgmental portrayal of female desire. But, as the critic bell hooks points out, *She's Gotta Have It* includes a scene in which Nola is raped by a man who repeatedly asks "Whose pussy is this?" until she answers "Yours," conceding ownership of the very sexuality that is her path to autonomy.

Recalling the bleakness of popular depictions of singlehood just a few decades ago makes it all the more extraordinary that today we are so surrounded by single women on television. It's this transition for which we have *Sex and the City* to thank, no matter our hesitations about it. Its focus not simply on single female life, but on relationships among single females, was revelatory.

Writer, director, and actress Lena Dunham has called female friendship "the true romance" of her show, *Girls*. And, indeed, the opening scene of its premiere episode showed Dunham's heroine, Hannah Horvath, waking up in bed, spooning her best friend, Marnie, who has taken refuge with Hannah both in an effort to escape being touched by her boyfriend, and because the two women wanted to stay up late watching *Mary Tyler Moore* reruns.

Dunham has spoken publicly about the struggles to not lose herself in her real-world friendship with political adviser Audrey Gelman. "What I want from my life and what you want from your life are very close but not identical," Dunham told Gelman in a 2012 joint interview, "and the job is to support your vision, not my vision of your vision. . . . Loving without judgment or fear of abandonment is. . . . the toughest activity known to mankind and I think with best friend that can be even more pronounced because you aren't my mom, we don't have kids together—but we do have matching tattoos." In the same interview, Gelman said that she couldn't imagine them ever parting ways, because "I think our souls are too commingled to ever split."

The 2011 comedy *Bridesmaids* was a box-office hit that made news ostensibly because it proved that women would pay to see other women star in a raunchy feature; it was also remarkable in that the central tension of the story was not between a heterosexual couple, but between best friends, struggling to survive the drift when one of them gets married and meets new people while the other flounders professionally.

The fury around that drift—the anger that is evidence of how badly a best friend can break your heart, especially when moved aside in favor of a more traditional romantic partnership—was also central to one of *Sex and the City*'s most memorable scenes, after Carrie Bradshaw quits her job in order to move to Paris with a man. When her best friend, the partnered mother and lawyer Miranda, questions Carrie's choice to abandon home and career for a relationship, Carrie yells back, "I cannot stay in New York and be single for *you!*" By the time *Sex and the City*'s television and cinematic run ended, three of its four protagonists were married. Tellingly, in order to sustain the project's narrative, which had always been driven by the friendships and not the love affairs of the women on the show, in the second feature film, writers sent all four characters to another country, Abu Dhabi. This geographic departure allowed them to behave as if they did not have husbands to crowd their lives, and thus continue to function as each other's primary relationships.

A decade after *Sex and the City*'s end, television has *Broad City*, which is even less apologetic about its vision of female friendship eclipsing hetero partnership. Television critic Rachel Syme has argued that it is "a love story . . . about two hapless, pot-smoking, sexually experimental, striving, swearing, struggling, inseparable young gal pals."[15] The two lead characters, Abbi and Ilana, Syme writes, "are intoxicated by . . . each other's presence, full partners in crime and life" who "live separately but share nearly everything: drugs, stomach issues, sexual fantasies . . ." Syme cites a scene that is the perfect distillation of the intimacy of their dynamic: one in which they cuddle under a blanket, discussing their fear of one day pooping during childbirth. "If it happens to me, you have my permission not to look," Ilana comforts. "I'm going to see you give birth, then?" Abbi asks. "Bitch, duh," is the reply. "Who else would be my focal point?"

This stuff, even the silliest of it, is important. It provides a proper acknowledgment of and an unembarrassed vocabulary about the role women play in each other's lives. In 2013, the website Buzzfeed ran a list called "22 Ways Your Best Friend is Actually Your Significant Other" (it included signs like cooking together and talking about growing old together, and ended with ". . . you don't mind people thinking you're a couple, because platonic or not, this is the best relationship you've ever been in.)" The same year, women's magazine *Marie Claire* published a story about women in their twenties, thirties, and forties who are each other's medical contact person, who get mortgages together, who help each other get pregnant. The story's author cited comedian Amy Poehler's joke, that on meeting her friend Tina Fey, she thought, "I finally found the woman I want to marry."

In 2013, science writer Natalie Angier gave the centrality of female friendship a zoological boost, pointing out that, "In animals as diverse as African elephants and barnyard mice, blue monkeys of Kenya and feral horses of New Zealand, affiliative, long-lasting and mutually beneficial relationships between females turn out to be the basic unit of social life."

Some West African chimpanzees, Angier reported, form female bonds that are "resilient, lasting until one member of the bonded pair dies," while female baboons form friendships as a way to combat the stresses—male aggression, bossiness, and infanticide—of baboon life. It all sounds pretty familiar, actually.

"You have to have somebody to hang onto," a researcher explained to Angier.

# CHAPTER FIVE

# My Solitude, My Self:
# Single Women on Their Own

Single. It's a word that's woven throughout cultural monuments to unmarried life, from *Sex and the Single Girl* to *Living Single* to the 1996
Cameron Crowe film *Singles* to Beyoncé Knowles's 2008 song "Single
Ladies (Put a Ring on It)," from which this volume derives its title. It's the
word that social psychologist Bella DePaulo relied on in her book, *Singled
Out,* as the base of her phrase "singlism," which she uses to describe the
"stereotyping, stigmatizing, and discrimination against people who are
single."

It's also a word that plenty of single women loathe.

Rebecca Wiegand Coale explained that one of her New Year's res-
olutions when she was unattached was to stop using the word *single* to
describe herself or any other woman. Rebecca, twenty-nine, saw her circumstances as an unpartnered woman as the opposite of single. When
she'd been in a relationship, she explained, she'd felt dependent on one
person for emotional support and companionship. She and her ex "did basically everything together, from laundry to going out," she recalled. The
relationship, she said, was a good one. "But it was kind of lonely, because
it was just the two of us."

When it ended, she said, she began to make friends through soccer
and bowling leagues. She made progress in her work life, and went on a
networking kick to meet new colleagues. In fact, Rebecca and her business partner and friend, Jessica Massa, coined the term "The Gaggle,"

on which they based a website and book, to describe the collection of romantic prospects in their life. "Suddenly," said Rebecca, "my life was so much richer and so much more *full* of people to depend on and relate to and connect with. I never felt more fundamentally lonely . . . than when I was in a relationship. And I've never felt more supported and connected and fully appreciated than when I was 'single!'" Rebecca has, in the years since she weighed in on the word "single," married a man with whom, she said in 2014, "I don't have to sacrifice the full, rich life I built" when unmarried. And she maintains that it was unmarried life, as opposed to her eventual marriage, that put the loneliness of her earlier relationship in perspective.

I thought of Rebecca's pushback to the idea of being "single" when I read a 2013 *New York* magazine profile of Fleetwood Mac singer Stevie Nicks. Questioned about her life as a woman who has never permanently settled with a romantic partner, Nicks replied, "I don't feel alone. I feel very un-alone. I feel very sparkly and excited about everything. I know women who are going, like, 'I don't want to grow old alone.' And I'm like, 'See, that doesn't scare me. . . . ' I'll always be surrounded by people. I'm like the crystal ball and these are all the rings of Saturn around me."

While the interplanetary part probably doesn't resonate for those of us who are not witchy rock icons, the part about not feeling solitary as an unmarried woman certainly does apply to many, including Rebecca and including me.

I saw more people every day when I was single than I do as a married person. I went out more, I talked on the phone with more people, knew more about other people's lives. I attended more baseball games and concerts; I spent more time at work, and certainly engaged more with colleagues and peers. When I met my husband, we turned in toward each other and our worlds got smaller.

But, while unpartnered life does not necessarily cut people off from the larger world, it is true that when women are not committed to a significant other, when they do not regularly begin and end their days with a romantic partner, they often wind up logging many hours by themselves, in their own homes, in their own heads. And, for many of them, that's just fine.

There is an assumption, put forth by everyone from greeting card companies to Bruce Springsteen, that nobody likes to be alone, least of all women. But many women, long valued in context of their relations to other people, find solitude—both the act of being alone and the attitude of being independent—a surprisingly sweet relief.

"I really value my time alone," said Kitty Curtis, a twenty-six-year old hair stylist from New Jersey. When she exited her last relationship, she first felt scared and was eager to find a new boyfriend immediately, but the feeling passed. "I started to value not having to worry about another adult agenda of any sort, not having to worry about anyone else," Kitty said, "and I got comfy and cozy in my new life. It's just a really easy life, being alone."

Kitty always wanted to travel, but in her two long-term relationships, she said, "I felt like I was constantly having to pull somebody along into a dream." Her vision of what she wanted "had to be compromised with whatever kind of vision they wanted . . . I was so, so smothered." By the time she ended her most recent relationship, she said, she felt unencumbered. "Now, I feel like there's so much to see in the world, so many more things to do. It's so much more exciting than the idea of combining my dreams with anybody else's."

For some, a desire to be left to their own designs remains a steady drumbeat throughout their lives. For others, the solitary impulse strikes at discrete periods, switching on and off with a yearning to cuddle up or hunker down with other human beings. But, in all cases, women's yearning for liberty can be just as keen as the pull toward companionship that has been much more widely advertised.

In her satirical Internet series about women in Western Art for The Toast, writer Mallory Ortberg included an entry entitled "What The Happiest Woman in the World Looks Like:" a painting of a woman sitting alone. "Do you know how rare finding a moment's peace has been for women throughout human history?" Ortberg wrote. "If you spent the rest of your days alone in a cottage on a solitary Alp, it would not *begin* to make up for the years your foremothers spent having to listen to men as a profession . . . A woman alone is a beautiful thing."[1]

## Freedom

Frances Kissling, a reproductive rights advocate who was, for a long time, in charge of Catholics for a Free Choice, was born in Queens, the oldest of four in a working-class family. After briefly joining a convent after high school and deciding that she didn't like it, Frances began her adult life as a sexually exuberant single woman. She has never married and never wanted to. "I'm going to be seventy next year and there is a thing about me, not about circumstances," Frances told me in 2013. "I am very suited to being alone. I *like* being alone. I *need* to be alone."

Frances lived with a couple of men and had one live-in relationship that bridged ten years of her twenties and early thirties. It was a good relationship by many measures, she said, until, "Ultimately, we just bored each other to tears." But, she continued, that relationship is evidence that she *can* be partnered: "It's not like I always wanted to be hermetic. But I'm quite a private person and most of the time I have more fun with myself than with other people." For years, Frances said, she couldn't fathom the appeal of marriage. As her married friends have aged, she conceded, she has watched some couples grow in complementary ways and has decided that a few "have something now that I find attractive. I'm not looking for it, but I definitely see the benefits for people who are healthy and can build a long-term meaningful connection with each other."

But, she added, the things those long-married friends have now derive from the very feature that she finds most repellent about marriage: the quotidian mechanics of cooperation with another human. "I cannot embrace the mundane things in life," Frances said. "When I was in relationships, the interruption of my very important thinking was intolerable. The occasional intrusion of worrying or caring or considering the *other person* in moments of spontaneity: suddenly you're with people and you decide you want to go out to dinner and you have to call this *other person* and tell them you're going to dinner, not because you need permission but because it's the right thing to do."

I felt this. After the man I dated in my early twenties broke up with me, I spent a miserable year getting over it. After that, I felt great; unencumbered in the way that Kitty and Frances described. My days belonged to me. A good mood was mine to sustain, a bad one mine to nurse. If I wanted to watch a television program, I watched it. If I didn't want to eat terrible Chinese take-out, I didn't eat terrible Chinese take-out just because my boyfriend had a craving. I got to build my life around my desires: *my* books, *my* music, *my* hours of sitting uninterrupted on my stoop smoking cigarettes, and thinking. Most important, I didn't have the constant *crick-crick-crick* of being in a relationship with a person who wasn't a good match scritching away at my brain, making me low-level unhappy even on the happy days.

Sometimes, when we're alone, living well feels like a form of revenge against whichever last partner did us wrong. Sometimes, it just feels like making a point, possibly to ourselves, that we don't have to be romantically attached to enjoy a rewarding, worthy—or even lush—existence. Nora Ephron once told me that, during her single years in her twenties in New York, she often consciously cooked and ate a full, lavish meal for herself, laying out place settings, napkins, and serving platters. On nights she spent at home, she said, "I would time it so that it came out at nine o'clock when there was something I wanted to watch on television with this little table in my living room and I would sit down with my meal for four in front of the TV." This was how she reminded herself that she could be alone but not have a diminished domestic experience, a way, Ephron said, to end her day and "not feel sad because you were eating yogurt."

For some, part of not feeling sad is not allowing filth or carelessness creep in, to not let the absence of what sociologist Eric Klinenberg has described as "surveilling eyes" diminish your living or behavioral standards. For others, it means the private space in which to let their freak flags fly.

In a 2012 *New York Times* story about people who live on their own, Sasha Cagen, founder of a website called Quirkyalone, described making herself dinners of a single sweet potato, while writer Kate Bolick, author of the 2015 book *Spinster*, confessed that she grazes on nuts and seeds and wears a pair of giant white bloomers. One unmarried woman told the paper, "I've been living alone for six years and I've gotten quirkier and quirkier," running in place during commercials, speaking French to herself, and keeping her clothes in the dryer, removing only the items she wants to wear that day. The ability to make unconventional choices about wrinkled wardrobes and seed-scattered pantaloons contribute to what Cagen described as "a freedom to really let loose and be yourself when you live alone that a lot of other people may envy."[2]

Until the worry sets in that you might not be able to undo your own attachment to independence and its attendant eccentricities. In the years I lived alone, I worried, and was regularly warned, that I was growing more intractable in my habits, becoming so set in my ways that I would never be able to make room for another person.

These anxieties were not entirely misplaced. It is true that when single, I swiftly chased off any men whose threatened disruption of my Saturday mornings, which I set aside for breakfast on my own and a ridiculous apartment-cleaning ritual that involved dancing, I found too irritating to bear. I felt smothered by suitors who called too often, claustrophobic around those who wanted to see me too frequently, and bugged by the ones who didn't want to try the bars or restaurants I liked to go to, or who pressured me to cut out of work earlier than I wanted to cut out. I got used to doing things my way; I *liked* doing things my way. These men just mucked it all up. I knew how I sounded, even in my own head: picky, petty, and narcissistic. I worried about the monster of self-interest that I had become.

In retrospect, however, I see that the fierce protection of my space, schedule, and solitude served as a prophylactic against relationships I didn't really want to be in. Maybe I was too hard on those guys, but I am also certain that I wasn't very interested in them. I am certain of that because when, after six years without a relationship that lasted beyond three dates, I met a man I was interested in and didn't think twice about Saturday mornings, about breaking my weirdo routines or leaving work early; I was happy every single time he called.

The difficulty that some people have in believing that others might truly relish a life, or even a portion of life, disconnected from traditionally romantic or sexual partnership can merge with a resentment of those who do appear to take pleasure in cultivating their own happiness. As the number of unmarried people steadily rises, threatening the normative supremacy of nuclear family and early bonded hetero patterns, independent life may swiftly get cast as an exercise in selfishness.

## Selfishness and Immaturity

Alison Turkos, the twenty-four-year-old health activist originally from Vermont, described the desire to absorb herself in her work and her social life, and not in anyone else's, as the chief argument for remaining single. She spends so much time at the office and out with friends and at evening events that she's rarely ever at home, she said, and when she is, "I don't want to hear about your day or talk about your day. I want to put on *Parks and Recreation* or a random Pandora station, call my best friend, open a bottle of wine and be with myself."

As Alison told me this, she paused, hearing how it sounded, and how discordant such admissions are in a world in which we're told young women are looking for love, or *should* be looking for love. She laughed and added, "Which is my being selfish, according to other people. Which is why I will always be single."

This unforgiving self-diagnosis is amply supported by cultural messages sent to unhitched women who find that they enjoy their independence.

"If you're single, chances are you think a lot about you," begins the "You're Selfish" chapter of Tracie McMillan's 2012 book, *Why You're Not Married Yet.* "You think about your thighs, your outfits, your nasolabial folds. You think about your career, or if you don't have one, you think about becoming a yoga teacher . . ." Part of the self-absorption McMillan was diagnosing as ugly and unhealthy stemmed from the audacity of belief that you might not even *require* partnership: "Sometimes you secretly wonder," she wrote, "if you even need a spouse. Maybe you're just fine on your own . . . Other people suck, frankly. They get in the way of eating cereal for dinner . . . They're always lying on the couch watching something you don't like on TV and eating something that smells disgusting unless you're the one eating it."

In "Marry Him," a 2008 blockbuster piece for *The Atlantic* that urged women to settle for less-than-perfect mates rather than live their adult lives alone, writer Lori Gottlieb leveled a similar, if subtler, charge: A woman in her late thirties, Gottlieb wrote, is discriminating. She has "friends who will know her more intimately and understand her more viscerally than any man she meets in midlife. Her tastes and sense of self are more solidly formed. She says things like 'He wants me to move downtown, but I love my home at the beach,' and 'But he's just not *curious*,' and 'Can I really spend my life with someone who's allergic to dogs?'"

McMillan and Gottlieb's logic was pernicious, absorbing some of the appealing building blocks of independent female adult life—commitment to careers, to friends, to health, pets, homes, and individual desires—and recasting them as itty-bitty personal concerns magnified to silly proportions by cartoonishly drawn examples of feminine self-absorption.

In fact, there's nothing so wrong with a woman who longs for a curious partner or who feels ambivalence about giving up a home she loves, nor is there anything petty about an adult who feels a responsibility to a pet. But Gottlieb, who herself has never married, was pathologizing unmarried women as flawed, sneakily laying out her self-interested female subject in comparison to a set of deeply ingrained cultural expectations: that a woman who *really* wants love and who is *worthy* of being loved should be willing to put her priorities second to those of a mate.

The notion that individuals, especially women, might be increasingly unwilling to make such accommodations in order to land husbands and create nuclear families sends some critics outside the self-help genre even further round the bend than McMillan and Gottlieb. In a furious review of Eric Klinenberg's book, *Going Solo*, about the record number of Americans now living on their own, critic Benjamin Schwartz sneered at the pursuit of individual fulfillment made more possible by the breakdown of marital and familial obligation.[3] The nation's founders, argued Schwartz, "greatly valued organic community . . . the internalization of civic values being the central bulwark against the deformation of liberty into license and chaos." Never mind that those civic values and founding communities depended on the disenfranchisement and enforced servility of entire races and genders. Per Schwartz, a society in which so many fail to couple, he complained in conclusion, indulges "the novel conceit that selfishness is a virtue."

But Schwartz is wrong that people living alone is equivalent to a breakdown in civic participation in a free society. For one thing, multiple studies have shown that single people behave *less* selfishly within their communities than their married peers.

Following in the (rather dispiriting) footsteps of previous generations of unmarried women, a 2011 report conducted by the Council on Contemporary Families showed that 84 percent of never-married women (and 67 percent of never-married men) offer practical help to their own parents, compared to 68 percent of married women (and 38 percent of married men). This higher percentage includes unmarried mothers. As Naomi Gerstel, one of the sociologists behind the study, told *The New York Times*, "It's the unmarried, with or without kids, who are more likely to take care of other people . . . It's not having children that isolates people. It's marriage."[4]

Never-married women in particular are far more likely to be politically active, signing petitions, volunteering time, and attending rallies. Eric Klinenberg has argued that people who live alone are more likely to attend lectures and be out in the world, while married adults tend to focus their energies within their own homes, perhaps volunteering for their own children's schools, but not necessarily for organizations that do not benefit themselves or their kin.

All of this compensatory energy thrown into the world by unmarried people is laudable and in line with the history of single women powering social movements. It also gets to the heart of an entirely different reason that aspersions of selfishness in women are overblown—because the default expectation of femininity, going back thousands of years has been self*less*ness.

In medieval Europe, where the powerful Catholic Church encouraged youthful unions, it also offered one of the only viable off-ramps: the cloister. Before the sixteenth-century reformation, many wealthy families regarded convents as a refuge (or dumping ground) for daughters they could not unload in, or who did not have dowries enough for, marriage.[5] But the trade-off, as always, was obvious: If they could not submit to marriage, these women would submit to Christ. In some places in Western Europe, there was an even more radical escape: the possibility of becoming a "beguine," an uncloistered, semireligious woman. Enough women availed themselves of this option that beguines came to be seen as a threat; in a report to the Council of Lyons in 1274, the Bishop Bruno of Olmutz suggested that beguines were troublesome insofar as they were "fleeing obedience both to priests and husbands."[6]

This objection hammered home the point of women's lives: they are meant, and have always been meant, to be dedicated to the giving over of self to others, if not to husbands, and kids, then to priests, to god, to parents, to community. Any time women do anything with their lives that is *not* in service to others, they are readily perceived as acting perversely.

Historian Lee Virginia Chambers-Schiller writes of the nineteenth century that "like their married sisters, many antebellum spinsters experienced debilitating illness, physical frailty, attacks of languor or morbidity, and even insanity." But, she continues, "There is general agreement that the roots of female distress grew in the barren soil of a culture which demanded great submission and dependence of women, and which encouraged them to find self-actualization in abnegation of self."[7]

It's this expectation of feminine self-denial that perhaps drives a contemporary obsession with the spending habits and acquisitiveness of contemporary women.

I myself judged *Sex and the City* for its reliance on expensive shoes and meals as symbols of female independence. But we are used to the idea of expenditure on familial, domestic trappings. I might have reared back from the scene of Carrie Bradshaw dropping hundreds of dollars on a pair of shoes, but would I have batted an eye at Carol Brady writing out a check for drapes?

The purchase of goods for oneself, especially if one's self is female, is a well-worn expression of hard-won liberty. When Susan B. Anthony began earning a salary as an elementary school teacher, at twenty-six, she had already turned down two marriage proposals in her quest to remain unmarried. She purchased for herself a fox-fur muff, a white silk hat, and a purple wool dress and wrote home, wondering if her peers might not "feel rather sad because they are married and can not have nice clothes."[8]

In 1979, the *Christian Science Monitor* reported on single women buying stereos, art, cookie jars, and furniture for themselves, since "single women deserve nice things too" and "who wants to sit on orange crates until you've got a wedding ring on your hand?[9]" It required some defensive effort to adjust to this new normal; the *Monitor* explained that if this new generation of unwed consumers was "a bit more self-indulgent than their mothers and grandmothers, it's because they've decided they're 'worth it.'"

But, as with many public estimations of female self-worth, a little goes a long way. In 1987, the *New York Times*, which thirteen years earlier had declared the news that single women were "self-assured, confident, secure,"[10] had changed its tune. "There is a single woman in New York, bright and accomplished," began a macabre mid-eighties story in the newspaper, "who dreads nightfall, when darkness hugs the city and lights go on in warm kitchens."[11] (Apparently, all that furniture the *Christian Science Monitor* had reported that single women were buying for themselves had not included lamps.)

Single women, the *Times* reported, while appearing to live lives full of "hard work and good friends, of stimulating days that end with cultural events, gymnasium workouts or Chinese and a soak in the tub" in fact "complain bitterly about their love lives and their marriage prospects" and are dogged by "nagging dissatisfaction." Strangely, many of the women interviewed did not seem that bitter or dissatisfied; one thirty-nine-year-old executive averred that she'd grown "increasingly satisfied with her single life." The *Times* reporter made reference, in a penultimate paragraph, to "several studies" showing that "single women are happier than their married sisters," but confidently noted that that research "flies in the face" of the opinion of one hairdresser who claimed that her single clients are very distracted by looking for a man.

Yes, many women who had pursued careers and not families experienced loneliness. But the question of whether that loneliness would be ameliorated by marriage—*any* marriage—was one that didn't get attention, even when another executive explained to the paper that some choices about remaining unmarried were made expressly to escape the unhappiness of an earlier generation of *married* women: "When you think of your mother as helpless, unable to choose her own life, you become determined never to be vulnerable."

The message to women, especially high-achieving women, was that their singleness was their fault: They'd opted for the gymnasiums and Chinese food, and thereby sacrificed the warm, well-lit kitchens. The underlying implication was that women's responsibility for their marriage-free fates lay in living lives that were *too* good, *too* full, and *too* powerful.

When people call single women selfish for the act of tending to themselves, it's important to remember that the very acknowledgment that women *have* selves that exist independently of others, and especially independent of husbands and children, is revolutionary. A true age of female selfishness, in which women recognized and prioritized their own drives to the same degree to which they have always been trained to tend to the needs of all others, might, in fact, be an enlightened corrective to centuries of self-sacrifice.

Amina Sow agrees. The advice she gives everyone is "Always choose yourself first. Women are very socialized to choose other people. If you put yourself first, it's this incredible path you can forge for yourself." Amina too understood how she sounded as the words were coming out of her mouth. "If you choose yourself people will say you're selfish," she said. "But *no*. You have agency. You have dreams. It takes a lot to qualify a man as selfish."

## Freakishness

Single women have never enjoyed a particularly glossy reputation. One Reformation-era proverb, which would be cited in different forms by John Donne and William Shakespeare, proclaimed that women who died unmarried were doomed to "lead apes in hell."

Despite the fact that living uncoupled for large portions or all of life has become the new normal, that fewer Americans are marrying and that those who are are doing so at later ages; despite the fact that people who live alone make up almost 30 percent of the population (more than nuclear families[12]), stigmas about single people, and especially women, as aberrant, weird, stunted, and perhaps especially as immature, persist.

In 2012, writer Deborah Schoeneman published an essay, "Woman-Child," about what she perceived as the indulgence of single women in childish extravagances, such as sparkly nail polish. Meanwhile, the conservative columnist Kevin Williamson laid into the HBO show *Girls*, for which Schoeneman herself had written: "[Lena Dunham] might have gone one better and called it *Thumbsuckers*," Williamson wrote, continuing that "The more appropriate title *Diapers* would terrify her demographic."[13] In not having and taking care of babies, Williamson felt, the unmarried female characters of *Girls* were themselves the babies.

In more serious quarters, single young adult life is often called "extended adolescence" or "adultescence;" unattached twentysomethings are sometimes referred to as "kidults." Psychologist Jeffrey Arnett has suggested that we use the term "emerging adulthood," acknowledging a new life stage, akin to the formal recognition of "childhood," "adolescence" itself, and "middle age": semi-defined periods within the human lifespan that have become recognized, often in response to adjustments in technology, medicine, industrialization, and civil rights. Images of "adultescence" are often summed up with a vision of grown but underemployed children sleeping on their parents' couches. Journalist Judith Shulevitz has asserted that "the twenties have turned into a lull in the life cycle," casting single life as a pause in adulthood.

While it makes sense to consider a period of grown-but-unmarried life as a new phase, the way it is cast as an inherently *im*mature stage isn't quite right. After all, unmarried life is not a practice round or a staging ground or a suspension of real life. There is nothing automatically adolescent about moving through the world largely on one's own—working, earning, spending, loving, screwing up, and having sex outside traditional marriage.

Yes, in a bad economy, grown children live with their parents. However, that's not a new familial configuration; historically and across classes, adult children have very often lived with their parents. We just didn't consider them quite so adolescent when they were married and had children dwelling with them in the multigenerational unit.

There is also a rather rich history of traditionally married adults behaving in childish ways: expecting to remain the center of attention and have their needs met by partners who feed them, entertain them, and do their laundry. Yet there has been little equivalent agonizing over the scourge of infantile husbands throughout history.

In many ways, the emotional and economic self-sufficiency of unmarried life is more demanding than the state we have long acknowledged as (married) maturity. Being on one's own means shouldering one's own burdens in a way that being coupled rarely demands. It means doing *everything*—making decisions, taking responsibility, paying bills, cleaning the refrigerator—without the benefits of formal partnership. But we've still got a lot of hardwired assumptions that the successful female life is measured not in professional achievements or friendships or even satisfying sexual relationships, but by whether you're legally coupled.

In turn, those assumptions are often undergirded by an unconscious conviction that, if a woman is *not* wed, it's not because she's made a set of active choices, but rather that she has not been selected—chosen, desired, valued enough. I remember keenly the day, in the midst of my bad first breakup, that an older male friend, trying to comfort me, explained why he'd decided to propose to his wife: because, "you don't let merchandise like that sit on the shelf." I let the implications of his remark wash over me as I sat glumly on my shelf, unpurchased and unloved.

"Among my very liberal, educated milieu," said Elliott, the forty-year-old novelist in Washington, "There is a sense of: 'What happened? How are you still on the shelf? You must be a defective product because nobody bought you." This is the message she absorbs every time a friend tries to be encouraging by telling her, "I would think everyone would be after you!"

Despite the fact that they are one of the largest growing demographic in the nation, women who remain single later than many of their peers often feel isolated, not simply in literal ways, but as if their experiences are unique.

While I was writing this book, I had dinner with a friend of my father-in-law, an unmarried academic in her fifties, living in a Midwestern community where the vast majority of her peers were married. While I held forth on the huge numbers of women now living outside marriage, she looked at me witheringly. This big, bustling world of single women that I (a traditionally married woman, no less) was describing did not match her experience of feeling socially excluded, aberrant, solitary—like the only single woman in a world of wives.

Nancy Giles, a fifty-two-year-old television commentator who lives in New Jersey, says that, even if she knows rationally that the world is now full of unmarried women, she still experiences an unconscious sensation that "single women's experiences have been cut off from each other and put on islands where each of us feels like we're freaks." Giles believes that feelings of freakishness stem from male confusion about women who, by choice or by happenstance, live life unattached. She remembered the perplexity she inspired in a former radio co-host, a white male comedian, who, she said, didn't know what to make of her. "He couldn't put me in a box," she said. "I wasn't a *Roseanne*-type housewife; I wasn't a woman he could tease for always dating the wrong men; I wasn't seeing anyone at the time; I wasn't gay. He would have denied that my being black made a difference. But he couldn't figure out how to deal with me, because I was just this kind of happy person. Why wasn't I having dating problems or being upset? Why wasn't I a man-hater? There was just this big giant question mark over his head."

In a 2011 study, researchers at the University of Missouri explored the pressures faced by middle-class, never-married women. They found that these women experienced a heightened sense of deviant visibility within their families and communities (especially at events like weddings, even more especially during bouquet tosses) and that, conversely, they were made to feel *in*visible and inconsequential in social environments in which the default expectation is that all adult women are wives and/or mothers. The study was headlined, "I'm a Loser, I'm Not Married, Let's All Just Look at Me."[14]

There remains an anxiety that a lack of marital affiliation might somehow be tied to a lack of *existence*, especially for women who have for so long been valued and lauded for their connections to others. It's in the line from *When Harry Met Sally*, in which Harry tells Sally that what she's in for, as a young woman headed to New York, is the risk of dying "one of those New York deaths where nobody notices for two weeks until the smell drifts out into the hallway." It's a funny line, but also a chilling one, especially for those of us who have feared, on occasion, that a lack of traditional ties leaves us unmoored, not just from nuclear family structures, but from the world.

## Loneliness

Loneliness is not directly tied to whether you're partnered. Journalist Judith Shulevitz has pointed to recent studies showing that chronic loneliness is a medical condition that takes place on a biological, cellular level,
that at least part of the propensity for the condition is hereditable and
that part of the rest of it has to do with conditions we face as newborns
and children, long before anyone is being encouraged or discouraged
from pairing off with another individual. Contemporary psychologists,
Shulevitz reports, "insist that loneliness must be seen as an interior, sub-
jective experience, not an external, objective condition." Loneliness, in
short, writes Shulevitz, "is the want of intimacy." And a want of intimacy
is not necessarily abated through marriage.

More than one in three adults over the age of forty-five report being
lonely; not all these adults are single. And, as anyone who's ever been in
a bad romantic or sexual relationship knows, intimacy doesn't just show
up and make itself at home when you have sex with someone, nor does
it necessarily creep in slowly over years; often, in fact, intimacy between
romantic partners can fade over time. And there may not be any loneliness as profound as the one you feel when you are lying next to a person
to whom you are supposedly tied tighter than anyone else and feeling
nothing but unknown, unseen, bereft of connection.

While reading Meghan O'Rourke's memoir of losing her mother to
cancer, I was struck by the way the grief seemed more intense to her because, in part, she felt it hers to bear alone. O'Rourke, who writes about
the disintegration of her marriage during her mother's illness, memora-
bly recalls an instance in the hospital in which she sees another young
woman about her age, obviously in pain, and feels a particular kinship
with her, until she sees the woman again, accompanied by a husband and
children, and immediately retracts the tentacles of shared experience.
"Your grief is not like mine," she decides.

O'Rourke's reasonable assumption is that the burden of her sadness
might be alleviated if she had a partner alongside whom she might work
through it. But in fact, the break from her husband, about which she
writes "it is impossible for me to know whether—or to what degree—the
separation was an expression of my grief," itself provides evidence that

romantic partnership does *not* automatically mitigate grief as she imagines it does for the married woman at the hospital; it is just as possible for conjugal bonds to fall victim to that grief.

O'Rourke's alienation from the married woman comes in part because she's filling in the imaginative blank of that woman's union with a fantasy of fulfillment. If loneliness is a want of intimacy, then being single lends itself to loneliness because the loving partnerships we *imagine* in comparison are always, in our minds, intimate; they are not distant or empty or abusive or dysfunctional. We don't fantasize about being in bad marriages, or about being in what were once good marriages that have since gone stale or sexless or hard, creating their own profound emotional pain. Rather, we fantasize about having a man or woman with whom to share our travails, someone with whom we can discuss our pain and our fears. The partner we conjure when we don't have one is our special assigned person, whose responsibility and pleasure it is to care for us when we're sick, to comfort us when we are sad, to rub our feet, and tell us that everything is going to be alright.

Elliott told me that she thinks, often, about "what would it be like to have someone in your corner, to have that unconditional person who's rooting for you and you're rooting for them? It would be so nice to just look at this other person and say, 'What a shitty day!' and give each other pep talks." And while she's grateful for the solitude she's had through her thirties, solitude that has afforded her time to do work she's proud of, she also sometimes feels, she said, "like there's a boat that's sailed and I missed it. I just had no idea, could never have predicted how intense the loneliness would be at this juncture of my life."

Of course, single people are lonely. Of course. We have all been lonely. For moments, for days, for endless, chilled seasons of sequestration. For some women, the loneliness may stem from, or be exacerbated by, the drain of having to be everything for yourself.

## Exhaustion

Living independently, even with the means to take care of oneself economically, can be physically and emotionally depleting; getting by alone *without* economic security, far worse. In addition to the emotional strain, there are the purely practical responsibilities: the cleaning of the house, the setting of the alarm, the job or jobs, the light bulbs, the leaks, clogged drains, the creaks in the night. As we marry later or not at all, we get tired.

In Rachel Crothers's 1910 play *A Man's World*, about unmarried bohemians in Manhattan, one female character, knackered after years of plying her way in the (then far less accommodating) world, sobs to a much-admired single friend, "I've tried just as hard as I can for ten years—and scrimped and scraped and taken snubs and pretended I was ambitious and didn't care for anything but my work, and look at me—I don't even know how I am going to pay my next month's rent. I'm so sick and tired of it all . . . I'd marry any man that asked me. . . . I would. I'd marry anything that could pay the bills. Oh, I am so tired—so tired of it all."

Much has been written, in recent years, about *opting out*, the proclivity of highly educated, often late-married professional women who, upon starting a family, leave their jobs, depending instead on a husband. I've often suspected that, as well as being symptomatic of the persistence of unequal divisions of domestic labor and responsibilities, contemporary opting out is also a symptom of the midlife burnout after having lived decades on one's own in an increasingly work-centered culture.

I see the raw desire to put one's feet up after years of having gone it alone with no wife to clean our houses and no husband to earn our money, in both my female and male contemporaries. I witness it in my economically stable single peers, some of whom, closing in on forty with no spouse and no children, have nonetheless quit their demanding jobs, or taken pay cuts in order to reduce their hours.

Marriage may be a historically constricting institution, but it's also provided a system for divvying up life's work, admittedly often on unequal terms: You do the earning, I'll do the cleaning. But when we do all the earning and all the cleaning ourselves—and then earn and clean and earn and clean and earn and clean some more, by the time we hit midlife, we are beat.

This speaks to something that many single people often don't get: socially approved pauses for life events. As I've now learned firsthand, there are few times in adult life during which people tell you with enthusiasm to take off, relax, take time for yourself. They come at the following moments: when you marry and when you have children. Of course, for most working Americans, the ideas of time off for honeymoons and paid leave after babies are pipe dreams, but in white-collar professions, single people, and those without children, often find themselves not only without the encouragement to take personal time of their own; they wind up compensating for their colleagues' breaks by making up the work, slogging through even more hours. In a country that still does not guarantee new parents a dollar of compensation for time taken after birth or adoption, it may seem crazy to suggest that we should start talking about paid time off for those without children or partners. Yet if we want to account for the growing numbers of unmarried people in the professional world, we must begin also to account for the fact that it is not just brides, grooms, and new parents who require the chance to catch their breath, to flourish, and to live full lives.

### Fear

Single life also, realistically, can entail a sensation of physical insecurity, a sense of danger that often hits at the very same moments that we are enjoying the whizzing highs of social liberty.

Some of the very best nights of my life in my twenties and early thirties were spent talking late into the night with friends, in various places in New York. Sometimes it was midnight, sometimes four in the morning, when I would begin to make my way home. Those nights always ended with me walking the sidewalks across my neighborhood, or from the subway, aware of the echoing sound of my footsteps on the pavement, happy, yes, but alert to my vulnerability on the street, the windows around me mostly dark. Who would know, not just if I were mugged, but if I simply tripped, sprained an ankle, hit my head? Who was waiting for me to come home? No one was.

It was the best of life and the worst of it all rolled into one, the meeting of the sublime and terrifying realities of independent existence that was addressed in an 1853 poem by astronomer Maria Mitchell. Written when Mitchell was in her mid-thirties, the poem was addressed to an unknown figure named Sarah. It read, in part:

> *Did you never go home alone, Sarah*
> *It's nothing so very bad,*
> *I've done it a hundred times, Sarah*
> *When there wasn't a man to be had . . .*
>
> *There's a deal to be learned in a midnight walk,*
> *When you take it all alone,*
> *If a gentleman's with you, it's talk, talk, talk,*
> *You've no eyes and no mind of your own.*
>
> *But alone, in dark nights when clouds have threatened*
> *And you feel a little afraid*
> *Your senses are all supernaturally quickened*
> *You study the light and the shade*
>
> *You have only to listen and words of cheer*
> *Come down from the upper air*
> *Which unless alone you never would hear*
> *For you'd have no ears to spare* [15]

The conjoined thrills and perils of life lived physically alone are felt even by those with extraordinary and rewarding social bonds, like Ann and Amina.

Ann, who described herself in her single Los Angeles life as "happy waking up every day alone and very happy to go to sleep alone," recalled a night out at a warehouse party with women she called "my core single ladies here in L.A." When she heard the first notes of Ginuwine's "Pony," she leapt to the dance floor, tripped, and found herself laid flat out on a concrete floor. She picked herself up and managed to dance through the rest of the night. But, on the way home with a friend, exuberant and heading for Fatburger, she threw her hands in the air and felt her shoulder pop from its socket. Ann's friend drove her to what she described as "a really janky twenty-hour urgent care center" at three in the morning.

As a freelancer with unsteady health insurance, Ann was worried that whatever was wrong with her arm was going to be expensive. They would not allow her friend in to see the doctor with her. Ann began to cry. "They were big fat tears," she said. "And I don't cry. Especially not in public. It's not a point of pride; it's just that I don't emote in that way. But there were these big fat tears; I was in a dirty party dress in urgent care."

The friend who'd brought her to the clinic was forced to leave; she had to drive to a wedding in Ojai the next morning. Alone, Ann soon remembered that her dress buttoned up the back. With her shoulder out of its socket in the middle of the night, it dawned on her that she would have to sleep in her dress until she could reasonably wake a neighbor to ask for help. She had already called Amina in a panic because Amina was the person who knew the details of Ann's health plan. But Amina then lived in Washington. "At five in the morning, when I have to get my dress off and get to sleep, that's not really helpful."

It was a moment that challenged Ann's view of her place in the world. "I am of the belief that there is nothing I, with the help of my friend network, cannot do to make myself one hundred percent happy," she said. "But, physically, that night, I just couldn't help myself. I honestly can't tell you another moment in my single life when I felt that way, but I got home and I cried some more."

No marriage or committed romantic partnership would have been a sure prophylactic against Ann's despair that night: A husband could have been out of town, could have been nasty about being awakened, could have been cruel, cold, or laughed. As a single woman, Ann might have just as easily hooked up and gone home with someone that night, someone who would have helped her more tenderly than some husbands. Her friend, had she not had to go to Ojai, would otherwise likely have helped her home and out of her dress.

But coupledom, at its best, provides the hope—and yes, often the practical reality—of companionship, of a warm body whose job it is to unbutton your dress, or to sit with you in the urgent care center when you're young and have dislodged an arm while dancing at a warehouse, or when you're old. When you're sick. When you're dying.

## Illness

There have been many studies, touted victoriously by social conservatives, showing marriage to have tremendous salutary benefits. "Marriage itself gives men and women healthier and longer lives," claim authors Maggie Gallagher (a vociferous anti-gay–marriage and antiabortion activist) and Linda Waite in their 2000 book *The Case for Marriage: Why Married People Are Happier, Healthier and Better off Financially*. "Researchers find that the married have lower death rates, even after taking initial health status into account. Even sick people who marry live longer than their counterparts who don't."[16] Or, as Tina Fey once joked, "Don't worry, lonely women, you'll be dead soon."

However, these studies cannot help but reflect the fact that generally healthy people are more likely to be in a position to marry to begin with, and that economically privileged adults—who can afford better health care, better food, and healthier environments in which to live—are those most likely to marry.

What's more, many of the same studies that turn up increased happiness and good health for married people also show unmarried people to be just as happy, and both groups to be far happier and healthier than those who are divorced, separated, or widowed—all states that derive directly from the condition of having been married. The claim that marriage—just *marriage*, as opposed to a *good* marriage—is a boon to general emotional and physical well-being is probably precarious at best.

But when it comes to chronic physical illness, there does seem to be persuasive evidence that being partnered helps. In 2013, a study published in *The Journal of Clinical Oncology* found that cancer patients who were married had better outcomes than those who were single,[17] noting that single patients, without partners to nudge them to get to doctors sooner, were 17 percent more likely to already have advanced stage cancer by the time they were diagnosed. Single cancer sufferers were also 53 percent less likely to get the therapy they needed than married patients, a statistic that likely speaks to the staggering logistical commitments of medical treatment: Having a person to support and love you may be salubrious; having a person to take care of children or earn money while you get chemotherapy or to drive you to that chemotherapy is definitely so.

This is part of what made Lori Gottlieb's paean to settling for someone, anyone, so compelling. In that original *Atlantic* piece, Gottlieb wrote, even of her less than blissfully married friends, "They, like me, would rather feel alone in a marriage than actually be alone, because they, like me, realize that marriage ultimately isn't about cosmic connection—it's about how having a teammate, even if he's not the love of your life, is better than not having one at all."[18]

Frances Kissling, who loves solitude and loathes the prospect of marriage more than almost anyone I spoke to while writing this book, spoke of the moment, in her late fifties, when she was caring for her mother, then dying of lung cancer. One day, Kissling was helping her feeble mother get dressed to go the doctor, Kissling recalled, "When she suddenly looked at me and said, 'Who. Is. Going. To. Do. This. For. You?'"

"It knocked me on my ass," Frances said. "Oh my god. Who *is* going to do this for me?"

Several years after her mother died, Kissling was diagnosed with kidney disease. "It was a crisis for me because my mortality was before me," she said. "Sickness is something you really deal with in a different way if you're alone." Kissling returned to therapy, wanting to revisit the decisions she'd made. "We talked about singleness and how there was now a deeper aspect of it to deal with: I am alone."

Of course, the cruel truth is that neither marriage nor children guarantee a different outcome. Those who take comfort that, in getting married, they are evading a future of lonely decline do not, often, consider the very realistic possibilities of divorce, abandonment, or the early death of a partner. We don't often consider that even in the very best case scenario, in which we bind ourselves to someone we love madly and reciprocally forever and ever—we are making a sad bet when it comes to the end of our lives. Because short of simultaneous expiration, marrying even happily leaves us with a fifty-fifty chance of dying last. For women, who have statistically longer life spans and are more likely to partner with men who are older than they, chances are higher than that. The average age of widowhood for women in the United States is around fifty-nine, and 2009 figures[19] showed that over 50 percent of women over seventy were widowed, more than double the percentage of men who were widowers. For the happiest wives, that means both suffering through the passing of our beloved and then, once again, facing the world—and our own ends— on our own.

Yes, perhaps we have children, whether we're single or married. Children, after all, provide another source of comfort, connection, and care. But, as anyone who has logged time in a nursing home or dementia unit can tell you, counting on offspring to be in a financial, professional, or emotional position to be there in one's final days, or months, or years is a gamble. This is especially true in a nation with widening class inequality and no structural support or compensation for those who, in the middle of life (and work and relationships and parenthood of their own) take time off to care for an aging parent or grandparent.

In 2013, the *New York Times* ran a story by a recent widow addressing how alone she felt. She had children, but reported that they could not understand her grief. She had no friends, she wrote. She was so consumed by her solitude that, one day, she became literally paralyzed, unable to move, while driving her car. This was a woman who had chosen to marry and have children. But, in her dotage, she nonetheless found herself alone and physiologically undone by the loss of the person to whom she had been wed.

"We're all alone, no matter," Frances agreed, but, noting that I am married and she is not, "You're alone in a different way from my aloneness. I have lots of friends, and very deep friendships. But essentially, I'm alone."

## Barbarous Institutions

One thing that seems certain *not* to provide a sure solution to the problems of solitude is a reinstatement of marriage as the norm to which all should aspire. In a society that has built an enormously lavish wedding industry, and in which women are far more likely to forego marriage than ever before, it's awfully easy to see marriage as the elusive solution, the institution where loneliness is ameliorated and solutions to personal challenges can be found.

And, indeed, when we fall in love, find companionship and support, and when our friends do, there is often a lot to celebrate, to be thrilled about, to feel grateful for. But it's an error to assume all marriages are good marriages, and to fall into the narrative trap laid by Disney and Shakespeare, the one in which a wedding is the satisfying conclusion of a story.

We have to remember that among the reasons that there are now so many *un*married women is that for hundreds of years, when marriage was practically compulsory, plenty of married women were miserable.

In the early twentieth century, Emma Goldman wrote of how marriage exacted from a woman the cost of "her name, her privacy, her self-respect, her very life 'until death doth part.'" Goldman alleged that marital expectation doomed women from the start. "From infancy, almost," she wrote, "the average girl is told that marriage is her ultimate goal. . . . Like the mute beast fattened for slaughter, she is prepared for that."

Pioneering English nurse and statistician Florence Nightingale wondered, "Why have women passion, intellect, moral activity . . . and a place in society where no one of the three may be exercised?" A woman who turned down multiple marriage proposals, Nightingale vowed to avoid marriage at all costs and considered the institution "an initiation[20] into the meaning of that inexorable word *never* . . . which brings in reality the end of our lives, and the chill of death with it."

Nineteenth-century author George Sand, pen name of Amandine Lucille Dupin, wrote that "there is only one happiness in life, to love and be loved," and famously partnered with the composer Frederic Chopin, but she called marriage, which she exited in her twenties with two children in tow, "a barbarous institution." And when Susan B. Anthony was in boarding school and received word that a friend from her youth was newly married to a middle-aged widower with six children, she wrote in her diary that "I should think any female would rather live and die an old maid."[21]

Even some men acknowledged the institution's drawbacks for women. George Burnap, a Unitarian minister and author of a series of lectures on the "Sphere and Duties of Women," wrote that "Marriage comes as the great crisis of a woman's existence . . . Perhaps if she knew what life has in store for her, she would shrink back."[22] He went on, even more darkly, to observe that "there is ever an undertone of sadness in the wedding's mirth; and when that bright being approaches, upon whom every eye centers and for whom every heart palpitates, I can almost fancy her bridal attire transformed to mourning, and her blushes changed to tears."[23]

Some nineteenth-century women reluctant or unable to find husbands turned for refuge, as others had for centuries before them, to the church. Membership in the celibate Shaker community rose in the years between 1810 and 1860, largely on the participation of women. And Quakers, who permitted women both to minister and to organize around the abolition of slavery from the early nineteenth century, drew a high proportion of single women.[24] By the mid-nineteenth century, 40 percent of Quaker women in Philadelphia were never married.[25]

In 1904, the *Independent* published a piece by "a Bachelor Maid" entitled "Why I Do Not Marry," which the paper claimed was an attempt "to explain the reluctance to enter into the matrimonial state so often manifested by intelligent and cultured women of today." The author, described by editors as "an attractive and able" young university professor, explained that her disinclination to wed stemmed from the fact "that I have been appalled by the hideous inequality of the conditions which marriage offers to the man and to me, when we have come up to the wedding point essentially alike in our past training and our ideals for the future." For men, in her view, marriage meant "the gaining of a home life which is an incentive to help his chosen profession rather than an obstacle;" but for herself, "[I]f I would have love and a home, the alternative presented is the renunciation of every other dear ambition."

The Bachelor Maid cited the case of a professor who left teaching to marry and have three children, prompting the question of why an accomplished woman should be "imprisoned in a nursery, her mental activity perpetually hampered by endless domestic burdens and bodily pain, while her brilliant and attractive husband . . . is lionized in every literary and social circle." The piece's tone reflected a brassy, almost profane, confidence not only in the normality, but the superiority of unmarried female life.

Critics hit back in tones that will be familiar to modern readers who have heard so much about selfishness, and about the tolls of too-high standards. In a 1907 piece in the *Atlantic* on the topic of why American marriage was in trouble, journalist Anna Rogers anticipated by one hundred years the pathologizing of pickiness that would make Lori Gottlieb and Tracie McMillan's work so popular. Rogers sneered at women who held out for a man who "must be a god physically . . . must have wealth, brains, education, position, a perfect temper, and a limitless capacity to adore her, kneeling." Rogers saw in new women's reluctance to settle "the latter-day cult of individualism; the worship of the brazen calf of Self."[26]

And, while marriage has improved dramatically from its nineteenth- and early twentieth-century form and feel, the conviction that it is the cure for unhappiness remains wholly unproven.

Psychologist Ty Tashiro suggested in a 2014 book that only three in ten married people enjoy happy and healthy marriages, and that being in an unhappy partnership can increase your chances of getting sick by about 35 percent.[27] Another researcher, John Gottman, has found that being in an unhappy union could shorten your life by four years.[28] Residual suspicion of the institution seeps into pop culture and media: the Website *Jezebel*'s section about weddings and marriage is titled "I Thee Dread." And, as critic Elif Batuman pointed out in 2014, the best-selling book and blockbuster movie *Gone Girl* got its hook in part from the acknowledgment that marriage itself is an abduction and that "wives are people who disappear." The distressing message laid out allegorically in *Gone Girl*, Batuman wrote, was "the revelation lying in wait for women when they hit the ages of marriageability and childbirth: that their carefully created and manicured identities were never the point; the point was for it all to be sacrificed to children and to men."

In short, while there may be all sorts of negative dimensions to life on one's own, there are certainly as many to marriage. Finding a strong marriage, a rewarding partnership, is hard and rare. And, ending up in a bad one remains a reasonably terrifying fate for many of us, yet we rarely read panicked pieces about the abundance of unhappy wives; we have rarely been treated to studies comparing the probabilities of them ever having great sex or satisfying careers to the probability of them getting killed by terrorists.

We are still wired to see marriages as the (happy) endings to women's stories, the resolution to their quests. We simply don't ask the same questions about the fates of women who marry, don't consider the crises (or even simply the fears, dissatisfactions, loneliness) that they may face within their unions as circumstances symptomatic of or particular to *marriage*; yet we easily and always consider single women's equivalent states as tied tightly to their unwed status.

And that's too bad. Because, as Karen Durbin wrote in her 1976 *Village Voice* piece "On Being a Woman Alone," "there are worse things than losing a man, alright; there's losing yourself."

## Reckoning

In 1950, one in ten Americans over sixty-five lived alone. Today, thanks to stretching life spans and high divorce rates, one in three do.[29] It's both a terrifying and a hopeful statistic. Because the increased pressure on a society in which human beings are not necessarily living, thriving, and dying within traditional family units anymore could force a more communal approach to healthcare, domestic cooperation, and to helping each other out of this world. Women's relationships with each other have long provided an imperfect but real alternative. As Frances Power Cobbe wrote in 1869, "Nor does the old maid contemplate a solitary age as the bachelor must usually do. It will go hard. But she will find a woman ready to share it."[30]

For her part, Frances Kissling, a believer in euthanasia, said that she and her like-minded friends have made agreements to help each other die in peace. "Had I been in the condition my mother was in, those agreements with others would have come into play," she said. And, in fact, there is no reason that we should assume that reliance on a spouse or child should be any greater than reliance on friends, or even, perhaps, neighbors.

The forced dependence of increasing numbers of single people on each other may hearken back to a lost feminist project: the socialization of care and domestic duty. There's also the building social recognition of relationships besides traditional heterosexual marriage, a fight that has been central to the gay rights, and specifically, to the gay-marriage movement. The ability to assign friends and nontraditional partners roles as next of kin, to permit them into hospital rooms and give them medical advocacy and end-of-life rights is key to the expansion of end-of-life care options for a population that will ever more frequently die unmarried. But, as singles advocate Bella DePaulo has argued, that's part of why the victories of the gay-marriage movement, with its emphasis on marriage as the ratifying union, remains incomplete. Even as gays and lesbians gain true, federally mandated marriage equality, DePaulo has written, "all those people who are single—whether gay or straight or any other status—will still remain second class citizens."

And some women seek more official stamps on their female partnerships.

Amina spoke to me of a "non-cheesy way to celebrate single people," noting that she's been taking care of herself since she was eighteen. "Everything I own I buy for myself. But there's nothing in society that celebrates me; in the eyes of my family I'm a failure because at this point I'm not partnered." She said that she and Ann have a running joke about doing a TED Talk about "how we should get married to each other for the benefits of marriage. The romantic stuff we're not interested in, but the economic reality of being single, man . . . You need to have a single person starter kit."

We also, of course, need to have affordable health care and housing, alongside stable social security and welfare systems. The state must play its role in supporting a population that no longer lives and dies within family units. Alongside social policy must come social recognition of the independent women turning to each other and relying on each other throughout their lives.

Imagined covenants of care, whether between women who want

to parent, or enjoy tax benefits, or seek support in old age or with the onset of illness, may seem unwieldy, dependent on the circumstances, fortunes, and reliability of those who enter into them. But, in this, they are not so radically different from traditional marriages, in which the promise of shared care for children is regularly shattered by divorce, by illness, by death, and the responsibility for caretaking through sickness and in health tends to be shouldered more heavily by one member of the pair, leaving the other alone.

Perhaps, if a future included more communal care between women, and if we saw models that flourished, those communal agreements could become more reliable and grow to contain more people, creating an expansive and resilient shield, in many ways more flexible than marriage, against the brutal realities of life and death, alone and together.

# CHAPTER SIX

# For Richer: Work, Money, and Independence

*"I truly believe that women should be financially independent from their men . . . Money gives men the power to run the show. It gives men the power to define value. They define what's sexy. And men define what's feminine. It's ridiculous."*

—Beyoncé, 2013

## Biological Determinism

Eleanor Ross was born in 1916, the daughter of a New England Telephone & Telegraph employee and a mother who stayed home and later worked in a bank. Eleanor grew up a lover of animals, the outdoors, and science. She wanted very much to be a doctor. By the time she attended Colby College in Maine, it was clear that there was not money to get her to medical school; she won a research fellowship at the University of Iowa, and took a train through the New England hurricane of 1838 to the Midwest, where she would earn an advanced degree in biology.

During her graduate-school summers, Eleanor worked at the Jackson Laboratory on Mount Desert Island in Maine, on a study conducted by a pioneering female scientist, Elizabeth Shull Russell, and published in the August 1940 *Journal of Experimental Zoology*, called "A Comparison of Benign and 'Malignant' Tumors in Drosophila Melanogaster." After completing her degree, Eleanor moved to Houlton, Maine, where her father had been transferred by the telephone company. In 1940, she took a job at Ricker Classical Institute, a local liberal arts college and its partner high school; she became the founding professor of Ricker's Biology Department.

By the time Eleanor began to teach, there had been generations' worth of arguments waged within the press and between friends about the possibility that women might feel professional aspirations or commitments that were comparable to men's. As "The Bachelor Maid" had written in 1904 of her impulse toward intellectual pursuits, "so far as I can discover . . . it is just the same sort of ambition that a man feels; not a thirst for a little cheap publicity as an 'intellectual woman,' much less the desire for a pseudo 'independence' and an individual bank account, but an honest love for the studies of which my school-days gave me a glimpse."

But wrapped up with "The Bachelor Maid's" very *raison d'être* was the fact that these ambitions were not, then, compatible with wifeliness and motherhood.

In *The Feminine Mystique*, Betty Friedan quotes the groundbreaking, never-married nineteenth-century doctor Elizabeth Blackwell as saying, "I am woman as well as physician . . . I understand now why this life has never been lived before. It is hard, with no support but a high purpose, to live against every species of social opposition . . . I should like a little fun now and then. Life is altogether too sober."[1]

The culturally enforced weighing of femininity (love, marriage, motherhood) against profession (intellectual engagement, money, public recognition) so fascinated writers and readers that, at the turn of the nineteenth century, three separate novels chronicled the pull between medicine and emotional life for women. William Dean Howells published *Dr. Breen's Practice* in 1881; in it, the doctor heroine realizes the error of her medical ambition and gives up her career for marriage. The next year, Elizabeth Stuart Phelps, who advocated the burning of corsets, wrote about unfair labor practices for women and the unjust financial dependency of marriage, and married in her early forties a man seventeen years her junior, published *Doctor Zay*, in which the heroine suggests a contract with her future husband, ensuring that she'll be able to continue practicing medicine after their marriage. In 1884, Sarah

Orne Jewett, herself a Mainer who never married, wrote *A Country Doctor*, in which the heroine sends her besotted suitor packing in favor of remaining a physician.

By Eleanor's lifetime, the turn-of-the-century tide of educated women pushing into the upper echelons of the professional world was already receding toward its midcentury low; even the most popular progressive calls for women to join the workforce were tempered by the promise that no amount of work could knock family from its primary perch within the female consciousness. Mystery writer Mary Roberts Rinehart, writing in *The Ladies' Home Journal* in 1921, made the scorching proposition that "Every young girl in the country today should be taught to be self-supporting, to do one thing well enough to earn by it when the necessity comes." And yet, she followed up, even the most avid professional, "if she is born woman . . . is born mate and childbearer," and must realize that her home "must be first."[2]

Eleanor did not marry at the age that many of her peers did. The year that she got her master's degree, finished work on the Drosophilia study, and became a biology teacher, the median age for first marriage for women in the United States was about twenty-one and a half;[3] she was twenty-four. But at the college where she taught, she met a political science teacher who also coached basketball, a potato farmer's son. They married in 1942, when she was twenty-six. There was no question but that she'd give up her job and move to the Air Force base in Arkansas where her husband would learn to fly before his World War II service in the Pacific. By 1943, he was based in Guam and Eleanor was back in Maine, expecting their first child, my mother.

In 1945, my grandfather returned and took over his parents' farm. He did not believe that mothers should work outside the home. Eleanor became a farm wife: a zealous homemaker, churner of butter, obsessive cleaner of dirt brought in from the potato fields, and a great cook who, during the harvest, brought enormous baskets of hot stews and pies out to the men and children for lunch. But as my mother remembered, "She was always sick, had headaches, back problems. She was obsessive about the floor; she scrubbed it three times a week on her hands and knees. She was not a happy lady; it was clear, even to me, as a kid."

In 1958, twenty years after Eleanor braved the hurricane to go get her biology degree, she had three children, aged four to fourteen. She had just lugged one of those hot lunches to the field, when the treasurer at the local college drove up, jumped out of his car, and explained that the school's biology teacher had just died. There was no one in the small town qualified to replace her. Could my grandmother fill in, just for a few weeks, until a replacement could be found?

My mother, a young teen who'd been working in the field that day, and remembered the conversation vividly, recalled that my grandmother looked for permission to her husband. He nodded; she should help out for a few weeks.

Eleanor retired twenty-two years later, after having been awarded an honorary doctorate.

My mother remembered, "When she went back to work, it was like night and day. She was busy; she didn't have to scrub the floor three times a week. She dressed up. She took more care with her appearance. She was happier. Everything about her changed."

I'm quite certain that my grandmother, who died in 2012, would have said that the most important role in her life was as a mother and wife and, later, as a grandmother. But I also know that, when I was young, the gifts I'd receive from her in the mail included the clipped wings of a dead blue jay and sea creatures preserved in jars of formaldehyde; she taught me how to gut fish and identify their internal organs; she'd walk me up the hill behind the farm and tell me the names of every wildflower; the photograph we had of her in our house showed her dissecting a cat. Even as a Nana, she was a scientist.

One Christmas, when she was in her early nineties and slipping into dementia so severe that she no longer recognized her children or grandchildren, my cousins and I heard her talking loudly—practically bellowing—from the guest bedroom where she was asleep. Curious and concerned, we gathered outside her door to listen to what she was yelling about.

She was teaching a lengthy and perfectly lucid biology class.

## Work

Work—in lucky cases, work that is engaging, but even in other less fortunate circumstances, work that permits economic autonomy or simply an identity outside a family—is just as crucial and as defining a pillar of adult life for women as it is for men. Which is to say: lots of women, like lots of men, find passion and fulfillment in work, just as lots of men, like lots of women, find passion and fulfillment in their personal lives.

But the assumption that a woman who works cannot really be a full and functional wife, remains so pervasive that, as Bella DePaulo recounts in her book, *Singled Out*, when television journalist Barbara Walters was stepping down from *20/20* in 2004, she gave a parting interview to her friend, journalist Ted Koppel, and proclaimed that one of the reasons that she was dialing back after forty years in the news business was to enjoy her personal life. Koppel reminded her that she had been twice divorced. He then asked, "Was it the job? If it had not been for the job, would you still be married to one of those men?"[4] Walters replied that she wasn't sure.

Sometimes, even today, the only class of women who can be comfortably understood as being ambitious or publicly powerful are those who are unmarried and childfree. Take, for example, Oprah Winfrey, Supreme Court Justices Sonia Sotomayor, and Elena Kagan, the longest-serving female senator Barbara Mikulski, and former Secretary of State Condoleezza Rice. They are all women whose unusual power and positions made sense, both because, yes, structurally and strategically, they had not been forced to divide their educational and professional attentions, but also because, without families, it could be assumed that their lives were otherwise empty. Never mind that men with wives and litters of children have held positions of enormous influence and responsibility since the beginning of time. For women, the assumption that a family *must* come first persists so strongly that, when Barack Obama nominated unmarried Janet Napolitano to be head of Homeland Security in 2008, former Pennsylvania governor Ed Rendell said that she'd be great for the job because "you have to have no life. Janet has no family. Perfect. She can devote, literally, nineteen to twenty hours a day to it."[5] (Napolitano's predecessors, Tom Ridge and Michael Chertoff, were each married, with two children).

The other traditionally acceptable pattern for ambitious women has been to enter the professional fray after children are grown. The fact of having *had* children renders this genus of women comprehensibly female, but doesn't scramble anyone's brain by suggesting that domestic and personal commitments might have existed equally and coterminously within the female brain. Ann Richards, the great Texas governor, didn't go into politics until after having had four children; she gave her career-highlight speech at the Democratic National Convention when she was fifty-four years old.

But this pattern of delay can gravely hobble women's ability to accrue power. In 2012, Nancy Pelosi, the former House Speaker, highest-ranking woman in Congressional history and a mother of five, was asked by Luke Russert, a twenty-seven-year-old reporter who got his first network job at twenty-three, whether her decision to remain at the head of her party at age seventy-two inhibited younger people from participation. Pelosi explained to Russert that her "male colleagues . . . had a jump on me because they didn't have children to stay home [with]. You've got to take off about fourteen years from me because I was home raising a family." Pelosi also said, "I want women to be here in greater numbers at an earlier age so that their seniority would start to count much sooner."

This is where the expanding generation of unmarried and later-married women comes in. When adulthood is not kicked off by marriage and motherhood, women can begin to accrue professional power earlier. This is true not only in politics and government—where female stars like Senators Kirsten Gillibrand and Amy Klobuchar, and Loretta Lynch, the first African-American attorney general, all dug their teeth into careers in law and politics *before* marrying or starting families, making it harder for those families to derail trajectories—but in the rest of the world.

Delaying marriage in order to set down professional roots, to build a solid reputation and an economic base, is an old tactic. Singer Marian Anderson turned down a marriage proposal in high school from suitor Orpheus Fisher for fear that marriage would wreck her career ambitions. She went on to become famous in Europe, befriending composer Jean Sibelius and scientist Albert Einstein, and had already sung her historic rendition of "My Country 'Tis of Thee" on the steps of the Lincoln Memorial in 1939 when she finally agreed to marry Fisher in 1943, at age forty-six.

The benefit to women of marriage postponement is so reflexively understood that, as former president Bill Clinton told the story in 2015, he had to ask his girlfriend to marry him, and come to Arkansas where he was pursuing a political career, three times before she said yes. He recalled telling Hillary Rodham, "I want you to marry me, but you shouldn't do it." Instead, he urged her to go to Chicago or New York to begin a political career of her own. "Oh, my God," he remembered Hillary responding at one point. "I'll never run for office. I'm too aggressive, and nobody will ever vote for me." She moved to Arkansas and married him, working as a lawyer, law professor, and for the Children's Defense Fund. She didn't put the gas on her own political career until after her husband left the White House and their daughter was in college.

Today, marriage delay is a move that women are making across the country and across classes, in both unconscious and *very* conscious ways, and the economic impact is clear. In 2013, Pew released census data revealing that, in the words of the report, "today's young women are the first in modern history to start their work lives at near parity with men. In 2012, among workers ages twenty-five to thirty-four, women's hourly earnings were 93 percent of those of men."[6] Those workers represent the very same generation of women who are remaining unmarried for longer than ever before. Between 2000 and 2009, the percentage of never-married adults in that same age bracket rose from 34 percent to 46 percent.

The millions of women who are staying single, whether for life or for some chunk of adulthood, play a transformative role in the way we perceive women's relationship to work. As universities and workplaces fill with more women who support themselves through wage-earning work, our eyes are slowly beginning to adjust. We're getting better equipped to discern and digest the reality of female ambition.

Single women are helping the world get used to working women.

## All About Our Mothers

In 2005, I watched from the audience as the usually flinty comedian, Tina Fey, began to cry, while accepting an award, as she described how her "brilliant" mother had been told by Fey's grandfather that she would not be going to college because "that was for boys." When it was Tina's turn for college, Fey recounted, her mother had taken an additional job in order to pay for it. Fey added that she hoped her mother derived satisfaction from the fact that her daughter had "found some success in [professions] that were just for boys."

Every generation has struggled to overcome the gendered obstacles set before the previous one and, often, eliminate those obstacles for the next. It's striking, when talking to women about their personal and professional choices, how deeply the experiences of mothers and grandmothers influence the decisions and strategies of daughters and granddaughters. It's easy to presume that each generation of women corrects in opposition to the last, with mothers and daughters ping-ponging back and forth between prioritizing work and wifeliness, engaging in feminism or antifeminist backlash. The truer story is that even the most intense waves of backlash have rarely fully undone the progress made previously. The story of women in America has moved slowly and sometimes circularly, but largely in one direction: toward more freedom to participate in public, professional, and intellectual life.

My mother has always said that watching her mother's transformation from thwarted scientist to reborn teacher inculcated in her a commitment to *never* stopping working. "When I saw that when she was working she stopped being so unhappy," my mother told me, shortly before retiring after almost five decades as an English professor, "That's when I knew I was never going to be a stay-at-home person." Eleanor's work, my mother went on, "was how she defined herself. And to be honest, it's one of the reasons I've looked at retirement with certain trepidation. Work is how I define myself. I mean, I love being everybody's grandmother and mother and wife and all of that—that's wonderful. But basically, there's got to be something that's *me*, and that's been my [working] life."

Columbia law professor Patricia Williams spoke with pride of a photograph of her own mother, marching in the procession to receive her Masters degree in 1951, visibly pregnant with Williams. Williams's mother was married. Williams's mother "didn't ever think that she should marry *instead* of getting an education. She always thought that you should never become dependent on anyone, including a man." Williams's grandmother also had a career, as the executive secretary to the president of a photography studio. Three generations of Williams women—descended from a slave-and-master union—had some college education.

A similar familial legacy was passed on to reproductive health activist Alison Turkos, raised by a mother who worked for the IRS and a father who worked for IBM. When Alison was a child, her father had more flexibility when it came to vacations and sick days, so he stayed home with her when she was ill, took her to doctors' appointments, and accompanied her on class trips. Her mother, meanwhile, remained intent on letting Alison and her sister know, from a young age, that one should never "enter a marriage or a relationship unless you could financially support yourself; you *always* had to have a job." Alison opened up a Roth IRA when she was twenty-two, after her first job as a nanny.

Turkos's and Williams's maternal models stand in stark contrast to Gloria Steinem's, yet had a similar impact. Steinem's mother, Ruth Nuneviller, had been a pioneering journalist in Toledo, Ohio, but stopped working entirely after becoming mired in an unhappy marriage to Steinem's father, and experiencing a series of mental health crises that left her nearly paralyzed by depression, cared for for most of her adult life by her daughters. Ruth's circumstances created in her younger daughter a very strong "desire to separate myself from my mother, so I wouldn't have the same fate," Steinem said. She also recalled how, when she briefly became engaged as an undergraduate, her mother offered this backhanded and ultimately prophetic observation: "It's a good thing that you're getting engaged early, because if you got a taste of being single, you'd never get married."

The eldest of five daughters, Carmen Wong Ulrich, president of a financial services firm, understood her Dominican mother to be a "renegade," because of her determination that all her daughters get college educations. Wong Ulrich explained that her mother had cultivated this obsession as a girl growing up in the 1950s and 60s, without any hope of pursuing a degree of her own. Pregnant and married at nineteen, Wong Ulrich's mother spent her life conscious of her dependence on her husband, a condition that turned her into a "super feminist," her daughter said. Wong Ulrich, a forty-one-year-old (divorced) single mother, gives financial advice on television and in magazines, regularly encouraging women to get their own credit cards and bank accounts, "so you can leave," she said.

This, she said, "is how my mother raised us: to not ever depend on a man, because you'll get stuck depending financially on someone who could be horrible, or who could go gallivanting, but who's got you by the scruff of your neck because they *have* something on you. That's how her life was." The freedom of having your own money, Wong Ulrich said, "has to be freedom to *not* marry the guy, to be free to *leave* the guy, and to support yourself as a single person, possibly with kids."

Here is the nexus of where work, gender, marriage, and money collide: Dependency. Dependency on men, primarily through marriage, was the perpetual condition of centuries of women. And many women, whether or not they are politically active, ideologically committed feminists, or whether they have simply considered the lives of their mothers and foremothers, understand, under their skin, that at the heart of *independence* lies money.

Letty Cottin Pogrebin explained to me that *her* mother, a middleclass Jewish woman, had divorced her abusive first husband back in 1927, when divorce, was considered "a *shonda*." Her mother had struggled financially for ten years, working for clothing designer Hattie Carnegie, before marrying Pogrebin's father. But, even in her second marriage, Pogrebin's mother did not forget how hard it had been to extricate herself from her first one. She began to amass a *knippel*: Yiddish for a married woman's secret stash of money, to be used as a life raft in a world in which access to money and power was patrolled by the men you married. When she was a teenager, Pogrebin's mother died, and Letty inherited her *knippel*; the money bought her a small blue French car, a Simca, which gave her freedom and flair. "My mother's *knippel*, which was the result of her single-woman experience," said Pogrebin, "allowed me to be a single woman." It also taught her, she said, "that you had to be independent; you *had* to be self-sufficient."

When my friend Sara moved to Boston to live with her boyfriend, she left a high-level job in New York and found herself in a city in which there were very few jobs in her industry. After months of applying, but not finding, work, Sara was spending her days in the apartment she shared with her boyfriend. She, like my grandmother before her, became obsessive about cleaning. She became unhappy. She felt cold through the Boston winter. She needed to buy warm boots. For her whole adult life until this point, she'd been able to buy her own boots. But suddenly, she was reliant on someone else's money; she had to justify her every purchase. The lack of autonomy was gutting; Sara got a job as a retail associate at Crate & Barrel; it had nothing to do with the career she'd left in New York. But, she said, it saved her sanity. She could buy her own boots.

That money is key to independence isn't a new notion. It's one that's newer, perhaps, to classes of people for whom money has historically been more plentiful and who have been able to take their autonomy for granted. For populations that have long lived in economic struggle, the ability of women to work for (fair) wages has been key to the fights for both gendered and racial equal opportunity. "No genuine equality, no real freedom, no true manhood or womanhood can exist on any foundation save that of pecuniary independence,"[7] said Susan B. Anthony at the turn of the twentieth century.

Just a few decades later, while my grandmother was giving up her work as a teacher to take her turn as a wife and mother, lawyer Sadie Alexander was expressing concern about the fact that "the labor turnover among women is greater than that among men, due . . . principally to the fact that women do not consider their jobs as permanent. They have not developed a philosophy of work under which they regard the production of price-demanding commodities as their life work." Women were conditioned to anticipate family events that would take them out of workforces, Alexander argued, which made them "slow to organize in unions" and in turn made men "slower to accept them" as professional peers. (In her thinking on women and work, Alexander was prefiguring not only Betty Friedan, but also Facebook COO Sheryl Sandberg, whose *Lean In* emphasizes what's wrong with contemporary women's lingering tendency to "leave before they leave.")

Alexander understood that out of financial necessity born of racial prejudice, "work for wages has always been more widespread among Negro than among white women" and suggested that this was, in fact, to the benefit of those women and their families and the world beyond. "The derogatory effects of the mother being out of the home are over balanced by the increased family income," Alexander wrote, going on to suggest that the salutary effects of women taking themselves seriously as wage earners extended far beyond individual families. "The increased leisure that is enjoyed by women who have entered the industrial and manufacturing enterprises is giving rise to an improved educational and social standard among Negro women."[8]

The economic necessities that have nudged women into the work force have, in turn, sometimes forced a rethinking of femininity. Back in the 1890s, Wilbur Fisk Tillett, a Methodist clergyman from North Carolina, wrote about how, before the Civil War, "self-support was a last resort to respectable women in the South. . . . so deeply embedded in Southern ideas and feeling was this sentiment of the nobility of dependence and helplessness in woman, and the degradation of labor, even for self-support." But, after the war, when resources were scarce, there was a recalibrating of expectation. Tillett reported in 1891, "Now . . . a woman is respected and honored in the South for earning her own living . . . Southern people, having passed through the financial reverses of the war, now realize as never before that a daughter's bread may some day depend upon herself, and so they want her well educated."[9]

## Daughters of the Revolution

Meaghan Ritchie is a twenty-year-old junior at Western Kentucky University, majoring in special education. Religiously home-schooled through most of high school, she and her family are Church of Christ Southern Baptists. Some of Meaghan's friends are already married now, but when she considers it, she thinks, "Oh, my goodness, I can't even *imagine* being married or having kids right now." Meaghan doesn't have a boyfriend, and said that she gets no pressure to settle down anytime soon from either her father, an electrical engineer, or from her mother, a full-time mother who babysits for local children in her home. In fact, her father has told her that she *cannot* get married until she graduates. Meaghan's mother was a college sophomore when her parents married; her dad got a job, and her mother dropped out of school to move to Texas, never graduating. "Maybe that's the reason my dad wants me to finish college," said Meaghan.

Even in socially and religiously conservative climes, the economically stabilizing effect of women finishing their educations and launching their own careers becomes ever clearer, prompting a reevaluation of marital and educational timelines. Academic drive, the urge to capitalize on educational opportunity, a plan to put off distracting romantic entanglement, all with the conscious desire to make later independence possible: These motivations were mentioned by nearly every college student or recent graduate that I interviewed for this book.

The daughter of a construction worker and a high school aide who emigrated to the United States from Albania in 2001, Yllka, twenty, attends a public university in New York City. The first person in her immediate family to go to college, Yllka is studying finance and wants to work in investment banking. Her parents urge her to learn to cook and clean, telling her "you're not going to get a husband otherwise," but they're also very supportive of her education and career. At the moment, Yllka doesn't want a husband or a boyfriend. For most of her friends, she said, relationships "feel like an extra class, organization-wise. [We] don't want to have a relationship. It's so much work. It takes a lot out of you and is a huge time commitment." Yllka's priority is her schoolwork, she said, precisely because "I don't want to be reliant or dependent on others. " If she someday meets the right person, she can imagine getting married. But, she emphasized, "If I do decide to go on that path, I want to provide for myself so we can both be equal in the relationship."

This sentiment directly jibes with the research of Elizabeth Armstrong, a University of Michigan sociologist who told the *New York Times* that women were choosing casual hookups over romantic entanglements, in the words of the *Times* reporter, "because they saw relationships as too demanding and potentially too distracting from their goals."

When Caitlin Geaghan, twenty-three, graduated from Virginia Commonwealth University in 2012, she ended her relationship with her boyfriend because she knew that, after six years together, the next step would be marriage, and she really didn't want to get married. She wanted to be an interior designer. She wanted to travel. "If I had chosen to stay with him," she said, "I would have been choosing to stay in one place." Caitlin told me that she loved her boyfriend, who was devastated by their breakup. But she never regretted her decision. Now living in Washington, D.C., working at a small interior design firm, Geaghan said that she works a lot, but that that's what she'd expected and wanted. She reads. She spends time alone. She is taking flying lessons, in order to get a private pilot's license. She'd like to go to London, or elsewhere in Europe, or perhaps start her own design firm. "As far as my personal life," she said, "I really don't have any plans for that. There is no age by which I want to get married. I don't anticipate it being anytime soon."

Alison Turkos, reproductive health activist, has serious professional goals: She wants to work to repeal the Hyde Amendment and increase access to abortion services for more people. In fact, she wants to work toward these goals every minute of every day. "I don't want to have to text a partner and say, 'Hey, I know we were supposed to do this but I want to do this other thing instead.' I want to put myself first and for me right now that means that I want to put my work first." Turkos said, "My career is the best partner I've ever had." Of her friends, some of them in relationships, she said, "They go to bed at night with their partners and I go to bed at night with *A Clinician's Guide to Medical and Surgical Abortion*. And I love it."

A drive to be financially independent from men is one of the things that motivates young people to work. But lucky women find in their educational or professional lives something equally sustaining: excitement, purpose, reward, recognition. For these women, it's not simply about economic practicality; the pursuit of education and professional ambition is also about experiencing other kinds of passion.

Nineteenth-century never-married doctor Elizabeth Blackwell once wrote, "How good work is—work that has a soul in it! I cannot conceive of any thing that can supply its want to a woman. In all human relations, the woman has to yield, to modify her individuality . . . but true work is perfect freedom, and full satisfaction."[10]

It was a satisfaction echoed by Cornelia Hancock, raised in a Quaker home in New Jersey to be a wife, who was twenty-three in 1863, when she took off to work as a volunteer nurse on the bloody, rotting fields of Gettysburg, where she slept outside on a cot. "[I]t seems to me that all my past life was a myth," she wrote in a letter home. "I feel like a new person . . . and walk as straight as a soldier, feel life and vigor which you well know I never felt at home . . . I cannot explain it, but I feel so erect." Hancock would go on to open a school for freed slaves in South Carolina, and was a founder of the Children's Aid Society of Philadelphia. She never married.[11]

In the decades since the Second Wave encouraged middle-class women to seek fulfillment and remuneration outside their homes, the flood of women into schools and workplaces has been immense. In 2010, women held the majority of all jobs in the country, along with 51 percent of all management positions. About a third of the nation's doctors are female, and 45 percent of its lawyers.[12] Women now graduate from high school more often than men; they receive about half of all medical and law degrees and more than half of master's degrees. The percentage of not just bachelor's degrees, but also of master's, law, medical, and doctoral degrees being awarded to women is the highest it has ever been in the history of the nation.[13]

But the eruptive enthusiasm of women for educational opportunity is no millennial fluke. The University of Chicago opened in 1892; by 1902, there were more female students than male, and more women than men in *Phi Beta Kappa*; fears that Chicago would come to be thought of as a women's institution led the university to implement a short-lived sex segregation policy.[14] Similar pressures applied at Stanford, which opened in the 1890s to such a crush of female applicants that the school's benefactor, Jane Stanford, capped women's enrollment at five hundred, lest the university become thought of as a "female seminary." By 1900, there were as many or more women than men in universities in California, Illinois,

Iowa, Kansas, Michigan, Minnesota, Missouri, Nebraska, Ohio, Texas, Washington, and Wisconsin.[15]

Back then, the academic doors that swung open to women slammed hard on marital expectation.

Among the alumnae of the first twenty-four Vassar classes, roughly one-third of graduates were married.[16] At Vassar in the 1870s, only two in five graduates would marry by the age of twenty-four. Fifty-three percent of Bryn Mawr students who graduated between 1889 and 1908 remained single, like 47 percent of female graduates of the University of Michigan in the same period.[17] During the 1870s,[18] according to Betsy Israel, the marriage rate among educated women plunged to 60 percent,[19] compared to 90 percent for all women in the general population. And for those pursuing advanced degrees in law, science, medicine, and academia, matrimony was even less likely. In 1890, over half of all female doctors were single, and of those women who earned PhDs between 1877 and 1924, three-quarters would not wed.

It's difficult to discern whether academic degrees and the professional opportunities that came with them made women less desirable to men looking for submissive wives; whether education broadened the hopes and ambitions, and perhaps raised the romantic standards, of female students; or whether universities and careers provided sweet escape for those already leery about entering early marriages. The reality was surely some combination of these and other factors.

But, even if the first explanation, the one most favored by the popular press—always looking to punish ambitious women—held, the steadily growing number of women eager to nonetheless matriculate was testament to the fact that marriage itself was becoming ever less the sole measure of female worth.

## Married to the Job

There's a phrase we use quite easily about a certain kind of professional man. We say that he is "married to his job." It's a gently critical appraisal, something that tells us that a man is committed, diligent, a workaholic.

Increasingly, it's possible to hear it, or the idea that it conveys, applied to women, but almost never with affection.

As married mother Eleanor Mills wrote in *The Times of London* in 2010 of her professionally driven, unmarried friends, "As they stare into a barren future . . . many singletons wish they'd put some of the focus and drive that has furnished them with sparkling careers, worn-out passports and glamorous social lives into the more mundane business of having a family." Mills reported that many of her ambitious cohort realized "too late . . . that no job will ever love you back," and added menacingly, "the graveyards are full of important executives."

Putting aside the fact that graveyards also contain large numbers of wives and mothers, Mills was wrong on another front: A job may very well love you back. It may sustain and support you, buoy your spirits and engage your mind, as the best romantic partner would, and far more effectively than a subpar spouse might. In work, it is possible to find commitment, attachment, chemistry, and connection.

In fact, it's high time that more people acknowledged the electric pull that women can feel for their profession, the exciting heat of ambition and *frisson* of success. It happens, here and there, as in the 2009 film *Julie & Julia*, an ode to professional passion, told through the stories of chef Julia Child in Paris in the 1950s and blogger Julie Powell in New York in the 2000s, women who yearn not for love but to do work that they care about and more, yearn to be recognized and well compensated for it. The film was a love letter to female ambition.

In *The New Yorker* online in 2013, Sasha Weiss wrote about comedian Kristen Wiig's sendoff from her seven-year gig as a cast member on *Saturday Night Live*. Wiig, co-writer and star of *Bridesmaids*, was leaving to pursue her suddenly hot Hollywood career. In the final skit, Mick Jagger conducted a high-school commencement ceremony, in which the only real graduate was Wiig, whom he joked was leaving to become a nun. Onstage to get her diploma, she doffed her cap and gown to reveal an off-white dress; she began to dance, happily and tearily, with all the other cast members to the Rolling Stones "She's A Rainbow."

"The graduation had morphed into a wedding," Weiss observed brilliantly. "But Wiig, who often plays women anxious about being single, seemed content to be marrying her career." Indeed, it was a cathartic, celebratory moment, a "relief" as Weiss described it, that "doesn't exactly defeat the problem of American women still earning, on average, seventy-seven cents for every man's dollar," but which was nonetheless stirring, celebratory. "It's heartening to see a raunchy, expressive, commanding female performer celebrated so publicly for her ambition," Weiss wrote, especially since the guy serenading her was Jagger, "that symbol of male sexual freedom . . . who seemed to regard Wiig not as under his thumb, but as a peer."[20]

The scene was not a moment of completely unalloyed joy: Wiig's heartbreak at leaving her job was evident on her face, and offered a glimpse of how deeply those of us lucky enough to enjoy our work attach ourselves to our workplaces, our coworkers, the identities that we've formed in relation to our work.

When I left my first journalism job at the place where I'd learned to write, been mentored, and also been underpaid and not particularly successful, I was thrilled to be moving on to a better position. I arranged to take a week's vacation between gigs. To my surprise and horror, I spent most of that week sitting in an armchair in my apartment, weeping. I had not been dumped by my job; I had dumped it. And yet, I cried, missing my office chair, my cluttered desk, my colleagues who were now eating lunch and talking about stuff without me; I cried because I wouldn't see my byline in the beautiful pink paper that week . . . or ever again.

I did wind up far happier in my next job. But, years later, when my old newspaper moved out of the building where I'd labored as a young reporter, I had a series of dreams about the old building, dreams from which I'd wake up shaken and sad. I had an emotional hangover, so deeply had I been shaped by that first, formative relationship to a job that was now, physically, permanently lost to me.

In 1861, when Sallie Holley was forced by the war to quit her antislavery lecturing crusade, she took to her bed and was administered a water cure to address her "torpidity of the liver." Nurse Clara Barton lost her voice and fell ill after her Civil War work came to an end. Barton later found more battlefield work during the Franco-Prussian War but, at its close in 1872, she lost her eyesight and was committed to the Danville

Sanitarium for ten years. Only when she began to organize the American Red Cross did her health return.[21]

When, after several years, my friend Sara left an all-consuming job she'd taken after returning to New York from Boston, she said, "It was extremely painful because of how deeply I loved and cared for it. But like a relationship that has run its course, I had to recognize it was time to move on . . . but, God, did it break my heart for a long time." Sara described the job as her "heavy-duty relationship from thirty-one to thirty-six," but then stopped, remembering that actually, she'd had a relationship with a man—a funny and lovable, but ultimately unreliable, man—in those years. "Perhaps it's interesting that he's who I chose to be with while I had the hardest job I will possibly ever have and one that I was extraordinarily passionate about," she ventured. In other words: the job was the passion. The (fun but unsuitable) partner was secondary.

In 2005, former Brandeis professor and lawyer Linda Hirshman wrote a scorching piece in *The American Prospect*, addressing those highly educated women she saw dropping out of the workforce to care for kids, and in doing so becoming dependent on their husbands. "Money," Hirshman argued, "usually accompanies power, and it enables the bearer to wield power, including within the family." But more than that, Hirshman suggested, for women, the family, "with its repetitious, socially invisible, physical tasks. . . . allows fewer opportunities for full human flourishing than public spheres like the market or the government."

Conservative columnist David Brooks responded in the *New York Times* by suggesting that "If Hirshman thinks high-paying careers lead to more human flourishing, I invite her to spend a day as an associate at a big law firm." (Brooks was apparently unaware that Hirshman spent decades working at big law firms and had argued twice in front of the Supreme Court). Brooks also suggested that while "the domestic sphere may not offer the sort of brutalizing, dominating power Hirshman admires . . . it is the realm of unmatched influence" and that "men are more interested in things and abstract rules while women are more interested in people. . . . Power is in the kitchen." Brooks's take was in service of precisely the paradigm of "power" that kept all those mothers and grandmothers dependent on husbands, and lacking the experience or skills that might enable them to earn their own livings. Several years later, Brooks would cite a study that claimed that "being married produces a psychic gain equivalent to more than $100,000 a year."

It's funny; when Sara finally left Boston, where she could have wound up married, she moved back to New York and became ascendant in her profession, in the job for which she felt such passion. It was a choice that produced an *actual economic* gain of over $100,000 a year, plus the psychic gain of no longer being in a relationship that had made her very unhappy.

## Their Way

Conservative polemicist Suzanne Venker (a niece of antifeminist crusader Phyllis Schlafly) wrote in a 2013 Fox News column, "Why Women Still Need Husbands," "Financial independence is a great thing, but you can't take your paycheck to bed with you."[22] What's more, Venker argued, if women have babies, which she felt they should only have with husbands, "There's no way to be a wife, a mother and a full-time employee and still create balance. But you *can* have balance by depending on a husband who works full-time and year 'round." Why not, Venker wondered, "let husbands bring home the bulk of the bacon so women can have the balanced lives they seek?"

Social conservatives, both men and the women who support a male-dominated paradigm of power, are always going to be threatened by the possibility that women might engage satisfyingly with their careers. Undergirding that potential for reward is the possibility that men might get pushed out, become accessories, see the space they would otherwise take up in the female life filled instead by wage-earning work.

It's threatening because it's true. But Venker and her compatriots make a mistake in holding up traditionally gender-divided marriages as an appealing alternative to career woman. Because when the choice is between an old-fashioned dependency relationship and work that satisfies, many women are going to choose the work. Research done by PEW, in 2013, reveals that among millennials, women are more willing than men to prioritize their work.[23]

Frances Kissling spoke of the advantages of being a single person in the workplace. "Professionally, there are certain things that accrued to me. I didn't have to think about the effect of my actions on a husband or children." In her line of work—social crusading and agitation—that had particular upsides. "If I got arrested, who cares?"

Holly Clark is a twenty-six-year-old television news camera utility, whose mother's life was devoted to raising her children. "I am unwilling to do what my mom did," Clark said, "and that's give up her life to raise my brother and me. I could never do that. Ever." Holly said her mother became financially dependent upon her father when she chose to be a stay-at-home mom, locking her into the marriage. Holly sees marriage and career as lifelong commitments, and said that, so far, she has always chosen work. "The minute a relationship has interfered with my career," she said, "it's out. Not even a second thought. You fuck with my career, you're done." And so, for now, she's single. "It's funny," she said, "people are making plans for New Year's and all I'm thinking about is hopefully working on a New Year's Eve special. Other people think 'Who am I going to give my midnight kiss to?' and I think, 'Where is the midnight shot going to be?'" Holly acknowledged that her devotion has scared off suitors, because, she said, "For many guys, strong women are not something that they want."

That's a note also sounded by Stephanie, a thirty-nine-year-old importer of Guatemalan art and Atlanta native who described her work as "like a love affair." She travels the world, partners with NGOs in artists communities, and aids in the aftermath of natural disasters, all of which she sees as "vehicles designed to make a global impact." Stephanie's mother has suggested, "Honey, maybe you shouldn't tell men all the things you're involved in, because I think it scares them." At the same time, Stephanie said, there are men who actively pursue her because of her accomplishments. "I think some men love the *idea* of a strong independent woman but they don't want to *marry* a strong independent woman," said Stephanie. "I hear that from a lot of my friends. Men love the idea of us—strong, independent women traveling the world, changing the world—but we frighten them."

Female professional success has often come at the cost of the attention of men, or at least the kind of men threatened by high-achieving women. Television commentator Nancy Giles told me, "To be a black woman, educated, with my own home and my own car . . . whether or not *I* feel like a woman packing a pistol or wearing a cone bra, that's how some men see me." Supreme Court justice Sonia Sotomayor was reported to have enjoyed her dating life prior to being appointed to the nation's highest court, and to have been dismayed when, upon taking the bench, it crashed and burned around her.[24] And one of the most resonant anecdotes from *Are Men Necessary?*, a 2005 book by *New York Times* columnist Maureen Dowd, was about the time one of her closest girlfriends, who sounds a lot like *New York Times* book reviewer Michiko Kakutani, called up, upon having been awarded the Pulitzer Prize, and announced that she would never be asked on a date again.

But loving and being lauded for one's work is its own kind of protection against another kind of dependency, not the financial sort. For if women really do hang all their hopes, dreams, and energies on love, they come to require not just economic support but fun, validation, and diversion from their mate. Education, work, and money can fill a woman's life, both in the absence of a partner, in addition to a partner, or when a partnership is extinguished. Educator Anna Julia Cooper understood this in the nineteenth century, when she wrote of the learned woman, "Neither is she compelled to look to sexual love as the one sensation capable of giving tone and relish, movement and vim to the life she leads."

The fact is, being married to your job for some portion or all of your life, *even if it does in some way inhibit romantic prospects*, is not necessarily a terrible fate, provided that you are lucky enough to enjoy your work, or the money you earn at it, or the respect it garners you, or the people you do it with.

## Earning, Spending

In 2013, while putting together statistics for her company, Maneto Mapping & Analysis, researcher Michelle Schmitt came across some figures that surprised her. As she looked at the population of women in Philadelphia who were classified as middle-income (those who make between

60 and 200 percent of the city's median income, which at the time translated to between $41,000 and $123,000) she noted that 48 percent were never married, up from 40 percent in the early seventies.

Never marrying or marrying late, Schmitt knew, was increasingly the pattern of both the very poor and the very privileged; her analysis also showed that while just 22 percent of high-income women were never married in the early seventies, that figure had risen to 40 percent between 2009 and 2011; the percentage of never-married low-income women had climbed from 49 percent to 61 percent in the same time period. But it was clear to her that the rise had now also become the pattern for those women in the middle. "These data make it clear that not marrying is becoming more common for all women, regardless of income level," said Schmitt.

Remaining unmarried through some portion of early adulthood, especially for college-educated women, has been revealed to be intimately linked with making money. The "Knot Yet Report," published in 2013, reported that a college educated woman who delays marriage until her thirties will earn $18,000 more per year than an equivalently educated woman who marries in her twenties.[25] Women without college degrees *also* gain a wage premium if they delay marriage into their thirties, though only an average of $4,000 a year.

An even more powerful suggestion of exactly why it's so important for the David Brooks of the world (including his conservative *Times* opinion page colleague, Ross Douthat, who has bemoaned modern woman's "retreat from child rearing") to convince women that power is in the kitchen: the Knot Yet Report also revealed the exact *opposite* pattern to be true for men.[26] Both college-educated and non-college–educated men earn more money if they marry *early*, and thus conform to the marriage model that has always supported their economic dominance and the resulting dependency of women on them.

Men don't just earn more by tying women down early: They do better at work.

A 2010 survey by the American Historical Association showed that it took, on average, a married female historian 7.8 years to get tenure, compared to the 6.7 years it took a single woman to earn the same promotion. For men, the pattern was reversed: Unmarried men became full professors in 6.4 years, compared to the 5.9 years[27] it took men with wives at home. For men, marriage, and presumably the domestic support derived from wives, boosted professional focus. For women, the *lack* of marriage and its attendant responsibilities is what allowed them to move ahead at a faster clip.

Maddeningly, having children enhances men's professional standing and has the opposite impact on women's. Sociologist Michelle Budig has been studying the gendered wage gap between parents for years, and in 2014 found—based on data from 1979 to 2006—that, on average, men saw a six percent increase in earnings after becoming fathers; in contrast, women's wages decreased four percent for every child.[28] The gap narrows significantly for women in upper echelon professions—also the population that tends to marry later, after careers have become more established—but another 2014 study of Harvard Business School graduates (as high-flying as it gets) found that even well-remunerated, super-educated wives weren't meeting their professional or economic goals, largely because, despite having comparable educations and ambitions, those women were allowing husband's careers to come before their own. Only seven percent of Generation X HBS graduates (and, less surprisingly, three percent of Baby Boomer women) said that they expected their careers to take precedence over their husbands'. More than 60 percent of Gen X men surveyed said that they expected *their* careers to be the top priority. Eighty-six percent of Gen X and Baby Boomer men said that their wives did most of the childcare.

There is much debate about whether having more women in the workforce—as colleagues and as bosses, slowly advancing to leadership positions—has much of an impact on these deeply entrenched patterns, whether it makes the professional world hospitable for more women or whether, as skeptics claim, it simply benefits those individual women who manage to plough through or around systemic obstacles. The argument made by Linda Hirshman in her manifesto *Get to Work*, is that the professional worlds—artistic, business, legal—would be much more anemic without these women.

But women's presence in the workforce doesn't just make an impact on their colleagues or clients, it also makes an impact on their husbands:

A 2013 study revealed that men whose wives *don't* work are likely to treat female coworkers poorly.[29]

When women work less, it reinforces ideas about a gender-divided world that, in turn, encourage and, in fact, force men to turn more of their attention to work.[30] Choices made by individuals have an effect on circumstances beyond individual or familial experience.

According to one study, unmarried, childless women in cities, between the ages of twenty-two and thirty, earned 8 percent more than their male peers in 2008.[31] It's a narrow, questionable statistic, but is bolstered by other research suggesting that nationally, childless, unmarried women earn nearly ninety-six cents for every male dollar, compared to seventy-six cents to the dollar earned by married mothers.[32] Postponing marriage has become a strategy by which women may make economic gains, positioning themselves closer to parity with their male peers.

For the first time in history, some single women are making real money. They're also spending it.

According to 2012 findings from the Bureau of Labor Statistics, single people spend more than 2 trillion dollars annually.[33] *USA Today* reported the same year that, by 2014, women would be influencing the purchase of $15 trillion in goods.[34] And NBC Universal Integrated Media's 2012 "The Curve Report," claims that single, childless, non-cohabiting women over the age of twenty-seven are spending more per capita than any other category of women on dining out, rent or mortgage, furnishings, recreation, entertainment, and apparel: $50 billion a year on food, $22 billion on entertainment, and $18 billion on cars.[35]

It's a worldwide phenomenon. In 2013, on November 11, a day that the Chinese have turned into an unofficial holiday acknowledging unmarried people, celebration quickly translated to purchasing power. Online sales at China's biggest online retail site, Alibaba, surpassed the United States' 2012 cyber-Monday tally, hitting $5.75 billion dollars by the end of the day. And, while it's impossible to know how many of the unmarried shoppers were women, Alibaba reported that in the first half of the day, shoppers purchased almost 2 million brassieres.

In 1974, the Equal Credit Opportunity Act made it illegal for mortgage lenders to discriminate against potential borrowers based on either gender or marital status. By the early eighties, single women comprised about ten percent of home buyers. Recently, that percentage nearly doubled, hitting a high of 22 percent in 2006, before the economy tanked, and it receded to about 16 percent in 2014.[36] Meanwhile, unmarried male home-buying has stayed steady, representing about eight percent of the market in 2014.[37] It is more common for an unmarried woman to purchase her own house than it is for an unmarried man. According to the National Association of Realtors, the median age of a single female homebuyer in 2010 was forty-one, and her median income $50,000.

The results of single women wielding an unprecedented amount of financial power are multilayered. There is an impact on future marriages, in which women who have become self-supporting earners will be less likely to give up salaries; spouses, with increasing frequency, elect to keep their finances separate.[38] There is also an impact on advertisers, who gear messages and products to unmarried women based on the assumption that unmarried women, unlike their married counterparts, do not have anyone else to spend money on, and will thus make purchases for themselves.

There is one particularly ironic wrinkle in the relationship between marriage delay and wealth accrual.

Elliott, the novelist in Washington, attended eight weddings the year she turned thirty-one. She spent money on travel, gifts, bridesmaid's dresses, showers, and bachelorette parties. "All my disposable income was going toward other people's weddings," she said. "I remember saying to my friends, 'You guys can all just buy my book when it comes out.'" At forty, she said, her money is going to baby showers.

As women's earnings have increased and marriage has been postponed, the wedding industry has transformed nuptial celebrations into yet another luxury good that women buy for themselves. Reliant in part on late-marrying, economically established couples with disposable income, the so-called marriage industrial complex has ballooned to dimensions that might be comical were they not also so wasteful. The average wedding costs nearly $30,000. And that's just for the spouses and their families. The bane of existence for many single women is the cash they lay out for their friends' weddings.

As writer Dodai Stewart told me, "There are resentments that crop up between friends who have been independent together, about the kinds of celebrations that happen around marriage ceremonies and not around single life." Dodai recalled an instance in which she lost her patience with a friend, after having made a bachelorette trip and gone to the wedding. "I was just done," she said. "Not with our friendship, just with showering her with presents. I'd much rather be spending money on myself. If these women are living in a dual income household, why am I buying them a present? What about single girl-showers?"

In fact, single-girl parties are not unheard of. Some high-earning un-married women are reclaiming their fortieth birthdays—the event that is supposed to signal the symbolic ticking out of the biological clock, the turning point at which we're told that our youthful appeal begins to ebb, the storied entrance not into adulthood but into middle age—as celebrations of the lives they have lived and the future in front of them. That is, at least in part, what we celebrate at weddings.

Kate Bolick, author of the 2015 book, *Spinster*, threw a lavish joint fortieth birthday party with a (married) best friend, an event she and her friend referred to as their "Platonic Lesbian Birthday Wedding." Bolick wrote about the event in *Elle,* acknowledging that "for me, this party actually was a bit like a wedding—it was the first time I'd asked my family and friends to take considerable trouble to gather together on my behalf, not to mention spend their money to get there. . . . Did I get points for sparing them the added expenditures of a bridal shower, bachelorette party, reception dinner, day-after brunch, and a gift, plus the bonus of knowing that, unlike nearly half of the weddings they go to, this celebration wouldn't end in divorce? If there was one thing I could assure my guests, it was that I'd be around until I was dead."

## High Costs

It's possible to acknowledge the economic leaps of the privileged as breakthroughs, but also crucial not to forget that the possibility of more comfortable vistas for some women has often, historically, come at a cost to others.

In the nineteenth century, industrialization alleviated white, middle-class women's responsibilities for grueling in-home production of food and textiles, and the Cult of Domesticity worked in tandem with expectations of Republican Motherhood (in which women's obligation was the instilling of civic virtue in offspring and the moral maintenance of husbands) to keep privileged women enclosed in their homes. Instead of community engagement, the emphasis came to be on family cohesion as the crucial moral and patriotic responsibility.[39] This enabled the wealthy to spend less time worrying about those less fortunate than they and, in a pattern that has remained steady, to suggest that blame for impoverishment might lie with the impoverished's failure to achieve domestic or familial sanctity.

Meanwhile, the cleanliness of middle-class homes, as well as the time cleared so that wives might spend it raising good citizens and offering moral succor to their husbands, was made possible by the new phalanxes of working women. Without servants to haul clean water and scrub a house, without female factory workers to produce the goods on which the family survived, historian Stephanie Coontz points out, "middle class homemakers would have had scant time to 'uplift' their homes and minister to the emotional needs of their husbands and children."[40]

Similar configurations existed in the midst of the twentieth century, as the postwar benefits that created the circumstances for an expanded white middle class meant the contraction of possibility for poor, working Americans, many of them Americans of color. Tending to home and hearth was held up as the feminine, familial ideal, but the actual scrubbing of the hearth was often done by poorer women, immigrants, and African-Americans who were in no economic position to depart the work force and attend to the cleaning and uplift of their own homes.

And, of course, when the Second Wave arrived to free many middle-class white women from their domestic prisons, many of those women continued to rely further on the low-paid labor of poorer women of color as nannies and housekeepers, rather than striking more equitable domestic bargains with their male partners.

Now, slowly but seriously improving economic circumstances of certain classes of privileged independent women—who earn and spend more freely than ever before—should not eclipse the grave economic realities faced by millions of other single women: the ones who continue to labor for low wages, making the goods and providing the services for the wealthy. Working-class and poor women are *also* living outside of marriage, at even higher rates than their more privileged peers. When it comes to unmarried women and money, the unprecedented economic opportunity enjoyed by a few is a small fraction of a far more complicated story.

# CHAPTER SEVEN

# For Poorer:
## Single Women and Sexism, Racism, and Poverty

Ada Li was thirty when she moved to the United States from China in 2001, just before the terrorist attacks of September 11, and found that, in their aftermath, especially for immigrants, life was hard: people were scared, suspicious; she sensed there were no jobs for her. She considered returning to China. Her friends in the United States urged her to stay, offering to help find her a husband who could support her.

Ada was not interested in finding a husband, but decided to stick it out and keep looking for work. A family friend hired her to make clothing on a sewing machine on Thirteenth Avenue in Brooklyn. After a year, she enrolled in manicure school. In these years, Ada recalled, she was "always busy, not a lot of time to go out or talk with friends. I was not taking English classes because I had no time. Just work." Ada worked six days a week from seven in the morning until nine at night, and on her day off, she took her manicure classes, returning to the sewing machine at night if there were still clothes to be made. "Hard life," she said, remembering how little money she made, how difficult it was for her to pay the rent.

For many women, the pursuit of work and money has far less to do with fulfillment, excitement, or identity than it does with subsistence. And, for many single women, scraping by is as hard as it has ever been. For most Americans, work is the center of life, not because they yearn for it to be, but because it has to be.

Beneath all the statistics about women spilling into colleges and uni-

versities and boardrooms—statistics that are important and unprece-
dented, and compiled adroitly in such books as Hanna Rosin's *The End of Men* and Liza Mundy's *The Richer Sex*, which both proclaim that women
are overtaking men in economic and professional realms—are piles and
piles of asterisks. These asterisks reveal that while some women *are* enjoying more educational, professional, sexual, and social freedom than
ever before, many more of them are struggling, living in a world marked
by inequity, disadvantage, discrimination, and poverty.

It's crucial to unpack what's true and what's not true about female
advancement—and *single* female advancement—across classes, rich,
poor, and in between. When it comes to female liberty and opportunity,
history sets an extremely low bar.

## Old Patterns

For centuries, women who did not find economic shelter with husbands
often discovered themselves nonetheless reliant on men, such as their
fathers, brothers, or brothers-in-law, for support. Jane Austen, who came
from comparative comfort, once accepted and then rescinded her acceptance of a marriage proposal, from a suitor to whom she did not wish
to yoke herself. She lived her life in her family home, and then in her
brother's homes. She wrote famously, "Single women have a dreadful propensity for being poor."

One "element of continuity in women's work (as in their lives,)" writes
historian Nancy Cott, "was its constant orientation toward the needs of
others, especially men." As professional opportunity expanded for women,
much of it was in service of male-run households as domestics, or working for male bosses: as secretaries, stenographers, retail clerks. Teaching
and nursing, two historically female-dominated professions that did not
necessarily entail answering to male superiors, involved the replication
of subservient female behaviors, the tending of children and sick people.
And none of the professions in which women have managed to thrive, so
many of which mimic the *unpaid* labors assigned to women historically,
have been known for being well paid.

Certainly, circumstances are improved compared to what they were two-hundred years ago, or fifty years ago (Women can open their own bank accounts! Get their own mortgages! Marital rape is less legal!). But men's economic and professional dominance has not in fact come to an end. In the United States, they are still very much on top. Men are the CEOs and the heads of universities, the scientists, and the acclaimed novelists; they dominate the world's most explosive field, technology; they are the firefighters and cops, the bankers and doctors; they are, for now, *all* the presidents and *all* the vice presidents ever to have been elected; they are 80 percent of Congress.

Men earn, on average, a dollar to women's 78 cents. That gap is far wider for women of color; it has remained mostly unchanged for more than a decade. The history of gendered and racial discrimination is not past; it has accrued, and often meant that money has *not* accrued, to women and especially to women of color. As Kimberlé Crenshaw reported[1] in 2014, the median wealth, defined as the total value of one's assets minus one's debts, of single black women is $100; for single Latina women it is $120; those figures are compared to $41,500 for single white women. And for married white couples? A startling $167,500.[2]

Women made up only 4.8 percent of *Fortune's* top CEOs in 2014.[3] Only twenty of the nation's thousand largest companies were run by female CEOs in 2012 (that's four percent) and, as *Forbes* reported, that number is a record; eleven of those CEOs were hired between 2011 and 2012.[4] Journalism professor Caryl Rivers wrote in 2010, "Nearly all American billionaires are male, or widows of males, with the exception of Oprah Winfrey."[5]

The study[6] showing that single childless urban women under thirty make eight percent more than men in their same age bracket is astonishing. But as Stephanie Coontz points out, the appearance of single urban female success can sometimes reflect the fact that (often predominantly white) educated women tend to cluster in the very same cities that are home to large populations of low-earning (often nonwhite) men without college educations. As discussed, some of the very services that make privileged, educated, single female life attractive and possible in cities—the restaurants and takeout and laundry and home maintenance that allow women who are not wives to live as if they *had* wives—are often provided, at criminally low wages, by poorer, often immigrant, women and men. If studies were done comparing women *only* to men with similar educational backgrounds, Coontz writes, "[M]ales out-earn females in every category." She also points to a 2010 survey showing that "female M.B.A.s were paid an average of $4,600 less than men in starting salaries and continue to be outpaced by men in rank and salary growth throughout their careers, even if they remain childless."[7]

That women are entering universities and the workforce in large numbers does not mean that they are earning or achieving throughout their lives at the same pace as the men who enter those universities and workplaces alongside them. Structural impediments, from the lack of paid family leave and pay gaps, to lingering and systemically reinforced negative attitudes about female leadership, combine to mean that, at some point, women fall behind men when it comes to earning, promotions, status, and reputation. These inequities can be obscured by the lavish coverage of increasingly abundant educational opportunities and the messages we send to young women about their potential achievement. Those messages may be righteous, but they are not the whole story.

A 2012 report by a compensation research firm found that, while amongst college graduates, pay growth remains about equal for men and women throughout their twenties, at age thirty, the growth in women's earnings slows while men's stays steady.[8] That's because it's in their thirties that many college educated women are now having their first children. But Cornell economics and labor professor Francine Blau has offered a further explanation: that men still remain more likely to work in high-paying fields, like business and law, that offer more opportunities to advance, while women are *still* more likely to work in low-paying fields built around service and care, including nursing and teaching, and these fields continue to have lower salary caps.

While the period immediately following Second-Wave feminism saw a change in the gender segregation of some professions, for example, women working as electrical engineers, that rearrangement has again reversed. And low-paying, traditionally feminized fields, including teaching and social work, have in fact become *more* female since 1980.[9] The expansion of other female-dominated professions, such as childcare and home health care, mean that more jobs may be becoming available to women, but they are the kind of jobs with few protections and reliably low salaries. Women make up about 90 percent of the home health business, among the fastest-growing industries in the nation, in which median pay hovers at about ten dollars an hour.[10] When California passed landmark paid sick-day legislation in 2014, home health care workers, disproportionately female and women of color, were exempted from receiving benefits.

The impact of all this persistent inequity on the economic (in)stability of unmarried women is profound. The question of what's to be done about it is at the heart of a fierce argument being waged between social scientists, politicians, and journalists.

## Divided by "I Do"

In an extensive 2012 feature in the *New York Times*, "Two Classes, Divided by 'I Do,'"[11] reporter Jason DeParle contrasted the circumstances of two white women in Michigan, colleagues at a day care facility, each with children and comparable salaries. One of them, Jessica Schairer, spent over half her income on rent, relied on food stamps, could not afford to enroll her children in extracurricular activities, or to take time off from work after surgery for cervical cancer. The other, Chris Faulkner, enjoyed a comparatively high household income, lived in a nice home, took vacations, and enrolled her kids for swimming lessons and Scouts.

"What most separates them" DeParle asserted, is "a six-foot-eight-inch man named Kevin." In other words, the fact that the more secure woman in the story was married to Kevin, a kind, involved, and employed husband. The single thing that DeParle was asserting would have helped Schairer make a more comfortable life for herself and her children was a husband.

But there is another thing that would have helped her situation: money. Money. And federal policy mandating paid medical leave. Despite being in management at the day-care center where she works alongside her slightly better paid counterpart, Schairer was paid just $12.35 an hour. After a surgery for cervical cancer, she returned to work, against doctors' orders that she take six weeks off, after just one week, because, as she told DeParle, "I can't have six weeks with no pay."

Higher wages would help Schairer. So would guaranteed paid leave.

The lack of adequate pay protections and social policies that disproportionately make an impact on women are symptomatic of systemic gendered economic inequality. As welfare expert Shawn Fremstad wrote in response to DeParle's story, "Why is it OK to pay the mostly female workers who take care of other people's children and of seniors and people with disabilities so little? . . . Why is it OK to not provide the vast majority of care workers with basic employment benefits like paid sick and disability leave?" Noting that even Faulkner, the wealthier woman in the set-up, didn't make much more than Schairer and, in fact, was so much better off only because her husband, a computer programmer with a comparable college degree and demographic background, made so much more, Fremstad asked, "Why does he, a computer programmer, earn more than *twice* as much as she does as a manager/director of a childcare center?" It wasn't simply that the married woman was *married*; it was that she was married to a man whose background was similar but whose wages were higher, in part because he worked in a male, and thus better paid, industry.

The problems of wage stagnation, pay inequality, unemployment, and social policies that presume women not to be breadwinners are often obscured beneath the persistent social and political calls to partner. Marriage, we are told repeatedly by our political leaders and pastors, will make it all okay.

Perhaps that's because this officially cheerful solution—going to the chapel and all that—is easier to talk about than the present stagnant economic climate and widening economic divide. In the decade *prior* to the economic collapse of 2008, the median family income dropped from $61,000 a year to $60,500;[12] even the privileged were graduating from college with mountains of debt and entering a parched job market. By 2012, two and a half million jobless adults were living with their parents.[13]

These are the financial circumstances faced by the unprecedented number of unmarried women now making their financial way in the world. And while it is not true that marriage is the answer, it is true that by simply living independently, they face an additional set of challenges in a world that remains designed with married Americans in mind. Single women foot more of their own bills, be they necessities like food and housing, or luxuries like cable and vacations; they pay for their own transportation. They do not enjoy the tax breaks or insurance benefits available to married couples. Sociologist Bella DePaulo has repeatedly pointed out that there are more than one thousand laws that benefit married people over single people.

According to *Atlantic* writers Christina Campbell and Lisa Arnold, "Marital privilege pervades nearly every facet of our lives." They found that health, life, home, and car insurance all cost more for single people, and report that "It is not a federal crime for landlords to discriminate against potential renters based on their marital status." Looking at income tax policy, Social Security, healthcare, and housing costs, Campbell and Arnold found that "in each category, the singles paid or lost more than the marrieds." At some point in their calculations, the authors confess, "We each wanted to run out and get a husband, stat."[14]

While single women purchase their own homes at a higher rate than single men, when compared to married adults, the unmarried lag far behind married couples. According to *U.S. News & World Report*, single people have "the lowest income levels . . . asset levels . . . [and] home ownership rates compared to other family structures."[15]

Anita Hill, who, as a law professor, specializes in issues of housing inequality, argued that housing costs are among the biggest issues facing unmarried women. "We can decide that we're going to be single," Hill said, "but we have to figure out how we're going to be able to put a roof over our heads. We're making eighty cents for every dollar a man makes. So there is a real issue with more and more women spending over 50 percent of their income on housing." Economic forces, Hill said, push women "into less independent relationships."

## The Price of Motherhood

Even within wealthy populations, the economic advantages of solo working life for women begin to melt when those women have children, both with partners and on their own: When they are forced to take time away from work and divide their attention in ways that are both physically and emotionally demanding, in ways that society still doesn't expect parenthood to be demanding of men.

Women who are pregnant or have young children find it harder than childless workers to switch jobs, harder to get hired. Sociologist Shelley Correll did a study in which she submitted fake resumes for high-status jobs. When the resumes included clues that the female applicant was a parent, the applicant was only half as likely to receive a call back about the job.[16] Correll has found that women earn approximately five percent less per hour, per child, than their childless peers with comparable experience, while sociologist Joya Misra argues that motherhood is now a greater predictor of wage inequality than gender on its own.[17]

The economic ramifications of having children are of course felt most keenly by unmarried mothers; a staggering 42 percent of people in families headed by single mothers live below the poverty line. One statistic bandied about in 2013 as evidence of how quickly women have advanced was a Pew Research Center finding about how nearly 40 percent of mothers are now the primary breadwinners in their families. But only 37 percent of those breadwinning mothers were women who out-earned husbands; this group enjoyed a median family income of $80,000. The rest—63 *percent*—were single mothers with a median family income of just $23,000.[18]

Forty-eight percent of first births in the United States in 2013 were to unmarried women; for those who haven't finished high school, it was eighty-three percent.[19] About 60 percent of American women who have their first babies before they're thirty have them out of wedlock.[20] Forty-one percent of *all* births are to unmarried women, a number that is four times what it was in 1970.[21]

Both poverty and single motherhood have historically been racialized in the public imagination, in part thanks to Moynihan-era assumptions about which Americans were having babies outside of marriage, and in part because the racialized Reagan-era caricaturing of so-called welfare queen black mothers has persisted as a talking point for people like Rick Santorum, who said in the 2012 campaign trail, "I don't want to make black people's lives better by giving them somebody else's money." And it's true that the country's history of racism and the multigenerational cycle of African-Americans being cut off from the kinds of economic securities—union-protected jobs, colleges, housing—that would allow them to build wealth has left a disproportionate number of blacks far more likely to be impoverished than their white counterparts.

However, the splintering of the American economy over the past forty years has diversified poverty, as well as the middle-income working classes, in which the incidence of unmarried motherhood is becoming most common. In 2000, around 22 percent of white households were run by single parents, the same percentage of black households that were single-parented when Daniel Patrick Moynihan published his report.[22]

Tim Casey, senior staff attorney at Legal Momentum and director of its Women & Poverty Program, says "There's this idea that all single mothers are black, which is not true." Though it remains true that the rate of single parenthood is higher among black women than among Hispanic women, which is in turn higher than among white women, Casey points out, "There is a high fraction of single mothers in *all* racial groups. In fact, there is growth in single parenthood in all high-income countries. It's just the new reality."

For their 2005 book, *Promises I Can Keep*, about poor single mothers, sociologists Kathryn Edin and Maria Kefalas spent years studying eight very low-income urban neighborhoods in Philadelphia and New Jersey, sampling Puerto Ricans, whites, and African-Americans. In a lecture at the University of Michigan, Edin said that there were only very slight distinctions between these groups: domestic violence was most common among whites and Puerto Ricans (in part because African-Americans in their study were less likely to live together); male incarceration rates were higher amongst African-Americans, unsurprisingly, given that the Bureau of Justice Statistics has estimated that nearly one-third of black men born at the turn of the century will be incarcerated at some point in their lives; infidelity was equally common amongst the groups. Mostly, Edin said that she and Kefalas were "absolutely astonished at how few racial and ethnic differences we found."[23]

In the eyes of some social conservatives, economists, and libertarians, including Charles Murray, author of *The Bell Curve,* and 2012's book on the class divide, *Coming Apart: The State of White America 1960-2010,* an aversion to marriage has, over the past forty years, spread from blacks to whites like some kind of sickness. Economist Isabel Sawhill, author of the 2015 book, *Generation Unbound: Drifting into Sex and Parenthood without Marriage,* has written that, "What we are seeing is alternative living arrangements that have spread from the poor, and especially poor blacks, to the rest of society. The consequences for children and for society have been far from benign."

There's truth in this, especially the first part of it. As with so many social developments for women that first stemmed from economic necessity—from working for wages to walking on the street unaccompanied to wearing shorter, lighter clothing—the possibility of not marrying, and of having children out of wedlock, developed amongst people for whom marriage was no longer the most economically beneficial option.

The nation's history has included many iterations of the privileged white co-option of black, and often poor, habits and behaviors, which, when performed by white populations, have drawn different kinds of attention. When white flappers danced to black jazz beats, they were culture-shifting rebels; when, in the mid-sixties, white women busted out of their domestic sarcophagi and marched back into workforces in which poor and black women had never stopped toiling, when Betty Friedan echoed Sadie Alexander by suggesting that work would be beneficial for both women and their families, *that* was when the revolution of Second Wave feminism was upon us. It has long been the replicative behaviors or perspectives of *white* women—and not the original shifts pioneered by poor women and women of color—that make people sit up and take notice and that sometimes become discernible as liberation.

In part, surely, it's because power is always more rigidly patrolled than powerlessness: When money and status are at stake, lines around who may access and transmit them (white men) and who is barred from them (women and people of color), remain firm. Marriage, historically, has been one of the best ways for men to assert, reproduce, and pass on their power, to retain their control. For those with fewer resources to protect, where less power is at stake, there has been a bit less watchfulness. There has also, of course, been more of an incentive for those who are struggling to find ways to survive, even if it means improvising new familial and coupling patterns. But it's only when more privileged people see how these new, more liberating, forms of behavior might disturb the power structure that people take a different kind of notice.

"The illegitimacy rate is now getting very large even across the board, among the white people," the antifeminist crusader Phyllis Schlafly told NPR host Michel Martin in 2012. Schlafly, like Murray and others, blames the increased number of single parent homes on welfare and social assistance programs that she believes allow women to substitute government for husbands (never mind that such programs have been radically cut during the years in which marriage rates have plummeted). "When Lyndon Johnson instituted lavish welfare," Schlafly said, "they gave the money only to the woman and that made the father irrelevant." It's all very grim, she concluded, because "we know that most of the social ills come out of mother-headed households."[24]

This last point is where the complicated interplay between economic disadvantage, greater independence for women, and increasingly diverse models for family structure get boiled down to two misleading messages.

The first is that the evaporation of the early marriage model leads to greater poverty. "Less marriage means less income and more poverty," is how Sawhill put it in an interview with *The Economist*. She's right only if one assumes that the imagined marriage partners in question would bring in additional income or domestic support, rather than cost additional money and time to feed, clothe, house, and clean up after.

The second and more spurious argument is that the American mothers who either choose to remain single or who find themselves unmarried are the generators and perpetuators of poverty; that they, and not the economically rigged system in which they make their way, are to blame for their families' economic circumstances. This is the message embedded in the now ubiquitous calls to tackle poverty not through stronger social-welfare policies, but through the promotion of marriage, and more than that, of early marriage.

As Ari Fleischer, former White House press secretary for George W. Bush, put it in a 2014 *Wall Street Journal* op-ed[25] unsubtly headlined "How to Fight Income Inequality: Get Married," in place of increased government support to impoverished Americans, "a better and more compassionate policy to fight income inequality would be helping the poor realize that the most important decision they can make is to stay in school, get married and have children—in that order." Robert Rector, one of the architects of the 1996 Welfare Reform legislation that made welfare harder to qualify for and assistance more temporary, wrote in 2012 for the conservative Heritage Foundation that marriage is "America's strongest anti-poverty weapon."

None of this makes much sense given that, in developed countries outside the United States, rates of poverty for single mothers are much lower than they are in the United States, and that this country's high child poverty rates extend across the board and include children living in *married* households. As Matt Bruenig at Demos wrote in 2014, "high child poverty in the U.S. is not caused by some overwhelming crush of single mother parenting. The lowest of the low-poverty countries manage to get along in the world with similar levels of single mother parenting just fine. . . . We plunge more than 1 in 5 of our nation's children into poverty because we choose to."[26]

But this reality doesn't prevent legislators from pouring both concern and funding into promoting *marriage*, and not social assistance, as the answer.

Claiming that marital decline drives up the rates of poverty and welfare dependence, Rector, who, in his Heritage Foundation piece asserted that "[Government] should clearly and forcefully articulate the value of marriage" and bemoaned that "under current government policies . . . marriage is either ignored or undermined," knows better than anyone that marriage has been anything *but* ignored by the government in recent decades.[27] Alongside conservative lawmakers, including Iowa Senator Chuck Grassley, Kansas Governor Sam Brownback, and Pennsylvania Senator Rick Santorum, Rector pushed George W. Bush in 2003 to enact the $300 million Healthy Marriage Initiative, a national program that diverted money from welfare programs in order to provide marriage education and encouragement to low-income populations.

Under the Bush administration, the project was nurtured by Department of Health and Human Services "marriage czar" Wade Horn, a psychologist who, according to *Mother Jones*, as the head of the National Fatherhood Initiative had once defended the Southern Baptist Convention's recommendation that "A wife is to 'submit' herself graciously to the servant leadership of her husband" and "serve as his helper in managing the household and nurturing the next generation."[28] Horn himself has cited Bible verse explaining that, "The husband is the head of the wife just as Christ is the head of the church."

Initially, the Healthy Marriage Initiative worked primarily through religious institutions, offering marriage seminars and classes to low-income people. It was renewed in 2010 under the Obama administration, though in its new incarnation, the focus shifted from faith-based intervention, and away from the enforcement of religiously grounded ideas about wifely submission, toward boosting employment alongside relationship advice.

Still, the Healthy Marriage Initiative has been shown to have little to no impact on marriage rates, which have continued to decline, or on divorce rates, which have remained relatively stable through the two presidential administrations that have now paid more than $800 million for it.[29]

The only public-policy approaches that have ever shown signs of boosting marriage rates and marital longevity haven't had anything to do with promoting marriage as an institution, but rather with providing people better financial resources in advance of, and to better facilitate, marriage. Among them was an expansion of welfare, from 1994 to 1998, when the Minnesota Family Investment Program allowed people to keep their welfare benefits, as opposed to cutting them off, even after they found work.[30] With the added economic security, the divorce rate for black women in the state fell by 70 percent.[31]

In approximately the same years, the New Hope Project was implemented in Milwaukee, Wisconsin. An antipoverty program, New Hope provided full-time workers whose earnings were below 150 percent of the federal poverty level with income supplements, offered those unable to find work community-service jobs and subsidized health and childcare.[32] In a study of marriage rates, researchers found that 21 percent of never married women who participated in the New Hope Project were married five years later, compared to 12 percent of never-married women who did not participate.[33] Income and wage growth also rose for participants, while depression decreased.

It seems clear that a government address of *poverty* is likeliest to make marriage more accessible to those who want it, while programs designed to shove marriage down the throats of Americans least equipped to enter it stably have little impact. If politicians are concerned about dropping marriage rates, they should increase welfare benefits. It's that simple. If they are concerned about poverty rates? They should increase welfare benefits. When asked what the single biggest step the country needs to take to address the needs of poor single mothers, Tim Casey from Legal Momentum said, "Step one: reforming welfare reform. Step two: reforming welfare reform. Step three: reforming welfare reform."

But Congress at the start of the twenty-first century isn't showing much interest in that, voting instead to reduce food stamp benefits, which disproportionately affect the ability of single mothers to feed themselves and their children. In 2014, Kentucky Senator Rand Paul suggested capping welfare benefits for single women who have children out of wedlock, telling a luncheon that "married with kids versus unmarried with kids is the difference between living in poverty and not."[34] What Paul did not acknowledge is that, in his state, there are fewer never-married parents living below the poverty line than there are married parents living below the poverty line.[35]

In North Carolina in 2013, Republican state senators proposed a bill that would require couples to submit to a two-year waiting period before divorcing.[36] And, in 2012, Republican State Senator Glenn Grothman, from Wisconsin, tried to pass a bill that cited single parenthood as a factor that contributed to child abuse. Happily, these legislative attempts have failed, but they showcase what's particularly dangerous about the combination of malevolence toward single women and a policy-enforced class chasm that leaves poor unmarried women vulnerable.

The irony, as *Slate*'s Amanda Marcotte has observed, is that conservatives are surely maddest at and most threatened by *powerful* single women—the privileged, well-positioned women who earn money, wield influence, enjoy national visibility, and have big voices: Anita Hill, Murphy Brown, Sandra Fluke, Lena Dunham. But there's only so much they can do to stop the surging power of those women, while there remain plenty of terrifying ways for them to take their aggressions out on poorer populations. While Republicans may not be able to stuff threatening wealthy women "back in the kitchen," Marcotte writes, "they can make life even harder for the single mother working two jobs who lives next door."[37]

## The Reversal of Order/Disorder

The Family Council, an Arkansas-based group associated with the socially conservative, anti-abortion group Focus on the Family, suggests that "there are four steps you can take in a specific order to reduce the chances your family will ever live in poverty. They are: 1. Graduate from high school. 2. Get married. 3. Have children *after you are married*. 4. Stay married. If you do those four things in that order, the chances you and your children will live in poverty are reduced by 82%." In 2013, the *Baltimore Sun* columnist Susan Reimer, in a column about the decision of affluent Kim Kardashian and Kanye West to have a child out of wedlock, noted that "in more affluent, educated communities, adults know—and make this clear to their children—that the path to success includes education, work, marriage, and kids. In that order." Reimer cited W. Bradford Wilcox at the University of Virginia's National Marriage Project, who called this education-work-marriage-kids progression "the success sequence." The foundation of a civil society. A specific order.

This traditional procession of marriage before children has indeed been reversed in recent decades across much of America. Researchers for 2013's Knot Yet Report, which detailed "the benefits and costs of delayed marriage in America," highlighted "the great crossover" moment, around 1990, when the age at which women have their first child became lower than the age at which they get married.

And, while the rate for out-of-wedlock births among college graduates has risen in recent years, those who have most dramatically scrambled the old familial sequence are Americans who have either not graduated from high school or those who have graduated and attended some college: most of the working and middle classes. The Knot Yet researchers described the crossover as "The moment at which unmarried motherhood moved from the domain of our poorest populations to become the norm for America's large and already flailing middle class."[38] They contrast it with the unmarried lives of privileged, college-educated populations, who they imagine "meeting friends or dates for sushi. . . . after a day consulting with bosses and co-workers from their cubicles . . . parlaying the twenties into a time of self-improvement: going to grad school, establishing a career track, and achieving some degree of financial independence."

It's true that many of the circumstances that stem from a lack of financial security—from random police interrogations to perpetual job insecurity to crumbling housing options—make life for most Americans terrifyingly unpredictable. But it's not quite right to portray wealthy choices around marriage as carefully calibrated and those choices made by poor women as examples of flailing. The decisions that women, even financially insecure women, are making about when to have children and when (or when *not*) to marry are not necessarily emblematic of disarrayed thinking, a lack of planning, or otherwise being out of control.

Struggling single women with children are often operating based on the same impulses that guide the sushi-gobbling grad students who stand for a new kind of unmarried autonomy: a desire to fill their lives with meaning and direction, to live independently. They're just doing it with far fewer resources.

Pamela grew up in the Bronx; her family received welfare. Pamela's mother, who suffered from physical and mental ailments, stayed at home, and her father cleaned streets to earn benefits. Pamela discovered she was pregnant when she was seventeen. For Pamela and her boyfriend, who was thirty-four, abortion wasn't an option; their first, firm decision, was to have the baby. The second decision, she said, was to make a financial plan. She didn't have a job; she was set on going to college, which she had hoped to do outside New York, away from her alcoholic father. That part of her dream got scuttled, but she refused to back away from the idea of an education.

Many of her peers from high school, she said, dropped out of school after having babies. "Those that did graduate and the spouse wasn't around," she said, "didn't go to college. They ended up working full-time jobs, maybe at McDonalds or at a clothing store. I knew I didn't want that." Pamela had worked a paid internship during high school, socking away money, so that she could move. "The money I had saved for something else was going to be used to raise my daughter."

Pamela and her boyfriend wanted to stay together; he got a second job. "We formulated a plan of how everything would work and what bills should look like," she said. "How much he should make so that he could feel he was able to pay for everything without me working and just going to school." Although Pamela insisted on living away from the instability of her parents' apartment, her mother helped by babysitting for the first two years of Pamela's daughter's life.

"I gave birth in August," Pamela said. "A week later I was in school. Because I knew that if I would have took a break I probably would not have gone back. So, I said, no. I'm not just going to be another statistic. I'm going to go to college and I'm going to graduate. And that's exactly what I did. But the only way I was able to do that was because I had help around me and I had money saved." She graduated from New York's City College in 2014.

Pamela had remarkable determination, a cooperative partner, and educational and financial opportunities that are not readily available to many young women. However, even among those who are poorer than she, sociologists have found that there is agency—and a good deal of active, engaged decision-making—in the choice to become a mother and remain unmarried.

In some cases, yes, a lack of sex education and impediments to making birth control and abortion available combine to mean that women have far fewer choices than they should about whether or when to become mothers. From a broader historical perspective, improved access to contraception and abortion has resulted in a decrease in teenage pregnancy; the rate of teen pregnancy was as low in 2012 as it has ever been.

Most unmarried mothers today are in their twenties and thirties.[39] Sociologists have found that many of those pregnancies are, if not consciously planned, then at least not unwelcomed by many economically disadvantaged single women who are seeking exactly the same thing their more affluent peers are seeking: meaning, connection, fulfillment, ballast, direction, stability, and identity. But many American women do not have college course work to throw themselves into or careers that offer anything like a promise of future economic stability. They could put off babies as long as they'd like without expecting to land an appealing job or gain access to a fast-moving career track.

Like their more privileged contemporaries, low-income women are wary of throwing themselves into early marriages that might not be economically stable and, therefore, might further encumber them without a promise of emotional fulfillment. So, as science writer Natalie Angier has described, "childbearing . . . offers what marriage all too often does not: lifelong bonds of love."

Kathryn Edin and Maria Kefalas have written of how motherhood, despite the high probability that it will push a financially strapped woman closer to or further below the poverty line, nonetheless has an overwhelmingly "positive valence" for the single women choosing to have babies out of wedlock, since it provides them with an opportunity to make a seemingly active, hopeful choice.

Tanya, a thirty-year-old urban farmer and social activist from the Bronx, told me, after having spoken in public about being pregnant with her fifth child by three different ex-partners, that she was tired of hearing from people who said things like, "You seem so smart, you don't seem like someone who's misguided; I don't understand how you can be on your fifth child!" Fields feels that she was far from passive, far from anyone's victim. "Every one of my children was a choice," she said. "My children are not the product of bad decision making. Every one of my kids is wanted, loved, and cared for."

There are very logical reasons for women who aren't wealthy to have children while they are young. In youth, women with fewer financial resources have advantages that are more likely to disappear as they age: good health, living and able parents and aunts and uncles and siblings who can help with childcare and possibly a place to live. For young women born in difficult circumstances in today's economically striated America, there is not the sense of an infinite future, but rather a very difficult one, in which work, good food, and quality healthcare will only get scarcer, not only for the woman in question, but for her network of friends and family. "Until poor young women have more access to jobs that lead to financial independence," Edin and Kefalas have argued, "until there is reason to hope for the rewarding life pathways that their privileged peers pursue—the poor will continue to have children far sooner than most Americans think they should, while still deferring marriage."[40]

Anita Hill has considered this circumstance and told me, "If you're saying that women are much better off if they have children later in life, you also have to say as a policy maker that they will have childcare, housing, health care. All these things that will benefit them and that they will need to raise children." But we certainly don't promise our citizens childcare, housing, or quality healthcare; we don't ensure them educational paths that can lead to advancement. And thus, there is logic in acting on the few advantages—youth, family—that life does offer. Having a baby is its own way of exerting control over the future.

Edin and Kefalas argue persuasively in *Promises I Can Keep* that, based on their studies, across races, motherhood is an organizing and often stabilizing factor in unmarried female life: the thing that prompts women to get up in the morning, to take better care of themselves, to settle down, to perhaps stop using drugs or staying out late, or to return to school or form closer bonds with other family members. Their interview subjects told them of the benefits, including "My child saved me."

Though the researchers acknowledge that the economic costs of *having* the children does not make poor women better off, the reasons behind motherhood have everything to do with the urge to bring structure and fulfillment to their lives. What motherhood provides, according to Edin and Kefalas, "is the possibility—not the promise—of validation, purpose, connection, and order. More importantly, children allow mothers to transcend, at least psychologically and symbolically, the limitations of economic and social disadvantage. These women put motherhood before marriage not primarily out of welfare opportunism, a lack of discipline, or sheer resignation. Rather, the choice to mother in the context of personal difficulty is an affirmation of their strength, determination, and desire to offer care for another."[41]

This matches what unmarried thirty-five-year-old Ana Perez, a high-school dropout who had her first baby at nineteen, but went on to become a vice president at a financial-services company, told the *New York Times*. If she had not had the baby, she said, "I would have been much less productive. I would have spent all my time just hanging out."

## Suitable Mates

Pamela is still with her boyfriend, the father of her daughter. But she doesn't want to marry him any time soon. "I always knew that marriage would not keep a man around," she said. "If I did get married and he wanted to leave, he would leave."

Pamela said that among her peers, not marrying is the norm. "I don't see people being married that often, and I see a lot of divorces if they were married," she said. "I see a lot of women being single mothers, and that's only what I see." Maybe in wealthier climes, she suggested, she'd know more legal couples. "But in an environment like I grew up in, the people around me have less education, probably didn't finish high school or just have their GEDs, and they don't have money."

Pamela considers herself fortunate to have a lasting relationship with the father of her baby. "I hear women becoming discouraged, saying there's not enough good men out there nowadays." She sees it, she says, in the South Bronx neighborhood where she was raised. "I don't feel like those men are somebody that I would like to marry or that I would like to raise a family with." When she was at City College, she said, "It's different; you see educated men. They're independent. They have something going for themselves and you can say to yourself, wow, you never know, there's a chance I can find someone who's educated, who's knowledgeable, that maybe I can connect with and build a relationship with. But I don't see that in my mother's neighborhood, and it's sort of discouraging."

Like the decision about whether and when to have children, the reasons that many women remain unmarried—even when they are in romantic relationships, often with the fathers of their children—aren't random, rash, or illogical. They are part of the story that has been unfolding for hundreds of years, in which women have come to understand that marriage, as a binding legal commitment entered into at the start of adulthood, may not be an institution that best serves their needs.

According to a Fragile Families and Child Wellbeing Study of unmarried couples with children, who were romantically together when their first child was born, there were a lot of good reasons for women to be hesitant about marrying their partners: 40 percent of fathers in the study had been incarcerated, a third earned less than $10,000 a year, 24 percent were unemployed. Forty percent of both the mothers and fathers in the study had dropped out of high school, and in 61 percent of couples, either the mother or the father had children by another partner.[42] Three years later, only 15 percent of the couples in the study had married, and 50 percent had broken up.

A shortage of eligible male mates is a phenomenon famously described by University of Chicago sociologist William Julius Wilson who argued in his seminal book, *The Truly Disadvantaged,* that the social and economic circumstances of impoverished urban neighborhoods has depleted the number of emotionally and economically robust young men. It's a serious argument. Just as surely as westward expansion drained the United States' East Coast of marriageable men, so, too, the systemic cycle of racism and poverty dramatically reduces the number of men available to marry. A 2014 Pew report[43] noted that for every 100 single women, there are only eighty-four employed single men; for every 100 single black women, there are only fifty-one employed single black men.

For African-American and Latino populations, this cycle includes sky-high incarceration rates. Thanks to long-time racial profiling and newer, codified stop-and-frisk procedures, black and Latino men—more likely to be poor—are far more susceptible to being stopped by police and put in jail for minor drug offenses. Nearly one-third[44] of black men born in 2001 are predicted to spend at least some time in prison during their lives.[45] A third of black high-school dropouts were in jail in 2010; that figure is less than half—just thirteen percent—for white high-school dropouts.[46] Over one million people are arrested for drug possession every year;[47] more than six hundred thousand for marijuana possession alone. Black people are incarcerated at about six times the rate of white people,[48] and the United States has more people incarcerated than the thirty-five top European countries combined.[49]

Having been convicted of a crime, in turn, makes it much harder for men to get jobs, leaving many with few choices other than to turn to illegal means of making money. In 1994, the federal government made it illegal for people in prison to receive Pell Grants.[50] People who have been convicted of a crime—and, in some cases, simply arrested[51]—can be evicted from public housing. As Michelle Alexander, author of *The New Jim Crow* puts it, once men have been to jail, "They're relegated to a permanent under caste. Unable to find work or housing, most wind up back in prison within a few years. Black men with criminal records are the most severely disadvantaged group in the labor market."[52] This makes it exponentially harder for them to be the stable mates on whom women might rely for economic or emotional ballast.

And again, economic struggle is not the exclusive domain of people of color. Hanna Rosin writes persuasively about how the collapse of blue-collar jobs around the nation—the shipping of manufacturing offshore—has resulted in decreased marriage rates around the country. Coontz points out that, even *before* the start of the recession, "the average employed guy with a high-school degree made almost $4 less an hour, in constant dollars, than his counterpart in 1979."[53] Even for those who are not living below the poverty line, the financial stress of unemployment, stagnated wages, high education costs, and the reverberations of the mortgage crisis make the prospect of partnering much more tenuous. Not just practically, but emotionally.

In a story about the pervasive health problems experienced by poor white women, journalist Monica Potts wrote, "In low-income white communities of the South, it is still women who are responsible for the home and for raising children, but increasingly, they are also raising their husbands. A husband is a burden and an occasional heartache rather than a helpmate." Poor women, Potts writes, "are working the hardest and earning the most in their families but can't take the credit for being the breadwinners. Women do the emotional work for their families, while men reap the most benefits from marriage."

Economists Betsey Stevenson and Justin Wolfers have explained that "money is related to love. Those with more household income are slightly more likely to experience that feeling. Roughly speaking, doubling your income is associated with being about four percentage points more likely to be loved." Perhaps, Stevenson and Wolfers guessed, having money makes it easier to find time to date, or maybe there are correlative reasons: "It's possible," the economists continue in a Valentine's Day editorial, "that other factors correlated with income, such as height or appearance, are the real source of attraction. Or maybe being loved gives you a boost in the labor market."[54]

It's also possible that *not* having money distracts a person from her personal life, or puts her in a dating pool with others who are *also* distracted by not having money. Financial tension makes marriages far more unstable. Impoverished communities have higher rates of depression, domestic violence, sexual abuse, and gun violence.

When (white) men had union-protected jobs at manufacturing plants and could get a good rate on a loan for a three bedroom house and had a pension plan, marrying one of them—especially when women didn't have these kinds of opportunities themselves—made sense. But when men are struggling and women are more capable than ever of economic, social, sexual, and parental independence, marriage doesn't just become unnecessary; bad versions of it can become burdensome and deleterious to women.

Jason DeParle's story about the two women in Michigan whose circumstances, we are to believe, are shaped by their marital status, reveals that the father of Schairer's three children "earned little, berated her often, and did no parenting." She later met and moved in with another man, but DeParle reports that, "It took a call to the police to get him to go." There's not much of a case that marrying either of these guys would have had a positive impact on Schairer's fortunes, economic or familial.

It's important to remember that, while poverty certainly makes single life harder, it also makes married life harder, so much harder that single life might be preferable. The number of married parents living below the poverty line increased by almost 40 percent between 2000 and 2012.[55] In his 2014 book, *Labor's Love Lost: The Rise and Fall of the Working-Class Family in America*, sociologist Andrew Cherlin points out that while the median income for dual-earning couples rose by 30 percent between 1980 and 2012, and the median income for single mothers rose by 11 percent, the median income for married but *single*-earning configurations did not rise at all. Marriage by itself did not automatically improve economic prospects; having two earners did.

Of course, single mothers in tricky financial circumstances might well benefit from a partner in non-economic capacities. Many women yearn for, and their lives might be significantly improved by, mates with whom they are in love, who offer them emotional support, who share the domestic labors, care for children, split the emotional burdens of life and family, whether or not they provide second incomes. But those good, well-matched, mates aren't simply available for the asking, and bad marriages—as well as the divorces that are often their conclusion—are economically and emotionally devastating, especially for women, and most especially for women who are already economically vulnerable.

## Future Weddings

Emmalee works as a customer service representative in Brooklyn. Twenty-four, she is the mother of a toddler and lives with, but is not married to, the father of her child. "With marriage comes divorce," she said. "I just feel like you're probably a bit more separated from each other." Emmalee likes the way things are now. "I like being together with someone but not married," she said, but by the time she's thirty-five, "I can see myself pushing [for it]: Like, okay, I'm getting old, maybe I should get married, especially if I'm still with him. In another ten years or so, I would look into that."

Because it is now *possible* for women to live without marriage, because they are more able than ever before to have independent professional, economic, sexual, and maternal lives, marriage has become potentially *more* meaningful than ever before. As Edin and others have argued, the lack of correlation between childbearing and marriage leads marriage to have a "high symbolic value;" it's something that women and men feel is worth holding out for, waiting for, being prepared to enter responsibly.

The problem is, once again, that, in low-income communities, the opportunities to gain that steady footing are far fewer than they are for those with access to good educations and good jobs.

One favorite spin on these structural inequities, frequently put forth by conservatives, including Phyllis Schlafly, is that economically disadvantaged people don't marry because combining incomes can push family earnings too high to qualify for help from the government. And because of the way welfare laws are structured, this is true for some.

In addition to her earnings as a customer service representative, Emmalee receives food stamps, Medicaid, and help from the Women, Infants, Children program (WIC), which provides supplemental nutrition for low-income women and children up to five years old. "I make ends meet," she said. "I'm able to survive. I get a little help from the government without being married. If I was married, I probably wouldn't get that extra help from them." Emmalee lives with her boyfriend, the father of her child. She said that the question of government aid wasn't wholly behind their decision not to marry. "Not my end result," she said, "but kind of, yeah."

So, there are logical reasons why economic need might have an impact on choices women make about marriage. But it certainly doesn't have *enough* of an impact to account for the number of unmarried women out there. As Tim Casey from Legal Momentum pointed out, "Welfare has such a negative image in society; it has such a stigma attached to it. Nobody wants to be on welfare." People accept government help because they really need government help, not because it is a rewarding alternative to marriage. Welfare benefits, contra Schlafly, have never been "lavish"— far from it—and their value has only diminished over the decades.

Those who blame the rise of the welfare state for falling marriage rates, write Edin and Kefalas, fail to take this into account: "The expansion of the welfare-state could not have been responsible for the growth in non-marital childbearing during the 1980s and 1990s for the simple reason that in the mid 1970s, all states but California stopped adjusting their cash welfare benefits for inflation. By the early 1990s a welfare check's real value had fallen nearly 30 percent. Meanwhile, marriage rates continued to decline while the rate of unmarried childbearing showed persistent growth."[56]

And then there's the fact that most struggling women are just as attached to the idea of their own financial independence and future stability as their more educated and privileged peers.

The Fragile Families study found that the factors most likely to influence whether a couple married within a year after the birth of a child were not only the man's employment and annual earnings, but also the woman's education and wage rate, showing that economic stability—coming from both partners in the relationship—is one of the keys to romantic stability.

Emmalee, who has an associate's degree, is determined to get more secure in coming years. "I would see myself in more of a career," she said, "Because [being a customer service representative] is not a career, this is just a job." Emmalee wants to be in law enforcement, she said, "Because I want a better life for my son. I want more for him." As a cop, she said, she'd have benefits and get pay raises. "I could probably get a house one day, and a car. The good stuff. And plus, I did go to college for something. What's really important to me right now that I can think of is more stability, definitely more stability, more certainty with my future."

Edin and Kefalas contend that work and economic ambition are keys to low-income women's vision of the future. The single mothers Edin spoke to, she said in a lecture at the University of Michigan, "believed it was vitally important and emphasized to us over and over again that both *they and* their partners are economically 'set' prior to marriage." Many of these women, Edin continued, "have a strong aversion to economic dependence on a man." They see their own economic stability, their jobs, as a "defense against patriarchal sex role expectations and a defense against bad behaviors," including substance abuse, cheating, and domestic violence, as well as "insurance" in case of a break up. "They're worried," said Edin, "that if they don't earn money they won't have the power to negotiate for equal say in the relationship."

For the hardest-working and lowest-paid Americans, it's easy to imagine that the dream might be *not* working, but staying home instead. But many of these economically challenged women feel that working for money is good for them and for their marriages. Adrianne Frech and Sarah Damaske did a study that showed that women who worked after having children were healthier physically and mentally by the time they hit forty than their peers who had not done paid work.[57] And, even for lower-earning women, who are far more likely to be exhausted, depressed, and hamstrung by inflexible shift work, *not working* did not provide relief. Stephanie Coontz cites a Gallup poll from 2012 revealing that women from low-income families who did not work outside the home were less likely than working mothers from the same income brackets to report having "smiled, laughed, or enjoyed themselves 'yesterday.'"[58]

"My family, they believe that the woman is supposed to take care of the children and even if they work, still their primary focus is on the children and the man really doesn't play a big role in that," said Pamela. "The man is just the moneymaker. The woman is supposed to cook and clean. I don't believe in that. I think the man should take a huge step in being involved in the child's life and being involved in the housekeeping." Pamela said that when she considers the gendered power dynamics of marriage, she thinks of "what my mother would take from my dad." Pamela described her father as "constantly abusive." She insisted that it's a situation she would never tolerate in her own life. "I'd be ready to walk away after the person doesn't change," she said. "You should be independent enough to not be treated that way."

Pamela wants to be a lawyer. "I feel pressure *not* to conform to gender roles because I don't want to be like my mom," she said. "My mom is stuck, and women [of her generation] who are like her are stuck. I honestly don't know why they feel that they're forced to stay with the man. . . ." Except, as she notes, that "If they are working, they're working as home-nursing aids or at a store; I don't see them taking more independent roles, like being a businesswoman or a teacher. That may be because they don't have the education to go ahead and fulfill those careers. But I do see most of them in the home."

The increased number of single mothers—and the fire in their bellies—is visible on a national stage. Even with the comparatively few women in positions of power, a number of them, including former Texas gubernatorial candidate Wendy Davis, Massachusetts Senator Elizabeth

Warren, Wisconsin Congresswoman Gwen Moore, and Maryland Senate candidate Donna Edwards, have lived and worked toward their professional goals as single mothers.

This presents another wrinkle. As one nurse wondered, in a marriage class attended by journalist Katherine Boo in "The Marriage Cure," her 2003 story on pro-marriage initiatives in Oklahoma, "How do you tell if he wants to marry you for the right reasons . . . ? When I wear my white uniform, guys around here know I'm working and chase me down the street to get their hands on my paycheck."[59]

Poor women are not rejecting marriage. They, like their wealthier peers, are delaying it until it's something they can be sure of, until they feel stable and self-assured enough to hitch themselves to someone else, without fear of losing themselves or their power to marriage. Rich, middle-class, and poor women all share an interest in avoiding the dangerous pitfalls of dependency that made marriage such an inhibiting institution for decades. They all want to steer clear of the painful divorces that are the results of bad marriages; they view marriage as desirable only as an enhancement in life, not a ratifying requirement.

The difference is that wealthier women have other avenues in which to direct their ambitions, have more hope of attaining economic independence, have the luxury of time and flexibility to delay childbearing and marriage while they pursue interests that, ironically, will put them in closer proximity to potential mates who share those interests and who themselves enjoy some stability. Thus, privilege replicates itself; the likelihood that better-off women will remain better-off on their own increases, as does the reality that many of them will eventually marry, and that, in turn, the marriages they enter into will further enhance their social, economic, and emotional lives.

But, critically, while they may be benefitting most publicly from the deferment of marriage, it's crucial to remember that privileged women no more invented liberation from marriage than they invented the idea of working to earn wages. These were all behaviors developed, out of economic necessity, by poor working women. When imitated by richer women who have more power to start with, they can be understood as beneficial; they can be seen as social progress and perhaps part of a movement, or at least a glamorized trend.

But in the disadvantaged communities in which they were born, these same shifts in behavior are read as vulnerability and victimhood and, yes, as pathology; they are cast as immoral, irresponsible, dangerous to communities and families, and as burdensome to the state. So, while it is true that we must address the cycle of poverty faced by single women and single mothers in low-income communities, it must begin with an understanding and acknowledgment that the high rates of singlehood in low-income communities are not accidental, and more crucially, that they do not signal a flaw in reasoning or morality.

As journalist Ta-Nehisi Coates has sensibly observed, "human beings are pretty logical and generally savvy about identifying their interests. Despite what we've heard, women tend to be human beings and if they are less likely to marry today, it is probably that they have decided that marriage doesn't advance their interests as much as it once did."[60]

# CHAPTER EIGHT

# Sex and the Single Girls:
# Virginity to Promiscuity and Beyond

Kristina, a lawyer and archeologist who works in Bismarck, North Dakota, is a brassy, open thirty-five-year-old who refers to herself as an "archaeological crime-fighting machine." Kristina was raised by liberal parents whose loving marriage was the second for each of them. They were very open with her about the unhappinesses of their first unions, and encouraged her to remain independent. When Kristina was in college and told her mother that she was going to move to Texas to be with a man, her mother was horrified. "You can't do that; you haven't had enough sex yet," Kristina remembered her saying.

Ultimately, Kristina agreed: She hadn't had enough sex yet. In her twenties, she said, she paid no attention to married culture and instead just enjoyed her single life. Her goal was "to make it to thirty single." Thus, she moved in and out of a series of monogamous relationships, and enjoyed a thriving casual sex life in between partners. Kristina said that she had sex with people who were interesting to her; "anyone who twirls me on a dance floor usually gets me going," she said. For her, sexual appetite was just one facet of what she called her "super passionate" personality. "I have a love for dogs," she said, "a love for my job, a love of running, a love of kids, and a love of physical contact. I love sex."

Kristina was shocked, she said, when she saw so many of her law-school classmates pair off, seemingly at random, "Men and women I never saw partying together or hanging out just got together and got married out of the blue," she said. This hasty coupling didn't appeal to her.

But, as she got older, she knew that she wanted children, and became increasingly interested in finding a partner with whom she might have some. She moved in with one boyfriend who turned out to have problems with alcohol and unreliability. She loved him, she said, "But there was no way I was making babies with him, because if I sent him out for milk and he didn't show up for two days, there was no way I was dealing with that." She moved to New Mexico and lived on the border of a Navajo reservation where poverty, racism, and lack of opportunity commingled to create an explosive, often unhealthy, social and sexual atmosphere.

"I entered a scene with people far younger and wilder than I am," she said. "I'd thought my twenties were wild, but my early thirties were the wildest time of my life sexually. There were orgies, multiple partners, threesomes, women, men."

Kristina enjoyed this sybaritic period, but realized, in retrospect, that it was accompanied by regular migraines and physical signs of overindulgence. Her father, with whom she maintains a very frank relationship, told her that he was glad she was having fun, but that she should perhaps consider that "running around with twenty-four-year-old death-metal musicians" wasn't making her very happy. Her next stop was Missoula, Montana, where she got a master's degree in archaeology, and where she fell in love with a man who was a devout Southern Baptist. Uncomfortable, having never lived with a woman before, Kristina's boyfriend turned more deeply to his faith. "This was a guy who said, 'Let's get married and make babies,'" said Kristina. "And I loved him and quickly jumped on board. But, suddenly, Jesus kept coming up. And I'm really not comfortable with Jesus."

Now in Bismarck, Kristina is single and, for the first time in her life, consciously trying to have *less* sex, instead of more. She says that it has to do with the sadness she's felt since breaking up with the Baptist, and a little bit with her increasing desire to have kids soon. "For one or all of those reasons," she told me, "today I choose not to have as much casual sex." She paused.

"I do sometimes," she went on, "because I can't help it if a pretty man approaches me. But a one-night stand is about all I'll do."

Kristina's only regret about her life of promiscuity is the people she may have hurt along the way. When she was younger, she considered herself "more of a muscle-myself-through-life kind of lady," she said. "Now, I'm a little bit more gentle, more thoughtful." She turned situations to her benefit in a style that popular culture mostly associates with men. "I'd say to a guy, 'Just so you know, I'm not looking for a relationship now, in fact I'm seeing someone else,'" she recalled. "And because they were guys, they were like 'Great! I don't like commitment!'" But then, they'd have a good time. Such a good time that it would continue to happen. "And then the guys would begin to make an assumption that I wasn't doing it with anyone else. But I was."

"I used to think that getting laid was the goal, and now it's not the goal anymore," said Kristina. "But I firmly believe everything I did put me where I am right now and I really, really love my life." She has noticed that both her sponsor at Al-Anon, where she goes to address issues of family alcohol dependence, and her therapist are sure that her youthful excesses were motivated by a lack of self-respect. But she strenuously disagrees. "I had a fucking blast," she said. "My whole life was a reckless, fun party. And I wasn't drunk driving or shooting heroin, I just always enjoyed myself."

## Juicy Stories

As I was writing this book, a respected professional mentor advised me to include "lots of juicy stories," since, he assured me, that would be the principal interest of any man who picked up a book about single women. His take was neither unfriendly nor censorious, but in a funny way, it reminded me of Rush Limbaugh's tirade against Sandra Fluke after her testimony on behalf of contraception coverage, in which he assuredly asserted that Fluke was fighting for her continued ability to have "so much sex."

What the two men had in common was their absolute certainty that single women must have an enormous amount of sex.

And it's true: Many unmarried women have sex. Some of them, like Kristina, even have "so much" sex. After all, the increased freedom to have socially sanctioned sex with contraception, with a variety of partners to whom they are not obligated to chain themselves for life, is one of the chief reasons that there *are* so many unmarried women.

When it comes to the stories that women tell (or don't tell) about sex, the interesting part isn't necessarily the fact of the sex; it's the increasing variety of sexual paths open to women, the diversity of choices made by different women, or sometimes by an individual woman, over the course of her adulthood. Some women have multiple partners, some have none. Many, like Kristina, have periods of promiscuity, periods of monogamy, and periods of chastity, all within a span of a decade or two—a decade or two that, a few generations ago, would most likely have been largely given over to married sex with one partner.

And it's not all juicy. Sex, after all, comprises the great and the abysmal: bad sex and violent sex and sex from which you contract a disease. It's a muck of physicality and emotion, of excitement and satisfaction and of betrayal and disappointment: The girlfriend who leaves you for a man. The man who leaves you for another woman. Anyone who leaves you. Or who you cut to the quick by leaving, or cheating on, or lying to.

The waggly-eye-browed (often older male) fantasy of single sex as an erotic wonderland rarely takes female discernment or disenchantment— or stretches of inactivity—into account, any more than it encompasses the comprehension that for many of us, sex is intermittently thrilling, occasionally satisfying, sometimes disappointing, but also not always the driving center of our lives. Even Candace Bushnell, the Grand Dame of Purportedly Sexy Single Sex, stated baldly in her first ever "Sex and the City" column that sex "can be annoying; it can be unsatisfying; most important, sex . . . is only rarely about sex. Most of the time it's about spectacle . . . or the pure terror of Not Being Alone . . ."

The sex lives of single women are studded with stories that can, these days—after centuries in which female desires and sexual predilections were not acknowledged, were a source of shame, and never to be put on public view—finally be told, with bravado or tenderness or humor or regret. Telling them is important, not because it excites the codgers but because, when we take the cover of marriage off the adult erotic lives of women, we learn more about the variety of things that drive and excite and hurt and engage them. We get a far more honest view of female sexuality and its complications and contradictions, its heat and its chills. And, in doing this, we finally begin to break apart the gender essentialist assumptions about "what women want" that have served often to steer too many women toward fates they've never desired.

## Not So Much Sex

For good and bad, our post-pill, sexually revolutionized era is one in which independent women and their sexual preferences and aversions can be put on display. However, it's not as though contemporary women invented sex, or the anxieties around it.

Earlier generations of unwed women had sex, sometimes with the approval of families who presumed that young women and their partners would wed.[1] Other single women who had sex before marriage, with lovers or otherwise committed men, managed to pull it off without terrible consequence. And then there were many more who lived by choice or need as prostitutes, or who moved through life degraded and in danger because of their sexual reputations. And, of course, enslaved women rarely had ownership of their own bodies or were able to exert control over their sexuality.

For those never-married women of the middle and upper classes, many of them pious, who left written records of their lives and loves, it was far more common to have lived chastely. However, that doesn't mean that they didn't think about sex or consider the way that sexual impulse and desire played a part in their lives.

Settlement House founder and activist Jane Addams argued in her book, *The Spirit of Youth*, that a redirection of sexual energy could foster engagement with other forms of beauty in the world. "Every high school boy and girl knows the difference between the concentration and the diffusion of this [sexual] impulse," wrote Addams. "They will declare one of their companions to be 'in love' if his fancy is occupied by the image of a single person . . . But if the stimulus does not appear as a definite image, and the values evoked are dispensed over the world, the young person suddenly seems to have discovered a beauty and significance in many things—he responds to poetry, he becomes a lover of nature, he is filled with religious devotion or with philanthropic zeal. Experience, with young people, easily illustrates the possibility and value of diffusion."[2] Addams's biographer, Louise Knight, described to me how another of her subjects, abolitionist Sarah Grimké, wrote directly about the imagined pleasures and value of sexual congress, as well as about how the ways in which it was practiced by men violated women's equal rights. Grimké wrote that marriage "finds its most natural, most sacred and intense outward expression in that mutual personal embrace."[3] However, she also argued that women must be afforded "an equality of rights throughout the circle of human relations, before she can be emancipated from that worst of all slaveries—slavery to the passions of man,"[4] a signal that while Grimké clearly "believed in marriage's possibilities," Knight said, she was "skeptical of its realities," including marital rape.

Many of the women left single, or who chose to remain single, in the wake of the westward migration in the nineteenth century, spent a good deal of time pondering what they had missed. Emily Greene Balch, a never-married economist and pacifist born in 1867, made no bones about the fact that she was sorry that, in electing to live unmarried, she had missed out on the emotional peaks and valleys of falling in love and having a family. Balch, who would win a Nobel Peace Prize, wrote that as an independent woman, "I am happy in my work . . . I have escaped the dangers of unhappy, or only half-happy marriage and the personal sufferings incident to the most successful marriage." But, she continued, "I have missed the fullness of life which I would prefer to any calm. . . . [I] have been shut out except in imagination and sympathy from the most human and deepest experiences."[5]

And yet, despite her melancholy over missed intimacies, Balch would write to her friend and fellow Nobel recipient Addams, during the period in which psychologists were attempting to pathologize nonconforming single women as perverse, that her peers had survived just fine without the sex that they might have been curious about. Balch wrote, "If the educated unmarried women of the period between the Civil War and the World War represent a unique phase, it is one that has important implications which have not yet been adequately recognized by those who insist upon the imperious claims of sex."

Sex and love might have been desirable elements in life, Balch believed. And yet, the absence of them, *even* for those women who wished it otherwise, was not an absence that necessarily deformed the rest of female experience.

The message that an active sex life was not simply a new freedom but, in fact, an imperative, a form of validating the worth of young women, has been one of the more convoluted messages to emerge in the century since Balch objected to the notion that sex had been made to mean too much.

Psychologist Paula J. Caplan has written about how the Second Wave, in combination with the invention of the birth-control pill, created for women "a strange combination of liberation and disturbing pressures with regard to sex." On the one hand was the revolutionary idea that "women should be as free as men to enjoy sex, and [that] those who did so ought not to be demeaned as a result." Countering that were the "greater pressures on women and even very young women: 'You won't get pregnant, and you're supposed to be free to enjoy sex, so you have absolutely no reason to refuse,' came the argument from many men."[6] The invention of the pill meant new carnal possibilities, yes, but also a new culture of public concupiscence and objectification and with it, new reasons for women—especially those already suspicious of male power—to fear exploitation, abuse, and degradation.

This was the thorny heart of the anxieties laid out by some radical Second-Wave feminists who famously objected to the gendered subjugations of marriage, but also saw unregulated sexual freedom as a new arena of objectification and diminishment for women. Back then, there were so few contemporary models of what unmarried female life might look like that even the most ardent antimarriage agitators had trouble making single sexuality sound terrifically appealing.

Feminist Shulamith Firestone was among those activists who was no fan of marriage, but saw no cheery alternative. In *The Dialectic of Sex*, Firestone advocated egalitarian partnership and romantic love, both of which she found wanting from the contemporary marital model. But she could not seem to envision actual independence from men, describing unmarried women as "consigned forever to that limbo of 'chicks,'" destined to become the "'other woman' . . . used to provoke his wife, prove his virility."[7] Firestone also argued that "those who do not marry and have children by a certain age are penalized: they find themselves alone, excluded, and miserable, on the margins of a society . . . (Only in Manhattan is single living even tolerable, and that can be debated.)"[8] In this formulation, to not be a wife was to not be one's self, but to be a wife-alternative who was still defined by abstention from marriage and now also by an identity tied to sexual degradation, still as passive objects of (inherently male) sexual impulse.

It's not hard to imagine Firestone or her radical colleagues looking with grief on Internet dating apps including Tinder, used by an estimated 50 million people in 2014,[9] where the process of erotic coupling has been taken to new consumerist heights. Online dating involves reciprocal evaluation—men and women selecting other men and women from real-time, steadily updating catalogs. But sites like Tinder, and their online buffets of willing partners, can also reduce the search for sex partners to its quickest and most commodified form. "You can swipe a couple hundred people a day," one young man told the *Vanity Fair* reporter Nancy Jo Sales in 2015. "It's setting up two or three Tinder dates a week and, chances are, sleeping with all of them, so you could rack up 100 girls you've slept with in a year."[10]

On Tinder, and other apps like it, including Hinge and Happn and OkCupid, men and women present versions of themselves that are photographed for maximum impact, describe themselves in just a few words and catchphrases, bringing the mid-twentieth century art of the singles ad or, for that matter, the centuries' old business of matchmaking, to a new technological age, making the process of pursuit and rejection swifter, the volume of potential choices higher. And because women remain more sexually objectified and less sexually empowered than men, troubled by more double standards and harsher aesthetic evaluations, the dehumanizing impact of dating apps, of sex apps, can be very real. "It's like ordering Seamless," another young man told Sales, "but you're ordering a person."

That's big talk, and it sounds pretty horrifying from a gendered perspective except that the sexual supply and demand patterns being reworked by apps and social media do not, in fact, all work in one direction. In a widely circulated 2015 piece, "The Dickonomics of Tinder," writer Alana Massey chronicled her use of Tinder after a heart-wrenching breakup, describing her approach to Tinder as hinging on one resonant mantra: "Dick is abundant and low value."[11] It was a phrase she cribbed from another woman whose words she read on Twitter, a lawyer and writer, Madeleine Holden, who had written that "there's this cacophony of cultural messages telling us that male affection is precious & there's a trick to cultivating it. They're all lies. To any women reading 'how to get a man' franchises or sticking around in stale dissatisfying relationships: dick is abundant and low value." To Massey, that last sentiment "emerged from the screen with their outer edges glowing like the inscription in the Dark Tongue of Mordor on the One Ring. I was transformed, nay, *transfigured,* by the message." It was an idea that enabled her to use Tinder to treat men as disposable, to give her the power of rejection, of being picky, knowing that the technology was presenting her with ample choice, and that "the centuries' long period of dick overvaluation is over." Massey knew that some would read her account of giddy evaluative dismissal of men as "evidence as a disturbing uptick in malevolent, anti-male sentiments among single straight women," but, she wrote, that's not true. Instead, "it is evidence of us arriving nearer to gender equilibrium."

For plenty of women, the experiences of sex and dating in the Internet age are somewhere in between objectification and liberation, or maybe comprise a bit of both, which is not so different from the stories of dating and sex in earlier eras. "My feelings about Tinder are complicated," said Amina. "Dating, period, is horrible. I don't think there is anything exclusive to Tinder that makes it worse." Amina said that despite press coverage suggesting that it's only a mechanism for commodified, brief, zipless erotic encounters, in life she knows plenty of happy "Tinder couples," "People who've gotten married or are in happy long-term stable relationships, and when I consider them, I don't know how they would have met without Tinder."

One of the challenges as people remain single later is that the contexts in which they are likely to encounter other singles narrow. There's not the romantic marketplace of college or fresh-out-of college social life. For people who don't like to date colleagues, or who work remotely, or who work all the time, there are few places to seek mates. Apps address this need.

The reality is that Tinder probably hasn't invented a new level of awful for women in dating. Rather, it has simply brought the human heartbreak and gendered inequities long threaded through heterosexual encounters to a new technological platform. "I don't think it's worse than sitting at a bar or even going out with people my friends have introduced me to," said Amina.

## No Sex

Today, in a culture that has more fully acknowledged female sexuality as a reality, it is perhaps more difficult than ever to be an adult woman who does *not* have sex. But there are plenty of such women out there, who feel varying degrees of pride or shame about their sexual inactivity. It may not define them any more than it did earlier generations of abstinent women, but it certainly occurs to them.

"I feel that it's one hundred percent worth waiting for [sex] to be within marriage," said Sarah Steadman, the twenty-nine-year-old Mormon schoolteacher from Utah. "I feel that sexual intimacy is a very sacred thing, and it's a beautiful gift we've been given to be able to express love and closeness with the person that we're married to." Yes, she acknowledged, "I sometimes think, 'Ah! Why do I have to wait?' Sure. I'm human and I have hormones. Lots of times I've even thought, 'Maybe I should marry this guy just so that I can.'"

Sarah has set guidelines as to how far she's willing to go, physically, within a relationship, and said that any time she's ever violated those guidelines, her relationships have been ruined. Some of that damage, she said, is based on self-recrimination and guilt about not having lived up to her own standards. But more, she said, the relationships suffer because "I see the act of waiting as caring enough to be completely committed to the one person. And [sex] is the final act that shows your complete commitment." Sarah said that she feels "a greater love for my boyfriend when we can control ourselves, as opposed to when sometimes we take things a little too far. Sure, taking things a little too far is pleasurable. But when we can control each other I know that he respects me, he loves me, and that we both have the desire to wait."

Meaghan Ritchie, the twenty-year-old undergraduate from Kentucky, is also holding out for marriage for religious reasons. "I do plan on saving myself for my husband," she said. "And I pray that my husband saves himself for me. That is just for marriage. Why give yourself away like that, emotionally and physically, especially when it can lead to pregnancy?" Meaghan's take on chastity echoes Jane Addams's; she sees her commitments and desires as rechanneled in other directions. "As a Christian," she said, "I feel that I am having a relationship with Christ. My number-one goal in life would be to bring glory to him. I'm very involved with my church, very involved with campus organizations. I just enjoy life." Ritchie has considered the possibility that she might never marry and thus, based on her beliefs, never have a sexual relationship. When this crosses her mind, she said, she comforts herself with two reminders: "First," she said. "I don't feel like God would give you desires if he wasn't going to fulfill them." But also, "If I *were* to be single, he would fill in that need. He's not going to make your life miserable if your goal is to glorify him."

For many women, the pressures to remain celibate come not from their own devotion, but from the religious beliefs enforced by parents and community.

Ayat, twenty-one, is the daughter of Palestinian immigrants and remains a virgin, though a sexually curious and experimental one. When asked if her parents knew about her sexual life she replied, "Oh, my God, I'd be shot in the face. They would go nuts. They definitely expect virginity first." She recalled a childhood conversation with her mother about whether she might have lost her virginity after slipping off a bicycle, and how her mother flipped out! She was like, 'This is a disaster!' It's definitely important to them. I would never say any stuff [about sex] to them, ever. Ever. Ever." But the cultural linking of adult femininity to sexual activity and identity plays on Ayat. Considering the question of what it means to be a woman versus a girl, she quickly returned to the subject of sex. "I would like to think I feel like a woman, but I haven't had sex yet," she said. "When I think about the fact that I haven't had sex, I feel like the process isn't complete yet or something. So, I guess, intellectually I think I'm a woman, but because of pop culture [its messages about sex] I don't feel like it."

Sometimes, abstinence can simply be the product of divided attentions. While most people feel sexual urges and desires, they aren't always quite strong enough to drive them to action, especially when other engagements are drawing their energies.

Remembering her late teenaged, collegiate life, Amina recalled, "I was too busy being good at math and science in college, and too busy making friends, to have a sex life. Then I felt like I needed to check off a box and was like, 'Okay, I'm going to do this now.'"

Amina said that this experience of first or early sex—almost as a chore to be dispensed with—was common among her compatriots. It certainly was true for some of my high-school and college friends, and for me. It wasn't as though we weren't curious about sex, that we didn't long for physical intimacy, engage in fantasy, or masturbate. It's just that when a suitable partner didn't make him or herself readily available, we busied ourselves with other things . . . things that in turn distracted us from any kind of laser-focused search for sexual intimacy.

This dynamic of having interest but no discernible opportunity to follow through on it leads to another, too rarely discussed, category of single women: the unintentionally chaste.

It's so easy, in high school or college, if you have not forged a specific sexual connection, if your energies, to use Jane Addams's term, have been diffused, rechanneled as enthusiasms for art or drugs or sports or science, to simply find yourself . . . not having sex. Not because you don't want to, not because you don't believe in it, but just because, well, appealing opportunities aren't always as plentiful as Hollywood summer movies would suggest.

Then, as the assumptions of the media and of peers grow surer, your virginity becomes more freighted. It comes to mean more, it gets harder to confess, looms larger every passing year. You become fearful that a friend, or a potential partner, might judge you for your lack of experience, might think you prudish or frigid or babyish, when really you were just busy.

So, you keep not having sex, and the not having it keeps getting more important. In 2013, the *New York Times* ran a story[12] by a thirty-five-year-old woman who wrote that when she was young, she'd held off out of fear of being hurt. But, as time passed, her expectations rose. "After so many years of holding out, I can't change now."

Too few people talk about this, but it happens. All the time. It happened to me. I was twenty-four when I lost my virginity, though I happily would have been done with it as a teen. The actress Tina Fey has said that she was twenty-four as well, joking that she "couldn't give it away." One close friend was well into her thirties by the time she first had sex; I'm less sure about others, now heading into their forties, because, as time has worn on, these brilliant, sexual, beautiful women find it ever harder to talk about their virginity.

A lack of sex, as much as a surfeit of sex, can come to define a woman. And, while protracted and cumbersome virginity is one thing, a formerly active sex life that goes fallow can provoke its own kind of self-reproach and self-doubt.

"Sex would be great," said fifty-two-year-old television commentator Nancy Giles. "But I have to like somebody. I can't just have sex for sex." It hasn't been for lack of trying. Giles has tried to be more casual. Once, she said, "I forced myself because it had been so long. I wasn't being celibate on purpose; it's just that no one really moved me." Giles attended a dinner party designed to introduce couples, and clicked with one of the guys. "I decided to go for it," she said. "But it was *so bad*. I remember thinking: 'Get me out; I wanted to get out of there so badly.'"

Still, Giles's lack of enthusiasm for unfettered encounters has made her feel bad, as though she was doing womanhood wrong. "It seemed for a long time like everyone knew the code for meeting people and having sex but me. It made me feel like I was a total fucking freak. But I can't even hug people if I don't like them." She tried a second time with the man she'd had bad sex with, and during their second liaison, she said, "the only thing that made it more interesting was that I was watching the Giants game over his shoulder" during sex. After that, she started feeling bad about having had sex with someone she didn't care about. It's only recently, Giles said, that "I finally have stopped feeling like a freak because I'm not dating."

## Nothing to be Afraid Of

"I'm not married, and I'm sexual," said Frances Kissling. "And that is about the scariest woman a patriarchal system can find." Frances recalled how, when she got out of her ten-year live-in relationship, she entered a phase that she described as "very, very, very, very sexually active." A Catholic advocate for contraception and abortion, she understood both that birth control can fail, and that while she *would* have an abortion, she didn't want to have to do it. She also knew that she never wanted children. So she had her tubes tied.

She remembered vividly, she said, the experience of having sex for the first time after her tubal ligation, and experiencing "this enormous feeling of freedom. I remember while we were having sex, saying 'This is how men feel!' There was just not the remotest possibility at all that I was going to get pregnant."

Frances's unapologetic verve for sex, but not for commitment, she said, makes her scary because it doesn't conform to what we think we know about what women desire, just as Kristina worries about hurting men by behaving rapaciously, in a manner that society most associates with male sexuality. When Frances meets a man, she explained, "I am never thinking 'Is he attracted to me? Is he going to ask me out? Is this a relationship?'" It's disconcerting. "When people can't figure out the mechanism by which they have power over you, you become very threatening," she said.

Indeed, sexual women have, in America's past, been viewed as such a threat that, in the mid-twentieth century, the language of female sexuality was tied to both pugilism and war. As Elaine Tyler May writes, physically violent words, including *knockout* and *bombshell*, began to be used in reference to sexual women; a photograph of pinup Rita Hayworth was attached to the hydrogen bomb dropped on the Bikini Islands. And those islands, site of explosive military action, gave their name to the two-piece bathing suit.[13]

In a more sexually open society, we are, very slowly, getting better at recognizing and acknowledging female *desire*, as opposed to just female sexual appeal. But it's still most digestible when it remains in a comfortable, old-fashioned framework: that women's active sex lives precede an inevitable marriage, that multiple partners are really a bunch of auditions for permanent commitment, that while women may get randy, they yearn most profoundly for emotional connection, that too much youthful promiscuity will provoke later regret, that the habitual pursuit of strings-free congress, as Kristina's therapist is sure, must be born of a lack of self-respect.

We get nervous when we are confronted with evidence that this model does not always hold, when we encounter women who are motivated by a spirit of conquest, who do not experience sexual hang-ups or guilt, who do not want touchy-feely ties with all or any of their sexual partners, and who do not in fact want to commit to them. This is (but) one of the ways that women get labeled sluts and deviants, considered unwell or unfit or unfeminine or damaged.

The slow realization that women's sexuality, when truly unleashed from hetero and marital expectation, might begin to look more like traditionally male sexuality is the stuff of social, economic, and sexual revolution. As Liza Mundy argued in her book *The Richer Sex*, which posited that women's growing economic power will reverse traditional heterosexual dynamics, "women are becoming the gender that wants sex more than men do." Mundy interviewed women who wanted to accumulate sexual partners "for maximum exploration." Mundy ventured that as economic power shifts further in favor of women, women will become "pickier about the appearance of the men they have sex with."[14]

Whether or not this upending of the sexual marketplace is as far underway as Mundy believes it to be, what's certainly true is that there is a far more robust dialog among women about the reality of intense and capacious female sexual appetites.

## Hooking Up

If there's anything the nation feels more anxiety about than sexually empowered adult women, it's sexually active girls in their late teens and early twenties, the women who are preparing to head into the world not necessarily to become wives, but to become people.

That anxiety has been made manifest most lately in the media obsession with so-called hookup culture. The term is meant to indicate the habits of high-school and college students, especially ambitious, high-achieving college students at high-end universities, who have physical encounters, generally understood to include anything from kissing to petting to oral sex to penetration, with peers to whom they do not commit.

Many of hookup culture's critics and defenders have framed this behavior as directly tied to the postponed marriage age and filling up of young female adulthood with other concerns. As *New York Times* reporter Kate Taylor explained in a 2013 article about the culture of casual sexual encounters at the University of Pennsylvania, the women she interviewed about their hookup habits "saw building their resumes, not finding boyfriends (never mind husbands), as their main job" at college.

The sloughing off of marital priority sends shivers down the spines of both entrenched social conservatives and nonideologically offended but, nonetheless, *very concerned* elders.

Hookup *agonistes* include writer Caitlin Flanagan, whose book, *Girl Land,* bemoaned the lost innocence of a time when girls could be girls who pined for boys without any pressure to have sex with them. Flanagan has written about how hookup culture has "forced [young women] to abandon" their investment in what she calls "The Boyfriend Story," in which they are meant to yearn for a boy who loves only them. Flanagan imagines teen girls as having been "hectored—via the post-porn, Internet-driven world—toward a self-concept centering on the expectation that the very most they could or should expect from a boy is a hookup."

Flanagan has found backup in Donna Freitas, author of *The End of Sex: How Hookup Culture Is Leaving a Generation Unhappy, Sexually Unfulfilled, and Confused about Intimacy.*" Freitas, who views hookup culture as "fast, uncaring, unthinking, perfunctory," and "so common, so obligatory, that it leaves little room for experimentation that bends the rules," has reported that 41 percent of students who have reported hooking up used negative words such as "regretful," "disgusted," "ashamed," and even "abused" in describing their experiences. She holds out for the "innocent wish for an alternative means of getting to know someone before getting physical,"[15] perhaps unaware that many hookups occur between young people who already know each other and share a social circle.

Former *New Yorker* and *Vanity Fair* editor Tina Brown reacted to Taylor's story about hookup culture at Penn by calling it "tragic" that "girls are completely editing out tenderness, intimacy, excitement, somebody respecting them. . . ."[16] Even in this new world of female ambition and success—a world that Brown herself has embodied—there is the presumption of sacrifice.

This mandated tradeoff becomes even more obvious when critics don't cast women as victims, but instead as cold, careerist tramplers on the budding flower of youthful commitment. In 2006, claiming that "young women are now as likely as young men to have sex and by countless reports are also as likely to initiate sex, taking away from males the age-old, erotic power of the chase," conservative commentator Laura Sessions Stepp blamed this power reversal for an increase in erectile challenges faced by collegiate men.[17] In this formulation, women are not just sacrificing their claim to tenderness, but also the very essence of their appeal.

What's certainly true is that whatever human connection collegiate women may or may not be seeking, many are upfront that it's not one that leads to marriage any time soon.

"I know it sounds hyperbolic," said Amanda Litman, who was a senior at Northwestern in 2012, "but I mean it when I say that getting married right now would ruin my life. I want freedom. I want the chance to pick up and move to a new city for a new job or for adventure, without having to worry about a spouse or a family. I need to be able to stay at the office until three in the morning if I have to, and not care about putting dinner on the table."

That Litman's vision of marriage is still as a gendered, servile relationship is telling. And a direct rebuke to the pundits who insist that a return to traditional roles might somehow "cure" hookup culture. It is, in fact, the lingering fear of falling into those traditional roles that *moti-*

*vates* at least some young women to keep their sexual encounters casual. "For so many of us," said Amanda, "getting into a serious relationship felt like compromising our ambitions and risking the independence needed to succeed careerwise. Hooking up—often in a friends-with-benefits style, but not always—was our way of exploring the physical side without having to devote the time or, more importantly, the emotional energy to someone else."

One of hookup culture's most vocal worrywarts, *New York Times* columnist Ross Douthat, has warned purportedly hook-up-happy college women to be careful what they wish for in their focus on careers. In an item headlined "Love in the Time of Hookups," Douthat fretted about (conservatively framed) studies that link the number of sexual partners a woman has to her likelihood of future divorce and depression, about how the delay of marriage results in having fewer children. "People pursuing neo-traditional paths to romance have a solid chance of finding, well, neo-traditional forms of happiness," he wrote, while "people taking a more career-minded path are more likely to see their careers benefit . . . but at the expense, potentially, of other areas of life."[18]

The flaw in Douthat's warnings is that the very people he's wringing his hands about—pre-professional, predominantly white, collegiate women postponing marriage—are precisely the demographic still most likely to find themselves ensconced in that most "neo-traditional form of happiness," marriage itself. Though privileged, educated women are marrying later than ever before, and at lower rates than ever before, they are, eventually, marrying far more frequently than their less economically advantaged peers.

What's more, those Americans with the most education and money, the ones marrying later but most reliably, are also the people currently enjoying the nation's lowest divorce rate. If his concern is "neo-traditionalism," the women engaging in what Douthat describes as "a sexual culture . . . well suited to careerism" and "the multiplication of sexual partners" are not its enemy, but its future.

As Salon writer Tracy Clark-Flory, a longtime advocate for and practitioner of casual sex, has written, "I, of all people, was supposed to end up alone. . . . that's what I was told" by culture warriors including Lori Gottlieb and Laura Sessions Stepp. "In my early twenties, I began passionately defending hookup culture from its critics and often used my own experiences with casual sex to make my case. According to their wisdom, which included such delightful gems as 'Why buy the cow when you can get the milk for free?,' I was destined to end up a sad cat-lady cliche. . . . Instead, I'm nearing 30, cohabitating, engaged, and talking about becoming a mom in the not-so-distant future." Clark-Flory married at twenty-nine.

There is simply no reason for Ross Douthat, or any of the other social conservatives, to break a sweat over the romantic and familial fates of these privileged and empowered women. Unless, of course, what they're actually worried about isn't their future marital happiness but rather that their circuitous route to getting there, which involves establishing themselves economically and professionally and thereby exerting more social and sexual control over their circumstances, is actually a signal of increasing female strength.

That's how Mundy sees it. And Hanna Rosin, who writes in *The End of Men* that the girls-as-victimized-by-casual-sex critique of hookup culture "downplays the unbelievable gains women have lately made, and, more important, it forgets how much those gains depend on sexual liberation." For young women who Rosin argues are "in their sexual prime," and also at the most potentially propellant moment of their careers and social lives, there is a recognition that "an overly serious suitor fills the same role an accidental pregnancy did in the 19th century: a danger to be avoided at all costs, lest it get in the way of a promising future."[19]

The fact that hooking up is a habit depicted in the media as of those most statistically likely to marry is just one of the facts that the hubbub over hookup culture often conveniently obscures. Among the other realities that you'd never quite absorb if you just read coverage of blow jobs and beer pong is that, actually, uncommitted physical encounters on campuses are not a particularly recent phenomenon.

"Hookup culture" was certainly the norm when I was an undergraduate in the mid-nineties. Back then, women made out with boys at fraternity parties and in dorm rooms; they performed oral sex (and more rarely had the favor returned); they had sex, sometimes one-night stands, sometimes recurring assignations, sometimes with strangers, but more often with friends with whom they also drank too much, and with whom they talked and gossiped and danced and ate dinner and breakfast. A few women got into very serious committed relationships that lasted months or years. One friend was with her boyfriend from high school; they stayed together through college and are still married, with three children. Lots more women rarely ever hooked up.

Assault and rape, Greek fraternity hazing and extreme binge drinking were serious, often horrifying, campus problems. But they were not hookup culture. Hookup culture was ordinary. Ordinarily fun, ordinarily frustrating, ordinarily heartbreaking, ordinarily weighted in favor of guys? Yes, like most of life. Completely ordinary for a bunch of sexually curious eighteen-to-twenty-two-year-olds living in close proximity to each other, beyond the reach of their families.

In fact, the only thing that is unfamiliar to me when I read the keening over the steady degradation of heterosexual collegiate relationships is that in my day, I don't recall many—or any—explicit female renunciations of commitment in favor of education or professional life, which is what leads me to believe that it's the careerism, and not the casual nature of the encounters, that is so rankling.

Lots of social scientists have backed up that hunch, with evidence that hookup culture is nothing new. University of Michigan sociologist Elizabeth Armstrong argues that sexual habits on campuses have remained largely unchanged since the sexual revolution of the mid-to-late twentieth century, and points out that today's college students are not having more sex than their parents.[20] The Centers for Disease Control and Prevention report that, between 1988 and 2010, the percentage of sexually active teenage girls dropped by 8 percent, from 51 to 43 percent.[21] As Rosin writes, "by many measures, the behavior of young people can even look like a return to a more innocent age." Research conducted by San Diego State University psychologist Jean Twenge and published in 2015 suggests that Millennials are on track to have fewer sexual partners, on average, than their Generation X and Baby Boomer predecessors. Although, interestingly, Twenge's research compares the number of partners people have had by age twenty-five, a cut-off point that is less final for today's young people, who are far less likely to be married by twenty-five than any generation before them.[22]

Paula England, an NYU sociologist, has done research that shows that students have an average of only about seven hookups, which may include anything from kissing to sex, over the course of their time at college. That means that they're getting busy with fewer than two people a year. She also found that a rather vast majority of college students, 80 percent, hook up less than once per semester.[23] In her story about hookup culture at Penn, Kate Taylor cites research that shows that three in ten college seniors have *never* hooked up during college, and that four in ten have either never had sex or had sex only with one person. Sociologist Lisa Wade turns up similar findings, estimating that somewhere between two-thirds and three-quarters of students hook up during college, but that about 32 percent of those hookups end with kissing, and 40 percent end with sex. As journalist Amanda Hess interpreted Wade's research, "that means . . . that [romantically unattached] college students are engaging in as little as *one makeout every four years*." Hess also crunched numbers to conclude that "less than fifteen percent of [single] college students are engaging in some form of physical contact *more than twice a year*."

The rest of the women, presumably, are doing different things: Some are in committed relationships; Rosin cites England's research showing that 74 percent of women, and about as many men, have had a college relationship that lasted six months or more.[24] Some are not in relationships. They're writing their honors theses on erotic art, they're wondering whether they're straight or queer, they're doing work-study jobs at the campus day-care center, or getting up early to work the breakfast shift at a sandwich shop and fantasizing about their shift manager. And a very few of them are planning their weddings, because yes, young people still do marry each other, just in far smaller numbers than ever before.

## Reality

What everyone is doing, in one way or another, is working out who they are and where they fit. They're figuring out who they want to be, what they want to do, who they want to do, whether they enjoy only meaningful sex or are excited by meaningless sex, whether they are sustained by the pacific companionship of romantic stability or electrified by the crackle of argumentative tension, or whether they prefer, simply, to be alone, or with their friends or their books or their pets.

"This is what the hookup trend pieces get wrong," writes Tracy Clark-Flory. "Women are different. We are not all the same. Some of us learn about ourselves and other people from serial live-in monogamous relationships; some of us gain more from pursuing the cutie at the end of the bar. Some of us want to get married; some of us do not. Some of us are straight; some of us are not. Some of us want kids; some of us do not. Even if we all wanted the same thing, there wouldn't be any reliable prescription for how to get it."

And there would be no reliable prescription for not getting hurt while at it, both as human beings, susceptible to hormones and cracked hearts, and as women who still, despite gains in power and sexual determination, tend to get stuck with the fuzzy end of the lollipop.

Sex and love, especially the sex and love we experience as young people, whose emotional cement is not yet dry, are full of risk, pain, and disillusionment for both sexes. England found that while about 66 percent of women confessed that they wanted their hookup to produce some longer connection, the notion that women are solely being left bereft and abandoned doesn't hold: 58 percent of men told her the same thing.[25]

It's true that increasing one's number of sexual partners almost certainly increases the risk of sexually transmitted disease and of unintended pregnancy. It increases the chance of having your soul stomped on, and of having really bad sex. It also, I should add, increases the odds of finding someone with whom you have terrific sex, and of learning more about what turns you on and what turns you off, how your body works and how other people's bodies work.

The fact that women experience any more disillusionment or shame than men in hookup culture is at least partly attributable to the remaining pressures on them to measure their worth by the degree to which they can hold male attention. And there is an argument that the lingering, systemic sexual injustices and pressures placed on women in a liberated sexual universe mean, for today's young women, a version of the unsatisfying sexual objectification that Shulamith Firestone so glumly imagined fifty years ago that, in liberating sexuality from marriage, women will be consigned to be "chicks," or the modern equivalent.

Rhaina Cohen, an undergraduate who worked as a researcher on this book, conducted interviews with women, gathered data, and talked endlessly about the subject of hookup culture with her undergraduate friends. She expressed reservations about my putting too positive a spin on a culture of casual sex. "Maybe the subject hits too close to home," she told me in 2014. "I've seen the way friends my age have turned to hooking up not for the reasons Kate Taylor writes about"—a deferment of commitment for professional ambition—"but because they think that's what's expected and it's all men will permit."

Are these dissatisfactions and double binds inherently worse than earlier iterations of sexual impossibility? By some measures, that doesn't matter, if you're the women living through them.

But the argument that this pain and disappointment is somehow tied to a biologically determined, as opposed to a culturally encouraged, female preference for long-term commitment has been thrown into question by journalist Daniel Bergner, who recently published *What Do Women Want?*, a lengthy study on the nature of female desire, in which he argued that gender bias has long made invisible the power of the female appetite for sex. One German study Bergner cited showed "women and men in new relationships reporting, on average, more or less equal lust for each other. But for women who've been with their partners between one and four years, a dive begins—and continues, leaving male desire far higher."

As Ann Friedman has written, "Women like having sex. They don't like being socially punished for it."[26] But they continue to be punished.

The studies quoted by Freitas and the experiences of emotional discontent and disappointment recounted by Rhaina Cohen speak to individual experiences of heartbreak, but also of something more gendered. They confirm that, despite the strides that women have made, they still wield less sexual power than men, are still more likely to feel commodified, to feel pressured into encounters that don't satisfy them physically or emotionally, to still sometimes feel bad about their sexual boldness, or their sexual acquiescence, then blame themselves for feeling bad.

As members of the gender that still holds most of the power, men remain the ones who get to dictate punishing sexual standards to which women are held. Male sexuality is considered normal, healthy; female sexuality is still liable to be viewed as immoral. Heterosexual male *abstention* from sex, meanwhile, is still often understood as a judgment passed on the desirability of a woman in question, while female abstention from sex is regarded as a symptom of prudishness, perversion, or lack of femininity. Male pleasure—the orgasm—is the accepted conclusion of the sex act; female orgasm is still considered a somewhat mysterious bonus. Young women give far more oral sex than they receive; pornography remains unduly focused on male release and is increasingly driven by an impossible, nearly inhuman vision of female physiology. The majority of sexual assaults are against women; the rape and assault of teen girls often ends with the victims being blamed not only by the alleged assailants but also by communities and media for being loose or "asking for it." Many of these inequities are on display in contemporary hookup culture. As a study reported by the *New York Times* in 2013 revealed that "women were twice as likely to reach orgasm from intercourse or oral sex in serious relationships as in hookups."[27]

But that doesn't make any of them the fault—or the creation—of hookup culture.

Inattention to female gratification and to women's anatomy extends back centuries; female pleasure has certainly not always been a reliable feature of supposedly serious relationships. According to historian Rachel Maines, it wasn't until the eighteenth century that doctors bothered to distinguish between the parts of the female reproductive anatomy, before they could tell "the vagina from the uterus," or were able to recognize a labia, a vulva, or a clitoris. Though it's true that other cultures and countries have at times been interested in female sexual climax (largely, as for example in the early Modern period in England, because they believed it to be necessary for conception) in more contemporary Western society, Maines points out, doctors and psychologists thought it "both reasonable and necessary to the social support of the male ego either that female orgasm be treated as a by-product of male orgasm or that its existence or significance be denied entirely." As recently as the 1970s, medical authorities "assured men that a woman who did not reach orgasm during heterosexual coitus was flawed or suffering from some physical or psychological impairment."[28] In addition, marital rape was legal in some states until the 1990s.

Long before colleges lifted their parietal rules and men and women lived in dorms together, women were raped, were treated badly, and felt shame, regret, and guilt—far more intense shame and regret and guilt than their counterparts today—about their desires and their sexual behaviors.

The differences were that, until recently, there was less chance that they might be able to safely open up to anyone, a friend or counselor or parent. There was little chance that, if they found themselves pregnant or suffering from an STD, they would have a safe or legal venue to seek help.

That's part of what made Helen Gurley Brown's *Sex and the Single Girl* so revolutionary in 1962, remembered Letty Cottin Pogrebin. It was, she recalled, "the meeting point between a former era and that next one that came after. It was so liberatory for a woman of my generation." As undergraduates in the 1950s, Pogrebin said, she and her friends used to gossip about a student who was openly sexually active, but, at a reunion twenty-five years later, they admitted to each other that none of them had been virgins at the time. "None of us were virgins and all of us were gossiping and putting her down," she said. "You had to live a lie, thinking you were the only one." Pogrebin, like many women of her generation, had had an abortion before college graduation, but had told no one. "I just didn't know what I was doing and there was no pill." Abortion, she said, "was everyone's deep, dark secret."

The cone of silence that shrouded women's physical and sexual experiences began to crack. "Helen outed us," said Pogrebin, "Gurley Brown outed the fact that single women have sex." It helped, she said, that she was "respectable enough and successful enough and old enough to make it not whorish." Without prompting, fifty years later, Pogrebin remembered that Gurley Brown had been thirty-seven when she got married.

Today's college student may indeed feel terrible for having gone home with a wretched guy who rubbed up against her at a frat party, and telling her that it might have been worse fifty years ago won't alleviate that pain. But the good, in fact, the *great*, news is that these days, she doesn't have to spend the rest of her life married to that wretched frat guy, or live in social purgatory should their encounter become public.

What's more, none of the inequities cited by hookup culture detractors are addressed, much less solved, by the alternatives they want to proffer. In Hess's words, "If young women can't find someone they like making out with just once, the solution is not to make out with the same person over and over again."[29]

Ambivalence about romantic commitment may be more evident today, but what it reveals is not necessarily a brand-new set of impulses, but rather a broader array of romantic and sexual preferences and metabolisms than have previously been on display. Now that we have greater freedom to consider doing other things with our lives, some individuals, women and men, might find they enjoy coupling cozily; others might enjoy sleeping around or being celibate. As with most developed preferences, it's hard for many of us to imagine desires that diverge from ours: Why do some people love opera and others love Nicki Minaj? Some people want to try every new restaurant and others want to stay home and watch NASCAR. Class, race, age, identity, opportunity, and community figure into these preferences; they shape the options we have available to us and the way the people around us behave; that's also true of relationship patterns.

But even given these contextual influences, what today's world allows is a diversity of romantic and sexual behaviors that we are still tempted to diagnose as aberrant or immature because they are not what we used to expect (or demand) of adults. But what we used to expect and demand is that everyone would get herded into the same conjugal channel. Quite suddenly, people are freer to take off in a number of directions, and they're taking advantage of that freedom.

That diversity of behavior is startling. It's different, uncharted, and admittedly a little scary. It certainly doesn't end well for everyone. But it's a grave mistake to argue that the single, narrow sexual chute into which most of us were once packed led more people to a greater number of happy endings.

# CHAPTER NINE

# Horse and Carriage:
# Marrying—And Not Marrying—
# In the Time of Singlehood

Letty Cottin Pogrebin remembers sitting in her garden apartment in Greenwich Village in 1963, having just returned from a work trip that had taken her to seven countries, and thinking "I'm never going to get married." She was twenty-three, and this recent trip, she said, short-circuited any lingering assumptions that she ever needed to become a wife, dependent on a husband. "Being single in a self-actualized way proves you can do things: I fixed my own toilet; I wired lamps; I changed tires. I didn't have somebody to do stuff for me. The things you do on your own, they buttress you so that you can't become poor dear wifey."

The next day, Pogrebin got a call from a man inviting her to spend her birthday on Fire Island. She went, and at the beach, first met a labor-and-employment lawyer, Bert. Six months later, they were married. Her husband, she said, is a committed feminist. Together, they came to the women's movement, reading feminist texts and raising three children on equal terms. The life she'd led on her own, she believes, permitted her to have an equitable marriage; she cofounded *Ms. Magazine* almost a decade after meeting Bert. "I've never had sex with anyone else in forty-eight years," said Pogrebin. "Which is so astonishing to me, given my past."

The great irony is that, as much as conservatives rage against the dying of traditional gender roles, by many measures, it's the people who are messing with the old marital expectations who might be credited with saving marriage as an institution.

Despite, or thanks to, the fact that Americans are staying single more often and for longer, have enjoyed increases in reproductive freedom and the ability to live promiscuously, engage in hookup culture, and have made gay marriage a reality, despite or thanks to all this: The majority of Americans will wind up married, or seriously committed to another person for some portion of their lives. And, right now, that sets the United States apart from many countries around the world.

In Japan, a nation with a downward-spiraling marriage rate, in competition with Germany for the lowest birthrate in the world, (with fewer babies born in 2014 than any other year on record) citizens have begun to abandon not just wedlock, but heterosexual sex itself, a trend the Japanese press refers to as *sekkusu shinai shokogun*, or celibacy syndrome.[1] One study found that over sixty percent of men and almost half of unmarried Japanese women between the ages of eighteen and thirty-four are not engaged in any sort of romantic relationship, numbers that are ten percent higher than they were just five years earlier. Yet another study, commissioned by the Japan Family Planning Association, showed that 45 percent of women under twenty-four claimed that they "were not interested in or despised sexual contact."[2] According to the Japanese magazine *Joshi Spa!*, 33.5 percent of Japanese people polled believe that marriage is "pointless."[3]

The rejection of straight coupling is closely linked to the inflexibility of gender roles in Japan. Japanese women are getting educations and making money, but find domestic expectations unadjusted. The Japanese workweek, designed for a man with a domestically submissive helpmeet at home, is strenuous, impossible to sustain for a woman who has a husband or children she is still supposed to tend with undivided attention. In Japan, working wives are referred to as "devil wives." And so, according to *The Guardian,* 90 percent of young Japanese women said, in a survey performed by Japan's Institute of Population and Social Security, that they would prefer to stay single than to enter into "what they imagine marriage to be like."[4] *Guardian* writer Abigail Howarth reported that an old Japanese saying "Marriage is a woman's grave" has today been repurposed to indicate that marriage "is the grave of [women's] hard-won careers." As one thirty-two-year-old woman told Howarth, "You have to resign. You end up being a housewife with no independent income."

Here is a cautionary tale about what happens to relations between the sexes when the scales are unbalanced, when societies fail to adjust to the increased liberty of their female population.

A similar phenomenon has emerged in Catholic countries, such as Italy, where there are rising cases of so-called *mammones*: mama's boys who, dissatisfied with the level of domestic devotion shown by their careerist female peers, continue to live with their cooking and cleaning mothers late into adulthood. The crude marriage rate (i.e., the number of marriages per 1000 inhabitants) fell in Italy from 7.7 in 1960 to just over 3 in 2013.[5]

In Germany, where working mothers are referred to, darkly, as *rabenmutters* or "raven mothers," and where, according to the Institute for Economic Research, only around 2 percent of senior management jobs were occupied by women,[6] the crude marriage rate has dropped by more than half, from 9.5 to 4.6 over the same period.

Compare those drastic declines in marriage rates to the Scandinavian nations, with more egalitarian social policy and attitudes, where women's increasing freedoms have been embraced both through social policy and cultural adjustment. In Finland, the crude marriage rate slid only from 7.4 in 1960 to 4.6 in 2013; in Sweden,[7] it dipped from 6.7 to just 5.4. Both those nations, in which the median age of first marriage for women is over thirty, used to have lower marriage rates than Italy and Germany; now their marriage rates are the same or higher.

Scandinavian citizens not only marry more often but form more stable committed unions outside marriage, evidence that progressive attitudes toward gender beget higher levels of heterosexual satisfaction and commitment. Cohabiting couples in Sweden are less likely than Americans to break up, and as sociologist Andrew Cherlin has pointed out, a child living with an unmarried pair of parents in Sweden "has a lower chance that his family will disrupt than does an American kid living with married parents."[8] Amina Sow remembered her most serious relationship, with a Swede. "He asked how much my birth control was so we could split it," she said. "Oh, my God, people who grow up in countries with equality!"

The United States, a comparatively youthful nation, born of Enlightenment thinking, with promises of individual liberty at its core, has also seen its marriage rates decline steeply over the past four decades. However, the crude marriage rate, in 2012, was 6.8,[9] higher than any other nation in the Americas, and than anywhere in Western Europe.

There's an argument to be made that Americans' continued propensity to marry is evidence of the tenacity of patriarchal expectation in a country whose promises of liberty were false at the start, and in which true parity—for women, for people of color, for gay people—has been hard won and remains elusive.

I believe the reverse: that, in fact, it is the progressive nature of a nation that permits continuing revisions to its bedrock institutions—its constitution, its electorate, its definition of marriage—that has allowed marriage to evolve, to become more inclusive, more equal, and potentially more appealing to more people.

At the heart of the long American fight to challenge gender inequity have been the women who have been single by choice or by happenstance, for some protracted period or for the whole of their lives. These women (and the men who are their partners or their allies), through argument or just through their existence, have forced the country to expand to make new space for them.

Today's enormous population of single women is *still* fighting hard for that space, some in the Japanese style: by abstaining from marriages that they imagine might be unjust. One 2013 study found only 66 percent of women, as opposed to 79 percent of men, felt that being married was a necessary component of having it all, and, as journalist Amanda Hess noted, "the proportion of women who don't prioritize relationships in their definition of success has almost doubled—from 5 percent to 9 percent— since last summer."[10] Similarly, sociologist Kathleen Gerson found, in researching her 2010 book, *The Unfinished Revolution*, that more than 70 percent of women would rather be unmarried than become housewives.[11]

But in Gerson's book about shifting domestic attitudes and social policy is a statistic that should give those worried about the fate of heterosexual partnership around the world hope for the United States: In addition to the 80 percent of the young American women Gerson sampled who desire egalitarian marriages in which wage earning, domestic duties, and childcare are divided equally, 70 percent of men now want the same thing.

The women who, for centuries, have been fighting to be able to stay single longer or forever, who have been blasting new paths and new space for themselves in the world, have made an impression on their fellow citizens. In delaying marriage, they have made it more conceivable to riff on it, to do it later, to do it differently, to do it better.

By demanding more from men and from marriage, it's single women who have perhaps played as large a part as anyone in saving marriage in America.

## Better Marriages Through Singlehood

In the United States, demographers continue to predict that eighty percent of Americans will marry[12] at some point in their lives. As the *New York Times* reported, the change in marriage patterns "is more about postponement than abandonment." While marriage has "declined precipitously among young women, both college graduates and women with less education" most "do eventually marry."

But the *postponement* of marriage has, throughout the country's history, been one of the chief strategies to get women closer to a better match, ensuring that female adulthood is not defined only by the man to whom a woman binds herself at its start.

Brittney Cooper, a scholar of black women's studies, who writes about African-American female public intellectuals of the Progressive Era, pointed out that many of the groundbreaking women she studies, including educator Mary Church Terrell, and activist, Ida B. Wells-Barnett, married late for their eras, delaying unions that might have limited their reach. Cooper said that most of the African-American women in her work wrote pointedly "about having progressive husbands who supported suffrage and supported their careers."

Church Terrell, the daughter of slaves who would go on to work as an anti-lynching activist, and a charter member of the NAACP, was among the first African-Americans to earn a college degree, in 1884. Her father wanted her to marry and settle down, and her defiance of his wishes and subsequent pursuit of her master's degree caused a family rift. Terrell became a Latin teacher and spent two years abroad, turning down a series of European suitors before marrying at twenty-eight. Wells had already toured Europe on an anti-lynching speaking tour and drawn the professional admiration of Frederick Douglass by the time she married at thirty-three. Wells would write of how, after she wed, her longtime friend and colleague Susan B. Anthony would "bite out" her married name, calling her only "Mrs. Barnett," and snipping to her, "since you have gotten married, agitation seems practically to have ceased."

But whatever Anthony's complaints from outside wedlock, the delay of marriage has often resulted in a building of individual capital for women, which has better allowed some to leverage demands for equity and freedoms *within* the institution.

Amelia Earhart was a world-famous aviator who had broken off one engagement, and turned down publisher George P. Putnam multiple times before she finally agreed to marry him, in 1931. In a letter to her husband on the day of their wedding, Earhart, who refused to change her name, wrote, "You must know again my reluctance to marry, my feeling that I shatter thereby chances in work which means most to me . . . Please let us not interfere with the other's work or play, nor let the world see our private joys or disagreements. In this connection I may have to keep some place where I can go to be myself, now and then, for I cannot guarantee to endure at all times the confinement of even an attractive cage."[13]

The tensions between public aspiration and wifely compliance that rightly worried Earhart have persisted into eras in which marriage has become more equitable. In 2003, Oprah Winfrey said of her multi-decade relationship with her beau, Stedman Graham, "Had we gotten married we wouldn't be together now. . . . Stedman's a traditional Black man, but I'm in no way a traditional woman, so to take on that role just doesn't fit."[14] The same year, she opined, "Stedman and I have a great relationship that allows me to be me in the fullest sense, with no expectations of wifedom and all that would mean."[15] It's worth noting that all the same, Winfrey referred to Graham as her fiancé for decades.

But women who have achieved on their own in advance, or instead, of marrying early are perhaps slightly more likely to find comparatively progressive men who encounter them, and pursue them, as independent, accomplished beings.

One of pop star Beyoncé's first interviews after marrying hip-hop star Jay Z, whose given name is Shawn Carter, was to *Seventeen Magazine*, the type of young women's publication that fifty years ago advised them as to how to land a husband before getting too old. Beyoncé had a different message, and spoke about how, when she started dating Carter at nineteen, she intentionally postponed marriage. "I really don't believe that you will love the same thing when you're twenty, as you do at thirty," she said. "So, that was my rule: before the age of twenty-five, I would never get married. I feel like you have to get to know yourself, know what you want, spend some time by yourself, and be proud of who you are before you can share that with someone else." When Beyoncé and Jay Z did marry, in 2008, she was twenty-six, and internationally famous on her own terms.

There is plenty of evidence today that marriage delay and higher rates of marital abstention seem to have had a positive impact on marriage quality. The states in which couples marry less frequently and at later ages—New York, Massachusetts, New Jersey, Illinois, and Pennsylvania—tend to boast the country's lowest divorce rates.[16] There is practically reverse symmetry for states where people marry youngest, with the exception of Utah, where Mormonism both encourages youthful unions and discourages divorce.[17] In Wyoming, Oklahoma, Arkansas, Kentucky, and Tennessee, marriage ages are low and divorce rates are high.[18]

Among other things, later starts to marriage permit men and women to spend more time together, and in more diverse circumstances than matrimony. Journalist Evelyn Cunningham once said that, "Women are the only oppressed group in our society that lives in intimate association with their oppressors." Citing that sentiment, blogger Feminist Griote wrote in 2010 of her realization, while "washing dishes in the sink that wasn't left by me" that "I would not last six months in a marriage to a man who expected me to be his wife, his whore, his cook, his maid, and personal secretary." In refusing to identify first, at the onset of adulthood, as maids and whores and wifeys, women break Cunningham's cycle of cohabiting oppression.

More than that, unmarried women alter assumptions about women by working alongside men who come to see them as colleagues and bosses; by drinking beer and arguing politics with men who come to regard them as friends; by having sex with men who (hopefully) come to understand that sex does not mean ownership. By existing on their own terms in the world, women force men to reckon with them as peers and as human beings, not simply as subordinate helpmates or sexual objects.

As Susan B. Anthony said, in her interview with Nellie Bly, who had already served as a foreign correspondent and circumnavigated the world in record time before marrying at thirty-one, "Once men were afraid of women with ideas and a desire to vote. Today, our best suffragists are sought in marriage by the best class of men."[19]

More than a century later, Anthony's argument, that women living independently in ways that once made them unattractive mates will eventually rearrange men's very tastes, is in tandem with shifts described by marriage historian Stephanie Coontz, who has pointed out that female college graduates and high earners, once the women least likely to find themselves hitched, are now among the *most* likely to one day become wives and to enjoy long-lasting unions.[20]

In part, that's because when we delay marriage, it's not just women who become independent. It's also men, who, like women, learn to clothe and feed themselves, to clean their homes and iron their shirts and pack their own suitcases.

The possibility of individual competence, leading to greater social parity, was fundamental to Anthony's vision of how an epoch of single women would work to equalize relations between the sexes. In her single utopia, men, she predicted, would visit the homes of single women not "to count their hostesses' chances in the matrimonial market," but rather visit "as they do to their gentlemen's clubs, to talk of art, science, politics, religion and reform. . . . They go to meet their equals in the proud domain of intellect."

It's what 1904's Bachelor Maid dreamt of when she wrote that the married life "of which I have permitted myself to dream contains a husband who may be an intellectual companion, who may be willing—even proud—to give me encouragement and inspiration to develop in my chosen field of work as I, in turn, would offer appreciative sympathy to him in his." But, alas, at the time, she complained, her "various lovers have desired in me [only] a mother for their children."

When I married my husband in 2010, I was thirty-five and he was forty-five; we had lived a combined eighty years without each other. There are downsides to this, almost all emotional: We will almost surely have a shorter number of years together than we'd like. I am also sad that, because of our ages and a desire to have children, we didn't get more time together on our own—to enjoy each other, by ourselves—before we had our children.

What was undeniably true was that one of us was not simply going to subsume the other. We had our own bank accounts; we had our own dishes; we had our own careers and our own social circles; we each knew how to do laundry and we each knew how to use an electric drill.

When you come at the work of life from a more equal starting point, tasks and responsibilities may be more appropriately apportioned to the person who is suited to them, not simply to the person who is stuck with them by dint of anatomy. In my marriage, we split the cooking, I do most of the cleaning, he does all of the laundry, we take turns with childcare. I don't advertise us, or any couple, as an aspirational model for any other couple; one of the freedoms of improving marriage is that the institution can be more easily molded around the particular talents and desires of the particular people entering into it. What I do know is that my life is a hell of a lot better, my daily load unimaginably lighter, my marriage far more equal than either my mother's or my grandmother's.

I'm not alone in this. A 2010 Pew Family Trends Research Center study revealed that 51 percent of respondents who were either married or cohabiting claimed that their relationship was closer than that of their parents. And of those who said that the relationship was better than that of the previous generation, 55 percent of women (as opposed to 46 percent of men) saw the improvement.[21]

By engaging in more equitable relationships with women, men have the chance to model more equitable future relationships for their children. Victoria Peng, a twenty-two-year-old, working at a law firm, recalled how she used to rib her self-employed business owner father, whose schedule was more flexible than her corporate mother's, for getting in touch with his feminine side when he'd pick her up from volleyball practice. Now, she said, "I want to find a man who is like my father."

In our epoch of female independence, men can be such kinder people, better friends, and peers. On my first traveling reporting trip after my first daughter was born, I was still breastfeeding. It was a male colleague—a competing reporter, a husband and father of two—who understood how a delayed press event might have an impact on my nursing situation. It was this male colleague who ran around the fish-processing plant where we were following the future senator Elizabeth Warren, finding me bags of ice to help keep the milk I was bringing home cold.

These are the halting steps of progress: On the one hand, the United States still lacks paid parental leave, anything resembling early maternal support from the government; many workplaces don't have rooms where new mothers can breastfeed when they come back to work; and in the House of Representatives, women only got their own *ladies' room* in 2011. And yet, the determination of American women to push through toward independence and parity, despite these systemic challenges, has produced an unquantifiable shift in attitude and behavior. We now work with, befriend, and partner with men who help us keep the breast milk cold.

Between 1965 and 2011, married fathers with children under eighteen went from doing four hours of housework a week to ten; the time they spent caring for their children went from two-and-a-half hours a week to seven.[22] And while there are gendered imbalances in how chores are divided—men rake the leaves and take out garbage, women do the dishes and clean bathrooms—the Bureau of Labor Statistics's Time Use Survey found that, from 2003 to 2014, the share of men who spent time cleaning and cooking increased from 35 percent to 43 percent; in the same span, the share of women doing domestic labor on an average day decreased 54 percent to 49 percent.[23] It's far from fifty-fifty, yet a hell of a lot closer than it's ever been before.

Surveys have found that, amongst millennials, the generation that still remains largely unmarried, work-life balance was prioritized above pay for *both* men and women when they chose a job.[24] A *New York Times* story about the rising number of men entering traditionally female professions like nursing, quoted Adrian Ortiz, who'd traded in his job as a lawyer in Mexico for a job as a bilingual kindergarten teacher in the United States, "My priorities are family, 100 percent."[25] Even some men in the most traditionally masculine-coded power positions are now more comfortable than ever acknowledging their domestic commitments. In 2015, Wisconsin Republican Representative Paul Ryan announced that his interest in taking the job of Speaker of the House—and becoming third in line to the presidency—was diminished by his desire not to "give up my family time." As a politician, Ryan has opposed childcare subsidies and paid leave legislation that would make spending time with families more realistic for more fathers and mothers, but it marks a fairly remarkable shift in the culture when a man can cite a domestic commitment as one that might stand in the way of a powerful (if also thankless and doomed) job.

Stay-at-home dads are still a rarity, but have become more common than they once were, especially in the upper economic echelons where women are slowly making their way to the top as exceptions, and where wealth allows one parent to stay home. According to the *New York Times*, the number of women working Wall Street jobs whose spouses stay home to take care of home and children has climbed by a factor of almost ten, from 2,980 in 1980 to 21,617 in 2011.

Across classes, the number of stay-at-home fathers in the United States almost doubled in the first decade of the twenty-first century.[26] One census study showed that among men married to wage-earning women with children under five, 20 percent of fathers served as primary caretakers. Those numbers have swelled thanks both to more mothers entering the paid labor force, and to fathers out of work as the result of the recession and the shrinking blue-collar labor force. Critics may dismiss the rise of primary caretaking dads as being simply symptomatic of economic distress, but high unemployment rates do not make those fathers any less fathers, just as generations of gendered prejudice that kept middle-class women out of workplaces didn't make them any less mothers.

Adjustment to new norms is more than possible; it's happening. Researchers from the University of Barcelona recently pored over census data from fifty-six countries, spanning 1968 to 2009, and determined that marriage patterns are, in fact, adjusting to the higher numbers of women attaining higher education, with more women marrying more men with lower education levels, a recent reversal of modern trends that had, until recently, left high-achieving women and low-achieving men single.[27] As researcher Albert Esteve said of the study, "What we see is that the composition of couples adapts quite well to these structural changes and that if these changes take place, sooner or later they will have an effect on the marriage market."

## Old Maids and Gay Marriage

In June 2013, after the Supreme Court overturned the Defense of Marriage Act, journalist Jess Oxfeld wrote a newspaper column entitled "Yesterday, An Oppressed Minority, Today, an Old Maid." Oxfeld's relationship with his boyfriend had ended the same week as the ruling. "I'm thirty-seven, single," wrote Oxfeld, "and I do want a husband." More than that, he argued, "all this heteronormativization is only encouraging my dull, heteronormative urges: I don't just want a husband, I want a husband while I'm at a marriageable age. . . . I want a wedding to be near the start of a life together, not near the end of it."[28]

In a *Slate* piece headlined, "Don't Be a Wife," commentator June Thomas produced an equally plaintive cry against the imposition of marital expectations on gay couples, specifically citing the feminist case against marriage as the reason for her discontent. "I've been in a blissfully happy monogamous relationship for going on 16 years," wrote Thomas. "We own property and are raising a cat together. I just don't want to be a wife—and I don't want a wife of my own." Thomas recalled her young adulthood in the women's movement: "although we didn't have marriage itself in the cross-hairs, on a certain level the institution represented the patriarchy and the tendency of some men to act as though they 'owned' their wives and could control their lives." Watching young lesbians and gays talk of marrying now that it's legal, she wrote, confused her. "Are they really going to mate for life, like swans in sensible shoes? That seems attractive at 35, but at 25 it's positively Amish."[29]

The recent, successful fight of homosexual couples to enter the institution from which so many women have struggled to distance themselves may appear counter to the progress we've made away from marriage as the only normative adult path. Stories like Oxfeld's and Thomas's seem to bolster the prediction of conservative columnist Megan McCardle, who wrote that the legalization of gay marriage would prove a "victory for the forces of staid, bourgeois sexual morality. Once gays *can* marry, they'll be expected to marry."

But the radical thing about gay marriage—well, there are many radical things about gay marriage—but, surely, one of the most crucial is that it reframes the power structure of the entire institution, disabling the gendered mechanism by which it historically exerted its oppressive power.

It is fully fitting that anarchist Emma Goldman, a woman far ahead of her time in her defense of homosexual connection, was also the person to predict, in 1911, of straight marriage, that "some day men and women will rise, they will reach the mountain peak, they will meet big and strong and free, ready to receive, to partake, and to bask in the golden rays of love . . . If the world is ever to give birth to true companionship and oneness, not marriage, but love will be the parent."[30]

Gay marriage, inherently and ideally based on love and companionship, and not on gender-defined social and economic power, will be key to our ability to re-imagine straight marriage.

Sure, individuals in all kinds of unions will continue to exert power over their mates. Spouses will be cruel and cold and passive and sad. They will grow bored with each other and manipulate each other and split. But the identity of the subjugated and the dominated will not be determined quite so reliably by the body into which a particular spouse is born. So, while marriage will never be perfect, it will become far more just and free for the women who enter it, both with other women and with men.

So profoundly has the notion of marriage's suddenly blunted inequities begun to sink in that, in 2013, *New York* magazine reported on straight couples who, anxious to find readings or text that represent the equitable unions they want to form, have chosen to read at their weddings from the Massachusetts Supreme Court case *Goodrich v Department of Public Health*, the first of its kind to legalize gay marriage.[31]

"Civil marriage is at once a deeply personal commitment to another human being and a highly public celebration of the ideals of mutuality, companionship, intimacy, fidelity, and family," reads the decision, in part. "Because it fulfills yearnings for security, safe haven, and connection that expressed our common humanity, civil marriage is an esteemed institution, and the decision of whether and whom to marry is among life's momentous acts of self-determination."

In this legal vision of marriage's nature and purpose, there is no hint of one power higher than another, no honor nor obeisance. There *is* mutuality, companionship, and the glorious choice, not only about *whom* to marry, but about *whether* to marry. In this new connubial world, there is a self, and it is determined.

## That Is Him

Ada Li was nineteen, living in Canton, China, when she met her first boyfriend. Now forty-one, she remembers him as a "very nice, nice boy." Her friends and family liked him, assured her that he was a good guy; it was obvious that he and Ada loved each other. After just a year of dating, he asked her to marry him. "Too young," recalled Ada. "I tell him I'm not ready. I say no."

Her boyfriend was devastated. She tried to explain that, in a few years, she might be ready. But he was so upset that he stopped speaking to her or returning her calls. Three months later, Ada learned that he had married someone else. "Then, *I* was so upset," she said. "He is a good guy, really nice. Why couldn't he wait?"

Ada, crushed, didn't want to risk further heartbreak with any of the other men who approached her in the wake of her breakup. "That feeling is horrible," she said. "You can't sleep, you can't eat." Three years later, she saw her ex on the street. He approached her and confessed that he was unhappy in his marriage. Ada asked him why he hadn't waited for her and he explained that the government company where he worked had been offering apartments to couples who married. So, Ada told me, almost two decades later, "He got married for an apartment. That is why. It was horrible. And that is why he doesn't feel happy. Because he knows [his wife] is not too good. They just want to marry for an apartment. That is stupid." Ada never saw him again, but her heartache lifted because, as she said, "After he tells me this story, I am not interested ever again."

As she got older, Ada faced tremendous pressure to marry. In her province in the 1990s, she said, being a single woman deep into her twenties was unusual. Her mother began worrying about her at twenty-five. She and her aunts directed young men her way. "They think maybe I am sick. Maybe she doesn't like man. It's like something is wrong when girl gets old and is still single." Ada was firm in her wish to not marry unless she was in love. "I don't want to marry a guy I don't love, just to marry with him," said Ada. "I don't care if he's handsome, I just want [that] I love him and he is good to me. That is what I want. But my parents and my aunt, they just want me married."

When Ada moved to New York in 2001 and worked as a seamstress, one of her coworkers kept trying to set her up with her nephew. Ada wasn't interested. The coworker suggested it again. Finally, Ada said, she agreed to call this man, since "sometimes, you need people to talk to."

She called him. "He is nice, talking," she remembered. She told him that if he wanted to meet her, he would have to take the train from Queens to Brooklyn; they planned to wear special jackets so that they would recognize each other on the street. When Ada saw the man in the long coat emerge from the subway, she thought, "That is him, maybe the person I want to marry. I just feel like that guy is nice. Maybe I will marry with him."

The man had married early and had two children; his wife had left him for another man. He had been raising his kids, then eleven and eight, by himself. Ada said she knew, immediately. "That man is good. It is really hard to take care of the two children." The two began dating, and Ada became pregnant. Despite obstacles with his mother, who worried that Chinese astrology portended poorly for the union, they married. They have been married for ten years and have a son together.

Recently, Ada's mother, sixty-two, and her father, sixty-eight, moved from China to live with her family in Queens. Her mother, born on a rice farm, educated only through the tenth grade, had entered her arranged marriage when she was nineteen, and later had two children. In New York, Ada said, her mother quickly blossomed. Her father, however, hated it, and quickly wanted to return to China. "My mom said, 'If you go back, you go back by yourself,'" said Ada. He did.

Now, Ada said, her mother looks happier, younger. In her first months in New York, Ada's mother, who does not read or speak any English, often got lost in the city's subway system. Now, said Ada, she takes buses and subways, zipping around Brooklyn, in and out of Chinatown. She has a job as a home-health aide.

"Now, she is so happy because she makes the money by herself," said Ada. The fact that she'd never had her own income, Ada suspects, had enabled her father to act meanly toward her mother. "When my mom would make breakfast for him, he would say, 'No, I don't want that!' That is not nice. It's why I sometimes say, 'Mom made it, just eat it, don't complain.' But that's why he went back to China. I always say to my mother, you need a change. Father, you need to change. The world is changed."

Mostly, Ada said, she is happy for her mother. "Her life is better," she said. "I think if time came back, she would want to do another thing, go to the school, don't get married early."

Today, Ada tells her twenty-two-year-old stepdaughter, Jennifer, "If you want to have power, do not just be thinking about getting married. You want your life to get better? Don't just think about being a wife." Ada credits her own decade of single life for her happiness. "Single time is when I learn how to take care of myself, how I know what I want," she said. "We have to understand that nobody can give you the best except for yourself. That is what I always tell Jennifer. I tell Jennifer don't get married too young. Make sure your boyfriend is nice, and that he push you to go the right way, not the wrong way."

Her stepdaughter, Ada tells me, often replies, "I am not that stupid. Don't worry."

Ada's story, her mother's history, and her stepdaughter's future, illustrate how, for all the statistics and numbers and data we can throw at the questions of marriage, singlehood, and how women move between the two, neither state is fixed. Transitions are fraught, complicated, unexpected. A doggedly single woman's mind can change with the emergence of a nice-looking man from a subway station; a lifetime of identifying as a dependent wife can be thrown off at sixty-two.

Or earlier.

## Marriage, Divorce, and In Between

Molly, a public defender in New York City, got married in her twenties to a kind man, whom she adored. Molly was raised in Utah, which, thanks to its large population of Mormons, has the lowest marriage age in the nation. Though she herself is not Mormon, Molly had absorbed some of the norms of the place where she grew up. When she met someone stable about whom she cared deeply, she married him. But, very soon into their union, she found herself feeling stifled. She and her husband shared professional and social passions, but she felt immobilized by their marriage. She recalled a night in which she tried to explain how she felt to her husband. "You're clipping my wings!" she wailed at him miserably. They divorced.

Molly's husband loved being married. In fact, he is married again, with children. He and Molly share custody of their dog and, until very recently, they shared office space. Molly, thirty-seven, did not love being married. She remains single.

While the improvements in marriage may make it more appealing to more women, they don't make it appealing to all women, who balk at its limitations, not just in advance of it but from inside it.

Heidi Sieck, forty-two, grew up in rural Nebraska, where most people got married early; she had a boyfriend whose parents hoped they'd marry. "I just didn't want to," she said. "I knew I needed to get out of Nebraska." She went off to college, and then to Washington, D.C., where she met a law student whom she described as being "out of a fairytale: tall and handsome and he went to Harvard and he was on *Law Review* and he played basketball and had a great family and was gregarious and fun." Sieck felt marriage was her guarantee of economic security and social status; she pushed to get engaged. However, as soon as she began planning the wedding, an eating disorder from high school reappeared, she began drinking too much, and stopped having sex with her fiancé. After their beautiful wedding, she had what she called "a full scale nervous breakdown."

Heidi began to understand that she had made "choices about marriage out of fear and economic insecurity and also out of scarcity—the fear that no man will ever love me." As it turned out, despite marrying a man who should have been the "perfect" partner, she hated being married. The union disintegrated. After five years of marriage and two years in couples' therapy, she asked for a divorce. They mediated a settlement without dispute within six months.

For the past twelve years, Heidi said, she has chosen to be single and self-sufficient. "I chose it, very specifically," she said. After the divorce, she quit drinking, pursued therapy, and earned a master's degree from Harvard, the institution that she used to brag about her husband having attended. "I'd thought I needed to marry into it, but my year there showed me that I could own it for myself," she said.

Heidi's husband loved being married. He is remarried, with children. Heidi and her ex remain friends; he was her lawyer for a business she started with some classmates from Harvard.

Through many lenses, the normalization of divorce has been terrifically liberating for women. It has allowed them to escape bad marriages, thus reducing rates of domestic violence; it has reduced the incidence of wives murdering their husbands and of children growing up in the shadow of miserably riven, but permanently bound, parents. For women like Molly and Heidi, divorce has been key to liberation.

It's also true, however, that divorce is among the most dangerous direct consequences of marriage. As numerous studies have shown, divorce leaves many women more unhappy, unhealthy, and impoverished than not marrying at all.

Thus, it is good news that women are marrying later and less frequently. The divorce rate, which skyrocketed in the 1970s, has been declining, slightly but steadily, since 1980, the years during which women increasingly opted to forego early marriage.[32] More strikingly, the people for whom the rates have plunged most dramatically are those who are staying single longest.

Interestingly, the segment of the population for whom the divorce rate has *risen* over the past twenty years is baby boomers (those born between 1946 and 1964), who married, often young, and at a moment before marriage had begun to be reformed.[33]

For those who are somewhere between single and married, or are unsure when or where or if they ever will land on one marital identity or another, there are millions of in-betweens. Hanna Rosin has described her realization that "we've invented this third kind of relationship which is sexually satisfying, emotionally satisfying, has a lot of intimacy and isn't on the road to marriage. It's hard to imagine, but it's a different kind of thing."[34]

I don't find it at all hard to imagine! It's how most of the people I've known of my generation have lived our lives: moving in and out of relationships of varying quality and duration. We have fallen in and out of love, in and out of lust. We've had great relationships that took us to new places, emotionally and sometimes geographically, and gruesome duds that have taught us volumes about what we *don't* want from life or partnerships.

Like our platonic friends, our partners, lovers, girlfriends, and boyfriends steer us through loss and grief and illness. I've had friends who have been with partners through cancer treatments and diabetes diagnoses, through the death of parents and the loss of jobs, who have later broken up with those people, with relief or with sorrow, good feelings or bitterness. But the experiences of having traveled through these defining moments of adulthood together are etched in them; the connection lingers. Our old partners don't cease to matter or to exist in our memories or in our makeup just because we don't marry them.

Journalist Jen Doll summed it up in her *Village Voice* piece on single women in New York: "The man who introduced you to really good bourbon; the guy with kids who helped you remember why you do, or don't, want them for yourself; the bisexual coworker; the 'poonhound;' the one that got away; and the one you let get away on purpose—they all have a place in your dating life. Don't regret them."

When and if we do decide to commit permanently to someone, we bring to the partnership the lessons and influence of our other, former partners. That's not a bad thing.

And while the marriage rate is low, our rates of unmarried cohabitation are surging. In a report about female reproduction in America in 2008, demographers found that nearly thirty percent of unmarried mothers were living with a committed partner, either of the same sex or the opposite sex.[35] Americans are not simply cycling through unmarried partners helter-skelter; they're moving in, committing to them in a way that may not be marriage, but is not any less real.

Living together without marrying works for lots of people who, for a variety of reasons, do not want to wed. It can assure legal independence, while giving couples a chance to see how they function together, how well they share space, whether they enjoy quotidian intimacy with each other. Cohabitation can be a leadup to marriage or an alternative to it, a way to gain some of the benefits of long-term partnership—daily contact and affection, bill splitting—without engaging a more formal and thus, confining, set of social and legal expectations. And they may be happier commitments.

The Gallup Organization visited 136 countries in 2006 and 2007, asking respondents if they had experienced a lot of love on the previous day. The groups least likely to have said that they experienced love were the divorced and widowed and, while married people responded affirmatively more often than single people, unmarried couples who lived together reported even more love than their married counterparts.[36]

### Independent Your Way to Loneliness

Anita Hill, pathologized as a desperate and crazed single woman in 1991, has, for many years, been in a long-term relationship with Chuck Malone. She met him at a restaurant not long after moving to Boston to teach at Brandeis University. The two live separately but see each other every day; they would marry, Hill said, "But I don't want to defer to convention. We'd marry each other, but we don't see why we should have to marry."

Their situation, Hill said, "Works. We are happy as we are."

"In some ways, I don't think of myself as the same single person status as I had before I got involved with Chuck," said Hill. "But I want people to understand that you can have a good life and not be married." This message is particularly important, she said, for black women. "We know what the numbers are and we know that specifically among African-American women the percentage of never-married women is higher than the general population," said Hill. "And I want everyone to understand that you can have a good life, despite what convention says, and be single. That doesn't mean you have to be against marriage. It just means that there are choices that society should not impose on you."

That Hill directs this message specifically at African-American women makes sense. They are the group who are most regularly told that their low marriage rates make them problematic. Many African-American women whom I interviewed for this book expressed a view that the partnership deck is stacked against them, in part because of their race and assumptions people make about them.

Journalist Dodai Stewart said that online dating worked best for her in her youth, because the men who clicked on her profile were just looking for a fun relationship. As she's gotten older, she imagines them saying, "I want to settle down and she's not going to be black." Stewart has had committed relationships with men who are Chicano and Korean, but said, "The numbers are against me. Black women are the bottom rung. Clicking through, men want to see young and they want to see white or Asian, maybe Latina. It's not just black guys. It's Asian guys, white guys . . . nobody wants black women, basically."

The dating site OkCupid studied this, and indeed found that "Men don't write black women back. Or rather, they write them back far less often than they should. Black women reply the most, yet get by far the fewest replies. Essentially, every race—including other blacks—singles them out for the cold shoulder."[37]

Meanwhile, television commentator Nancy Giles despairs of the shortage of attractive men for black women to partner with. She recalled watching Barack Obama speak at the Democratic convention in 2004 with a college friend, and both of them joking "Where was *he* at Oberlin? Where are all those guys and this new breed of educated, smart, funny black guys? When we went to school they weren't really there." When she considers online dating, she feels torn about pursuing men who aren't black. "It's difficult as a woman of color, because there are all these issues of betraying your race," she said, recalling a black friend who ignored the cat-calling of a homeless man on the street, only to have him yell after her, "You probably prefer white men! You're what's wrong with the black race!"

These are among the grim and often contradictory messages thrown at black women: you're too independent, no one will want you; there aren't any black men if you do want them; why don't you want a black man? Do you think you're too good for a man? You're what's wrong with the race. What's wrong with you?

"It all goes back to that *Newsweek* article about getting killed by a terrorist," said Giles. "It's mean and depressing. It's not even subliminal messaging, it's pretty much liminal: that smart women are going to end up getting punished." In that old *Newsweek* article, researchers asserted that an unmarried, thirty-year-old, college-educated woman had a 20 percent chance of marriage and, by forty, no more than a 2.6 percent shot. It was part of a panicky news cycle catalogued scrupulously by journalist Susan Faludi in her 1991 best-seller, *Backlash*, in which the message sent to independent women was that they faced a purported shortage[38] of men to marry.

The message that high-achieving women will be punished by spinsterhood has not abated in the past three decades, despite the evidence that high-achieving women are increasingly the *most* likely to marry. And, while almost no ethnicity or religion has been spared pro-marriage messaging, perhaps the most relentless spotlight has been trained on black women, not just by white conservatives looking to punish them politically, but by black men obsessed by black female independence, despite the fact that, as journalist Tami Winfrey Harris has pointed out, while 45.5 percent of black women over fifteen have never been married, 48.9 percent of black men in the same category haven't been either.[39]

Entertainer Steve Harvey has co-hosted several television specials focusing on successful black women whom he has urged to lower their standards to find men. In 2009, he published the best-selling dating advice book, *Act Like a Lady; Think Like a Man*, and took a similar message to *Oprah*. In 2011, R&B singer Tyrese gave an interview in which he spoke to black women "on this independent kick [who say] I don't need no man." To those women, Tyrese said, "You're going to independent your way into loneliness."[40]

In the midst of all these messages, it's easy to miss a reality: While patterns of marriage and independent life for African-Americans have *always* differed from the patterns of their white counterparts, the purported crisis of permanent singlehood for black women isn't quite as extreme as it's made out to be. In the *New York Times*, Angela Stanley, writing about how "few things are more irritating than the unsolicited comments I get that black women, like me, are unlikely to marry," refuted the popular claim that more than 70 percent of black women have never been married by pointing out that that percentage only applied to women between the ages of twenty-five and twenty-nine, and that, by the time black women turned fifty-five, only thirteen percent of them had never been married.

"Black women marry later," wrote Stanley. "But they do marry."

Susana Morris, English professor at Auburn University in Alabama, said that, while, in her thirties, most of her white friends are married and her black friends remain single, she doesn't feel anxiety about *marriage*, "I just would like to go on a date." Morris wants to find someone she can have a conversation with. "I'm interested in partnership [more than] marriage," she said. What *is* anxiety provoking, she continued, "Is that every time you open a magazine, a book, or turn on the television, you hear that something's wrong with you as a black woman. You're too fat, too loud, don't nobody want to marry you. *That* is anxiety producing." Echoing Stanley and Anita Hill, Morris argued that the "purposeful misdirection and misinformation" of the media's pathologizing of single black womanhood masks the fact that "single people are living in a variety of healthy ways that are just not being accounted for."

Writer Helena Andrews wrote, in 2012, about how "according to the data—and the media that are obsessed with it—I'm screwed. As a thirty-one-year-old, college-educated black woman who's never been married, everywhere I turn, the odds of finding a good man are against me. That is, of course, until I turn over every morning to the man sleeping next to me. He is (gasp) black. He is (*quelle surprise!*) college educated. He isn't a felon, a deadbeat, a father of illegitimate children, or a cheat—all the categories women like me are forced to choose from, according to the seemingly never-ending stories about the 'crisis' of black marriage. Attention, media! There is no crisis in my bedroom."[41]

## Marriage Has Its Benefits

When talking about her unmarried relationship with Chuck Malone, Anita Hill acknowledged that the improvisational nature of their bond is made easier by the fact that they do not have children. "It becomes much more complicated for women who want children and who would like to have a partner raising children with them," she said. Hill has also begun to understand some of the disadvantages that come with choosing to remain unmarried in a world still designed for married people.

Yes, as unromantic as it sounds, in a time when options for how to live and how to love have become more varied, the questions of whether and when and why to marry often come down to technicalities: benefits, health care, access, rights, and recognition. In fact, the desire for hospital access, next-of-kin proximity, of inheritance, and of healthcare were part of the root of the gay-rights movement's push for marriage.

Getting hitched remains the best, and often the only, way to secure a visa for someone not born into the United States, the precise problem that novelist Elizabeth Gilbert, who had sworn off marriage after the painful divorce that produced her runaway best-selling memoir, *Eat, Pray, Love*, encountered when her committed partner was barred from reentering the United States. They decided to marry, a circumstance so traumatic that it provoked Gilbert to write a follow-up book, *Committed*, that sifted through her deep ambivalence about the institution.

Until the recent enactment of the Affordable Care Act, people often married to secure health insurance. "I love my husband, live with him, and plan to stay with him indefinitely," wrote Nona Willis-Aronowitz in 2011, "Also, I wish we had never gotten married." Nona and her boyfriend got hitched only after an emergency-room visit resulted in questions from a health-insurance administrator about whether she could legally continue to cover him as her domestic partner. Nona's own parents, feminist cultural critic Ellen Willis and sociologist Stanley Aronowitz, both divorced after very youthful marriages in the mid-twentieth century, married each other "grudgingly" when Nona was fifteen, "only because they were worried that their partnership wouldn't adequately protect their property and assets." Nona didn't even attend their wedding; she was busy studying.[42] When Nona and her husband married, in order to get him on her health plan, she wore a black dress and flip-flops to Chicago's City Hall.

## Hard Out There

Here's the thing: for many of us, finding a person whom we want to marry, or move in with, or go on vacation with, or split bills with, is not so easy.

"There are such beings in the World perhaps, one in a Thousand, as the Creature You and I should think perfection," Jane Austen wrote to a niece. "Where Grace & Spirit are united to Worth, where the Manners are equal to the Heart & Understanding, but such a person may not come your way, or, if he does, he may not be the eldest son of a Man of Fortune, the near relation of your particular friend & belonging to your own Country."[43] Austen understood that it was not even a matter of finding the right person, but the rather more complicated prospect of finding the right person at the right time under the right conditions.

As it becomes more possible for us to provide for ourselves, it makes sense that our standards might rise even higher—far higher, in fact—than the standards of Austen's day, when alternatives to marriage were so grim. Contemporary women are perhaps likelier to have a full life that requires protection from the potential harm of a *bad* match, even when they badly wish to fall in love.

Elliott, the novelist from Washington, D.C., described herself as deeply sad that she hadn't settled down with anyone, yet acknowledged that she didn't regret not *settling*. "What's complicated," she said, "is that if I *had* really wanted to marry, I would have settled for one of the not-quite right relationships I had in the last ten years, but I didn't." On the one hand, she said, "I'm proud that I never settled for less than I wanted, but it's not like in return I got exactly what I did want."

Elliott has noted the changing nature of dating. "You don't sort of sweep each other off your feet anymore," she said. The realities of the world become known and better understood. She recalled going on dates with a man who admitted he was more than $100,000 in debt. "There was a time when that wouldn't have mattered," said Elliott. "But I don't have any debt, and I have to admit that it's scary, if you've been fiscally responsible and made your way in the world, to think about partnering up with someone who is so in the red."

Sweep-you-off-your-feet-debt-free potential mates do not grow on trees. And the fact that our lives can now be full enough *without* those spectacular others makes our standards soar even higher. The heightened bar is a side effect of all our independence: Back when women needed a man, truly *needed* one, to earn money, provide social standing and a roof, *needed* to be married in order to enjoy a socially sanctioned sex life or have children who wouldn't be shunned, standards could be lower. They were necessarily lower. A potential mate could more easily get away with offering only a pay check, a penis, and a pulse.

Today, women want much more, and holding out for better partners is part of how we're improving—and thereby saving—marriage.

The lion's share of finding love is luck, in tandem with privilege, since key to propitious circumstance is opportunity: the opportunities on offer to us when we are born, the resources and options made available to us as we grow.

These were the circumstances by which I wound up married: One night I was headed back to my apartment; I was planning to work late. When I got off the subway, I decided to stop at a favorite neighborhood restaurant, a place I frequented with my girlfriends, to get some takeout pasta. After I ordered, I sat at the bar to drink a glass of water, and noticed a handsome man sitting next to me, eating by himself at the bar. He was reading a magazine and drinking a glass of wine. I watched him in the mirror above the bar and felt, suddenly, that I wanted to know him. Unconsciously, I dropped my glass of water and it broke on the bar. He looked up, and we began a conversation.

I was neither looking nor *not* looking for love; I was looking for dinner.

There was no strategy. It might just as easily never have happened. There was nothing special about what I was doing or wearing or how I was acting or my approach to the relationship or whether he called me back. In fact, he was in the late stages of grief and initially hesitant about entering a relationship: If I had listened to the advice from *He's Just Not That Into You* I would never have pursued him, never wound up discovering exactly how easily we fell into each other.

The only action I took in my life that had a direct impact on meeting the man I wound up marrying was that I didn't marry anyone before him. This wasn't on purpose: I had wished many times that I could will myself into non-excellent relationships, because I had little evidence that better ones existed, and I thought that maybe I just needed to come to grips with the fact that if I really wanted to be in love, it wasn't going to be perfect.

But, mostly, I didn't pursue people I wasn't crazy about because I was busy doing other things that I enjoyed more than I enjoyed being with men I wasn't crazy about. That abstention meant that, when a good relationship with someone I *was* crazy about became a possibility, I was free to pursue it.

I wound up happily married because I lived in an era in which I could be happily single.

### Her Best Jeans

When she was sixty-six, Gloria Steinem, the feminist leader who said that she didn't want to marry because she couldn't mate in captivity, who said, "We are becoming the men we wanted to marry," who once called marriage a union of one-and-a-half people and ran away from her collegiate fiancé, got married.

She married David Bale, a South African environmental and animal-rights activist, in rural Oklahoma.

As Steinem tells the story of her long single life before Bale, "I had realized at about the time that feminism entered my life that a) I didn't have to get married," that "people (even women) could choose different lives and b) I couldn't marry anyway because I would be giving up my civil rights (credit rating, legal residence, name—etc. etc.)" Her adulthood was filled with relationships she entered "without imagining that they could or should lead to marriage, all the more so because I had discovered I was happy without children."

The same would have held true with her relationship with Bale, she said. "We loved each other and were together, but at our age—he was 59 and I was 65 when we met—there seemed to be no reason on earth for us to get legally married."

Except for all those pesky benefits.

Bale had been in the United States on a type of visa recently eliminated by Congress. He was concerned about immigration. The pair consulted with lawyers and was told that the surest way for Bale to secure a green card was through marriage.

Steinem said that she spent time considering how the women's movement had worked to improve marriage laws. She felt she would no longer lose her civil rights by marrying. She consulted with her close friend, Wilma Mankiller, former principal chief of the Cherokee Nation, who considered the question overnight, under the stars, and then advised Steinem to do it.

Steinem and Bale were already scheduled to travel to the Cherokee National Holiday powwow in Oklahoma. Once there, they drove to a small Oklahoma courthouse to get their marriage license. Steinem said that she was given a bag of detergent and various household cleaning samples that local merchants gave with each license. One of Bale's daughters, along with a couple of Steinem's friends who were already present for the Cherokee Reunion, were able to be there.

At dawn, Mankiller's husband, Charlie Soap, performed the marriage ceremony in Cherokee around an outdoor sage fire. Then a female judge and friend of Mankiller's did the legal ceremony. "We had a wonderful breakfast," said Steinem, "and that was it!"

Steinem said she was surprised by how quickly the press found out about their rural nuptials. Within a day, there was a lot of coverage, including a few bleats of disappointment from women who had wanted her to hold out, and a couple of hearty exclamations of victory that she had succumbed to the institution she had worked so hard to resist and alter. Mostly, though, reaction was warm; there was no anxiety that, at sixty-six, Steinem had forsaken any part of her independence, and people seemed happy that, for whatever reason, she had decided to do this thing she had not previously wanted to do.

When O, *The Oprah Magazine*, asked to print a wedding photo, she even sent a few in. "I got a message back: No, we want a *wedding* photo—you're wearing jeans in these." But, Steinem explained, "They were my *best* jeans!"

Before and during her marriage to Bale, Steinem recounted, he would attend campus events and speeches with her, and always wound up talking to the students for hours afterward. Steinem noticed how eager these students, mostly young women, were to "talk to a man who—because of our relationship and also because of who he was—showed [them] that you could be loved by a man without giving up yourself." Steinem hadn't realized, she said, "just how deep that hunger was, and how few the examples to feed it."

As it turned out, getting married was the right decision for Steinem and for Bale. "If we had not been married, David would not have been covered by my health insurance," she pointed out. "When he became ill with what was finally diagnosed as brain lymphoma about two years later—and was hospitalized or in a nursing home for almost a year—it would have financially broken everyone, including his children."

Bale died three years after marrying Steinem.

Retrospectively, Steinem said that, "the intensity of that time profoundly changed all of us." In a way, she continued, Bale's illness made her realize "what people mean when they say about a painful and tragic event: *But I wouldn't have had it any other way*. I think I was sent into his life to help him enjoy it more before leaving it. He was sent into mine to help me live intensely in the present."

Steinem's experience with marriage, she said, made her understand what she feels to be "the biggest remnant of old thinking" about the institution: idealizing and valuing it above all other types of loving relationships.

"Some people still assume that, because we got legally married, he was the love of my life—and I was his," said Steinem. "That's such a misunderstanding of human uniqueness. He had been married twice before and he had wonderful grown children. I had been happily in love with men who are still my friends and chosen family. Some people have one partner for life, but most don't—and each of our loves is crucial and unique."

# CHAPTER TEN

# Then Comes What? And When?
## Independence and Parenthood

Amanda Neville is a brand-and-content strategist, who was raised in Germany and Virginia, and now lives in New York City. In her early thirties, she got out of a serious relationship. Amanda had been interested in adoption ever since she'd seen a 2003 CBS special about older kids who needed homes, struck by the children's descriptions of what it felt like to go to adoption fairs, hoping that somebody picks you. "It broke my heart and planted a seed," she said. "I couldn't stand the thought of somebody not having a family or feeling like they have to do something to make somebody love them." Married very briefly to her college sweetheart in her early twenties, Amanda had discussed the possibility of adoption with her husband, but they had split before the plan grew serious.

She and the boyfriend she'd had into her thirties had already started the process of looking into adoption. She didn't intend to let a breakup stop her. "I haven't made any decisions in my life based on having a partner or not having a partner. Why would I make this one? It makes no sense." Single in her thirties, and eager not to let the absence of a partner derail her, she continued the adoption application process for Ethiopia, which permitted single-parent adoption at the time. While waiting for a match, she received a message from her adoption agent, telling her of a special child in Russia. Amanda visited Russia three times. She was thirty-five when she brought four-year-old Nina, who is deaf, home to New York with her.

"She is an amazing kid, loving and sweet and funny and I'm so glad the universe put us together," said Amanda. "But she is also a handful; it's been really hard." Nina, five, has new cochlear implants and is slowly learning to interpret sounds and some language; she and Amanda communicate by signing. Money is tight; Amanda runs her own consulting business; in 2013, she opened a wine shop. Childcare, even with Nina in public school every day until three, costs at least a thousand dollars per month. And because Nina sometimes has tantrums—a symptom, Amanda feels, of having spent so long in an orphanage where it was her only route to attention—they don't go out much. Amanda said the experience "has been really, really isolating."

Among the oft-cited trepidations of single women who are increasingly free to decide whether to have children on their own is this social isolation, and the accompanying fear that they will be putting romance on hold. But, soon after Nina came home, Amanda got an email from a man she'd met some months before, offering to help her. "He wrote and said 'I can't even imagine what you're going through, I don't know where I can even start, but I know how to cook and I can fix things and if there's anything you need, let me know.'" Amanda invited the man over. They soon began dating. At the end of 2013, he moved in with Amanda and Nina.

In reproductive biology, female liberty meets limits. Perhaps the most compelling evidence of the size, strength, and determination of America's single women to preserve their independence is the lengths to which they have gone, over the past four decades, to push right up against, bypass, and even alter, the deadlines set upon them by their bodies and reproductive systems. Contemporary women are redefining whether, when, and how they become mothers.

However, easy alternatives to the cold equations of child-bearing are not plentiful. Here is the math: There are a limited number of years during which most women's bodies can easily bear children. When most women got married and started families in their late teens and early twenties, the window of reproductive opportunity matched the window of marital expectation, binding the conjugal and the marital in a way that seemed, for a long time, inextricable. But those windows no longer overlap so neatly.

## Chicken or Frozen Egg

One of the big questions of changed marriage patterns for women and, with them, the delay of childbearing, is whether the mass movement toward later partnership and parenthood is what kick-started the explosive, enormously profitable field of fertility technology, or whether the development of new ways for women to extend their fertility created space and hope that allowed women to feel more comfortable postponing marriage and motherhood. It's impossible to say for certain which development caused the other, but they have blossomed coterminously.

The technology that now allows women to have babies later in life was not developed with single or late-partnered women in mind, but it was born in the same decade that would give rise to the professional, political, and sexual liberations on which today's single women have built full early adulthoods.

The first successful human product of in-vitro fertilization was born in 1978. Louise Joy Brown was referred to by a breathless press as a "test-tube baby;" she was the daughter of thirty-year-old Lesley Brown, who had married in her early twenties, and had been trying unsuccessfully to conceive for nine years. Two British doctors, Robert Edwards and Patrick Steptoe, had been thinking about how to fertilize an egg outside the human body since the 1950s, and had been working in earnest for over a decade on methods for how to achieve their futuristic goal. Before it was even successful, word of the work had leaked and inspired doomsday fears in the scientific community and popular press. James Watson, a Nobel Prize–winning biologist who in 1953 co-discovered DNA, told a 1974 congressional committee that the practice of making babies in Petri dishes would lead to "all sorts of bad scenarios" and that "all hell will break loose, politically and morally, all over the world."[1]

Watson was correct. When it comes to who can make babies, and how and when they do, all hell *has* broken loose; the rules and limitations that governed and shaped family life for generations have come apart. Today, around five million babies have been born thanks to in-vitro fertilization. In 2010, Robert Edwards, who had outlived his partner Steptoe, was awarded a Nobel Prize himself for pioneering IVF technology and changing the world.

The impact of what IVF makes possible for some women is truly astounding, and can be unsettling. In 2012, a sixty-one-year-old Brazilian woman gave birth to twins. The number of Australian women who gave birth after age fifty, has risen from eleven in 1996 to twenty-two in 2006 to fifty-three in 2011.[2] In England in 2010, 1,758 babies were born to mothers forty-five and older, compared to 663 in 2000.[3]

Fertility technology has changed the scope of reproductive possibility for single women who wish to have a baby without a partner and can now do so via sperm donor; it's changed the world for women who, for any number of reasons, find themselves wanting to have a baby deeper into their thirties, forties, and, yes, fifties, and for same-sex couples who want children. It has also remade the landscape for the women for whom it was invented: traditionally heterosexually partnered young women who might even have married young, but who experience fertility challenges and now have a better chance of having children.

The ability to fertilize an egg outside of a woman's body, without sexual congress between two human beings, has led to a host of other advances and reproductive improvisations that can extend and expand the scope of possibility for when and with whom (if anyone) we can have our children. Women and men now turn to egg donation, create a variety of surrogacy plans, freeze eggs for later use, and test the health and viability of embryos before even implanting them in uteruses.

Make no mistake: Fertility technology is no unalloyed good. It is prohibitively expensive for most people, costing thousands of dollars, sometimes hundreds of thousands of dollars, depending on the technology in question and the number of rounds it takes before success. It involves pumping hormones into bodies. And it often doesn't work, creating cycles of pain and loss and regret: The Centers for Disease Control and Prevention have reported that only 22 percent of medically assisted reproductive cycles lead to live births for forty-year-old women, and that number plummets to five percent by age forty-four,[4] though success rates change all the time, and new technologies, including egg donation and freezing, continue to alter the likelihood of success with every passing year.

Despite these drawbacks, the push of increasingly independent women against the barrier of their own fertility has not relented. The market that has been created for extended reproductive possibility is huge: Americans now spend around $5 billion on fertility treatments each year.[5] And, as marriage recedes decades deeper into female adulthood, the startling advances in fertility technology have helped make the worst fears of social conservatives more real: IVF has helped to make the heterosexual, nuclear family structure far less of a cultural, social, or biological imperative. It is no longer the only approved mechanism through which American society might reproduce itself. The world now brims with an infinite variety of familial configurations.

## Old Mamas

Among the most striking results of protracted female independence is that women are having babies later than ever before. The average age of first motherhood in the United States has shot from 21.4 in 1970 to 26 in 2013. More than four in ten births in 2010 were to women over the age of thirty, and one in seven was to women over thirty-five.[6] More than that: Of *first births*, eight percent in 2009 were to women over thirty-five, compared to just one percent in 1970.[7] The number of women giving birth after age thirty-five rose by 64 percent between just 1990 and 2008.[8]

The postponement of parenthood has brought its own set of challenges and peculiarities, among them the likelihood that if you are an unmarried woman over the age of twenty-four, you've read, heard, or been told something that has made you quite certain that your ovaries are withering and your eggs are going bad. Right now. This second. As you're reading this and *still* not doing anything about getting pregnant.

I was twenty-six in 2001, when the American Society for Reproductive Medicine put up ads all over New York City featuring an image of a baby bottle shaped like an hourglass, running out of milk. *Tick-tock, tick-tock.* "Advancing age decreases your ability to have children," read the copy. I remember watching a bus pass by me bearing this chilling message, followed directly by a bus plastered with an image of Carrie Bradshaw.

I was twenty-seven the next year, when economist Sylvia Ann Hewlett published her blockbuster book, *Creating a Life: Professional Women and the Quest for Children*, in which she warned that ambitious women were making a mistake by not marrying and gearing up to have babies in their twenties, because their egg quality began declining at twenty-seven, and plummeted at thirty-five. We were all deluding ourselves, she warned; we didn't know about our fast-fading fertility. *Tick-tock*.

The Hewlett book was a sensation. *60 Minutes* ran a segment on it. *Time* published a cover story called "Baby vs. Career;" it was either/or. *Tick-tock, tick-tock*. "Baby Panic" was the headline at *New York* magazine, where journalist Vanessa Grigoriadis interviewed one twenty-nine-year-old who described seeing the *60 Minutes* episode, then waking up the next morning, "and it's on the cover of *Time* magazine and *The View*. Everywhere I go, everyone's talking about the baby panic. It's like an epidemic! It's as though a disease broke out in New York and everyone's trying to *alert* you. 'Stay indoors! Emergency Broadcasting System: Your eggs are declining!'"

Grigoriadis, then twenty-eight herself, confessed her own fears. Through her twenties, she wrote, she had concentrated on her own plans, which "were about conquest and adventure: becoming a better writer, traveling the world, experimenting as much as I could before settling down at the last possible moment to start the perfect family, the one that I was sure to get if I lived life as I wanted to. . . . These days, the independence that seemed so fabulous—at least to those of us who tend to use that word a lot—doesn't anymore."[9] *Tick-tock*.

The egg-panickers' concern was not intended to be malevolent; it was intended to prevent young women from accidentally becoming the woman from that spoof of a Lichtenstein cartoon, the woman who cries "Oh, my God, I forgot to have a baby!"

But the intensity of this anxiety had its roots in other eras—truly. Writer Jean Twenge, who wrote a story about her own early thirties post-Hewlett meltdown about dwindling fertility, dug around and discovered that the oft-cited claim that only 30 percent of women between the ages of thirty-five and thirty-nine will get pregnant after a year of trying—a claim that was published in 2004 in the science journal *Human Reproduction*—was actually based on French birth records from 1670 to

1830. As Twenge pointed out, millions of women were being told when to get pregnant "based on statistics from a time before electricity, antibiotics, or fertility treatment."

Then there was more recent history: the post-Second-Wave generation who had hoed harder rows than we, their descendants. They had existed in smaller numbers, had more limited choices and harsher judgments imposed upon them, been bound more tightly by ideas about traditional family structure and timing. As a result, the birth rates for the paltry number of women who had had high-powered corporate careers were low.

But Hewlett and her cohort were making an error in assuming that past patterns would so directly apply to the vastly higher number of single women who were now overrunning the nation's cities, staying single—and keeping men single—later, and already helping to create a market that would push reproductive technology further than it had ever gone. After all, Hewlett published *Creating a Life* when she was fifty-six, the mother of five children, the youngest of whom was five. Sylvia Ann Hewlett had gotten pregnant, thanks to fertility treatments, at age fifty-one.

It was a testament to how committed professional single women were to the new kinds of lives they were living, that the terrifying threats of egg decline did not set off a wave of early marriage and dramatically lower the age of first birth.

Maybe single women didn't want to heed the warnings. More likely, it was because even if those warnings *were* provoking anxiety, there wasn't all that much they could do about it. Singlehood wasn't some outfit you could simply change out of when someone pointed out that it wasn't keeping you warm enough; the husband-free existences women were living couldn't change course with a snap of the fingers. These were their lives. What were they going to do?

I was twenty-seven, when my warm, maternal gynecologist finished an exam and updated me on the state of my fibroids, the benign tumors that were growing in my uterus, and would need to be surgically removed when I wanted to have children. I loved this doctor. As I sat up, she smiled and said "They're still growing, but everything else is fine. I just wish you would hurry up and get married, so we can stop worrying about them!"

I never went to see her again. This was my life. What was I going to do?

In her story, Jean Twenge smartly recalled a *Saturday Night Live* sketch from 2002. "According to Sylvia Hewlett, career women shouldn't wait to have babies, because our fertility takes a steep drop-off after age twenty-seven," began "Weekend Update" host Tina Fey. "And Sylvia's right. I *definitely* should have had a baby when I was twenty-seven, living in Chicago over a biker bar, pulling down a cool $12,000 a year. That would have worked out great."

Rachel Dratch was up next, noting, "Yeah, Sylvia. Thanks for reminding me that I have to hurry up and have a baby. Uh, me and my four cats will get *right* on that."

Amy Poehler added, "My neighbor has this adorable, cute little Chinese baby that speaks Italian . . . so, you know, I'll just buy one of those."

And Maya Rudolph said, "Yeah, Sylvia, maybe your next book should tell men our age to stop playing Grand Theft Auto III and holding out for the chick from *Alias*."

At the time they did this sketch, none of these four comedians had children. Today, as Twenge pointed out with satisfaction, they have nine between them, all but one born after they were thirty-five.

It's not that late parenthood is a perfect solution. The fact is, for many of my cohort, it *has* been harder to get pregnant than it might have been in our twenties. And, while so far, nearly all my friends who have availed themselves of fertility treatments eventually have had children, the few who haven't yet become parents have experienced terrible pain and high costs.

What's more, parenting in your late thirties and forties and fifties is physically taxing. As parents get older, the risks for having children with chromosomal abnormalities, developmental disabilities, and autism get higher. The fertility treatments endured by some older mothers who are having trouble conceiving can be grueling, and doctors do not yet seem completely sure that the high doses of hormones do not have any long-term side effects.

Another impact of older parenthood is that parents often wind up with fewer children than they might have otherwise. According to Lauren Sandler, whose book, *One and Only,* documented the rising number of only-child households, the percentage of women who have only a single kid has more than doubled between 1990, when it was just 10 percent and 2010, to 23 percent in 2013.[10] In part, that's because, when you start late, there's less time to keep going, and chances of secondary infertility are higher. But it's also true that many women who have delayed childbearing have done so for a reason: because of other commitments or hesitations, economic concerns or responsibilities against which they weighed the desire to have children. For these women, fewer children is not necessarily a negative outcome. In a country that continues to make it difficult for women to balance domestic and professional life, having one child can be a strategy to preserve financial stability, a good marriage, a robust sex life, a satisfying career.

Further, the realizations just beginning to dawn on America's women and men, thanks in large part to the number of them living independently for longer, is that while the world is full of people who love their children and are crazy about being parents, for many of them, parenthood is simply not the only, or the primary role from which they derive meaning and identity.

### Child-free by Choice

So hard-wired are our old assumptions about what shapes and motivates the lives of women, that the notion that some women may authentically, truly, in their deepest of hearts not want children has been among the hardest for us to wrap our minds around. A 2002 piece about Hewlett in *Time* magazine suggested to readers, "Listen to a successful woman discuss her failure to bear a child, and the grief comes in layers of bitterness and regret."[11] Embedded in this is the blanket assumption, so central to our lingering beliefs about gender identity: that for a woman not to have a baby is a *failure*.

But not according to lots of non-failing women.

"If I had kids, my kids would hate me," Oprah Winfrey recently told an interviewer. "They would have ended up on the equivalent of the

*Oprah* show talking about me; because something [in my life] would have had to suffer and it would've probably been them."

Winfrey seems to understand that when it comes to desires around motherhood, women are not all built alike. She compared her own personal trajectory to that of her best friend Gayle King, whom she explained was "the kind of kid who, in seventh-grade home-ec class, was writing down her name and the names of her children," said Winfrey. "While she was having those kind of daydreams, I was having daydreams about how I could be Martin Luther King."[12]

In 2009, Food Network star Rachael Ray, questioned by journalist Cynthia McFadden about how she had "famously said that you're too busy for children," explained, "I'm forty years old, and I have an enormous [number] of hours that have to be dedicated to work." Like Winfrey, Ray couldn't imagine a world in which work obligations would give way to childcare. "I feel like a borderline good mom to my dog. So I can't imagine if it was a human baby. Plus I also literally don't think . . . I can't imagine anybody giving me three or six months off to go physically have a child and take even a baby break. There is too much momentum and I feel like it would be unfair, not only to the child but to the people I work with."

It is too rarely acknowledged that there are millions of ways that women leave marks on the world, and that having children is but one of them. Motherhood has for so long been the organizing principle of female life that women's maternal status is often treated as the singularly interesting thing about them, often eclipsing all the other interesting things about them. When pioneering rocket scientist Yvonne Brill, the inventor of a system that prevented satellites from slipping out of orbit in space, died at age eighty-eight in 2013, her obituary in the *New York Times* began, before identifying her professionally, with this paragraph: "She made a mean beef stroganoff, followed her husband from job to job and took eight years off from work to raise three children. 'The world's best mom,' her son Matthew said."

Queries about whether childless women want kids, or are planning to have kids, or whether they regret not having them are posed often, whether the person in question is being interviewed about children or her professional life. "I'm not going to answer that question," thirty-three-year-old actress Zooey Deschanel told an interviewer profiling her for *Marie Claire* in 2013 who asked if children were on her priority list. "I'm not mad at you for asking that question, but I've said it before: I don't think people ask men those questions."

They don't. But, if they did, no one would be surprised to hear men cite other priorities, commitments, different ambitions, and other forms of attachment that they'd formed in the world as reasons why they don't have children, or as satisfactions that make it okay that they don't have children. Women have those other ambitions and satisfactions as well.

In a post called "Daughters of Dorothy Height," writer Robin Caldwell wrote of legendary civil-rights leader, who had just died, "Dorothy Height died childless, having never married. To some women that would be a sin and a shame. To me and countless others who appreciated her presence as a civil-rights activist and women's 'club' movement leader, she died leaving a multitude of daughters."[13]

In 2015, former *Sex and the City* star Kim Cattrall, asked about being childless, replied "I am a parent. I have young actors and actresses that I mentor. I have nieces and nephews that I'm very close to. . . . There is a way to become a mother in this day and age that doesn't include your name on the child's birth certificate.[14] You can express that maternal side of you very, very clearly, very strongly. It feels very satisfying."

In these sentiments, Cattrall and Caldwell are preceded by the original single monarch, Elizabeth Tudor, who replied to one of Parliament's periodic requests that she marry in 1558: "I beseech you, gentlemen, charge me not with the want of children, forasmuch as everyone of you, and every Englishman besides, are my children and relations"[15] and "after my death you may have many stepdames, yet shall you never have a more natural mother than I mean to be unto you all."[16]

Even if they don't have subjects, women have responsibilities to other human beings, to their work, their colleagues, to families who are not their own.

In the 1970s, one in ten American women concluded her childbearing years without having a kid. In 2010, it was almost one in five.[17] Some of the increase in childless women—around half,[18] in fact—can be attributed to the number of women who want children, but do not find a path to having them before their clocks tick out. The other half represents a population of women who, with alternate models of female life more visible and available to them than ever before, conclude that they do not want to have children, at least not as much as they want to do other things.

Historian Louise Knight spoke of how, for some of her subjects and for herself, a drive to create and write overwhelms the drive to procreate. "There is a real feeling, something inside of them that needed to be expressed," she said of Jane Addams and Sarah Grimké. "And I understand that for some women that thing is being a parent. That isn't inside of me, and if it were, I would have made other choices." Knight clarified that she didn't mean to imply that women who *do* have children don't have an urge for self-expression as well. "But they have child fire as well." Knight recalled being seven years old, watching her sister play with a baby carriage and doll, and experiencing complete befuddlement. "Why would you do that?" she recalled thinking. "But singlehood freed people like me to not pretend they have child hunger when they don't."

The freedom accrues not just to people like Knight, who have never married, but to women who *do* marry and don't feel a pull toward parenthood. The internet is home to thousands of sites that support the notion of coupled adults who are childfree by choice.

Journalist Piper Hoffman, a religious Jew, has written of how she and her husband slowly came to the realization that neither wanted to give up their work to raise children, despite intense pressure from religious family members and friends. She writes of how liberating it was to discover that there were communities of other people just like them, people who "lacked the drive to make and raise babies" and that they were happy! "They described enticing benefits, one of which particularly stood out for me: having their beloved to themselves and cultivating a devoted, satisfying relationship."[19]

Gloria Steinem told me that she regularly gets asked about whether she regrets not having had children, recalling the most memorable version of the question, which came at a women's center in a poor neighborhood in India. "Somebody asked me, 'Don't you regret not having children?' And I thought, 'If I'm honest, I'll lose them, because this is a very traditional [community]' but then I thought 'Well, what's the point of not being honest?' so I told the truth, which is 'Not for a millisecond.' And they applauded. Because they *have* to have children, so they were glad to know that you didn't have to."

The freedom of not "having" to have babies! It's real and it's making an impact on the world.

In his 2012 *New York Times* column, "More Babies, Please," Ross Douthat surmised that "the retreat from child rearing is, at some level, a symptom of late-modern exhaustion—a decadence that first arose in the West but now haunts rich societies around the globe. . . . It embraces the comforts and pleasures of modernity, while shrugging off the basic sacrifices that built our civilization in the first place."

Of course, some people's "decadence" is other people's "liberation;" the exhaustion with child-bearing and child-rearing that Douthat finds so troubling is the weariness of the women who have borne the children and, until very recently, raised them largely on their own, their "basic sacrifices" the sacrifices of individual identity, social relationships, or the pursuit of equality in the world.

And, while women may have nudged partnerships ever closer to parity and more evenly split sacrifice, the double-punch of biology and social policies still designed around breadwinning-men and baby-making wives mean that it's still women who must do the lion's share of the arithmetic: the tallying and risks and rewards, of lost wages and promotions, sick days and leave policies, pumping rooms and corner offices, that come with kids. Women are all too mindful of the variety of losses they incur should they choose to bear children.

"We're well aware that we lose fertility at a certain age," wrote Ann Friedman, "but also that we lose professional power after we have kids." [20] Singer Vanessa Carlton told journalist Jada Yuan about how her mentor, Stevie Nicks, once explained why, in her rock-and-roll youth, she never saw herself as a mother. "She said, 'I wanted to be respected by every single dude on that stage, and if I walked out and I'd made that choice, the dynamic would have been different.'"

## And By Circumstance

It's estimated that about half of women between forty and forty-four who have not had children aren't childless because they chose it, but because it happened to them.

Melanie Notkin's book, *Otherhood,* chronicles what she calls "circumstantial infertility," which she calls the "unrequited love story of our generation." For women like Notkin, not having kids wasn't a decision, and certainly not her desired fate. "The heartache over our. . . . childlessness due to being without a partner is exacerbated by the inexhaustible myth that we have chosen not to be mothers,"[21] she writes. Notkin calls women who yearn for children but do not have any of their own "childfull:" "We choose to fill our lives with the children we love like our nieces and nephews and friends' children."

Kristina leads a Girl Scout Troop in Bismarck. When she filled out the application, she said, "It seemed kind of creepy for a woman with no children." But Kristina loves kids. Plus, she said, "I think it's important for these girls to see that you can be thirty-five and be successful in your career outside of a marriage and having babies." For her, the Girl Scouts, "has been a vehicle to be part of children's lives and I guess maybe exercise my parenting muscles."

But an attachment to other people's children doesn't always fulfill the women who are childless not by choice, and not exactly by accident, but for some complicated set of reasons that fall somewhere between the two. It's not that these women haven't considered doing it on their own. As it becomes more common, it's almost impossible *not* to consider doing it.

Elliott, the D.C. novelist, described a conversation with a distraught friend who is thirty-eight and not in a relationship. "She always wanted to have kids, always wanted to be married and have a family," said Elliott. "But she has been crunching the numbers and feels like it is absolutely not possible [to do it on her own]. She's a teacher and is barely making it month to month."

Elliott herself moved to D.C. to be closer to her two nieces. Partly, she said, that move was about resigning herself to a future in which she would not have kids of her own. Financially and emotionally, she said,

"It would be too much work to do it on my own. I was never one of those people for whom it was going to be the be all, end all. So, making my peace with not being a mother was actually easier than making my piece with not having a partner."

In her mid-thirties, Elliott said, her maternal urges grew stronger. Then she wrote a book. "Part of why I no longer have that yearning is because I've given birth to another thing, and have been very satisfied, creatively." Elliott has started a second book, and said, "Maybe things work out the way they're supposed to. I'm really lucky to have had so much mental space to write."

When she was thirty-nine, Dodai Stewart wrote, in *Jezebel*,[22] of the "Ambivalence. Indecision. Fear." she faced at the realization that she might not wind up with kids: "As friends and colleagues get hitched and have babies, sometimes I start to feel like a straggler at a party. Everyone's gone home, what am I still doing here?" Stewart wrote of how the entertainment media bombards women with "mommy propaganda" about celebrity baby bumps and post-pregnancy weight loss, and the ongoing saga of actress Jennifer Aniston's empty uterus, in which, Stewart wrote, "[Aniston] is not a person but a character, a woman smiling and fit and happy yet apparently deeply sad that she's unmarried and childless." That narrative, Stewart observed, "Is a haunting reminder that if you're not doing what's expected of you—pairing up, mating, reproducing—you must be doing something wrong. Actually: *There must be something wrong with* you."

In a perfect world, Stewart went on, "It wouldn't even be an issue, it would be like, hey, you do you, I do me, everything's cool . . . But this world is baffling: you're meant to make something of yourself, work hard, contribute to society in a meaningful way. And once you fight tooth and nail to establish yourself. . . . you're chastised: 'What, no kids?'" Maybe, Stewart wondered, "instead of picturing myself as the straggler at the party, it's important to see beyond all the baby mama drama, recognize that on this side of the fence, there's plenty of love, good time, late nights, late mornings, travel, shopping, joy, indulgence, pleasure, accomplishment. . . . If I end up staying at this party instead of heading to the other party, it's still a party, and if we're not praised, we should praise ourselves."

Indeed, even for those who are bereft about childlessness, there can be other unexpected rewards.

Television commentator Nancy Giles said that throughout her life, she had always envisioned herself being a mother with one little daughter. At thirty-eight, she lost her mother. "After my mother died and I saw mothers and daughters on the street, I was in pieces," she said. When her mother died, both of her sisters were married with kids. "It was something they could fall back on: I gotta get up, gotta get the kids ready for school. They had a family unit to focus on. I was completely adrift, and I felt so alone." But, in the wake of her mother's passing, Giles wound up spending time with her father, something her sisters could not do. She forged a new and improved relationship with him. "For the first time in my life, I'm a daddy's girl!" she remembered telling her therapist. "Reconnecting with my father and feeling a kind of special love from him was wonderful. It happened late."

At no point, Giles said, could she imagine having had children on her own.

## Sisters Doing It for Themselves

But there are lots of women who do it.

Pamela, a twenty-four-year-old senior at City College, got pregnant accidentally, when she was seventeen. "I was stigmatized," she said. "I had all of these people on top of me saying what was I going to do, who was the father, and if he did exist, was I going to get married to him?" She did have a boyfriend, and lots of people, she said, pushed marriage on her, but she didn't see the benefit. "I wasn't going to tie him down if I got married," she said. "There wasn't going to be anything different if I got married." She's glad, in retrospect, that she did not rush to City Hall. Pamela believes that women making decisions about single motherhood need to carefully sift through the reasons they want to have children, with or without a partner. "You don't want to have kids, and then be financially dependent on somebody," she said. "You want to be able to sustain a life, even if the person did walk away, even if you didn't have the father there to help you out. I don't think there's a timeline to get married. I don't think it is necessary to get married."

But, she went on, "Society stigmatizes women who don't have kids." And it lays complicated traps for them. "People say you're not ready to have kids when you're eighteen to twenty-two, because you're still in school; it's too difficult. And it's true. It's difficult every single day. But, at the same time, later, I may have a career that requires my full attention, so when will I have time to have kids then? So, when am I going to have a kid? So, I don't know if there's a certain time frame when people should start trying to have kids."

Single motherhood is a norm for women in low-income communities, where early marriage has largely faded, but where parenthood can provide women with meaning and direction. It is also an increasingly accepted and available option for privileged women. For those who are single, but quite sure they want to have kids, and who decide they have the resources to do it, even conceiving of the possibility of having a child on one's own can be enormously liberating.

By the time I turned thirty, I'd been single for several years and my fibroids were worse than ever. I knew I was going to have to have surgery to remove them and, that, after the surgery, there would be a window of time before they grew back during which I might be able to get pregnant. In other words, I anticipated a curtailed reproductive window, and I had never been in a romantic relationship that I had ever found sustaining.

At thirty, I made a plan, determined to address the feeling I'd had when I left my gynecologist's office three years before: This was my life. What was I going to do?

I would plan to have a baby on my own. My parents would be supportive; they told me so. I would put away money, begin to prepare. When I turned thirty-four, I would have the operation, with an eye to getting pregnant, perhaps by a sperm donor, or maybe with one of my male friends, when I was thirty-five. A girlfriend and I spoke about the possibility of doing it at the same time, moving into adjacent apartments, helping each other with childcare and meals and companionship.

Even beginning to consider this scenario was incredibly freeing. It's not that I relished the idea: I hoped fervently that it wouldn't come to pass, that some person who was right for me would pop into my life by the appointed moment. But the fact that this other part of what I wanted from life—to make a family—didn't have to be lashed to that passive hope was exhilarating. The notion of even imaginatively separating the question of partnership from the question of parenthood felt liberating.

As it turned out, the timeline I'd mapped out as a single person fell into place, except with a partner. I fell in love at thirty-two, had major surgery at thirty-three, a baby at thirty-five and another at thirty-nine. I was unimaginably lucky, timing-wise, love-wise. I cannot say what would have happened in real life had I not been. I make no claim to the bravery that single motherhood entails, only to the fact that the imagined possibility of it enabled me to move forward with energy and optimism and a sense of familial agency.

Kristina, thirty-five and working in Bismarck, North Dakota, has been thinking about making the same kind of plan I did. She's begun to divorce the idea of marriage from children, prompted by her father, who suggested that she read an article about how you didn't necessarily need to do both at the same time. She recently went to a new gynecologist in Bismarck. "I was frightened. I knew I was thirty-five, and I really want kids." Kristina had an IUD set to expire when she was in her late thirties, and the new doctor remarked that they probably wouldn't have to fit her with a new one; Kristina freaked out at the implication that she'd be infertile by her late thirties.

But, to her surprise, her North Dakota doctor said, "You want kids? Well, just do it, Kristina!" It turned out that the doctor herself had had her first child when she was single and in med school. Kristina's New Year's resolution, she said, "is to prepare myself for when I hit thirty-six. I'm going to take care of myself, so I can make a baby. I am taking prenatal vitamins, and my nails and hair are awesome."

Law professor Patricia Williams was forty when a relationship in which she "most wanted my biological clock to be respected and it didn't happen" broke up. She said that it was at that moment that she "hit that crossroads where you ask yourself: Do you give up on the idea of having children?" She was fortunate enough, she said, "to have a marvelous career and remarkable parents who communicated to me that my ability to have children was not hooked onto a man, necessarily."

Williams had long felt that the boundaries placed around family and race were social constructions, and she was put off by the amount of money charged for in-vitro reproduction, wary of the idea that "a woman isn't a full woman until she has a baby." Williams was also interested in "alternative models of family, tribal models, adoptive models, kinship models. There are so many other alternatives to this very econometric model of family and marriage we have now."

Just on the cusp of her fortieth birthday, "People were basically saying 'It's now or never.' I didn't feel it was now or never, but that relationship ending was the moment that I really deeply felt that I could unhook the ability to have a child from the necessity of having a man."

Williams adopted a son.

The impact on how people viewed her, she felt, was immediate. Prior to adopting, she said, "I was viewed as this strong black woman who was a professional striver, a triumph of the race." The day she adopted, she said, "I was a single black mother." When her son was just five weeks old, she recalled, she was attending the Republican National Convention and wound up on a panel with Ralph Reed, of the Christian Coalition. Reed lit into her, upset, she said, that "I could adopt a child without a father. It wasn't just Ralph Reed. There were members of my family who felt exactly the same way." Within New York's private school system, Williams said, "People just assumed that because I was a single mother that I was somebody's nanny, whose generous family was paying for my son's education."

But the other line she got, she said, "Was that I was Mother Teresa and this child wouldn't have had a chance in the world. I hate that even more than the black single mother thing. This idea that he was a lost soul. He was a healthy, beautiful baby. I hate the narrative of necessary gratitude that I picked him up from the gutter. His biological parents were college students. But people just assumed that he was a crack baby."

Often, single motherhood is less of a consciously planned and considered identity.

When Letisha Marrero was thirty-five, and in a long-distance relationship that was coming to a close, she allowed herself a final romantic fling and fell pregnant. "At that point, I wanted to be a mother more than I wanted to be a wife," she said. "That was my purpose in life. And all the depression I've gone through, all the ups and downs all melted away once I got pregnant. For the first time in my life it became completely clear what I had to do. I never loved myself more than when I was pregnant. I had natural childbirth because I knew I might not have it again. I wanted to breastfeed as long as humanly possible."

When she was pregnant, Letisha was a copy editor for *Star* magazine. Her maternity leave paid half her salary but, when it was time to return to work, the reality of fifteen-hour workdays with no partner and a breastfeeding newborn hit her. She quit her job, and said that she lost three or four subsequent opportunities for work because of her inability to combine childcare with reasonable work hours. Her daughter's father has remained present in their lives but, when she lived in New York, he was only able to visit a few times a year, and he, too, struggled financially. After moving around the city, to ever cheaper apartments and rougher neighborhoods, Letisha recently moved to Virginia, where life is more affordable.

Through it all, Letisha said, "I was just going to forge a way. Forge a way for this little girl to have a life. She's never known if I had thirty-five dollars in the bank or thirty-five hundred."

## Baby Panic

There are a thousand things about the changing familial structures that result in later and fewer marriages for women that have critics on all ends of the ideological spectrum panicking. Some of the concern—Women having babies outside of marriage! And so few of them!—that sound like the Jackie Mason joke about the restaurant with terrible food and small portions. But the levels of nationally voiced anxiety about the damage that single and late-married women are doing to themselves and the nation is not at all funny for the women who find themselves caricatured and chastised by columnists and presidents for their part in altering the marital patterns that had for so long restrained them.

It is true that, as women marry later and not at all, and spend the non-wifely portions of their lives doing things besides or in addition to having children, there are fewer children being born in the United States. The general fertility rate has fallen, hitting an all-time low in 2013, with just 62.5 live births to 1,000 women of childbearing age, close to half the rate in 1957, when the baby boom hit its peak with nearly 123 births per 1,000 women.[23] No matter that that baby boom number was a socially constructed, freakishly high modern anomaly, and not a steady norm by which any of us should wisely measure the health of reproductive life in this nation. . . . some people are nonetheless *very* concerned.

Jonathan Last is concerned. His 2013 book, *What to Expect When No One's Expecting,* was subtitled "America's Coming Demographic Disaster." In a *Wall Street Journal* story about the low fertility rate, echoing the arguments Teddy Roosevelt had made about "race suicide" a hundred years earlier, Last wrote, "The root cause of most of our problems is our declining fertility rate," and that the fertility decline, while tied to wage stagnation, was also largely the doing of women. "Women began attending college in equal (then greater) numbers than men," wrote Last. "More important, women began branching out into careers beyond teaching and nursing. And the combination of the birth-control pill and the rise of cohabitation broke the iron triangle linking sex, marriage and childbearing."[24] While careful to note that some of these developments were positives, Last was clear that, "even social development that represents a net good can carry a serious cost." And that white, educated American women, whom he deems "a good proxy for the middle class," with their fertility rate of 1.6, meant that "America has its very own one-child policy. And we have chosen it for ourselves." Conservative columnist Megan McCardle is also concerned, and has warned that those who think that declining birth rates are no big whoop should look no further than Greece, to see "what a country looks like when it becomes inevitable that the future will be poorer than the past: social breakdown, political breakdown, economic catastrophe."

It's not just conservatives who are concerned. It's also our Democratic president, who does not publicly worry as much about population decline as he does the scourge of single-parented households. In a 2008 guest sermon on Father's Day, Obama framed his argument as a scolding of absent fathers—and specifically black fathers—whom he referred to as

"AWOL" and "MIA," and as "acting like boys." He blamed absent fathers as being partially responsible for poorer outcomes for black children, for higher dropout and incarceration and teen pregnancy rates.

Obama was careful to celebrate "heroic" single moms, rightly suggesting that "We need to help all those mothers out there who are raising kids by themselves . . . they need support," but ultimately concluding that the help they need is "another parent in the home," because "that's what keeps the foundation . . . of our country strong." In this, Obama—himself the son of an absent father, and yet the president—was reductively asserting that there is a single healthy and correct model for family, foundation, support. He affirmed that the two-parent, partnered home is the type of home to which we are all to aspire.

As Melissa Harris-Perry wrote about Obama's approach to single-parent homes, "President Obama is right when he points to the importance of loving, involved, financially responsible men in the lives of their children and their communities," but that he "lacks some imagination when it comes to analyzing the necessary ingredients for childhood success . . . odd given that the recipe is readily apparent in his own biography." That recipe, Harris-Perry suggested, included "an intergenerational support network, access to quality education, and opportunities for travel and enrichment."[25]

Obama is not alone in his conviction that single mothers are bad for kids. A 2010 Pew study showed that 69 percent of Americans believed the increase in single motherhood was a "bad thing for society" and that 61 percent believe a child needs both a mother and a father to grow up happily.[26]

Other liberal critics, including Gloria Steinem, worry that embracing not just single parenthood but single motherhood as a new normal has worrying implications. "It's really, really, really important that children see men as loving and nurturing parents," said Steinem, adding that, "It doesn't have to be your biological parent, not even your relative. But if we don't grow up knowing that men can be loving parents, or can parent, can nurture, then we're back in the stew of gender roles where we think only women can be nurturing."

Of course, societies need time, and generations, to adapt to profound changes in family structure. When women are freed from old expectations, new ways of coping or reorganizing the world are not instantly in place. We must work to adjust and change. Kathy Edin's follow-up work to *Promises I Can Keep* was a 2013 book on single fathers, *Doing the Best I Can*, written with Timothy Nelson. Edin spent time with inner-city, economically disadvantaged men who were more determined than the absent fathers of previous generations to forge bonds with and take responsibility for their offspring. Human beings change behaviors and then change again to accommodate new patterns. We cannot now simply look around us and say that this is how things will always be.

Yet for those women and men and children who *are* alive now, in today's conditions, these worriers have a serious—a very serious—point, backed up by research. Social scientists at the Brookings Institute found, in 2014, that kids whose mothers were married were far more likely to fare well economically than those of single parents.[27]

And as Bowling Green social scientist Susan Brown has written, roughly half of all children can now expect to spend some of their lives outside of a married parent family. Brown presents a number of studies that suggest that "Children living with two biological married parents experience better educational, social, cognitive, and behavioral outcomes than do other children, on average." But, in part because single parenthood is more prevalent in low-income communities, it's difficult to separate how many of the outcomes are influenced by the absence of married parents and how many are influenced by the economic challenges presented by poverty. As Brown writes, "Solo parents (typically mothers) who lack a partner to cooperate and consult with about parenting decisions and stressors tend to exert less control and spend less time with their children although those associations are confounded with socioeconomic disadvantage."[28]

As Brown writes, neither marriage by itself nor biology by itself is enough to explain the different outcomes for children in different family structures, and that "the task for future research is to develop more nuanced theory and richer data to decipher the mechanisms driving these differentials." Part of that theory and data is reliant on accepting new family structures, new roles for women and men, and examining how these new roles are supported by or thwarted by the social policy that still treats men and women as if they are all married to each other. What we must do is accept that we are living in a new world, and try to make that world more humane for all kinds of individuals, couples, and children.

Katie Roiphe, opinion writer and polemicist who, in her late twenties, described how her cohort of perpetual singletons enjoyed casual sex and professional ambition, but harbored not-so-secret longings for Jane Austen's connubial conclusions, by her early forties found herself the unmarried mother of two children by different men.

Roiphe now writes regularly, and compellingly, about single motherhood. In one *New York Times* piece she noted her own economic and educational privileges, acknowledging that while she may not be a "typical single mother . . . there is no typical single mother any more than there is a typical mother." It's the persistent ideas that an unmarried mother is one way—an aberrant way—Roiphe argued, "that get in the way of a more rational, open-minded understanding of the variety and richness of different kinds of families."[29]

Roiphe cites Sara McLanahan's ongoing Fragile Families studies, which show that the chief risks of single motherhood stem from poverty, and to a lesser extent from the introduction of a series of love interests to the family structure (possibly itself a danger worsened by poverty, with its higher risks that those love interests will be depressed, jobless, abusive, or a toll on the family finances), not from the simple setup of having children and not being married. In fact, Roiphe extrapolates from the Fragile Families study, "a two-parent, financially stable home with stress and conflict would be more destructive to children than a one-parent, financially stable home without stress and conflict."

"What gets lost in the moralizing conversation," writes Roiphe, "is that there is a huge, immeasurable variety in households," and that "no family structure guarantees happiness or ensures misery."[30]

## The Next Frontier

Like in-vitro fertilization, egg freezing was not invented as a panacea for single women. In fact, it was developed in the early 1990s by Italian doctors whose mission was to circumvent the Roman Catholic prohibition on embryo freezing that was preventing married women from using IVF to have kids.[31]

Until 2012, egg freezing was considered "experimental" by The American Society for Reproductive Medicine; in a 2012 statement, the society declared that in a series of trials, there seemed to be no marked difference between using fresh or frozen eggs in in-vitro fertilization treatments.

While egg freezing, in its early years, wasn't particularly reliable, new flash-freezing technology, called vitrification, which prevents ice crystals from damaging the egg, has raised success rates, which are now around 40 percent.[32] And, while the ASRM still does not endorse the procedure "as a means to defer reproductive aging," clinics are springing up in regions across the nation that are home to high concentrations of single and later-marrying women.

The freezing of eggs, as opposed to embryos, theoretically would allow women to preserve their eggs in advance of having met, or chosen, a man whose sperm they would use to fertilize them. This makes it the perfect technology for single women who still hope to meet a partner, but who do not want to risk losing their fertility in the process.

Like most of the technologies being developed to help women exert control over their reproductive lives, egg freezing does not come without costs, starting with the ten to twenty thousand dollars women must pony up for retrieval, freezing, and storage. The procedure involves hormone injections. There is still very little data showing exactly how effective it might be: Sarah Elizabeth Richards, author of *Motherhood, Rescheduled*, has pointed out that most women freeze eggs as a precaution, not because they are actively planning to use them. As a result, while, by the end of 2013, over ten thousand women had had the procedure, fewer than 1,500 had come back to use their eggs.[33]

And even though it's a tool that will, potentially, extend a woman's fertile years, it's also one that doesn't work nearly as well once you get past your peak fertility. Women over thirty-eight are often discouraged from freezing eggs that may have already declined in quality enough that freezing them would be a waste.[34]

That means that, if women are ever to really use egg freezing as a means to reliably extend their fertility, the price has to come down, and it needs to be an option that's encouraged in the middle of their fertile years, not at the end. That's a tough sell to young women, most of whom do not have or cannot fathom spending the money; do not necessarily want to go through the medical process, and who also want to believe that sometime down the road, they'll be in a position to do it the old-fashioned way. For most women, the idea of children remains tied to the idea of partnership. It's mentally very difficult to pull the two relationships apart in advance of a natural realization that they might not happen along the same timeline.

However, as egg freezing improves as a practice and shows higher success rates, some doctors—and bosses, including ABC anchor Diane Sawyer, who married for the first time at forty-two, and did not have children of her own—are urging women to consider egg freezing earlier. Nicole Noyes, one of the specialists at the NYU clinic to which Sawyer recommends patients, told *Newsweek* that three-quarters of her patients come to her because they aren't ready to have children yet, and that many of them are sent by their parents. One childless woman in her forties told *Newsweek*, "I want to send Diane a basket of flowers for what she's doing." In 2014, some Silicon Valley companies, including Apple and Facebook, announced that they would begin paying for egg freezing as part of their benefits packages.

Sarah Richards reported in the *Wall Street Journal* in 2013 that the age of egg-freezing candidates "is slowly coming down;" one study of the 240 women showed that the average age of women who got fertility consultations at a reproductive organization in New York between 2005 and 2011 dropped from thirty-nine to thirty-seven, and, Richards writes, "Several doctors say they are seeing a trickle of women under thirty-five—the turning point when a woman's fertility goes downhill and she is labeled 'advanced maternal age' on medical charts."[35]

It's an early hint of what a future could look like: It's not one in which everyone will be freezing eggs for exorbitant amounts of money, but in which our attitudes about the inseparability of childbearing from partnership begin to change. It's a future in which women might take in a measure of Hewlett's warning—*tick-tock*, don't forget to have a baby—and apply it to their increasingly independent young adult lives; a future in which it will be easier for them to distinguish between their choices about children and the mates who may or may not show up at the time they want them to.

While writing her book on egg freezing, Richards found that critics of the process for nonmedical reasons claimed that "biological deadlines serve a purpose in life," and that once removed, women would no longer have an incentive or drive to seek out a partner. But the women Richards interviewed, she wrote, "didn't use their frozen fertility as an excuse to date their DVRs. In fact, they said that egg freezing motivated them to take charge of their lives. They relaxed. They dated, married and thawed."

## This Is Not the End of the Story

In April 2013, my friend Sara turned thirty-nine. Since her return from Boston, she had had a series of jobs, found a new apartment that she loved, and extended and strengthened her social circle. She'd traveled (with me) on a work trip to Africa, visited Iceland and Cuba and celebrated the fortieth birthday of a single girlfriend with a week at surf camp in Costa Rica.

Sara had been in and out of relationships in her eight years back in New York. Some of them were casual, some long-lasting. As she entered her fortieth year, Sara missed some of her exes, but was making peace with being single, continuing to meet people, living the very full life she had built for herself.

About two months after her thirty-ninth birthday, she and I were on our way home from a dinner when she told me that she was going to see a doctor about having her eggs frozen. I was stunned. We had talked about children, but she had always maintained to me that she would never do it alone, that she was a romantic, that she was determined to hold out for partnership.

A week later, she called from outside the doctor's office: She was a good candidate; she was going to start the process immediately. She was giddy, as exhilarated and thrilled as I'd perhaps ever heard her.

"As soon as I got in there and started talking to the doctor," she told me in a rush, "I felt so sure, so empowered." Sara was invigorated. "I just suddenly felt like there was something that was in my control."

In fact, though the doctors had explained the timeline and suggested she begin it in a couple of months, Sara, who had gotten her period that very morning and understood that the process began at the start of her cycle, insisted that they start right then and there. By the next day, she was administering shots to herself.

Sara's procedure went beautifully. She produced lots of eggs and the doctors rated them as being very healthy. It was hard on her body: the hormones, the trigger shots, the extraction, the swelling of ovaries. She felt awful. And, also, when it was over, a little let down. She'd been through the hormone swings and whizzing excitement of baby-making-related activity, without actually having made the decision to get pregnant. But her eggs were frozen. She'd done something about her future family life that felt right for her.

In early November, Sara was over, and after dinner, she told me that she was beginning to feel a little lukewarm about a guy she'd been seeing casually. Maybe she still wasn't over a particular ex, she said. Then she paused and looked at me. "Or maybe," she went on, "I'm just figuring out that I am who I am, and that's a single person."

After freezing her eggs, she said, she had begun to reckon a little bit more with her own self-sufficiency, the fact that she was at her best when she was acting independently. "Maybe I'm just built to be on my own," she said, "And maybe that's really what makes me happy."

Ten days later, she phoned and warned me to sit down.

"I got married," she said.

To the guy she'd been seeing casually? I asked, shocked. No. To her ex-boyfriend, the one she'd had a hard time getting over. Their story was complicated, but the short version was that he'd gotten in touch, told her he wanted to spend his life with her. He knew about the eggs. He wanted to have kids. He loved her and didn't want to live without her. They'd gotten married at City Hall four days later in a dress she'd bought the afternoon before.

She was really happy.

Several weeks into her marriage, Sara and her husband were having some trouble adjusting to life together; they were thinking of perhaps keeping separate residences. And, while the notion appealed to them both equally, Sara was having difficulty reconciling it with her ideas of what "marriage" meant, based on the union of her parents, who that summer had celebrated fifty years together.

"It's just that we're both such independent people," she explained to me. "I've lived alone, just by myself; it's been eleven years since I've even had a roommate. Maybe that's how I like it, even though I love Bryan and want to make a life with him. I just can't process how different that would be from what I always thought of as *marriage*."

Sara wasn't sure what would happen: if they'd move in, if they'd have kids, if they'd stay together or decide to end it. She was sure of one thing: "Getting married that way, that quickly and without any fanfare," she said, "was the most freeing thing I've ever done, next to freezing my eggs."

Maybe, I said, it was because it best reflected their quirky dynamics as a couple. "Maybe," she said. "Or maybe it's just that it best reflected me, and what I want and don't want."

Sara wanted me to make clear that her marriage wasn't some kind of bow that tied her life up tight and happy. Sara was forty, right in the middle of her life. "And it's just so different from my parents' life," she said to me. She has no idea how it will turn out.

"Just please don't make it sound like the wedding was the end of my story," she begged.

# Conclusion

During the election cycles in the early part of the twenty-first century, much attention was paid, by both Democrats and Republicans, to single female voters, largely because of the dawning realization that they wield enormous electoral power.

In 2012, Barack Obama's campaign released a bit of campaign propaganda that featured a cartoon character woman named Julia. It illustrated how Julia was born, got a college degree, had a career and a child thanks, in part, to the aid to of government-sponsored programs. According to Julia's bare-bones timeline, her life did not include marriage. Conservatives went bananas. One *Washington Post* op-ed writer called her "Mary Tyler Moore on the government's dime," lamented that while single parenthood used to be a disgraceful state, single mothers now present "a new and proud American demographic," and called a world in which independent women benefit from their government a pitiable "hubby state" in which missing husbands are replaced by Uncle Sam.

The notion that what the powerful, growing population of unmarried American women needs from its government is a husband is of course problematic. It reduces all relationships women have to marital ones, and suggests that they are, by nature, dependent beings, in search of someone—if not a husband then an elected official or a set of public policies—to support them.

But putting aside what's wrong with those implications, both critics and celebrants of single women's impending union with government are getting it a little bit right. In looking to the government to support their ambitions, choices, and independence through better policy, single women are asserting themselves as citizens—full citizens—in ways that American men have for generations.

For if single women are looking for government to create a "hubby state" for them, what is certainly true is that their male counterparts have long enjoyed the fruits of a related "wifey state," in which the nation and its government supported male independence in a variety of ways. Men, and especially married wealthy white men, have long relied on government assistance. It's the government that has historically supported white men's home and business ownership through grants, loans, incentives, and tax breaks. It has allowed them to accrue wealth and offered them shortcuts and bonuses for passing it down to their children. Government established white men's right to vote and thus exert control over the government at the nation's founding and has protected their enfranchisement since. It has also bolstered the economic and professional prospects of men by depressing the economic prospects of women: by failing to offer women equivalent economic and civic protections, thus helping to create conditions whereby women were forced to be dependent on those men, creating a gendered class of laborers who took low paying or unpaid jobs doing the domestic and childcare work that further enabled men to dominate public spheres.

But the growth of a massive population of women who are living outside those dependent circumstances puts new pressures on the government: to remake conditions in a way that will be more hospitable to female independence, to a citizenry now made up of plenty of women living economically, professionally, sexually, and socially liberated lives.

We have to rebuild not just our internalized assumptions about individual freedoms and life paths; we also must revise our social and economic structures to account for, acknowledge, and support women in the same way in which we have supported men for centuries.

And while previous generations of women have offered their time and energies to the pursuit of social progress—abolition, suffrage, temperance, labor—today's single women are applying a more diffuse set of pressures: their very existence pushes us to alter the foundational policies, as well as the cultural and social expectations, that have historically made it difficult for women to thrive outside of marriage. Single women require new sets of protections that support their free lives in ways that will enable them to enjoy opportunities equal to those that their male peers have long enjoyed.

Of course, the policies that have held up the marriage model as the only model are incredibly varied: They range from the lack of subsidized childcare and school days that end in the mid afternoons (*Who*, after all, is meant to do the childcare if everyone is working? And who is supposed to pay for it if it is to be done by someone other than a nonworking parent?) to the Hyde Amendment, which prevents poor women from using any federal money to pay for abortions, making it difficult for them to exert control over the size of their families, their careers, their bodies.

As Anita Hill told me in 2013, the real fear of politicians and society about the increase in numbers of single women is the growing recognition that if women had sexual and professional agency, it would force us, as Hill said, "to think about women's work experiences differently, about the hours and days in the workplace, about the economic implications, the cultural and political implications" of women being full adults in the world.

"Single motherhood is not the bogeyman," Hill told me, by way of example. "The problem really is a lack of support for women who want to raise children. Part of the fear is that politically we have to make different decisions if we are forced to acknowledge that women might have children on their own. . . . There would be economic implications, cultural and political implications which we are still trying to sort through."

Single women are taking up space in a world that was not built for them. We are a new republic, with a new category of citizen. If we are to flourish, we must make room for free women, must adjust our economic and social systems, the ones that are built around the presumption that no woman really counts unless she is married.

In short, it is time to greet the epoch of single women that's upon us with open eyes and curious minds. If we do, we will travel the progressive path that Susan B. Anthony imagined winding away in front of her, the path that is now in front of us. By truly reckoning with woman as both equal and independent entity, we can make our families, our institutions, and our social contract stronger.

If our grandmothers and great-grandmothers, and their unmarried compatriots, could envision the radical future in which we are now living, it is incumbent on us to honor the work they did and walls they broke down by adjusting our own lenses. It's time to rebuild the world for the diverse women who live in it now, more freely, than ever before.

# Appendix

Here, then, are some policies, and some attitudes, that must be readjusted and readjudicated as the swelling numbers of unmarried American women move forward into the world:

- Stronger equal pay protections. This is perhaps the heart of what independent women require economically: the guarantee that their labor will not be discounted, in part because of leftover attitudes that they are not breadwinners, or that they are, by dint of their gender, likely to be supported by husbands.

- A higher federally mandated minimum wage. This is a benefit that would accrue to women and men, but from which women would especially profit, since they make up two-thirds of all minimum wage workers. A higher minimum wage would help to alleviate the burdens of poverty on America's hardest and least well-remunerated workers, bettering the lives of independent women, and also their potential romantic partners, friends, and family members with whom they are likely to live and perhaps raise families.

- We need a national healthcare system that encourages all women, across classes, to better monitor and care for their reproductive systems. We also need to have a system that covers reproductive intervention, so that those women who want to have babies on their own, or who wait until they are older—whether because they are waiting for a partner,

saving money, or doing other things besides parenting with the first decades of their adult lives—are able to avail themselves of the best medical
technologies to support parenthood, whether they are married or single,
and regardless of their income.

• Additionally, mandating that insurance companies cover IVF and
other assisted reproductive procedures would cut down on some of the
medical complications of assisted pregnancies, since prohibitive costs
would become less of a determinative factor for women choosing the
(often dangerous) option of implanting multiple embryos.

• We need to create more housing for single people, perhaps offering housing subsidies (and then, attendant tax breaks) for those single-
dwelling Americans who choose to live in small spaces that work better
for them and are better for the environment. This will also require reform
of the many state and local provisions that make it difficult for unrelated
adults to legally cohabit, since communal living is likely to be an ever
more frequent option for unpartnered Americans.

• We need government-subsidized or fully funded day care programs
that allow more families of every structure to thrive, and that create
well-paying jobs for childcare workers.

• Government must mandate and subsidize paid family leave for
women *and* men who have new children or who need to take time off to
care for ailing parents or family members. These policies would support
families of every shape and, if mandated for all new parents, go a long
way toward erasing stigmas associated with full-time fatherhood, creating the possibility of more equal domestic arrangements for women and
men, partnered or single.

• We need universal paid sick day compensation, regardless of gender, circumstance, or profession. Women who live independently or
within family units must be able to take sick days to care for themselves
or others without fear of losing their livelihoods.

• We should increase, rather than continue to decrease, welfare
benefits for all Americans, acknowledging that government assistance
has *always* been fundamental to life, liberty, and the pursuit of happiness in America, that stronger economic foundations help create the
conditions in which families, and partnerships, may be better able to
flourish.

• We need a system of economically supported leave time for Americans, regardless of whether they have children or parents to care for, so that they might care for *themselves*. And so that emotional, physical, and mental health benefits of leisure and time away from work do not accrue only to those who have traditional families.

• We must protect reproductive rights, access to birth control, and sex education, so that women do not get herded into dependency relationships due to unplanned pregnancies. To that end, we must eradicate the Hyde Amendment, which prevents poor women from exercising their right to obtain legal abortions. We must afford women in every economic bracket as much control as possible over when, if, and under what circumstances they have children.

• We need to support alternate family structures, including cohabiting friends, people who live on their own and in clusters, people who parent with partners and without. We need to adjust our eyes to a new normal that includes personal and familial configurations that do not look anything like the hetero married units of our past.

• There must be adjustments in the American attitude toward work, leisure, and compensation. We are increasingly a land of free people, who at various times in our lives enjoy companionship and care, and, at other times, do not. We must not continue to function as if every worker has a wife caring for his home and his children for free, or as if every wife has a worker on whose paychecks she must depend. We need shorter workdays, and more space cleared for social, emotional, psychological, and familial thriving.

# Where Are They Now?

**Dodai Stewart** is still single, but "feeling better, more relaxed and less rigid about dating these days. Not lowered standards, just more open-minded. I spent last year traveling a lot as well as going on Tinder and OkCupid dates. I'm currently seeing a guy who happens to be (significantly) younger, and that's been fun. In general, I feel pretty happy being free—I have been chatting with a few friends who are either divorced, going through a divorce, or just unhappily married and thinking about divorce, and I see myself through their eyes—what a luxury it is to live selfishly or self-indulgently, the Zen delight that comes from stretches of peaceful solitude (or uninterrupted book/Netflix time). I'd love to be in love but I've definitely reached new levels of self-love and self-acceptance. Things are good."

**Kitty Curtis** has moved from New Jersey to Florida, where she works as a hair stylist. She remains single, is making friends, and is very happy.

**Ann Friedman** still lives in Los Angeles. She recently moved in with her partner, who moved from his home in England to join her in Los Angeles. In 2015, she and Amina launched a podcast about long-distance friendship, titled "Call Your Girlfriend."

**Aminatou Sow** lives in Northern California. She and Ann co-host "Call Your Girlfriend." She is single.

**Ada Li's** father decided he didn't like living without his wife in China, and so returned to join her in the United States. But things are different now. Ada's mom happily works two jobs, has her own money, and, said Ada, "Tells my dad *no*. Everybody's happier now. She is really independent." Ada's stepdaughter remains unmarried and has begun graduate school. She has a boyfriend whom Ada likes very much.

**Patricia Williams** has, in her early sixties, begun "a relationship with a man with whom I reconnected after decades. We'd been good friends in our twenties before losing touch. Having been quite resolutely independent most of my life, it's both odd and wonderful to be grappling anew with the intimate negotiation that deep commitment requires. It helps that we were friends to begin with, yet, at this stage of life, I think we're both more able to sustain a solid, quietly grounded union. I don't think we would have had the same lovely ease in our twenties as we have now. It was worth the wait."

**Caitlin Geaghan** did take flying lessons and became engaged to her instructor. "I couldn't be happier," she said. "He has been more supportive of me than anyone else in my life." Caitlin said she's doing well at work, and has recently been promoted to a senior project management position. She travels frequently, including recent trips to Ireland, California, and Utah. "I realize this is quite a change" from her earlier rejection of youthful marriage, Caitlin said. "I just happened to stumble upon the right person earlier than I thought I would." Caitlin said she still believes that early marriage is risky. "I don't think that it never works, but I do feel that it is a rare thing to make a marriage work at any age, especially with the societal pressures that have historically been put on women."

**Elliott Holt** has moved to Paris and was startled to remember how she'd felt about being single at the time of our interview. "When you interviewed me a few years ago, I was still working my way through grief about the end of a serious relationship," she said. "I was still mourning the life I might have had, as part of a couple. I still yearned for a partner and life companion. But now, I savor my life of solitude. I'm grateful that I never married and I have no desire to pair up with anyone. Even dating seems like too much work. I don't want to give up my precious time to go on dates with people I don't know. When I socialize, it's with people I've known for years. I may be single, but I have plenty of love in my life (the love of friends, of my sisters, of my three nieces, and my nephew). I love living on my own terms. I'm committed to my single life and I can't imagine giving it up."

**Alison Turkos** is "single, living in Brooklyn, most likely funding abortions or talking about her deep love of Vermont. She's still completely confident that she does not desire to parent or get married—but thanks for checking!"

**Sarah Steadman** got married "to the guy I was dating during the interview for this book. We just recently moved to San Antonio where I will be teaching sixth-grade social studies. Married life is great and I'm happy!"

**Amanda Neville** says, "In a six-month period, my mom died, a beloved pet died, my partner and I broke up, and then another pet died. I spent months reading *Dinosaur's Divorce* to Nina every night and Nina held funerals for her stuffed animals and dolls for weeks. It was like being in a riptide with a child on my back—I was engulfed in grief but I had to keep it together for her. We eventually adopted two more pets and, that summer I made sure to plan lots of fun things for us to do together and we slowly started to feel normal again. Nina is thriving and I'm slowly healing. I still have days where I feel really raw, but I feel strong. I know it will take time and I'm focusing on taking care of her, our pets, and myself in the meantime."

**Meaghan Ritchie** graduated from college in the spring of 2015, and began a job teaching at an elementary and middle school, working with students who have moderate to severe disabilities. She also worked as a student teacher for four weeks in Piacenza, Italy, which she called "one of the best experiences of my life." Meaghan is "still single, and in no rush to change that. I firmly believe you have to be happy and content with yourself before you can be happy with someone else. I have never been happier and I'm so excited to see what the Lord has planned for me. For now, I am just living life and trying to bring glory and honor to Him."

**Carmen Wong Ulrich** left her job as president and co-owner of a financial planning firm to work in entertainment. Her feelings about economic independence have changed since the time of her interview. "Now, I feel we have to be careful that with our independence we reject the possibility of interdependence. We're human and if we're lucky enough we'll live a long time, which means we'll suffer setbacks. We're not invincible as women and there's nothing wrong with asking for help or accepting it."

**Nancy Giles** had been looking for "a guy with two basic requirements: a great sense of humor and the ability to return phone calls." She unexpectedly connected with one with that and more, and they've "been calmly keeping company."

**Kristina** is now in a committed relationship with a man. As soon as she met him, she made it clear that she was planning to have children, on her own if need be. In the past year, she lost two pets and had her IUD removed. She is happy.

**Letisha Marrero** and her daughter Lola moved from their cramped apartment in Virginia to a home in Maryland where they now live with Lola's father. Although marriage isn't on the table at this juncture, the couple is committed to each other and to raising their now ten-year-old daughter together. While finding work-life balance and managing finances remain ongoing challenges, Letisha wouldn't trade her experiences of being a mom for anything.

**Holly Clark** said that she respects "the women who decide motherhood is for them, but now I have a career to be proud of, and I have found a man who is just fine with the amount I work. We are going to be house searching in the next few months and marriage and children are something in our future. And I won't have anything to give up."

**Susana Morris** is happily single and living in Atlanta.

**Pamela** is working as a legal assistant at the Office of the Bronx District Attorney. She says she is "applying to law school and hoping for the best."

She is expecting her second daughter and remains with the same partner; they are not married.

**Sara** and her husband are no longer together. Sara left. Not because she didn't want to be married, but because all the things she took that leap for were not happening. She struggled with the idea of getting out of a marriage quickly, she said, emphasizing "I looked at it like a true partnership, whether with a friend or a man . . . For me, it didn't have to match with prevailing ideas of what marriage should look like, but it had to be truthful about what it was. And it wasn't truthful and it didn't work for me."

# Acknowledgments

When I set out to write this book, I had a gut feeling that Marysue Rucci would be its editor. I'm so lucky that it worked out that way. She has remained patient and clear-eyed as its size and scope have shifted; she has steered me capably. At Simon & Schuster, I am grateful for the enthusiasm of Jonathan Karp, and for the diligence and good will of Emily Graff, Laura Regan, Sydney Tanigawa, Sarah Reidy, Cary Goldstein, and Ebony LaDelle. My wonderful agent, Linda Loewenthal, has supported me through many stages of book writing; I thank her always.

Rhaina Cohen was just an undergraduate when she first offered me her research services. Yet I could not have conjured a more brilliant, dedicated, or capable associate; her work was fundamental to the shape and content of this volume.

This book profited from those with expertise in fields outside my own. Thanks to Michelle Schmitt, Brittney Cooper, Susana Morris, Louise Knight, Emily Nussbaum, Mikki Halpin, and Virginia Heffernan for corrections and affirmations. I learned much from discussions with friends and colleagues including Leslie Bennetts, Katha Pollitt, Linda Hirshman, Nora Ephron, Gail Collins, Anna Holmes, Irin Carmon, Amina Sow, Adam Serwer, Joan Walsh, Lizzie Skurnik, Dahlia Lithwick, Jen Deaderick, Michelle Goldberg, Kate Bolick, Eric Klinenberg, Molly Gallivan, Alice Rubin, and Mark Schone. Thanks to J. J. Sacha for brokering a couple of introductions and to Madeleine Wattenbarger for careful transcription. I am forever indebted to Erin Sheehy for her thorough fact-checking.

I'm especially grateful to those who read portions of this book at its earliest stages: Zoë Heller, Katha Pollitt, Rich Yeselson, Michelle Goldberg, Irin Carmon, Anna Holmes, Barbara Traister, and Jean Howard.

To all those I interviewed, on and off the record, who were so generous with their stories: thank you. My deep admiration also for the dozens of scholars cited in these pages. As the daughter of academics, I am keenly aware of my own scholarly limitations and am grateful for the historians, sociologists, literary critics, and economists on whose work I have drawn here. I feel lucky to know the historians Rachel Seidman and Amy Bass well enough to have asked them to take a look, and lucky too to have had the voice of Northwestern's Carl Smith in my head for twenty years, nudging me always toward history. I've learned so much from the faculty and students at the many colleges and universities I've visited, and especially thank Denise Witzig at St. Mary's in California, who shared with me her syllabus for a class about the Bachelor Girl and provided this project its earliest roadmap.

Thanks to those editors who have born with me, including Lauren Kern, Adam Moss, Laurie Abraham, Lisa Chase, Robbie Myers, Greg Veis, Chloe Schama, Gabriel Snyder, Ryan Kearney, Michael Schaffer, Franklin Foer, Kerry Lauerman, and Joy Press.

Friendships with Kimberly and Lin-Lee Allen, Judy Sachs, Lisa Hollett, Becca O'Brien Kuusinen, Michael Freidman, Abbie Walther, Benedicta Cipolla, Heather and Edward McPherson, Tom McGeveran, Lori Leibovich, Hillary Frey, Zoe Heller, Katie Baker, Allison Page, and Merideth Finn have long sustained me. To Sara Culley and Geraldine Sealey, this book is, by many measures, for you.

Finally, deep gratitude to, and for, my family. Barbara and Daniel Traister provided a retreat from domestic responsibilities; feeding me and giving me space to work for weeks at a time. Aaron and Karel Traister kept me laughing and Pheroze Wadia kept me talking. Jean Howard and Jim Baker regularly saved the day. Rosie was born days after this book was sold, Bella days after the manuscript was handed in; Marion Belle has provided exceptional care for them and in doing so, made my work and my husband's work possible. Rosie and Bella, your lives will be filled with possibilities that your great-grandmother, whose story is recounted here, could never have fathomed, and I'm so excited to see what you make of them. And to Darius: we were each whole people when we met, and you've made the whole of me happy, every minute of every day since. Thank you for our crowded, crazy life.

# Selected Bibliography

Addams, Jane. *The Spirit of Youth and the City Streets.* New York: MacMillan, 1909.

Alcott, Louisa May. *An Old-Fashioned Girl.* Seven Treasures Publications: 2009.

Alexander, Michelle. *The New Jim Crow: Mass Incarceration in the Age of Color Blindness.* New York: New Press, 2010.

Bartlett, Elizabeth Ann, ed. *Sarah Grimké: Letters on the Equality of the Sexes and Other Essays.* New Haven: Yale University Press, 1988.

Baxandall, Rosalyn and Linda Gordon, eds. *America's Working Women: A Documentary History, 1600-The Present, Revised and Updated.* New York: W.W. Norton & Company, 1976 & 1995.

Bennett, Judith M. and Amy M. Froide, eds. *Singlewomen in the European Past, 1250–1800.* Philadelphia: University of Pennsylvania Press, 1999.

Bolick, Kate. *Spinster: Making a Life of One's Own.* New York: Crown, 2015.

Brown, Kathleen M. *Good Wives, Nasty Wenches, and Anxious Patriarchs: Gender, Race and Power in Colonial Virginia.* Chapel Hill and London: The University of North Carolina Press, 1996.

Burnap, George Washington. *The Sphere and Duties of Woman: A Course of Lectures.* Baltimore: John Murphy, 1848.

Chambers-Schiller, Lee Virginia. *Liberty, A Better Husband: Single Women in America: The Generations of 1780–1840.* New Haven and London: Yale University Press, 1984.

Chevigny, Bell Gale. *The Woman and the Myth: Margaret Fuller's Life and Writings.* Revised ed. Boston: Northeastern University Press, 1994.

Clinton, Catherine and Michele Gillespie, eds. *The Devil's Lane: Sex and Race in the Early South.* New York: Oxford University Press, 1997.

Collins, Gail. *America's Women: Four Hundred Years of Dolls, Drudges, Helpmates and Heroines.* Paperback ed. New York: Harper Perennial, 2004/2003.

———. *When Everything Changed: The Amazing Journey of American Women from 1960 to the Present.* New York: Little, Brown and Company, 2009.

Coontz, Stephanie. *Marriage, A History: From Obedience to Intimacy or How Love Conquered Marriage.* New York: Viking, 2005.

———. *A Strange Stirring: The Feminine Mystique and American Women at the Dawn of the 1960s*. New York: Basic Books, 2011.

Cott, Nancy. *Public Vows: A History of Marriage and the Nation*. Cambridge: Harvard University Press, 2000.

———. *The Bonds of Womanhood: "Woman's Sphere" in New England, 1780–1835*. New Haven: Yale University Press, 1977 and 1997.

DePaulo, Bella. *Singled Out: How Singles are Stereotyped, Stigmatized, and Ignored, and Still Live Happily Ever After*, New York: St. Martin's, 2006.

Dubois, Ellen Carol, ed. *Elizabeth Cady Stanton and Susan B. Anthony: Correspondence, Writings, Speeches*. Introduction by Gerda Lerner. New York: Schocken Books, 1981.

Edin, Kathryn and Kefalas, Maria. *Promises I Can Keep: Why Poor Women Put Motherhood Before Marriage*. Paperback ed. Berkeley and Los Angeles: University of California Press, 2011 and 2005.

Ephron, Nora. *Crazy Salad: Some Things About Women*. New York: Alfred A. Knopf, 1975.

Faludi, Susan. *Backlash: The Undeclared War Against American Women*. New York: Crown, 1991.

Firestone, Shulamith. *The Dialectic of Sex: The Case for a Feminist Revolution*. New York: Bantam Books, 1971.

Friedan, Betty. *The Feminine Mystique: Twentieth Anniversary Edition*. New York: Laurel Books, 1983.

Giddings, Paula. *When and Where I Enter: The Impact of Black Women on Race and Sex in America*. New York: Bantam Books, 1984.

Gilbert, Elizabeth. *Committed: A Love Story*. New York: Penguin, 2010.

Glenn, Cheryl. *Rhetoric Retold: Regendering the Tradition from Antiquity Through the Renaissance*. Southern Illinois University: 1997.

Goldman, Emma. *Anarchism and Other Essays*. Second revised ed. New York and London: Mother Earth Publishing, 1911.

Goldstein, Dana. *The Teacher Wars: A History of America's Most Embattled Profession*. New York: Knopf Doubleday, 2014.

Gordon, Ann D. *The Selected Papers of Elizabeth Cady Stanton and Susan B. Anthony, Volume I, In the School of Anti-Slavery, 1840–1866*. New Brunswick: Rutgers University Press, 1997.

Gould, Stephen Jay. *The Mismeasure of Man: The Definitive Refutation to the Argument of the Bell Curve*. New York: W.W. Norton & Company, 1996.

Gunning, Sandra. *Race, Rape, and Lynching: The Red Record of American Literature, 1890–1912*. Oxford and New York: Oxford University Press, 1996.

Guy-Sheftall, Beverly, ed. *Words of Fire: An Anthology of African-American Feminist Thought*. Afterword by Johnnetta B. Cole. New York: The New Press, 1995.

Hadfield, Andrew, ed. *The Cambridge Companion to Spenser*. United Kingdom: The Press Syndicate of the University of Cambridge: 2001.

Hamilton, Susan, ed. *Criminals, Idiots, Women & Minors,* second ed., Ontario: Broadview Press, 2004.

Hayden, Dolores. *The Grand Domestic Revolution*. Cambridge and London: The MIT Press, 1981.

Henry, Astrid. *Not My Mother's Sister: Generational Conflict and Third-Wave Feminism*. Bloomington: Indiana University Press, 2004.

Hill, Anita Faye and Emma Coleman Jordan, eds. *Race, Gender, and Power in America: The Legacy of the Hill-Thomas Hearings*. New York: Oxford University Press, 1995.

Israel, Betsy. *Bachelor Girl: 100 Years of Breaking the Rule—A Social History of Living Single*. Paperback ed. New York: Harper Perennial, 2003.

Kessler-Harris, Alice. *Out to Work: A History of Wage-Earning Women in the United States*. New York: Oxford University Press, 1982 & 2003.

Klinenberg, Eric. *Going Solo: The Extraordinary Rise and Surprising Appeal of Living Alone*. New York: Penguin, 2012.

Last, Jonathan. *What to Expect When No One's Expecting: America's Coming Demographic Disaster*. New York: Encounter, 2013.

Le Faye, Deirdre, ed. *Jane Austen's Letters, Fourth Edition*. Oxford: Oxford University Press, 2011.

Lovett, Laura. *Conceiving the Future: Pronatalism, Reproduction and the Family in the United States, 1890–1938*. Chapel Hill: University of North Carolina Press, 2007.

Maines, Rachel P. *The Technology of Orgasm: "Hysteria," The Vibrator, and Women's Sexual Satisfaction*. Baltimore: Johns Hopkins University Press, 1999.

May, Elaine Tyler. *Homeward Bound: American Families in the Cold War Era*. New York: Basic Books, 1999.

———. *Barren in the Promised Land: Childless Americans and the Pursuit of Happiness*. Cambridge and London: Harvard University Press, 1995.

Meyerowitz, Joanne. *Women Adrift: Independent Wage Earners in Chicago, 1880–1930*. Chicago: University of Chicago Press, 1988.

Moran, Rachel F. "How Second Wave Feminism Forgot the Single Woman." *Hofstra Law Review*. Volume 33, Issue 1, article 5. 2004.

Morton, Patricia, ed. *Discovering the Women in Slavery: Emancipating Perspectives on the American Past*. Athens: University of Georgia Press, 1996.

Norton, Mary Beth. *Founding Mothers and Fathers: Gendered Power and the Forming of American Society*. New York: Alfred A. Knopf, 1996.

———. *Liberty's Daughters: The Revolutionary Experience of American Women 1750–1800*. 1996 paperback ed. (Cornell Paperbacks). Ithaca: Cornell Press, 1980.

Peiss, Kathy. *Cheap Amusements: Working Women and Leisure in Turn-of-the-Century New York*. Philadelphia: Temple University Press, 1986.

Randall, Mercedes Moritz. *Improper Bostonian: Emily Greene Balch, Nobel Peace Laureate, 1946.* New York: Twayne Publishers, 1964.

Roiphe, Katie. *Last Night in Paradise: Sex and Morals at the Century's End.* New York: Little, Brown and Company, 1997.

Rosenberg, Rosalind. *Beyond Separate Spheres: Intellectual Roots of Modern Feminism.* New Haven: Yale University Press, 1982.

Rosenthal, Naomi Braun. *Spinster Tales and Womanly Possibilities.* Albany: State University of New York Press, 2002.

Sandler, Lauren. *One and Only: The Freedom of Having an Only Child and the Joy of Being One.* New York: Simon & Schuster, 2013.

Sawhill, Isabel V. *Generation Unbound: Drifting into Sex and Parenthood Without Marriage.* Washington: Brookings Institution Press, 2014.

Smith, Margaret, ed. *The Letters of Charlotte Brontë, Volume Three: 1852–1855.* Oxford and New York: Oxford University Press, 2004.

Smith-Foster, Frances. *Till Death or Distance Do Us Part: Love and Marriage in African America.* New York: Oxford University Press, 2010.

Smith-Rosenberg, Carroll. *Disorderly Conduct: Visions of Gender in Victorian America.* Paperback ed. New York: Oxford University Press, 1986/1985.

Stansell, Christine. *City of Women: Sex and Class in New York City 1789–1860.* Paperback ed. Urbana and New York: University of Illinois Press, 1987/1982.

Sugrue, Thomas J. *Sweet Land of Liberty: The Forgotten Struggle for Civil Rights in the North.* Paperback ed. New York: Random House, 2009.

Traub, Valerie. *The Renaissance of Lesbianism in Early Modern England.* Cambridge: Cambridge University Press, 2002.

Trimberger, Ellen Kay. *The New Single Woman.* Boston: Beacon Press, 2005.

Vapnek, Lara. *Breadwinners: Working Women and Independence, 1865–1920.* University of Illinois, 2009.

Walsh, Joan. *What's the Matter with White People: Finding Our Way in the Next America.* New York: Simon & Schuster, 2012.

Watson, Elwood and Darcy Martin, eds. *There She Is, Miss America: The Politics of Sex, Beauty and Race in America's Most Famous Pageant.* New York: Palgrave MacMillan, 2004.

Willard, Frances and Hannah Whitall Smith. *The Autobiography of an American Woman: Glimpses of Fifty Years.* Evanston: National Women's Christian Temperance Union, 1889.

# Notes

### Introduction

1. Mather, Mark and Diana Lavery, "In U.S. Proportion Married at Lowest Recorded Levels," *Population Reference Bureau*, 2010 http://www.prb.org/Publications/Articles/2010/usmarriagedecline.aspx.

2. According to Robert B. Bernstein at the Census Bureau, in 1979, the median age rose to 22.1.

3. Mather and Lavery, "In U.S., Proportion Married at Lowest Recorded Levels," 2010.

4. Cohn, D'vera, Jeffery S. Passel, Wendy Wang and Gretchen Livingston, "Barely Half of U.S. Adults Are Married—A Record Low," Pew Research Center, December 14, 2011, http://www.pewsocialtrends.org/2011/12/14/barely-half-of-u-s-adults-are-married-a-record-low/.

5. Mather and Lavery, "In U.S., Proportion Married at Lowest Recorded Levels," 2010.

6. Betts, Hannah, "Being Single by Choice Is Liberating," *The Telegraph*, March 21, 2013.

7. Roiphe, Katie, *Last Night in Paradise,* via *New York Times* excerpt, 1997, http://www.nytimes.com/books/first/r/roiphe-paradise.html.

8. Gardner, Page, "Equal Pay Day: Unmarried Women Bear the Brunt of the Pay Gap," The Voter Participation Center, August 13, 2015, http://www.voterparticipation.org/equal-pay-day-2015/.

9. Mather, Mark and Beth Jarosz, "Women Making Progress in U.S. But Gaps Remain," Population Reference Bureau, 2014, http://www.prb.org/Publications/Reports/2014/us-inequality-women-progress.aspx.

10. "America's Families and Living Arrangements: 2014: Adults" (Table 1A), United States Census Bureau http://www.census.gov/hhes/families/data/cps2014A.html *via* Lake Research Partners, "The Power of Unmarried Women," The Voter Participation Center, March 2012.

11. Fry, Richard, "No Reversal in the Decline of Marriage," Pew Research Center,

November 20, 2012, http://www.pewsocialtrends.org/2012/11/20/no-reversal-in
-decline-of-marriage/#src=prc-newsletter.

12. Anthony, Susan B., "The Homes of Single Women," October, 1877. Anthony's essay
is cited in many texts, including *Elizabeth Cady Stanton and Susan B. Anthony:
Correspondence, Writings, Speeches*, with critical commentary by Ellen Carol Du-
Bois and a foreward by Gerda Lerner (New York: Schocken Books, 1981), 148–149.

## Chapter One: Watch Out for That Woman

1. See also, "drapetpomania" a purported mental illness reported by physician Sam-
uel Cartwight to be suffered by slaves fleeing captivity. Here is the imagination of
disease when someone who has been disempowered becomes empowered. Cited
by Melissa Harris-Perry on "Melissa Harris-Perry," MSNBC, April 7, 2014.

2. Safire, William, "The Plot to Savage Thomas," *New York Times*, October 14, 1991
http://www.nytimes.com/1991/10/14/opinion/essay-the-plot-to-savage-thomas
.html.

3. Hill, Anita Faye, "Marriage and Patronage in the Empowerment and Disempower-
ment of African American Women," in *Race, Gender and Power in America*, 283.

4. Patty Murray in conversation with Karen Finney at *The Atlantic*'s "Women in
Washington" event, September 25, 2013.http://www.murray.senate.gov/public
/index.cfm/newsreleases?ContentRecord_id=bc16d80a-aca9-43cc-864a-c645ab
30c2cd.

5. "Social Indicators of Marital Health and Well-Being," State of Our Unions Report, 2011, http://www.stateofourunions.org/2011/.social_indicators.php.

6. *Anita: Speaking Truth to Power*, directed by Frieda Mock, Goldwyn Films,
2013.

7. Quayle, Dan, "The Murphy Brown Speech," May 19, 1992 via Michael A. Cohen's *Live From the Campaign Trail*, 2008, http://livefromthetrail.com/about-the
-book/speeches/chapter-18/vice-president-dan-quayle.

8. Hymowitz, Kay, Jason S. Carroll, W. Bradford Wilcox, Kelleen Kaye, "Knot Yet:
The Benefits and Costs of Delaying Marriage in America," The National Marriage Project at the University of Virginia, The National Campaign to Prevent
Teen and Unplanned Pregnancy, and the Relate Institute, 2013, http://twenty
somethingmarriage.org/summary/.

9. Friedan, Betty, *The Feminine Mystique*, 1963/1983, 1.

10. "1.4 million copies . . ." Menand, Louis, "Books as Bombs: Why the Women's
Movement Needed *The Feminine Mystique*," *The New Yorker*, January 24 2011.
"Credited with having kicked off . . ." attributed to, among other places, Nora
Ephron's "Miami," published in *Crazy Salad*, 37–46.

11. Henry, Astrid, *Not My Mother's Sister*, 64.

12. Episode One, *Makers: Women Who Make America*, PBS, February 26, 2013.

13. Friedan, Betty, "The National Organization for Women's 1966 Statement of Purpose," October 29, 1966.

14. Guy-Sheftall, Beverly, *Words of Fire*, 97. Via Coontz, *A Strange Stirring*.

15. "In 1970 . . ." from "Median Age at First Marriage: 1890 to the Present," U.S. Census Bureau, Decennial Censuses, 1890 to 1940, and Current Population Survey, Annual Social and Economic Supplements, 1947 to 2014 and via The U.S. Census Bureau.

16. Friedan, Betty, "Up From the Kitchen Floor," *The New York Times Magazine*, March 4, 1973.

17. Friedan, Betty, *The Feminine Mystique*, 18–19.

18. "Gloria Steinem 'Irons Out' a Few Things with Moses Znaimer," CBC, November 4, 1968, http://www.cbc.ca/player/Digital+Archives/CBC+Programs/Television/The+Way+It+Is/ID/2575079962/.

19. Steinem, Gloria, letter to *Time*, September 16, 2000.

20. Moran, Rachel F., "How Second Wave Feminism Forgot the Single Woman," *Hofstra Law Review*, vol.33, issue 1, article 5, 2004.

21. Cott, *Public Vows*, 199.

22. Faludi, *Backlash*, 108.

23. Moran, Rachel F., "How Second Wave Feminism Forgot the Single Woman," *Hofstra Law Review*, vol. 33, issue 1, article 5, 2004.

24. "Percent Never Married Among Those Aged 35 and older by Sex: 1890–2010" from Elliott, Diana B, Kristy Krivickas, Matthew W. Brault, and Rose M. Kreider, "Historical Marriage Trends from 1890–2010: A Focus on Race," 2012. U.S. Decennial Census (1890–2000) American Community Survey (2010), http://www.census.gov/hhes/socdemo/marriage/data/acs/Elliottetal PAA2012figs.pdf.

25. Rivers, Caryl, "Newsweek's Apology Comes 20 Years Too Late," *Women's eNews*, June 14, 2006, http://womensenews.org/story/uncovering-gender/060614/news weeks-apology-comes-20-years-too-late.

26. This exact figure is 57.5 percent, according to the Centers for Disease Control.

27. "Marriage, More than a Century of Change," National Center for Family and Marriage Research at Bowling Green State University, July 18, 2013.

28. Martin, Jonathan, "A New Firm Sets Out to Secure Women's Votes for a Vulnerable G.O.P.," *New York Times*," November 11, 2013.

29. Lake Research Partners Election Eve Omnibus, November 4–6, 2012.

30. Last, Jonathan V., "Start a Family . . . And Before You Know It, You'll be Voting for the GOP," *Weekly Standard*, April 22, 2013.

31. Stan, Adele M., "After a Generation of Extremism, Phyllis Schlafly Still a Leading General in the War on Women," *Alternet*, April 22, 2012.

32. Kotkin, Joel, ""Demographic Dead End?" Barack Obama's Single Nation," *The*

*Daily Beast*, October 18, 2012, http://www.thedailybeast.com/articles/2012/10/18
/demographic-dead-end-barack-obama-s-single-nation.html.

33. Gardner, Page, "How Unmarried Women Can Change the World," *Role Reboot*,
August 18, 2015, http://www.rolereboot.org/culture-and-politics/details/2015-08
-how-unmarried-american-women-can-change-the-world/.

34. Babbin, Jed, "Fluke the Welfare Queen," *The American Spectator*, March 12,
2012, http://spectator.org/blog/29164/fluke-welfare-queen. Via Joan Walsh,
*What's the Matter With White People*.

35. Sawhill, Isabel V., "Beyond Marriage," *New York Times*, September 13, 2014.
http://www.nytimes.com/2014/09/14/opinion/sunday/beyond-marriage.html.

36. Wakeman, Jessica, "Bad Advice? Or Worst Advice? Mitt Romney Urges 3012
College Grads to Get Married, Have Kids," *The Frisky*, May 1, 2013, http://www
.thefrisky.com/2013-05-01/bad-advice-or-worst-advice-mitt-romney-urges-2013
-college-grads-to-get-married-have-kids/

37. Last, Jonathan V., "America's Baby Bust," *The Wall Street Journal*, February 12,
2013.

38. Carmon, Irin, "Pregnancy is Patriotic!" *Salon.com*, February 21, 2013, http://www
.salon.com/2013/02/21/decoding_the_fertility_panic/?source=newsletter.

### Chapter Two: Single Women Have Often Made History

1. "That it please your Majesty . . ." Hadfield, Andrew, *The Cambridge Companion
to Spenser*, 191; "I have long since . . ." Glenn, Cheryl, *Rhetoric Retold*, 162; "one
mistress and no master . . ." *Oxford Dictionary of Political Quotations*, 2012; "If I
am to disclose to you . . ." Traub, Valerie, *The Renaissance of Lesbianism in Early
Modern England*, 128.

2. Bennett and Froide, *Singlewomen in the European Past*, 6–7

3. Nellie Bly interview with Susan B. Anthony, *The World*, February 2, 1896, http://
www.rarenewspapers.com/view/621269?acl=851761768&imagelist=1#full-im
ages&rc=blog.

4. Gordon, Ann D., *The Selected Papers of Elizabeth Cady Stanton and Susan B.
Anthony*, 316.

5. Norton, Mary Beth, *Founding Mothers and Fathers*, 39–40; 41.

6. Baxandall, Rosalyn and Linda Gordon, *America's Working Women*, 17.

7. Kessler-Harris, Alice, *Out to Work*, 11.

8. Cott, Nancy, *Bonds of Womanhood*, 27.

9. Chambers-Schiller, *Liberty: A Better Husband*, 11.

10. Dubler, Ariela, "In the Shadow of Marriage: Single Women and the Legal Construction of the Family and the State," *The Yale Law Journal*, May 1, 2003, http://
www.highbeam.com/doc/1G1-102910521.html.

11. Cott, *Bonds of Womanhood*, 22.

12. Moran, Rachel F., "How Second Wave Feminism Forgot the Single Woman," *Hofstra Law Review*, vol. 33, issue 1, article 5, 2004.

13. Norton, *Liberty's Daughters*, 299.

14. Chambers-Schiller, *Liberty, A Better Husband*, 1.

15. Goodbeer, Richard, *Sexual Revolution in Early America*, 200.

16. Foster, *Till Death or Distance Do Us Part*, 37. Foster's book also included the reference to Harriet Ann Jacobs' *Incidents in the Life of a Slave Girl*, 1861.

17. Hanger, Kimberly S., "The Fortunes of Women in America: Spanish New Orleans's Free Women of African Descent and Their Relations With Slave Women," in *Discovering the Women in Slavery*, 153–178.

18. Hanger, Kimberly S., "Free Black Women in Colonial New Orleans," in *The Devil's Lane*, 226.

19. *The Young Lady's Book: A Manual of Elegant Recreations, Exercises and Pursuits.* London: Vizetelly, Branston and Co, 1829, 28.

20. Welter, Barbara, "The Cult of True Womanhood: 1820–1860," *American Quarterly*, Volume 18, Issue 2, Part 1, Summer 1966.

21. Collins, *America's Women*, 92.

22. Chambers-Schiller, *Liberty, A Better Husband*, 41.

23. Burnap, George Washington, *The Sphere And Duties of Woman: A Course of Lectures*, Baltimore: John Murphy, 1848, 121–122. Via Chambers-Schiller, *Liberty, a Better Husband*.

24. Chambers-Schiller, *Liberty, A Better Husband*, 54.

25. Ibid., 10.

26. Goldstein, Dana, "The Chicago Strike and the History of American Teachers," *Dana Goldstein*, September 12, 2012, http://www.danagoldstein.net/dana_gold stein/2012/09/the-chicago-strike-and-the-history-of-american-teachers-unions .html.

27. Goldstein, "The Woman Upstairs and the Pedagogy of Love," http://www.dana goldstein.net/dana_goldstein/2013/06/the-woman-upstairs-and-the-pedagogy-of -love.html.

28. Betsey "A Letter About Old Maids," *The Lowell Offering*, October 1840, 4–5.

29. Olson, Lynne, *Freedom's Daughters: The Unsung Heroines of the Civil Rights Movement 1830–1970*, New York: Scribner, 2001. Via excerpt, *The New York Times*, http://www.nytimes.com/books/first/o/olson-daughters.html.

30. Israel, *Bachelor Girl*, 33; *Encyclopedia of African American History, 1619–1895*, Paul Finkelman, ed. 332.

31. Governor's Address on "the emigration of young women to the West," March 29, 1865, http://archive.org/stream/reportma00mass/reportma00mass_djvu.txt. Via Collins, *America's Women*.

32. Vapnek, Lara, *Breadwinners*, 19–20.

33. Chambers-Schiller, *Liberty. A Better History*, 7–8.

34. "The Stakeholder: A quarterly publication of the Cherokee Strip Regional Heritage Center," Winter, 2008.

35. Chambers-Schiller, *Liberty, A Better Husband*, 2–3.

36. "Transcript of the Morrill Act," 1862, http://www.ourdocuments.gov/doc.php ?flash=true&doc=33&page=transcript; Linda Eisenmann, *Historical Dictionary of Women's Education in the United States*, 275. Via Chambers-Schiller, 191.

37. Peischl, Bridget Smith, "The History of Mississippi University for Women," *Mississippi History Now*, March, 2012, http://mshistorynow.mdah.state.ms.us/articles/379/the-history-of-mississippi-university-for-women.

38. Chambers-Schiller, *Liberty, A Better Husband*, 176.

39. Ibid.

40. "Myra Bradwell v. State of Illinois," 1873.

41. Gould, Stephen Jay, *Mismeasure of Man*, 135–137. Also via Chambers-Schiller.

42. Gould, Stephen Jay, *Mismeasure of Man*, 135–137.

43. Chambers-Schiller, *Liberty a Better Husband*, 192.

44. Ibid.

45. Ibid., 196.

46. Cott, *Bonds of Womanhood*, 7.

47. Peiss, Kathy, *Cheap Amusements*, 34.

48. Goldstein, Dana, "The Chicago Strike and the History of American Teachers' Unions," *Dana Goldstein*, September, 12, 2012, http://www.danagoldstein.net /dana_goldstein/2012/09/the-chicago-strike-and-the-history-of-american-teachers-unions.html.

49. Giddings, Paula, *When and Where I Enter*.

50. Peiss, *Cheap Amusements*, 57–58.

51. Ibid.

52. Coontz, *A Strange Stirring*, 41.

53. Coontz, *Marriage: A History*, 200.

54. "Before the Mother's Conference," *A Compilation of the Messages and Speeches of Theodore Roosevelt*, 576.

55. Lovett, Laura, *Conceiving the Future*, 91–92.

56. I first found reference to this in Coontz, *Marriage a History*, 201, though some discrepancy about Sumner's date of death led me to Bruce Curtis, "Wlliam Graham Sumner on the Family, Women and Sex" in *Victorians Abed*, 101.

57. Hamlin, Kimberly A., "Bathing Suits and Backlash: The First Miss America Pageants, 1921–1927," in *There She is, Miss America*, 28.

58. Coontz, *A Strange Stirring*, 45.

59. May, Elaine Tyler, *Homeward Bound*, 95.

60. Ibid, 101.

61. Heidel, Don, "Coeds: Is It Too Late? Manless Juniors Said Old Maids," *The Florida Flambeau*, February 22, 1957. Via Gail Collins, *When Everything Changed*. https://news.google.com/newspapers?id=4vsyAAAAIBAJ&sjid=4hAGAAAAI BAJ&pg=2112%2C606968

62. Collins, *When Everything Changed*, 38.

63. Coontz, Stephanie, "Marriage: Saying I Don't," *Los Angeles Times*, January 19, 2012. http://articles.latimes.com/2012/jan/19/opinion/la-oe-coontz-marriage-201 20119.

64. Friedan, Betty, *The Feminine Mystique*.

65. Episode One, *Makers: Women Who Make America*, PBS, February 26, 2013.

66. Davis, Kingsley, *Contemporary Marriage*, The Russell Sage Foundation, 1985.

67. Elliott, Diana B., Kristy Krivickas, Matthew W. Brault, Rose M. Kreider, "Historical MArriage Trends from 1890–2010: A Focus on Race Difference," SEHD Working Paper Number 2012-12, 12–13. https://www.census.gov/hhes/socdemo /marriage/data/acs/ElliottetalPAA2012paper.pdf.

68. Margo, Robert A. "Explaining Black-White Wage Convergence, 1940–1950," *Industrial and Labor Relations Review*, Vol. 48, No. 3, April 1995, 470–481, http:// www.jstor.org/stable/2524775?seq=1#page_scan_tab_contents.

69. Katznelson, Ira, *When Affirmative Action Was White: An Untold History of Racial Inequality in Twentieth Century America*, New York: W.W. Norton and Company, 2005. Via Ta-Nehesi Coates, "A Religion of Colorblind Policy," *TheAtlantic .com*, May 30, 2013. http://m.theatlantic.com/national/archive/2013/05/a-religion -of-colorblind-policy/276379/.

70. Sugrue, Tom, *Sweet Land of Liberty: The Forgotten Struggle for Civil Rights in the North*, Via Ta Nehesi here: http://www.theatlantic.com/national/archive/2013/02 /the-effects-of-housing-segregation-on-black-wealth/272775/

71. Sugrue, *Sweet Land of Liberty*, 200–201.

Chapter Three: The Sex of the Cities

1. Wile, Rob, "This Southern City has the Most Single Person Households in America," *Business Insider*, April 26, 2012.

2. Klinenberg, Eric, *Going Solo*.

3. Venugopal, Arun, "New York Leads in Never Married Women," wnyc.org, September 22, 2011, http://www.wnyc.org/story/160010-blog-new-york-never-mar ried-women/.

4. Nanos, Janelle, "Single By Choice," *Boston Magazine*, January 2012. "The median age . . ." from same story, supported by Population Reference Bureau charts drawing on five-year American Community Survey, 2009–2013, http://www.prb.org /DataFinder/Topic/Rankings.aspx?ind=133.

5. Bennett and Froide, *Singlewomen of the European Past*, 2–3.

6. Kowaleski, Maryanne, in Bennett and Froide's *Singlewomen of the European Past,* 53–54.
7. Stansell, Christine, *City of Women,* 13–14.
8. Israel, *Bachelor Girl,* 58.
9. McDougald, Elise Johnson, "The Double Task: The Struggle of Negro Women for Sex and Race Emancipation," *Survey* 53, March 1, 1925, 689–691. Via Giddings, *When and Where I Enter.*
10. Peiss, *Cheap Amusements,* 13.
11. Nellie Bly interview with Susan B. Anthony, *The World,* February 2, 1896, http://www.rarenewspapers.com/view/621269?acl=851761768&imagelist=1#full-images&rc=blog.
12. Peiss, *Cheap Amusements,* 58.
13. Israel, *Bachelor Girl,* 106.
14. Kaufman, Gena, "Where the Single Men Are," *Glamour,* June 5, 2013, http://www.glamour.com/sex-love-life/blogs/smitten/2013/06/where-the-single-men-are-um-ev.
15. "The Woman with the Flying Hair," *Swarthmore College Bulletin,* February 1991, http://bulletin.swarthmore.edu/bulletin-issue-archive/index.html%3Fp=1052.html.
16. Israel, *Bachelor Girl,* 112.
17. Stansell, *City of Women,* 255.
18. Stansell, *City of Women,* 84.
19. Meyerowitz, Joanne, *Women Adrift,* 80.
20. Chambers-Schiller, *Liberty, a Better Husband,* 72.
21. Ibid., 74.
22. "between a third and a half . . ." Moran, "How Second Wave Feminism Forgot Single Women." "Each member . . ." from Katherine Snyder, "A Paradise of Bachelors: Remodeling Domesticity and Masculinity in the Turn of the Century New York Bachelor Apartment," *23 Prospects: An Annual of American Cultural Studies,* 1998, quoted in Moran.
23. Gray, Christopher, "For Career Women, A Hassle-Free Haven," *New York Times,* June 28, 2012.
24. Israel, *Bachelor Girl,* 4.
25. Dvorak, Petula, "A City Divided and Increasingly Unaffordable," *The Washington Post,* April 3, 2014.
26. Wax, Emily, "Home Squeezed Home: Living in a 200 Square Foot Space," *The Washington Post,* November 27, 2012.
27. Thompson, Lynn, "Critics of Micro-Apartments Calling for a Moratorium," *Seattle Times,* April 23, 2013.
28. North, Anna, "What the Single Ladies Have Wanted for More Than A Century,"

*The New York Times*, April 24, 2015, http://www.nytimes.com/2015/04/24/opin
ion/what-the-single-ladies-have-wanted-for-more-than-a-century.html.

29. Stansell, *City of Women,* 72.
30. Meyerowitz, *Women Adrift*, 115.
31. Stansell, *City of Women*, 221.
32. Lovett, Laura, *Conceiving the Future*, 88.
33. "A Deadly Encounter" *Dateline, NBC*, January 20, 2007, http://www.nbcnews
    .com/id/16713078/ns/dateline_nbc/t/deadly-encounter/#.UbtL8yMkchw.
34. Nussbaum, Emily, "Difficult Women," *The New Yorker*, July 29, 2013.

### Chapter Four: Dangerous as Lucifer Matches

1. Angier, Natalie, "The Changing American Family," *New York Times*, November 26, 2013, http://www.nytimes.com/2013/11/26/health/families.html.
2. Smith-Rosenberg, Carroll, *Disorderly Conduct*. 61–62.
3. Bennett and Froide, *Singlewomen in the European Past*, 85.
4. Smith-Rosenberg, *Disorderly Conduct,* 60.
5. Ibid., 71–75.
6. Norton, Mary Beth, *Founding Mothers and Fathers*, 354.
7. Lincoln, Abraham, "Dear Speed, Springfield, Ills., Feby 13. 1842," *Collected Works of Abraham Lincoln*, http://quod.lib.umich.edu/l/lincoln/lincoln1/1:292?rgn=div1 ;view=fulltext, via Jennie Rothenberg Gritz, "But Were they Gay? The Mystery of Same-Sex Love in the 19th Century," *The Atlantic.com*, September 7, 2012.
8. Gritz, "But Were They Gay?" *The Atlantic.com*.
9. Willard, Frances, *The Autobiography of an American Woman*, 642.
10. Chevigny, Bell Gale, *Margaret Fuller the Woman and the Myth* 113.
11. Coontz, *Marriage, A History*, 205–206.
12. All letters cited were written between August and October 1854, from Margaret Smith, ed., *The Letters of Charlotte Brontë: Volume Three 1852–1855*.
13. Mailer, Norman, "The Mary McCarthy Case," *The New York Review of Books*, October 17, 1963, in Nussbaum, Emily, "Hannah Barbaric," *The New Yorker*, February 11, 2013.
14. Episode One, *Makers: Women Who Make America*, PBS, February 26, 2013.
15. Syme, Rachel, "The Broad Strokes," *Grantland.com*, January 14, 2015, http:// grantland.com/features/broad-city-season-2-comedy-central-abbi-jacobson-ilana -glazer/.

### Chapter Five: My Solitude, My Self

1. Ortberg, Mallory, "What the Happiest Woman in the World Looks Like," *The Toast.com*, February 11, 2015, http://the-toast.net/2015/02/11/happiest-woman -world-looks-like/#GjSEZ1Sf1HaxYbj6.99.

2. Kurutz, Steven, "One if the Quirkiest Number," *The New York Times*, February 22, 2012.

3. Schwartz, Benjamin E., "Selfishness as Virtue," *The American Interest*, June 10, 2012, http://www.the-american-interest.com/article-bd.cfm?piece=1272#sthash .RdgQ6T9c.dpuf.

4. Parker-Pope, Tara, "In a Married World, Singles Struggle for Attention," *The New York Times*, September 19, 2011, http://well.blogs.nytimes.com/2011/09/19/the -plight-of-american-singles/?_php=true&_type=blogs&_r=0.

5. Bennett and Froide, *Singlewomen in the European Past,* 60–63.

6. Farmer, Sharon, in Bennett and Froide, *Singlewomen in the European Past,* 87.

7. Chambers-Schiller, *Liberty, A Better Husband,* 159.

8. Goldstein, Dana, *The Teacher Wars,* 33.

9. Walker, Ruth, "Why Wait? Single Women Want to Live in Style," *Christian Science Monitor,* February 4, 1979. Via Israel, *Bachelor Girl.*

10. Faludi, Susan, *Backlash,* 108.

11. Gross, Jane, "Single Women: Coping With a Void," *The New York Times*, April 28, 1987, http://www.nytimes.com/1987/04/28/nyregion/single-women-coping-with -a-void.html?pagewanted=all&src=pm.

12. Klinenberg, Eric, *Going Solo,* 5.

13. Williamson, Kevin, "Five Reasons Why You're Too Dumb to Vote," *National Review.com,* September 28, 2014, http://www.nationalreview.com/article/388945 /five-reasons-why-youre-too-dumb-vote-kevin-d-williamson.

14. DePaulo, Bella, "That Spinster Stigma Study: Others are Intrusive or they Ignore You," *Psychology Today,* June 10, 2010, http://www.psychologytoday.com/blog /living-single/201006/spinster-stigma-study-others-are-intrusive-or-they -ignore-you.

15. Maria Mitchell Papers Diary 1854–1857; Box One, Folder One. Courtesy of the Nantucket Maria Mitchell Association.

16. Gallagher, Maggie and Linda Waite, *The Case for Marriage*, New York: Crown, 2002, 52.

17. Parker-Pope, Tara, "Married Cancer Patients Live Longer," *New York Times*, September 24, 2013. http://well.blogs.nytimes.com/2013/09/24/married-cancer-pa tients-live-longer/?hpw&_r=1.

18. Gottlieb, Lori, "Marry Him! The Case for Settling for Mr. Good Enough," *The Atlantic,* March 2008.

19. Kreider, Rose M. and Renee Ellis, "Number, Timing, and Duration of Marriages and Divorces, 2009," U.S. Census Bureay, May 2011, http://www.census.gov/prod /2011pubs/p70-125.pdf.

20. Israel, *Bachelor Girl,* 42.

21. Goldstein, *The Teacher Wars,* 31.

22. Burnap, George Washington, *The Sphere And Duties of Woman: A Course of Lectures*, Baltimore: John Murphy, 1848, 64. Via Chambers-Schiller, *Liberty, a Better Husband*.

23. Chambers-Schiller, *Liberty, a Better Husband*, 50.

24. Ibid, 55.

25. Collins, *America's Women*, 138.

26. Rogers, Anna A., "Why American Marriages Fail," *The Atlantic Monthly*, Cambridge: The Riverside Press, 1907, via Coontz, *Marriage: A History*.

27. Esfahani Smith, Emily, "Science Says Lasting Relationships Come Down to Two Basic Traits," *The Atlantic.com*, November 9, 2014.

28. Barker, Eric, "These Four Things Kill Relationships," *Time.com*, August 26, 2014, http://time.com/3174575/these-4-things-kill-relationships/.

29. Klinenberg, *Going Solo*, 157.

30. Cobbe, Frances Power, "Celibacy vs. Marriage," in *Criminals, Idiots, Women & Minors*, Susan Hamilton, ed, 57, via Israel, *Bachelor Girl*.

### Chapter Six: For Richer

1. Friedan, *The Feminine Mystique*, 158.

2. Rinehart, Mary Roberts, "A Home or a Career?" *Ladies Home Journal*, April 1921. Via "These Working Wives: The 'Two-Job' Woman in Interwar Magazines," a paper presented by Jane Marcellus in 2004.

3. "Estimated Median Age at First Marriage, by Sex, 1890 to Present," US Bureau of the Census, 2010.

4. DePaulo, *Singled Out*, 144.

5. Brown, Campbell, "Sexism Sneaks In Over and Open Mic," *Cnn.com*, November 19, 2008.

6. "On Pay Gap, Millennial Women Near Parity—For Now," Pew Research Center, December 11, 2013, http://www.pewsocialtrends.org/2013/12/11/on-pay-gap-millennial-women-near-parity-for-now/.

7. Chambers-Schiller, *Liberty, A Better Husband*, 68.

8. Guy-Scheftall and Johnnetta Cole, *Words of Fire*, 99.

9. Gunning, Sandra, *Race, Rape, and Lynching*, 122.

10. Chambers Schiller, *Liberty, a Better Husband*, 66.

11. Ibid, 98.

12. Rosin, Hanna, "The End of Men," *The Atlantic*, July/August 2010, http://www.theatlantic.com/magazine/archive/2010/07/the-end-of-men/308135/.

13. "Percentage Degrees Awarded to Women," *The Washington Post* online, May, 2013, http://www.washingtonpost.com/blogs/wonkblog/files/2013/05/its_getting_better-degrees-women.jpg.

14. Mercado, Monica and Katherin Turk, "On Equal Terms: Educating Women at

the University of Chicago," The University of Chicago Library, http://www.lib
.uchicago.edu/e/webexhibits/OnEqualTerms/NoneDebateOverSexSegregation
.html.

15. Rosenberg, Rosalind, *Beyond Separate Spheres: Intellectual Roots of Modern Feminism*, 44.

16. Bronski, Peter, "A Woman's Place," *Vassar Alumnae Quarterly*, January 2011, http://vq.vassar.edu/issues/2011/01/features/a-womans-place.html.

17. D'Emilio, John and Estelle B. Freedman, *Intimate Matters: A History of Sexuality in America*, 1988, 190.

18. Israel, *Bachelor Girl*, 30.

19. Ibid., 39.

20. Weiss, Sasha, "A Study in Farewells: Kristin Wiig and Peggy Olson," *The New Yorker.com*, June 1, 2012, http://www.newyorker.com/online/blogs/culture/2012/06/a-study-in-farewells-kristen-wiig-and-peggy-olson.html.

21. Chambers-Schiller, *Liberty a Better Husband*, 164.

22. Venker, Suzanne, "Why Women Still Need Husbands," foxnews.com, December 6, 2013, http://www.foxnews.com/opinion/2013/12/06/why-women-still-need-husbands/.

23. "Many Millennials Say Women Are More Focused on Careers than Men," in "On Pay Gap, Millennial Women Near Parity, Pew Research Center, December 10, 2013, http://www.pewsocialtrends.org/2013/12/11/on-pay-gap-millennial-women-near-parity-for-now/sdt-gender-and-work-12-2013-0-08/.

24. Flock, Elizabeth, "Book Says Supreme Court Crashed Sonia Sotomayor's Personal Life," *USNews.com*, July 17, 2012.

25. Klein, Ezra, "Nine Facts About Marriage and Childbirth in the United States," *The Washington Post*, March 25, 2013, http://www.washingtonpost.com/blogs/wonkblog/wp/2013/03/25/nine-facts-about-marriage-and-childbirth-in-the-united-states/.

26. Ibid.

27. Coe, Alexis, "Being Married Helps Professors Get Ahead, but Only if They're Male," *TheAtlantic.com*, January 17, 2013.

28. Miller, Claire Cain, "The Motherhood Penalty vs. The Fatherhood Bonus," *The New York Times*, September 6, 2014.

29. Lemmon, Gayle Tzemach, "I'm Not Your Wife! A New Study Points to a Hidden Form of Sexism," *The Atlantic.com*, June 5, 2012.

30. Rikleen, Lauren Stiller, "Are Working Women Held Back?" *Harvard Business Review*, December 2012.

31. Alazraki, Melly, "Young Single Women Now Earn More than Men," *DailyFinance.com*, September 1, 2010, http://www.dailyfinance.com/2010/09/01/young-single-women-earn-more-than-men/.

32. Miller, Claire Cain, "The Motherhood Penalty vs. The Fatherhood Bonus," *The New York Times*, September 6, 2014.

33. Cardona, Mercedes M.,"Single Minded Marketing: A Multitrillion Dollar Opportunity," cmo.com, April 17, 2013, http://www.cmo.com/articles/2013/4/16/single _minded_marketing.html.

34. Swartz, Jon, "How Women are Changing the Tech World," *USA Today*, June 6, 2012.

35. "Indie Women," *The Curve Report*, NBC Universal, http://thecurvereport.com /category/films/indie-women/.

36. Bolick, Kate, "For Women, Is Home Really So Sweet?" *The Wall Street Journal*, February 18, 2012.

37. "Field Guide to Women Homebuyers," Realtor.com, June 2015, http://www.real tor.org/field-guides/field-guide-to-women-homebuyers.

38. Elmer, Vickie, "Wed, in all but Finances," *New York Times*, July 5, 2012, http:// www.nytimes.com/2012/07/08/realestate/mortgages-wed-in-all-but-finances .html?_r=1&hp.

39. Coontz, *Marriage a History*, 168.

40. Ibid., 169.

## Chapter Seven: For Poorer

1. Crenshaw, Kimberlé Williams, "The Girls Obama Forgot," *The New York Times*, July 7, 2014.

2. Hollar, Julie, "Wealth Gap Yawns, and so does Media," FAIR Fairness and Accuracy in Reporting, June 1, 2010, http://fair.org/extra-online-articles/wealth-gap -yawns8212and-so-do-media/.

3. Fairchild, Caroline, "Number of Fortune 500 Women CEOS Reaches Historic High," *Fortune.com*, June 6, 2014, http://fortune.com/2014/06/03/number-of-for tune-500-women-ceos-reaches-historic-high/.

4. Howard, Caroline, "The New Class of Female CEOs" *Forbes*, August 22, 2012, http://www.forbes.com/forbes/welcome/.

5. Rivers, Caryl, "The End of Men? Not so Fast," *The Huffington Post*, http://www .huffingtonpost.com/caryl-rivers/the-end-of-men-eyewash_b_624309.html.

6. Luscombe, Belinda, "Workplace Salaries: At Last, Women on Top," *Time*, September 1, 2010.

7. Coontz, "The Myth of Male Decline," *New York Times*, September 29, 2012, http://www.nytimes.com/2012/09/30/opinion/sunday/the-myth-of-male-decline .html?pagewanted=all.

8. "On Pay Gap, Millennial Women Near Parity for Now," Pew Research Group, December 11, 2013, http://www.pewsocialtrends.org/2013/12/11/on-pay-gap-millennial -women-near-parity-for-now/. And "Do Men Really Earn More Than Women?" *Payscale.com*, http://www.payscale.com/gender-lifetime-earnings-gap.

9. Coontz, "The Myth of Male Decline," *New York Times*, September 29, 2012.

10. Schwartz, Madeleine, "Opportunity Costs: The True Price of Internships," Winter 2013, http://www.dissentmagazine.org/article/opportunity-costs-the-true-price-of-internships.

11. DeParle, Jason, "Two Classes, Divided By I Do," *New York Times*, July 7, 2012, http://www.nytimes.com/2012/07/15/us/two-classes-in-america-divided-by-i-do.html.

12. Confessore, Nick, "Tramps Like Them: Charles Murray Examines the White Working Class in 'Coming Apart,'" *New York Times*, February 10, 2012.

13. Rampell, Catherine, "Bundled Households," *New York Times*, November 12, 2012, http://economix.blogs.nytimes.com/2012/11/12/bundled-households/.

14. Arnold, Lisa and Christina Campbell, "The High Price of Being Single in America," January 14, 2013, http://www.theatlantic.com/sexes/archive/2013/01/the-high-price-of-being-single-in-america/267043/.

15. Palmer, Kimberly, "Why Single People Are So Financially Stressed," *USNews.com*, October 17, 2010.

16. Correll, Shelley, Steven Bernard, In Paik, "Getting a Job: Is there a Motherhood Penality?" *American Journal of Sociology*, Vol. 112, No. 5, March, 2007, 1297–1339, http://gender.stanford.edu/sites/default/files/motherhoodpenalty.pdf.

17. Coontz, Stephanie, "Progress at Work, But Mothers Still Pay a Price," *New York Times*, June 8, 2013, http://www.nytimes.com/2013/06/09/opinion/sunday/coontz-richer-childless-women-are-making-the-gains.html.

18. Wang, Wendy and Kim Parker and Paul Taylor, "Breadwinner Moms," Pew Research Center, May 29, 2013, http://www.pewsocialtrends.org/2013/05/29/breadwinner-moms/.

19. Hymowitz, Kay and Jason S. Carroll, W. Bradford Wilcox, Kelleen Kaye, "Knot Yet Report: What Does the Rising Marriage Age Mean For Twentysomething Women, Men and Families?" 2012, http://twentysomethingmarriage.org/.

20. Castillo, Michelle, "Almost Half of First Babies in US Born to Unwed Mothers," CBS News, March 15, 2013, http://www.cbsnews.com/news/almost-half-of-first-babies-in-us-born-to-unwed-mothers/.

21. Angier, Natalie, "The Changing American Family," *The New York Times*, November 26, 2013, http://www.nytimes.com/2013/11/26/health/families.html.

22. Sawhill, Isabel, "The New White Negro," *Washington Monthly*, January/February 2013, http://www.washingtonmonthly.com/magazine/january_february_2013/features/the_new_white_negro042050.php?page=all.

23. Edin, Kathryn and Maria Kefalas, "Why Poor Women Put Motherhood Before Marriage," published by the National Poverty Center, March 12, 2013, https://www.youtube.com/watch?v=wRUj_C5JdHs. Talk stems from *Promises I Can Keep* by Edin and Kefalas.

24. "Phyllis Schlafly Still Championing the Anti-Feminist Fight," *Tell Me More*,

NPR, March 30, 2011, http://www.npr.org/templates/story/story.php?storyId=13 4981902.

25. Fleischer, Ari, "How to Fight Income Inequality: Get Married," *The Wall Street Journal*, January 12, 2014.

26. Bruenig, Matt, "The Single Mother, Child Poverty Myth," Demos, April 14, 2014, http://www.demos.org/blog/4/14/14/single-mother-child-poverty-myth.

27. Rector, Robert, "Marriage: America's Greatest Weapon Against Child Poverty," The Heritage Foundation, September 5, 2012, http://www.heritage.org/research /reports/2012/09/marriage-americas-greatest-weapon-against-child-poverty.

28. Mencimer, Stephanie, "The GOP's Dead End Marriage Program," *Mother Jones*, June 25, 2012, http://www.motherjones.com/politics/2012/06/gops-dead-end -marriage-program.

29. Covert, Bryce, "Heritage Panel tells Women that the Road to Economic Security is Marriage, not Feminism," *Think Progress*, April 1, 2014, http://thinkprogress .org/economy/2014/04/01/3421603/heritage-marriage-poverty/.

30. "Minnesota Family Investment Program," Minnesota Department of Human Services.

31. Fremstad, Shawn and Melissa Boteach, "How Progressive Policies Can Strengthen Marriage and Family Life," *Family Studies,* February 10, 2015, http://family-stud ies.org/how-progressive-policies-can-strengthen-marriage-and-family-life/.

32. "New Hope Project," Promising Practices, http://www.promisingpractices.net /program.asp?programid=269.

33. Gassman-Pines, Anna and Hirokazu Yoshikawa, "Five Year Effects of an Anti-Poverty Program on Marriage among Never-Married Mothers" *Journal of Policy Analysis and Management,* Vol. 25, No. 1, 2006, 11–30, http://steinhardt.nyu.edu /scmsAdmin/media/users/jr189/Five_Year_Effects_of_Antipoverty_Program.pdf.

34. Covert, Bryce, "Senator Floats Idea to Penalize Low-Income Women Who Have Children," *Think Progress*, January 29, 2014, http://thinkprogress.org/economy /2014/01/29/3220881/rand-paul-welfare-cap-children/.

35. "Rand Paul and the Extent of Marital Poverty in Kentucky," CEPR Blog, Center for Economic and Policy Research, January 30, 2014, http://www.cepr.net/blogs /cepr-blog/rand-paul-and-the-extent-of-marital-poverty-in-kentucky. Via Shawn Fremstad,"Temporary Assistance Doesn't Help Impoverished Married Parents," TalkPoverty.org, May 1, 2015, http://talkpoverty.org/2015/05/01/temporary-assis tance/.

36. Senate Bill 518, General Assembly of North Carolina, Session 2013, April 1, 2013, http://www.ncleg.net/Sessions/2013/Bills/Senate/PDF/S518v1.pdf.

37. Marcotte, Amanda, "The Worst State for Women?" *The American Prospect*, January 13, 2013, http://prospect.org/article/worst-state-women.

38. Hymowitz, Kay and Jason S. Carroll, W. Bradford Wilcox, Kelleen Kaye, "Knot

Yet Report: What Does the Rising Marriage Age Mean For Twentysomething Women, Men and Families?" 2012, http://twentysomethingmarriage.org/.

39. Angier, Natalie, "The Changing American Family," *The New York Times*, November 26, 2013, http://www.nytimes.com/2013/11/26/health/families.html.

40. Edin, Kathryn and Maria Kefalas, "Unmarried with Children," *Contexts,* Vol. 4, No. 2., May, 2005, http://ctx.sagepub.com/content/4/2/16.abstract.

41. Edin, Kathryn and Maria Kefalas, *Promises I Can Keep,* 185.

42. Fragile Families and Child Wellbeing Study, cited by Kathryn Edin Study cited by Edin and Kefalas in ""Why Poor Women Put Motherhood Before Marriage" speech.

43. Wang, Wendy, "The Best Cities for Women Looking to Marry," Pew Research Center, October 2, 2014, http://www.pewresearch.org/fact-tank/2014/10/02/the-best-and-worst-cities-for-women-looking-to-marry/.

44. Knafo, Saki, "1 in 3 Black Men Will Go To Prison in their Lifetimes, Report Warns," *Huffington Post*, October 4, 2013, http://www.huffingtonpost.com/2013/10/04/racial-disparities-criminal-justice_n_4045144.html.

45. Porter, Eduardo, "In the U.S., Punishment Comes Before the Crimes," *The New York Times*, April 29, 2014.

46. Coates, Ta-Nehesi, "The Black Family in the Age of Mass Incarceration," *The Atlantic*, October, 2015.

47. Via the Federal Bureau of Investigation.

48. "Criminal Justice Fact Sheet," National Association for the Advancement of Colored People, naacp.org, http://www.naacp.org/pages/criminal-justice-fact-sheet.

49. Angier, Natalie, "The Changing American Family," *New York Times*, November 26, 2013, http://www.nytimes.com/2013/11/26/health/families.html.

50. Discussion between Marian Wright Edelman, Vivian Nixon, Glenn Martin, Bob Herbert on *The Melissa Harris Perry Show*, MSNBC, July 14, 2012.

51. "Know Your Rights: Housing and Arrests or Criminal Convictions," The Bronx Defenders, October 2, 1010, http://www.bronxdefenders.org/housing-and-arrests-or-criminal-convictions/.

52. Alexander, Michelle, "The Zimmerman Mindset: Why Black Men Are the Permanent Undercaste," July 29, 2013.

53. Ludden, Jennifer, "Can Marriage Save Single Mothers From Poverty?" *Morning Edition*, NPR, September 13, 2012, http://www.npr.org/2012/09/13/161017580/can-marriage-save-single-mothers-from-poverty.

54. Stevenson, Betsey and Justin Wolfers, "Valentine's Day and the Economics of Love," *Bloomberg View*, February 13, 2013, http://www.bloombergview.com/articles/2013-02-13/valentine-s-day-and-the-economics-of-love.

55. Fremstad, Shawn, "Temporary Assistance Doesn't Help Impoverished Married

Parents," TalkPoverty.org, May 1, 2015, http://talkpoverty.org/2015/05/01/tempo rary-assistance/.

56. Edin and Kefalas, *Promises I Can Keep*, 199.

57. Coontz, Stephanie, "The Triumph of the Working Mother," *New York Times*, June 1, 2013, http://www.nytimes.com/2013/06/02/opinion/sunday/coontz-the -triumph-of-the-working-mother.html?ref=global-home.

58. Ibid.

59. Boo, Katherine, "The Marriage Cure," *The New Yorker*, August 18, 2003.

60. Coates, Ta-Nehesi, "Of Baguettes and Black Families," *The Atlantic*, September 13, 2013, http://www.theatlantic.com/national/archive/2013/09/of-baguettes -and-black-families/279678/.

### Chapter Eight: Sex and the Single Girls

1. Coontz, Stephanie, *Marriage: A History*.

2. Addams, Jane, *The Spirit of Youth and the City Streets*, 15–16. Via Louise Knight.

3. Grimké, Sarah, "Marriage," in Sarah Grimke, *Letters on the Equality of the Sexes and Other Essays*. Elizabeth Ann Bartlett, ed., 148.

4. Ibid., 148.

5. Randall, Mercedes Moritz, *Improper Bostonian: Emily Greene Balch*, 398.

6. Caplan, Paula J., "Sex and the Myth of Women's Masochism," *Psychology Today*, August 14, 2012, https://www.psychologytoday.com/blog/science-isnt-golden /201208/sex-and-the-myth-women-s-masochism.

7. Trimberger, Ellen Kay, *The New Single Woman*, 14.

8. Firestone, Shulamith, *The Dialectic of Sex: The Case for Feminist Revolution*, 152.

9. Bilton, Nick, "Tinder, The Fast Growing Dating App, Taps and Age-Old Truth," *New York Times*, October 30, 2014, http://mobile.nytimes.com/2014/10/30/fash ion/tinder-the-fast-growing-dating-app-taps-an-age-old-truth.html?referrer=& _r=0.

10. Sales, Nancy Jo, "Tinder and the Dawn of the 'Dating Apocalypse,'" *Vanity Fair*, August 2015, http://www.vanityfair.com/culture/2015/08/tinder-hook-up-culture -end-of-dating.

11. Massey, Alana, "The Dickonomics of Tinder," *Matter*, April 30, 2015, https://me dium.com/matter/the-dickonomics-of-tinder-b14956c0c2c7.

12. McCracken, Amanda, "Does My Virginity Have a Shelf Life?" *The New York Times*, November 13, 2013, http://opinionator.blogs.nytimes.com/2013/11/13 /does-my-virginity-have-a-shelf-life/?smid=tw-share.

13. Tyler May, Elaine, *Homeward Bound*,.

14. "Sex Will Change Totally, Liza Mundy Predicts in New Book, 'The Richer Sex,'" *Huffington Post*, March 19, 2012, http://www.huffingtonpost.com/2012/03/19

/sex-richer-liza-mundy-gender-gap_n_1363917.html#s790489title=Women_Will
_Refuse.

15. Freitas, Donna, "Time to Stop Hooking Up (You Know You Want To)" *The Washington Post*, March 29, 2013.

16. Plank, Elizabeth, "There's A Way to Discuss Hookup Culture and this Wasn't It," *mic.com*, July 15, 2013, http://mic.com/articles/54701/there-s-a-way-to-discuss-hook-up-culture-and-this-wasn-t-it.

17. Sessions Stepp, Laura, "Cupid's Broken Arrow," *The Washington Post*, May 7, 2006, http://www.washingtonpost.com/wp-dyn/content/article/2006/05/06/AR2006050601206.html.

18. Douthat, Ross, "Love in the Time of Hookups," *New York Times*, July 18, 2013, http://douthat.blogs.nytimes.com/2013/07/18/love-in-the-time-of-hookups/.

19. Rosin, Hanna, "Boys on the Side, *The Atlantic, September 2012,* http://www.theatlantic.com/magazine/archive/2012/09/boys-on-the-side/309062/3/.

20. Ingeno, Lauren, "Let's Talk (Differently) About Sex," *Inside Higher Ed*, July 29, 2013, http://www.insidehighered.com/news/2013/07/29/changing-hook-culture-conversation-college-campuses.

21. Rosin, Hanna, "Boys on the Side, *The Atlantic, September 2012,* http://www.theatlantic.com/magazine/archive/2012/09/boys-on-the-side/309062/3/.

22. Paquette, Danielle, "Why Millennials Have Fewer Sex Partners than their Parents Did," *The Washington Post*, May 6, 2015, http://www.washingtonpost.com/news/wonkblog/wp/2015/05/06/why-millennials-have-sex-with-fewer-partners-than-their-parents-did/.

23. Ingeno, Lauren, "Let's Talk (Differently) About Sex," *Inside Higher Ed*, July 29, 2013, http://www.insidehighered.com/news/2013/07/29/changing-hook-culture-conversation-college-campuses.

24. Rosin, "Boys on the Side," *The Atlantic*.

25. Ibid.

26. Friedman, Ann, "When Women Pursue Sex, Even Men Don't Get It," *New York*, June 4, 2013, http://nymag.com/thecut/2013/06/when-women-pursue-sex-even-men-dont-get-it.html.

27. Kitroeff, Natalie, "In Hookups, Inequality Still Reigns," *New York Times*, November 11, 2013, http://well.blogs.nytimes.com/2013/11/11/women-find-orgasms-elusive-in-hookups/.

28. Maines, Rachel P., The Technology of Orgasm: "Hysteria," the Vibrator, and Women's Sexual Satisfaction. Via *New York Times* excerpt, http://www.nytimes.com/books/first/m/maines-technology.html.

29. Hess, Amanda, "Abstinence Won't Solve Hookup Culture," *Slate*, April 1, 2013, http://www.slate.com/blogs/xx_factor/2013/04/01/abstinence_won_t_solve_the_hookup_culture_donna_freitas_is_wrong_about_sex.html.

## Chapter Nine: Horse and Carriage

1. Waldman, Katy, "Young People in Japan Have Given Up on Sex," *Slate*, October 22, 2013, http://www.slate.com/blogs/xx_factor/2013/10/22/celibacy_syndrome_in_japan_why_aren_t_young_people_interested_in_sex_or.html.

2. Haworth, Abigail, "Why Have Young People in Japan Stopped Having Sex?" *The Guardian*, October 20, 2013, http://www.theguardian.com/world/2013/oct/20/young-people-japan-stopped-having-sex.

3. "Survey Shows One Third of Japanese Think Marriage Is 'Pointless,'" *Japan Daily Press*, July 2, 2013, http://japandailypress.com/survey-shows-one-third-of-japanese-think-marriage-is-pointless-0231559/.

4. Haworth, "Why Have Young People in Japan Stopped Having Sex?" *The Guardian*.

5. Eurostat, Statistics Explained, http://ec.europa.eu/eurostat/statistics-explained/index.php/Main_Page.. Via Hillary White, "Italians Not Having Kids and Now, Not Getting Married Either, New Stats," *Lifesite News*, June 6, 2011.

6. Evans, Stephen, "Is the German Insult 'Raven Mothers' Holding Back Women at Work?" BBC News, March 11, 2011, http://www.bbc.com/news/business-12703897.

7. Eurostat, Statistics Explained, http://ec.europa.eu/eurostat/statistics-explained/index.php/Main_Page.

8. Luscombe, Belinda, "Who Needs Marriage? A Changing Institution," *Time*, November 18, 2010, http://content.time.com/time/magazine/article/0,9171,2032116,00.html.

9. "Crude Marriage Rate," Chartsbin.com, http://chartsbin.com/view/3219

10. Hess, Amanda, "When It Comes to 'Having it All,' Men Want More," *Slate*, October 31, 2013, http://www.slate.com/blogs/xx_factor/2013/10/31/work_life_balance_study_professional_men_are_more_likely_than_women_to_want.html.

11. Wade, Lisa, "Most Women Would Rather Divorce than be a Housewife," *The Society Pages, December 29, 2013,* http://thesocietypages.org/socimages/2013/01/28/mens-and-womens-gender-ideologies-ideals-and-fallbacks/.

12. Cherlin, Andrew J., "In the Season of Marriage, a Question: Why Bother?" *New York Times*, April 27, 2013, http://www.nytimes.com/2013/04/28/opinion/sunday/why-do-people-still-bother-to-marry.html?pagewanted=all.

13. Adelman, Lori, "Amelia Earhart's Prenup from the 1930s Lays Out a Pretty Darn Modern Vision of Marriage," *Feministing.com*, December 12, 2010, http://feministing.com/2012/12/10/amelia-earhart-prenup-from-1930s-lays-out-a-pretty-darn-modern-vision-of-marriage/.

14. Cotten, Trystan T. and Kimberly Springer eds., *Stories of Oprah: The Oprahfication of American Culture,* University Press of Mississippi, 2010, 23.

15. Tauber, Michelle, "Oprah at 50: Prime Time of Her Life," *People*, February 2, 2004.

16. Rauch, Jonathan, "Red Families, Blue Families, Gay Families and the Search for a New Normal,"*Journal of Law and Inequality,* Summer 2010, via http://www .jonathanrauch.com/jrauch_articles/red-blue-and-gay-marriage/. And "Women's Median Age at First Marriage by State," *LiveScience.com,* March 18, 2013, http:// www.livescience.com/27974-women-media-age-marriage-states.html.

17. "Women Who Get Hitched Early, Divorce Early," *Indian Express,* November 10, 2011.

18. "U.S. Divorce Rate Statistics," Centers for Disease Control, National Survey of Family Growth, May 23, 2015.

19. Nellie Bly interview with Susan B. Anthony, *The World,* February 2, 1896, http:// www.rarenewspapers.com/view/621269?acl=851761768&imagelist=1#full-images &rc=blog.

20. Coontz. Stephanie, "The Disestablishment of Marriage," *New York Times,* March 23, 2013, http://www.nytimes.com/2013/06/23/opinion/sunday/coontz -the-disestablishment-of-marriage.html?pagewanted=all.

21. "The Decline of Marriage and Rise of New Families," Pew Research Center, November 18, 2010, http://www.pewsocialtrends.org/2010/11/18/the-decline-of -marriage-and-rise-of-new-families/3./

22. Parker, Kim, "5 Facts About Today's Fathers," PEW Research Center, June 18, 2015, http://www.pewresearch.org/fact-tank/2015/06/18/5-facts-about-todays-fa thers/.

23. "American Time Use Survey—2014 Results," Bureau of Labor Statistics, U.S. Department of Labor, June 24, 2015, http://www.bls.gov/news.release/pdf/atus.pdf.

24. Chernoff, Allan, "The Millennials—Ever Optimistic about Jobs," *CNN Money,* May 18, 2011.

25. Dewan, Shaila and Robert Gebeloff, "More Men Enter Fields Dominated By Women," *The New York Times,* May 20, 2012, http://www.nytimes.com/2012 /05/21/business/increasingly-men-seek-success-in-jobs-dominated-by-women .html?pagewanted=2&_r=1&emc=eta1.

26. Livingston, Gretchen, "Growing Number of Dads Home with Kids," Pew Research Center," June 5, 2014, http://www.pewsocialtrends.org/2014/06/05/grow ing-number-of-dads-home-with-the-kids/. Via Miller, Claire Cain, "More Fathers Who Stay at Home By Choice," *New York Times,* June 5, 2014 http://www .nytimes.com/2014/06/06/upshot/more-fathers-who-stay-at-home-by-choice .html.

27. Esteve, Albert and J. Garcia-Roman and I. Permanyer, "The Gender-Gap Reversal in Education and Its Effect on Union Formation: The End of Hypergamy," *Population and Development Review,* vol. 38, issue 3, September 2012, http:// www.sciencedaily.com/releases/2012/10/121030093739.htm.

28. Oxfeld, Jesse, "Yesterday an Oppressed Minority, Today an Old Maid," *New York*

*Observer,* June 2013, http://observer.com/2013/06/yesterday-an-oppressed-mi
nority-today-an-old-maid/#ixzz2nJtZg4lX.

29. Thomas, June, "Don't Be a Wife: I'm a Lesbian and I'm Never Getting Married. Why Are You?" *Slate.com,* November 2012.

30. Goldman, Emma, *Anarchism and Other Essays,* 233–245.

31. Issenberg, Sasha, "With These Words," *New York,* July 27, 2012.

32. Walsh, Susan, "The Chances of Divorce May Be Much Lower Than You Think," *Hooking Up Smart,* June 13, 2012, http://www.hookingupsmart.com/2012/06/13 /relationshipstrategies/your-chances-of-divorce-may-be-much-lower-than-you -think/.

33. Angier, Natalie, "The Changing American Family," *The New York Times,* November 26, 2013, http://www.nytimes.com/2013/11/26/health/families.html.

34. North, Anna, "Hanna Rosin: Hookup Culture is Changing," *Salon.com,* September 1, 2013, http://www.salon.com/2013/09/01/hanna_rosin_hookup_culture_is _changing/.

35. Lewin, Tamar, "Census Finds Single Mothers and Live-In Partners," *The New York Times,* November 5, 2010.

36. Stevenson, Betsey and Justin Wolfers, "Valentine's Day and the Economics of Love," *Bloomberg View,* February 13, 2013, http://www.bloombergview.com/arti cles/2013-02-13/valentine-s-day-and-the-economics-of-love.

37. Rudder, Christian, "How Your Race Affects The Messages You Get," *Ok Trends Dating Research,* okcupid.com, October 5, 2009, http://blog.okcupid.com/index .php/your-race-affects-whether-people-write-you-back/.

38. Faludi, *Backlash,* 1.

39. Harris, Tami Winfrey, "Marriage Is Like Kitchenware and It Doesn't Matter What Men Want," *Clutch,* February, 2013. http://www.clutchmagonline.com/2013/02 /marriage-is-like-kitchenware-and-it-doesnt-matter-what-men-want/.

40. "Real Talk: Tyrese Says You Need a Man," *Essence.com,* November 17, 2011.

41. Andrews, Helena, "Setting the Record Straight," *Marie Claire,* April 12, 2012, http://www.marieclaire.com/sex-love/advice/a7010/interracial-relationships/.

42. Aronowitz, Nona Willis, "I Wish I Wasn't Married: In Defense of Domestic Partnerships for Straight Couples," *Good,* July 16, 2011, http://www.good.is/posts/do mestic-partnerships-should-be-an-alternative-to-marriage-for-all-couples.

43. *Jane Austen's Letters,* 292.

## Chapter Ten: Then Comes What?

1. Garber, Megan, "The IVF Panic: All Hell Will Break Loose, Politically and Morally, All Over the World," *The Atlantic,* June 25, 2012, http://www.theatlantic .com/technology/archive/2012/06/the-ivf-panic-all-hell-will-break-loose-politi cally-and-morally-all-over-the-world/258954/.

2. Davey, Melissa and Philip Ly, "Doctors Warn Women Not to Rely on IVF As More Give Birth in their 50s," *Sydney Morning Herald,* June 15, 2013.

3. Martin, Daniel, "Number of Babies Born to Women 45 and Older Trebles in Just Ten Years,: *Daily Mail,* January 27, 2012.

4. Kluger, Jeffrey and Alice Park, "Frontiers of Fertility," *Time,* May 30, 2013, http://healthland.time.com/2013/05/30/frontiers-of-fertility/.

5. Ibid.

6. "Common Myths About Having a Child Later in Life," CBS News, August 7, 2012.

7. "Births: Final Data for 2013," National Vital Statistics report, Centers for Disease Control, http://www.cdc.gov/nchs/data/nvsr/nvsr64/nvsr64_01.pdf.

8. Livingston, Gretchen, and D'Vera Cohn, "The New Demography of Motherhood," Pew Research Center, May 6, 2010, http://www.pewsocialtrends.org/2010/05/06/the-new-demography-of-american-motherhood/.

9. Grigoriadis, Vanessa, "Baby Panic," *New York,* May 20, 2002, http://nymag.com/nymetro/urban/family/features/6030/index2.html.

10. Aronowitz, Nona Willis, "Mo' Children Mo' Problems," *The American Prospect,* June 14, 2013, http://prospect.org/article/mo-children-mo-problems.

11. Twenge, Jean, "How Long Can You Wait to Have a Baby?" *The Atlantic,* July 2013, http://www.theatlantic.com/magazine/archive/2013/07/how-long-can-you-wait-to-have-a-baby/309374/.

12. Rothman, Michael, "Oprah Winfrey Reveals Why She Never Had Children," *Good Morning America,* ABC News, December 12, 2013.

13. Caldwell, Robin, "The Daughters of Dorothy Height," *politic365.com,* April 21, 2010, http://politic365.com/2010/04/21/the-daughters-of-dorothy-height/.

14. Interview with Kim Cattrall, "Woman's Hour," BBC, September 14, 2015.

15. Glenn, Cheryl, *Rhetoric Retold,* 162.

16. Hadfield, Andrew, *The Cambridge Companion to Spenser,* 192.

17. Sandler, Lauren, "Having It All Without Having Children," *Time,* August 12, 2013, http://time.com/241/having-it-all-without-having-children/.

18. Abma, J., and G. Martinez, "Among Older Women in the United States: Trends and Profiles," *Journal of Marriage and the Family,* Vol. 68, 2006, 1045–1056.

19. Hoffman, Piper, "Be Jewish and Multiply? Perhaps Not," JTA.org, November 20, 2013, http://www.jta.org/2013/11/20/life-religion/be-jewish-and-multiply-perhaps-not#ixzz2nlqB7srr. not#ixzz2nlqB7srr.

20. Friedman, Ann, "The Real Reason Twentysomething Women Are Worried," *New York,* December 17, 2013, http://nymag.com/thecut/2013/12/real-reason-20-something-women-are-worried.html.

21. Notkin, Melanie, "The Truth About the Childless Life," *Huffington Post,* October 1, 2013.

22. Stewart, Dodai, "When Motherhood Never Happens," *Jezebel.com*, May 8, 2012, http://jezebel.com/5908514/when-motherhood-never-happens.

23. Jacoby, Jeff, "The Baby Bust Generation," *The Boston Globe*, December 6, 2012, http://www.jeffjacoby.com/12678/the-baby-bust-generation.

24. Last, Jonathan, "America's Baby Bust," *Wall Street Journal,* February 12, 2013.

25. Harris-Perry, Melissa, "Obama and the Black Daddy Dilemma," *The Nation*, June 17, 2009, http://www.thenation.com/article/obama-and-black-daddy -dilemma/.

26. "Disapprove of Single Mothers," Pew Research Center, January 6, 2011, http://www.pewresearch.org/daily-number/disapprove-of-single-mothers/.

27. Kurtzleben, Danielle, "Two Parents, Not Just Two Incomes, Are What Help Kids Get Ahead," *Vox.com*, September 16, 2014, http://www.vox.com/2014/9/16/613 5445/marriage-cohabitation-inequality-social-mobility-children-contraception.

28. Brown, Susan L.,"Marriage and Child Wellbeing: Research and Policy Perspectives," *Journal of Marriage and Family*, vol. 72, October 2010, 106201063.

29. Roiphe, Katie, "In Defense of Single Motherhood," *New York Times*, August 11, 2012, http://www.nytimes.com/2012/08/12/opinion/sunday/in-defense-of-single -motherhood.html?pagewanted=all.

30. Ibid.

31. "Why I Froze My Eggs," *Newsweek,* May 1, 2009, http://www.newsweek.com /why-i-froze-my-eggs-79867.

32. Dana, Rebecca, "The Vitrification Fertility Option," *Newsweek, January 23, 2012,* http://www.newsweek.com/vitrification-fertility-option-64265.

33. American Society of Reproductive Medicine.

34. Richards, Sarah Elizabeth, "We Need to Talk About Our Eggs," *The New York Times*, October 22, 2012.

35. Richards, Sarah Elizabeth "Why I Froze My Eggs (And You Should Too)" *The Wall Street Journal,* May 3, 2013.

Simon & Schuster Paperbacks
Reading Group Guide

# ALL THE SINGLE LADIES

## BY REBECCA TRAISTER

### ABOUT THIS GUIDE

This reading group guide for *All the Single Ladies* includes an introduction, discussion questions, ideas for enhancing your book club, and a Q&A with author Rebecca Traister. The suggested questions are intended to help your reading group find new and interesting angles and topics for your discussion. We hope that these ideas will enrich your conversation and increase your enjoyment of the book.

### INTRODUCTION

In a provocative and groundbreaking work, Rebecca Traister traces the history of unmarried and late-married women in America who have radically shaped our culture through political, social, and economic means.

When award-winning journalist Rebecca Traister started writing about the twenty-first-century phenomenon of the American single woman, she thought that it would be a work of contemporary journalism. But over the course of more than a hundred interviews with social scientists, academics, and prominent single women, Traister discovered that the phenomenon of the single woman in America was far from new. In fact, she found that women having options beyond heterosexual marriage resulted in massive social changes, from abolition to temperance and beyond.

Destined to be a classic work of social history and journalism, *All the Single Ladies* is a fascinating look at contemporary American life and how we got here, through the lens of the single American woman.

1. In her note about the interviews, Traister writes, "when I realized, late in the process, that I had written more than three hundred pages of a book in which only a handful of men were cited, I felt bad" (p. xvi). What do you think of Traister's disclosure? Do you think including more male voices and scholarship changed the book? If so, how?

2. Frederick Douglass wrote that women would occupy a large part of the true history of the antislavery movement because "the cause of the slave has been peculiarly woman's cause" (p. 48). Although, as Traister notes, "Marriage and slavery were not equivalent practices" (p. 43), the intersection between the two illustrates how marriage could be used as a means to control a population. In what ways did slave owners use marriage to both control and further exploit their slaves? Why might women have been particularly involved in the cause of abolition?

3. Writer Dodai Stewart says, "My long-term relationship is with New York" (p. 83). What does she mean? What does New York represent to Dodai? Many young, single women settle in cities. What do women gain from urban spaces? Have you ever felt about a city the way that Dodai Stewart feels about New York? Talk to your book club about the experience. Why did you feel so connected to that location?

4. Traister writes "Female friendship has been the bedrock of women's lives for as long as there have been women" (p. 97). How was the role of friendship in women's lives changed as the age of marriage has been delayed? What have female friends historically offered each other that husbands cannot? Discuss Ann and Amina's friendship. What do they mean when they describe each other as "my person"? Do you have any friendships in your life like Anne and Amina's?

5. When Traister first moved to New York City, HBO's *Sex and the City* had captured the national zeitgeist. She recalls nursing a "seething grudge" (p. 92) against the show. Why was Traister resentful of the show? Did it change the perception of single women living in cities? In what ways? Traister takes umbrage with *Sex and the City*'s reliance on expensive consumer products as symbols of female empow-

erment. How might the act of buying an expensive item for oneself be an expression of independence? Compare Traister's reaction to the show to that of television critic Emily Nussbaum.

6. Amina Sow says, "It takes a lot to qualify a man as selfish" (p. 134), whereas women are chastised for being selfish if they choose to focus on themselves. Discuss the roots of this double standard. How does it contribute to the message to women that they are to blame for their single status?

7. According to psychologist Paula J. Caplan, the combination advent of the birth-control pill and Second Wave feminism created "a strange combination of liberation and disturbing pressures with regard to sex" (p. 217). Discuss this statement. How did attitudes toward sex change with the invention of the birth-control pill? What are some of the pitfalls that women experienced as a result?

8. According to Traister, Gloria Steinem's "most powerful gift was her ability to synthesize radical sentiments into appealingly pithy, era-defining sound bites" (p. 26). Discuss Steinem's role in the feminist movement. How did the way she lived her life—with male suitors and a healthy sexual appetite—make her particularly useful to the movement? What was the general reaction to Steinem's marriage, at sixty-six, to David Bale?

9. Sara, Traister's best friend, begs her, "please don't make it sound like the wedding was the end of my story" (p. 295). Why is this so important to Sara? How does Sara's story reflect a seismic shift in ideals of marriage? Why do you think that Traister chooses to end the penultimate chapter of *All the Single Ladies* with this statement?

10. Discuss the impact that Anita Hill had on the national discourse. How did her allegations against Clarence Thomas lead to a dialogue about sexual harassment? How was Anita Hill treated by the Senate Judiciary Committee and the press? What was the effect of bringing up her status as a single woman?

11. In June 2013, The Defense of Marriage Act was overturned by the Supreme Court, enabling gay and lesbian couples to marry. Traister

notes that the successful fight of homosexual couples to enter an institution that many women are struggling to distance themselves from only appears counterintuitive. Do you agree? Why may gay couples want to partake in the institution of marriage? What makes gay marriage so radical, according to Traister?

12. How does Traister define "hookup culture"? Contrast the media depictions of hookup culture with the reality that Traister outlines. Why do you think that there is such a stigma against hookup culture today?

13. Traister writes, "Having a baby is its own way of exerting control over the future" (p. 200). How does having a child give a mother a sense of control? Why might women make the choice to have a child out of wedlock? Describe some of the ways that single mothers have been vilified by popular culture. Do the arguments made against single motherhood have merit? Explain your answer.

## ENHANCE YOUR BOOK CLUB

1. Traister writes, "Austen's novels had been as much ambivalent cries *against* the economic and moral strictures of enforced marital identity for women than they were any kind of reassuring blueprint for it" (p. 7). Read one of Jane Austen's novels with your book club and discuss it within the context of Traister's statement. In what ways does Austen's writing condemn the institution of marriage?

2. *That Girl* starring Marlo Thomas and *The Mary Tyler Moore Show* were groundbreaking at the time they premiered. Watch old episodes of the shows with your book club and discuss what made them so revolutionary? If you watched them when they initially aired, discuss if your perception of them has changed. If it has, in what ways? Are there any television shows today that are similarly groundbreaking? What are they?

3. In a commencement address at Wellesley College, writer Nora Ephron recalled how she and her classmates "weren't meant to have politics, or careers that mattered, or opinions or lives; we were meant to marry them" (p. 65). Read some of Nora Ephron's work and discuss

the feminist aspects of it. How is her reaction to the pressure to marry reflected in her writing?

4. To learn more about Rebecca Traister, read reviews of *All the Single Ladies*, and to find out if she'll be in a city near you, visit her official website at www.rebeccatraister.com.

## A CONVERSATION WITH REBECCA TRAISTER

**You thank "all those [you] interviewed, on and off the record, who were so generous with their stories" (p. 312). Can you tell us how you found your subjects? How did you ensure that you had a diverse cross section of women who were contributing to your research?**

At first, I went through colleagues and friends who brought me their own colleagues, friends, and friends of friends. I interviewed many people who had written or spoken publicly about living singly (which is part of why, as I acknowledge in my introduction, there are more writers represented here than there are in the real world). I put out feelers in specific areas of the country—the South, the West. Especially as I got deep into work on the book I simply began talking to people everywhere I went; I interviewed women I met on buses and in airports and on the subway. And then, I worked with a remarkable researcher, Rhaina Cohen, who was more than ten years younger than I and went through completely different channels. She tracked down dozens of subjects from around the country.

**Was there anything you found particularly surprising while conducting your research? Can you tell us about it?**

As I describe in the book, the richness of the history of single women in America came as a surprise to me. I went into this project thinking I was writing a book of contemporary journalism and wound up writing a book that covers an enormous amount of this country's history. Of course, that added about three years of research and writing to my timeline.

**Although *All the Single Ladies* relies almost exclusively on the scholarship and experiences of women, you note that men are a crucial part of the story about female independence. Did you**

**consider adding more male voices to the book when you realized only a few were included?**

No, I didn't consider adding men's voices just for the sake of gender balance. This is a book about women. There are a lot of books about men and about the male experience and there remain many more to be written, including a chronicle of men's lives in a world in which heterosexual marriage has become rarer. But this was not that book. This is a book about women's experiences and perspectives and place in the world.

**The *New York Times* lauded *All the Single Ladies* as "an informative and thought-provoking book for anyone—not just the single ladies—who wants to gain a great understanding of this pivotal moment in the history of the United States." Were you writing the book with a specific audience in mind?**

I probably assumed it would be read mostly by women (and have been surprised by how many men have read it!) but I didn't assume it would be read exclusively by single women. There are millions of women (including me) who have been single for long periods or in formative ways but are now married; there are plenty of people who know and love single women—their friends and parents and grandparents and children. And plenty of women (and, it turns out, men) who, married or unmarried, are simply curious about the history of women in America.

**Your first book, *Big Girls Don't Cry*, was critically acclaimed and named as a *New York Times* notable book when it was published. How did the experience of writing *All the Single Ladies* compare? Since your first book was so critically acclaimed, did you feel added pressure while writing it?**

The nice thing about my first book is that it was critically acclaimed but didn't sell, so I had plenty of room for improvement. I always feel pressure when I write to make it good, fresh, and accurate, and to say something new. The real pressure here was that the book took so long; with every passing month and year I felt more and more driven to make sure it was worth the time and effort. And also, of course, something I think people don't acknowledge enough: books that take a long time to write take up work time over years, which produces an enormous financial pressure, too.

**Do you have any advice for aspiring writers and journalists? Is there anything that you wish you had been told at the start of your writing career?**

Well, in part because I feel the aforementioned pressure to always be good, I often cling to something an editor told me fifteen years ago about regular journalism: "If a quarter of your pieces are great, you're ahead of the game." I haven't really internalized this, but I say it to myself sometimes to remind myself that it's just a job, and some days you'll do the job better than other days. As far as advice for young journalists, unfortunately, my best advice isn't always achievable in today's media climate: it's to treat journalism as a learned, practiced skill, like plumbing: learn the rules, the ethics, the structure, how to write on deadline. Then when you get really good at that you can start writing with more voice and authority. But there aren't so many places anymore, such as local papers, where you can learn those skills. Mostly, these days, the best advice I can give is: if you can find a job, great! Take it seriously, work hard at it, and help take the profession into the future.

**Gloria Steinem has said that getting married made her understand what "she feels to be 'the biggest remnant of old thinking' about the institution: idealizing and valuing it above all other types of loving relationships" (p. 265). Did your experience of getting married as you were writing *All the Single Ladies* cause you to see marriage in a different light? If so, how?**

The way I feel about marriage as an institution is wholly separate from how I feel about my husband. To me, "marriage" as a concept is almost meaningless except insofar as its legal implications; people's marriages are all so different from each other; their quality and meaning depend on the two people involved and their individual dynamic as a couple. The huge transition in my life was simply falling in love with the person I fell in love with. He is an extraordinary man, and I'm very much in love with him. But that doesn't mean that *marriage* provided me happiness, just that this particular man and I happen to make each other very happy. It also doesn't blot out or diminish the life, years, and relationships I had when

I wasn't married or in love with a partner: my connections to my friends and family and my work and city are no less central to who I am or who I became than my connection to the man who is now my husband. Also, being married has allowed me to personally witness how isolating marriage can be, which is the opposite of what everyone tells you. But when I fell in love and then got married and had kids, my world turned inward. I saw less of the outside world, was able to spend less time with friends, stayed in my home more. Everyone says that single people are isolated, but I participated much more in the outside world when I was single than after I was partnered.

**Paramount Television has acquired the rights to develop *All the Single Ladies* for television. Can you tell us more about that? What has that experience been like?**

It's still in such early stages that I can't tell you anything except that it's an exciting possibility.

**What would you like your readers to take away from *All the Single Ladies*? What compelled you to write it?**

I am happy when readers take away anything of value. If they find their own experience reflected, great. If they gain insight into the lives of loved ones, great. If they learn about history that interests them, terrific. I suppose I'm extra excited if the book makes them rethink women's relationship to the government and to economic and social policy because I believe that that's the stuff that must change if we're to move into a more equal future: we need higher wages, pay equality, subsidized daycare, and paid family leave and sick days—a stronger welfare system. And of course partisan leanings can make plenty of Americans dubious about those kinds of shifts, but I hope that this book offers an argument about why they make practical sense in today's world.

**Are you working on anything now? Can you tell us about it?**

I'm covering the presidential election! My day job is as a journalist who writes about women and politics, so I pretty much can't see into the future beyond November 8, 2016. After that: who knows. I can't even talk about after that, because the possibilities are too frightening.

Also by *New York Times* bestselling author

# REBECCA TRAISTER

A *NEW YORK TIMES* NOTABLE BOOK OF 2010

"Certainly one of the things that's changed about presidential elections is the very existence of books like this one. Girls, these days, can not only run for president, they can also brilliantly analyze presidential campaigns, too."—Maureen Corrigan, NPR's *Fresh Air*

# BIG GIRLS DON'T CRY

## THE ELECTION THAT CHANGED EVERYTHING FOR AMERICAN WOMEN

## REBECCA TRAISTER

Pick up or download your copy today!

SIMON &
SCHUSTER
A CBS COMPANY